The Emerging Law of Forced Displacement in Africa

Development and implementation of the Kampala Convention on internal displacement

Allehone M. Abebe

Routledge
Taylor & Francis Group
LONDON AND NEW YORK

First published 2017
by Routledge
2 Park Square, Milton Park, Abingdon, Oxon OX14 4RN

and by Routledge
711 Third Avenue, New York, NY 10017

First issued in paperback 2018

Routledge is an imprint of the Taylor & Francis Group, an informa business

British Library Cataloguing in Publication Data
A catalogue record for this book is available from the British Library

Library of Congress Cataloging in Publication Data
Names: Abebe, Allehone M.
Title: The emerging law of forced displacement in Africa : development and implementation of the Kampala Convention on Internal Displacement / Allehone M. Abebe.
Description: New York : Routledge, 2016. |
Series: Human rights and international law | Includes bibliographical references and index.
Identifiers: LCCN 2016016381| ISBN 978-1-138-66921-5 |
ISBN 978-1-315-61822-7 (e-book)
Subjects: LCSH: African Union Convention for the Protection and Assistance of Internally Displaced Persons (2009 October 22) | Internally displaced persons—Legal status, laws, etc.—Africa. | Forced migration—Africa. | Migration, Internal—Law and legislation—Africa. | Refugees—Legal status, laws, etc.—Africa.
Classification: LCC KQC567 .A24 2016 | DDC 342.608/3—dc23
LC record available at https://lccn.loc.gov/2016016381

The views expressed herein are those of the author(s) and do not necessarily reflect the views of the United Nations.

ISBN 13: 978-1-138-62392-7 (pbk)
ISBN 13: 978-1-138-66921-5 (hbk)

Typeset in Galliard
by FiSH Books Ltd, Enfield

The Emerging Law of Forced Displacement in Africa

As of the end of 2015, there were 40.8 million civilians who had been internally displaced by conflicts and effects of natural disasters in various parts of the world. Internally displaced persons (IDPs) are currently the largest group of persons receiving assistance from some of the main international humanitarian organisations. With the largest concentration of internally displaced persons (IDPs), the African continent has been the worst affected region. While previously IDPs have largely been neglected under international law, the first-ever continental binding treaty on internal displacement, the African Union Convention on the Protection of and Assistance to Internally Displaced Persons (the Kampala Convention), entered into force on 6 December 2012. As of January 2016, 25 states have ratified the instrument while 40 states have become signatories.

This book significantly contributes to the study, policy making and practice on managing internal displacement by presenting the first major systematic examination of the evolution, elements and implementation of the Kampala Convention. It explores the responsibility of the state for the protection of IDPs particularly those who are most vulnerable during armed conflicts, internal strife, natural disasters, human rights violations and other circumstances. The status of ratification of the Convention is reviewed as well as the steps currently being undertaken by governments to implement the Convention. It also analyses the contribution by human rights mechanisms, inter-governmental bodies and UN peace-keeping missions in the implementation of the Convention. The book casts the Kampala Convention in broader institutional and normative developments in Africa and beyond. It demonstrates how concepts such as 'responsibility to protect' and 'sovereignty as responsibility' have begun to make inroads; influencing some of the more progressive instruments adopted by the African Union. It also sheds light on the relationship between the Convention and some regional instruments. In assessing the effectiveness of the Kampala Convention Allehone Abebe argues that the link between the Convention and initiatives on development, human rights and governance in Africa should be fully fostered.

Allehone M. Abebe is a Senior Protection Officer (UNHCR). He served as a senior diplomat at the Permanent Mission of Ethiopia in Geneva (2007–2011). He has written widely on human rights, migration and forced displacement.

Human Rights and International Law

Series Editor: Professor Surya P. Subedi, O.B.E.

This series will explore human rights law's place within the international legal order, offering much-needed interdisciplinary and global perspectives on human rights' increasingly central role in the development and implementation of international law and policy.

Human Rights and International Law is committed to providing critical and contextual accounts of human rights' relationship with international law theory and practice. To achieve this, volumes in the series will take a thematic approach that focuses on major debates in the field, looking at how human rights impacts on areas as diverse and divisive as security, terrorism, climate change, refugee law, migration, bioethics, natural resources and international trade.

Exploring the interaction, interrelationship and potential conflicts between human rights and other branches of international law, books in the series will address both historical development and contemporary contexts, before outlining the most urgent questions facing scholars and policy makers today.

A full list of titles in this series is available at:
www.routledge.com/Human-Rights-and-International-Law/book-series/HRIL.

Available titles:

Human Rights and Charity Law
International perspectives
Kerry O'Halloran

Human Rights and Development in International Law
Tahmina Karimova

The Emerging Law of Forced Displacement in Africa
Development and implementation of the Kampala Convention on internal displacement
Allehone M. Abebe

Forthcoming titles:

Adoption Law and Human Rights
International perspectives
Kerry O'Halloran

The Right to Truth in International Law
Victims' rights in human rights and international criminal law
Melanie Klinkner and Howard Davis

To Girumyee and Dagiyee

Contents

Acknowledgements

I owe a great debt of gratitude to Professor Walter Kälin and Dr Chaloka Beyani for their guidance and assistance during the research and writing of the material for this book. My mentor and good friend, Mr Minelik Alemu shared exceptionally useful comments and observations. Several officials and experts at the African Union, United Nations High Commissioner for Refugees, and International Committee of the Red Cross and Permanent Missions provided invaluable information about the process of drafting the African Union Convention on the Protection and Assistance of Internally Displaced Persons.

A very special thanks to my wife Eskedar and my two sons, Girumkal and Dagmawi, for their unwavering love and support. My parents and sisters have all created a circle of support and encouragement. I immensely thank all of them.

List of abbreviations

ACHPR	African Commission on Human and Peoples' Rights
ACRWC	African Charter on the Rights and Welfare of the Child
AMIS	African Union Mission in Sudan
AMISOM	African Union Mission in Somalia
APRM	African Peer Review Mechanism
AU	African Union
AUC	African Union Commission
AUPSC	African Union Peace and Security Council
BPETR	Bureau for the Placement, Education and Training of Refugees
CAR	Central African Republic
CCAR	Coordination Committee on Assistance to Refugees
CEDAW	Convention on the Elimination of All Forms of Discrimination Against Women
CESR	Centre of Economic and Social Rights
CEWARN	Conflict, Early Warning and Response Mechanism
CNDP	National Congress for the Defence of the People
COP	Conference of Parties
CSO	Civil society organisations
CRM	Country Review Mission
CSSDCA	Conference on Security, Stability, Development and Cooperation in Africa
DRC	Democratic Republic of Congo
EAC	East African Communities
ECOMOG	The Economic Community of West African States Monitoring Group
ECOSOCC	The Economic, Social and Cultural Council
ECOWAS	Economic Communities for West African States
FARDC	Forces Armées de la République Démocratique du Congo
FDLR	Forces démocratiques de libération du Rwanda
FGM	Female Genital Mutilation
GA	General Assembly
HARPD	Humanitarian Affairs, Refugees and Displaced Persons Division
IASC	Inter-Agency Standing Committee
ICC	International Criminal Court

ICGLR	International Conference of the Great Lakes Region
ICJ	International Court of Justice
ICRC	International Committee of the Red Cross
ICTR	International Criminal Tribunal for Rwanda
ICTY	International Criminal Tribunal for Former Yugoslavia
IDMC	Internal Displacement Monitoring Centre
IDPs	Internally displaced persons
IFRC	International Federation of the Red Cross
IGAD	Inter-governmental Authority on Development
IHL	International Humanitarian Law
ILC	International Law Commission
IOM	International Organisation for Migration
LRA	Lord Resistance Army
MONUC	United Nations Mission in the Democratic Republic of the Congo
MONUSCO	Mission of the United Nations Organisation Stabilisation in the Democratic Republic of Congo
MOU	Memorandum of Understanding
NAWOCO	National Women Councils
NEPAD	New Partnership for Africa's Development
NGO	Non-Governmental Organization
NHRI	National human rights institutions
OAS	Organisation of American States
OAU	Organisation of African Unity
OCHA	Office for the Coordination of Humanitarian Affairs
OHCHR	Office of the High Commissioner for Human Rights
OSCE	The Organization for Security and Co-operation in Europe
PRC	The Permanent Representatives Committee of the African Union
PSC	Peace and Security Council
SADC	South African Development Community
SARRED	International Conference on the Plight of Refugees, Returnees and Displaced Persons in Southern Africa
SC	Security Council
RSG	Representative of the Secretary General
TFG	Transitional Federal Government
UN	United Nations
UNAMID	United Nations-African Union Mission in Darfur
UNAMIR	The United Nations Assistance Mission for Rwanda
UNDRO	United Nations Disaster Relief Organization
UNHCR	United Nations High Commissioner for Refugees
UNITA	The Union for the Total Independence of Angola
UNSC	United Nations Security Council
UPR	Universal Periodic Review
WFP	World Food Program

1 Introduction

The world is confronted with the largest and most complex forced displacement of populations since the Second World War. Armed conflicts and communal tensions have displaced more than 60 million civilians, both within their own countries and across international borders. Natural disasters have also fuelled this displacement crisis. Among the displaced civilian population, IDPs constitute the largest group of population with humanitarian needs. IDPs are defined as

> persons or group of persons who have been forced or obliged to flee or to leave their homes or places of habitual residence, in particular as a result of or in order to avoid the effects of armed conflict, situations of generalized violence, violations of human rights or natural or human-made disasters, and who have not crossed an internationally recognized border.[1]

Over the decades humanitarian concern for refugees, those individuals who fled their country as a result of persecution, resulted in the development of an international refugee law and the establishment in 1951 of the office of the United Nations High Commissioner for Refugees (UNHCR) with the mandate to coordinate the response to their welfare. However IDPs are currently the largest group requiring assistance from international humanitarian organisations.

By the end of 2014, 38 million people were internally displaced, up from 33.3 million in 2013. Out of this large number of displaced persons, 11 million IDPs were newly displaced during 2014.[2] The African continent has been the worst affected region. During the same period there were 11 million IDPs in sub-Saharan Africa. Central African Republic, South Sudan,

1 Introduction, Guiding Principles on Internal Displacement, 22 July 1998, E/CN.4/1998/53/Add.2.

2 Internal Displacement Monitoring Centre. (2015) *Global Overview 2015 People Internally Displaced by Conflict and Violence*. Available at www.internal-displacement.org/publications/2015/global-overview-2015-people-internally-displaced-by-conflict-and-violence.

Nigeria, the Democratic Republic of Congo and Somalia have a significant number of their population internally displaced. In 2015 the number of internally displaced persons increased to 40.8 million. Conflicts remain the main triggers of displacement. Millions across the continent are leaving rural areas to urban centres, seeking better opportunities but often becoming invisible to authorities and service providers. Major public infrastructure and development projects put pressure on local livelihoods and displace communities. The effects of climate change, urbanisation and competition among communities over resources have also become sources of great concern.

The scale and complexity of internal displacement in Africa poses major challenges not only to humanitarian action but also to disaster response and to initiatives on conflict resolution, peace building, development and rule of law. Each year significant resource is committed to humanitarian activities to address the needs of IDPs and to finding solutions. There has also been an international effort to develop international collaboration through the 'cluster approach' and to support a further dissemination and implementation of the 1998 UN Guiding Principles on Internal Displacement (the Guiding Principles). Progress in the field of human rights, international humanitarian law, international criminal law and most recently, laws dealing with natural disasters supported this trend. More than ever, the UN are engaged in activities aimed at protecting civilians from harm and risks of violations.

Almost two decades after the adoption of the Guiding Principles, the impact of the international framework on the protection of and assistance to IDPs is at best mixed. Despite the welcome trend of internationalisation of the issue of internal displacement, crafting a robust international legal and institutional instrument for the protection of IDPs remains to be achieved.

Some of the most innovative legal developments concerning internal displacement have taken place in Africa. The first-ever continental binding treaty on internal displacement – the African Union Convention on the Protection of and Assistance to Internally Displaced Persons (also known as the Kampala Convention) – is a significant development. As of January 2016, 25 states have ratified the instrument while 40 states have become signatories. By consolidating existing norms and breaking new legal grounds, the Kampala Convention addresses the protection and assistance needs of IDPs in a continent that is disproportionately affected by the problem of internal displacement. Another significant milestone had been achieved when the Protocol on the Protection and Assistance to IDPs was adopted in 2006. The 2008 Annotations prepared by the former Representative of the UN Secretary General on the Human Rights of Internally Displaced Persons (RSG) duly acknowledges the adoption of the Protocol as an important legal development.[3]

3 Walter, Kälin, *The Guiding Principles on Internal Displacement: Annotations*, Second Edition (Washington, DC: The American Society of International Law, 2008).

The relationship between this regional legal development and the fast evolving international protection mechanisms, and its impact on existing protection standards and norms must be sufficiently explained. The Kampala Convention does not redefine the concept of sovereignty. Its provision derives from the premise that the state assumes the primary responsibility for protecting and assisting IDPs. In this sense, they clarify the responsibilities of states and non-state actors with regards to the protection of IDPs, particularly to those who are most vulnerable.

Explaining the evolution, scope and implementation of the Kampala Convention is the main theme of this book. The research explores factors that underpinned the regional codification of legal instruments on internal displacement in Africa. African regional development will be contrasted with past developments at the international level. It seeks to explore why perceptions and developments made the utility of an approach, deemed impractical at the international level, attractive to a regional setting. The question of whether this approach then translates into the effective protection of and assistance to IDPs needs to be answered. Both primary and secondary sources are considered. The drafting of the Kampala Convention took into account current developments and decisions of the African Commission on Human and Peoples' Rights (ACHPR), of the Inter-American Court of Human Rights, of the International Court of Justice and those of the European Court of Human Rights. Hence, decisions by regional and international tribunals, international and regional treaties and domestic legislation has been consulted as appropriate. The author conducted a series of interviews with experts, humanitarians and diplomats involved in the negotiation. The author has also closely examined the background documents of the drafting of the Convention whenever possible.

The relevance of the Convention's innovative provisions in addressing contemporary challenges such as displacement induced by environmental stress and climate change will be discussed. The book will further explore the normative and institutional, regional and national factors with the potential of affecting its implementation. The book is organised as follows. Chapter 2 traces the history and modality of formulating the Guiding Principles and examines the factors which have hindered the development of a binding international instrument for the protection of IDPs. Chapter 3 studies the evolution of the African Union's normative regime applicable to the protection and assistance needs of IDPs, and in particular, it looks at how codification has been rationalised and justified. Chapter 4 will then discuss the drafting background and history of the Kampala Convention. Important aspects of the regional instrument dealing with issues such as the definition of IDPs, the role of states and non-state actors, access to humanitarian assistance, protection of vulnerable groups, humanitarian assistance, and accountability for crimes are discussed in Chapter 5. Chapter 6 will lay out some of the challenges of implementing the Kampala Convention, and discuss how effective reinforcement requires a workable link among mechanisms at the national, regional and international levels, while Chapter 7 will conclude with the salient findings of the research.

2 Developments and gaps in international law concerning internal displacement

Introduction

The legal framework dealing with internal displacement brings together a myriad of norms from discrete fields of international law. Thus, it is imperative to examine the relevance of key developments, particularly in international human rights and humanitarian law. Treatment of IDPs had for long been considered a matter of state sovereignty. Considerable international developments have occurred since the 1990s. The formulation of the Guiding Principles in 1998 is an important milestone in international standard setting.[1] The Guiding Principles is the first authoritative framework that recognises the rights and freedoms of IDPs.

The following decade witnessed consolidation of these standards. First, the convergence and cross-fertilisation of doctrines across formerly 'self-contained' legal fields such as refugee, international humanitarian and human rights law have become commonplace.[2] Second, there has been a greater appreciation of the need for an effective international response to issues previously considered falling within the domestic jurisdiction of states. Third, though the initial ambivalence to normative standards on internal displacement gradually subsided, the idea of a binding international treaty for the protection of IDPs has largely been resisted. Last, but certainly not least, states have increasingly adopted national legislations and policy instruments specifically dealing with IDPs. These instruments borrow notions from the Guiding Principles. In Africa, Angola, Kenya, Uganda, Sierra Leone, Somalia and Sudan have already adopted national legislations or

1 Guiding Principles on Internal Displacement, 22 July 1998, E/CN.4/1998/53/Add.2; Compilation and Analysis of Legal Norms, E/CN.4/1996/52/Add.2 (1995); and Compilation and Analysis of Legal Norms, Part II, E/CN.4/1998/53/Add.1 (1998).

2 Joan Fitzpatrick, 'Human Rights and Forced Displacement: Converging Standards', in Anne Bayefsky and Joan Fitzpatrick, eds., *Human Rights and Forced Displacement* (The Hague, The Netherlands: Martinus Nijhoff Publishers, 2000), 3; Bruno Simma, 'Self-Contained Regimes', *Netherlands Yearbook of International Law*, Vol. 16 (1985), 11–136.

policies dealing with internal displacement.[3] Others are in the process of doing so.

The application of international law to IDPs and its impact on regional and national developments is still evolving. Africa's recent legal and institutional innovations should not be considered in isolation, but must be examined taking into account the nature and complexity of this evolution. The development by the African Union of a legal framework to deal with internal displacement should lay bare the increasing role of regional organisations. By identifying key developments particularly in the fields of human rights and humanitarian law relevant to the protection and assistance of IDPs, this chapter examines the African Union's initiative from the perspective of international law. It attempts to examine the relevance of the doctrine of state responsibility, and the basis on which international law for an international response with respect to IDP can be justified. The relevance and limitations of concepts of humanitarian intervention and responsibility to protect will also be analysed. By discussing the codification history of the Guiding Principles, the chapter will identify lessons learnt from international efforts to elaborate an international legal instrument to regulate internal displacement and highlight some of the approaches that were considered in addressing this 'normative gap'.

Recent developments in international law

Internal displacement is not a concept well-recognised under international law. The latter neither defines IDPs nor grants them special status.[4] An inquiry into the treatment of internal displacement under international law is also made more difficult by the absence of a legal instrument which specifically deals with the issue.[5] Notions of sovereignty and non-intervention have been used to shield states' relationship with their nationals from the purview of public international law.[6] Whenever the issue of internal displacement is discussed by the United Nations, states often invoke the principle that international response should be 'based on an appeal by the

3 Brookings LSE Project on Internal Displacement. (2011) *National and Regional Laws and Policies on Internal Displacement: Index*. Available at www.brookings.edu/projects/idp/Laws-and-Policies/idp_policies_index.aspx.

4 Guy Goodwin-Gill and Jane McAdam, *The Refugee in International Law*, Third Edition (Oxford: Oxford University Press, 2007), 482.

5 The former UN Representative of the Secretary General States, 'Existing international law as applied to IDPs consists of a highly complex web of norms originating from a variety of legal sources which makes its application in specific situation of internally displaced difficult'. See Compilation and Analysis of Legal Norms, E/CN.4/1996/52/Add.2 (1995), para. 4.

6 Patrick Schmidt, 'The Process and Prospects for the UN Guiding Principles on Internal Displacement to become Customary International Law: A Preliminary Assessment', *Georgetown Journal of International Law* 35(2003–2004), 489.

7 Article 3 of the Annex to General Assembly Res 46/182, 19 Dec. 1991.

affected state'.[7] States also conveniently make public reference to the United Nations' Charter prohibition of 'the threat of force or use of force against the territorial integrity or political independence of any state',[8] and intervention 'in matters which are essentially within the domestic jurisdiction of any state'.[9] They opposed the formal adoption of the Guiding Principles fearing that the later may be used as tools of intervention.[10] These challenges made some authors consider it 'unrealistic to believe that international law can be overstretched to effectively address the issue of IDPs'.[11] However, international law incorporates useful standards and norms that are directly relevant to internal displacement.[12] The former RSG examined the extent to which international law provides protection to IDPs. The conclusions of this exercise resulted in two important documents which were later submitted to the former UN Commission on Human Rights. This work underlined that international human rights and humanitarian law embodies relevant standards for the protection of IDPs. These include (a) prohibition and criminalisation of forced displacement, (b) protection from eviction based on grounds that are not permissible under international law, (c) recognition of the basic human rights of all including IDPs, and (d) provision of state obligations to address the consequences of displacement on the enjoyment of other entitlements. It served as a basis for the development of the Guiding Principles.[13]

As was noted by the former RSG, though the above mentioned fields of international law may serve as sources of legal protection for victims of forced displacement, 'grey areas' and 'gaps' persist.[14] Human rights norms

8 Article 2, para. 4 of the United Nations Charter, 24 October 1945, 1 UNTS XVI. See also Article 3 of the International Law Commission's Draft Declaration on the Rights and Duties of States, adopted by the General Assembly Resolution 375 (IV) of 6 December 1949. See also Declaration on Principles of International Law Concerning Friendly Relations and Co-operation among States in Accordance with the Charter of the United Nations, Annex, General Assembly Resolution 2625 (XXV) of 24 October 1970.

9 Article 2(7) of the United Nations Charter.

10 Thomas Weiss and David Korn, *Internal Displacement: Conceptualisation and its Consequences* (Oxford: Routledge, 2006), 12, note 23.

11 See Mohammad Alborzi, *Evaluating the Effectiveness of International Refugee Law: Protection of Iraqi Refugees* (The Netherlands: Martinus Njihoff Publishers, 2006), 5; See also Elizabeth Ruddick, 'Note: The Continuing Constraint of Sovereignty: International Law, International Protection and the Internally Displaced', *Boston University Law Review* 77(1997): 429, 440, 452. Catherine Phuong, *The International Protection of Internally Displaced Persons* (Cambridge: Cambridge University Press, 2004), 233; see also Francis Deng, 'Frontiers of Sovereignty: A Framework of Protection, Assistance and Development for the Internally Displaced', *Leiden Journal of International Law* 8(1995): 247.

12 E/CN.4/1996/52/Add.2, at para. 25; See Walter Kälin, 'The Guiding Principles on Internal Displacement as International Minimum Standard and Protection Tool' *Refugee Survey Quarterly* 24(2005): 28.

13 See Compilation and Analysis of Legal Norms, E/CN.4/1996/52/Add.2 (1995) and Compilation and Analysis of Legal Norms, Part II, E/CN.4/1998/53/Add.1 (1998).

14 Compilation and Analysis of Legal Norms, E/CN.4/1996/52/Add.2 (1995), paras. 410 and 411.

only implicitly recognise protection from arbitrary displacement.[15] Their application may also be limited by notions of limitation and derogation. International humanitarian law does not prohibit all forms of forced displacement.[16] Whereas a specific right of a displaced person is well recognised in one branch of international law, its existence may not be as certain in other contexts.[17] The ambivalence and uncertainty of international law towards internal displacement, however, started changing due to recent developments in human rights, international humanitarian law and criminal law.

International human rights law

It is only recently that human rights instruments began making specific references to IDPs. The Vienna Declaration and Plan of Action for Human Rights calls on states to give 'special attention including through intergovernmental and humanitarian organizations and finding lasting solutions to questions related to internally displaced persons including their voluntary and safe return and rehabilitation'.[18] The Convention on the Rights of Persons with Disabilities includes provisions covering issues related to the protection and safety of 'persons with disabilities in situations of risk, including situations of armed conflict, humanitarian emergencies and the occurrence of natural disasters'.[19] The United Nations Declaration on the Rights of Indigenous Peoples provides for protection from forced removal of indigenous people from their traditional land.[20]

International humanitarian law

International humanitarian law applies directly to internal displacement generated by armed conflicts. Its rules prohibit the transfer of populations in occupied territories unless such measures are justified on the basis of security

15 These relevant human rights norms include, among others, freedom of movement and choice of residence, freedom from arbitrary interference, and the right to housing. Ibid., para. 10.

16 See Eritrea Ethiopia Claims Commission: Partial Award in Ethiopia's Central Front Claims, 43 ILM 1275(2004), para. 53.

17 The right of humanitarian assistance is well recognised under international humanitarian law, but 'no legal instruments explicitly acknowledge the existence of such a right' in disaster situations. See, Preliminary Report on the Protection of Persons during Disasters, Mr Eduardo Valencia-Ospina, Special Rapporteur, International Law Commission, 60th Session, A/CN.4/598, para. 54.

18 Vienna Declaration and Programme of Action of the World Conference on Human Rights, held at Vienna, 14–25 June 1993, United Nations document A/CONF.157/23, Part I, para. 23.

19 Convention on the Rights of Persons with Disabilities, adopted by the General Assembly, 24 January 2007, A/RES/61/106, Art 11.

20 Art 10, United Nations Declaration on the Rights of Indigenous Peoples, General Assembly Resolution, A/61/L. 67, Annex., 7 September 2008.

or military necessity.[21] International humanitarian law also embodies general obligations to facilitate the return of persons once hostilities cease. International humanitarian law stipulates strict rules which aim to limit conditions under which vulnerable groups such as children may be evacuated.[22] Civilians subjected to evacuation must be treated in a manner which meets minimum standards. Belligerents are obligated to prevent family separation and facilitate family reunification.[23]

International humanitarian rules applicable to non-international armed conflict have not been as elaborate as those that are directly implementable to situations of international armed conflict. In recent years, however, a welcome trend has emerged which expands the reach of humanitarian rules. A seminal study by the International Committee of the Red Cross on customary international humanitarian law is one important indication of such trend. It recognises that the provisions of Geneva Convention IV and Protocol II concerning the prohibition of forced movement of populations have archived the status of international customary law.[24]

The relevant section of the study is incorporated in rules 129–133. Rules 129 and 130 underline the prohibition of deportation or forced transfer of population. When displacement occurs, 'all possible measures must be taken in order that the civilians concerned are received under satisfactory conditions of shelter, hygiene, health, safety and nutrition and that members of the same family are not separated' (Rule 131). Displaced persons have a right to voluntarily return in safety to their homes or place of residence as soon as the reasons for their displacement ceases (Rule 132). They also enjoy the right to the protection of their property (Rule 133).

The significance of the study and its normative contributions should not be underestimated. It further develops rules applicable to non-international armed conflict. By reviewing a body of state practice and jurisprudence of international tribunals, the International Committee of the Red Cross (ICRC) study clarifies the application of international humanitarian rules to internal displacement.[25]

International criminal law

International criminal law is directly relevant to situations of forced displacement. The Statute of the International Criminal Court (ICC) includes

21 Article 49 of the Geneva Convention IV; Article 17 of Protocol II.

22 See Articles 78(1) and 4(3)e of Protocol I and Protocol II respectively.

23 See Articles 26 and 74 of Geneva Convention IV and Protocol I respectively.

24 Jean-Marie Henckaerts and Louise Doswald-Beck, *Customary International Humanitarian Law, Volume I: Rules* (Cambridge: Cambridge University Press, 2005), Rule 129(B).

25 Ibid., Rules 129–133.

unlawful forced displacement in the list of war crimes[26] or crimes against humanity.[27] The International Criminal Tribunal for Former Yugoslavia (ICTY) has jurisdiction under its statute to look into situations of unlawful deportation and transfer of civilian population both during international and non-international armed conflicts.[28] The Court reaffirmed this rule in a number of its judgments.[29] ICC Statue also allows the court to consider deportation as a crime against humanity.[30]

State responsibility

States assume the primary responsibility for providing protection and assistance to their nationals including IDPs. There has been a growing interest to apply the doctrine of state responsibility to examine laws relevant to forced displacement.[31] International law provides guidance for determining the legality of acts by the state causing forced population displacement, and its responsibilities in preventing and mitigating such phenomenon.[32] Now it is accepted that state responsibility extends to conducts of states resulting in breaches of international human rights obligations[33] and conducts by non-state actors which may be attributable to states.[34] Yet the doctrine is still evolving.[35] The International Law Commission (ILC) notes that 'international law today lays more and more obligation on the state with regard to

26 The Statute of the International Criminal Court, UN Doc, A/CONF.183/9, 17 July 1998, Arts 8(2) (b) (viii) & 8(2) (e) (viii).

27 Article 7(1) (d).

28 Note 24 above.

29 *The Prosecutor v. Radislav Krstic*, Judgment of Trial Chamber I, IT-98-33, 2 August 2001, paras. 519–532 and *Prosecutor v. Milorad Krnojelac* (Trial Judgment), IT-97-25-T, International Criminal Tribunal for the former Yugoslavia (ICTY), 15 March 2002, paras. 472–485.

30 Statute of the International Criminal Tribunal for Rwanda, 1994, 33 ILM 1602, Art 3(d).

31 See Guy Goodwin-Gill, 'State Responsibility and the 'Good Faith' Obligation in International Law', in *Issues of State Responsibility before International Judicial Institutions*, eds Fitzmaurice, Malgosia and Sarooshi, Danesh (Oxford: Hart Publishing, 2004); Christian Tomuschat, 'State Responsibility and the Country of Origin', in *The Problem of Refugees in the Light of Contemporary International Law Issues*, ed. Vera Gowlland Debbas, 59–81. (The Hague: Kluwer Law International, 1996); Pierre Bertrand, 'An Operational Approach to International Refugee Protection', *Cornell International Law Journal* 26(1994): 495–500.

32 See Chaloka Beyani, 'State Responsibility for the Prevention and Resolution of Forced Population Displacement in International Law', *International Journal of Refugee Law* (Special Edition, 1995): 131–137.

33 Ian Brownlie, *Principles of Public International Law*, (3rd ed., 1976) (Oxford: Oxford University Press, 1976): 512–3..

34 Articles 9 & 10 of ILC Draft Articles. International Law Commission, Draft Articles on Responsibility of States for Internationally Wrongful Acts, November 2001, Supplement No. 10 (A/56/10).

35 Guy-Goodwin, note 4 above, 132.

the treatment of its nationals'.[36] However, the Commission's Draft Articles on State Responsibility chiefly govern the inter-state relationship.[37] Goodwin-Gill contends that the Draft Articles,

> leave open, and are even equivocal on, the issue of consequences of breach where the primary beneficiary of the obligations is not a state, for example, in human rights cases, or where a state is unable or unwilling to invoke rights on behalf of individual persons.[38]

Accordingly, state responsibility primarily deals with the responsibility of states, presenting a clear challenge to those who wish to see non-state actors having clearer responsibility for human rights breaches; perhaps importantly also to victims of forced displacement. Whenever third-party states invoke state responsibility for violations of human rights without showing any specific interest of injury, rules of non-intervention and sovereignty apply. Crawford identifies norms including the distinction between the state and the private sector, the lack of criminal responsibility of non-state actors, and the principles of non-intervention underpinning the doctrine of state responsibility which risk diminishing its utility for implementation of human rights.[39] Moreover, factors generating forced displacement such as natural disasters, famine, epidemics and so on 'are not phenomenon that can be directly imputed to human activity'.[40] It is true that public international law provides that unlawful treatment of individuals even by their government may result in *erga omnes* obligations.[41] This may provide an opportunity for third-party states to invoke state responsibility. This is particularly relevant to those states which 'without specially affected by the breach, participate in a specific legal regime from which legal obligation *erga omnes* partes derive'.[42]

36 Report of the International Law Commission to the General Assembly. Commentary on Article 3 of the Draft Articles on State Responsibility, para. 12, reprinted in *Year Book of International Law Commission 2* (1972): 179.

37 See Edith Weiss, 'Invoking State Responsibility in the Twenty-first Century', *American Journal of International Law* 96(2002): 798.

38 Guy Goodwin-Gill, note 4 above, 76.

39 See James Crawford, *Human Rights and State Responsibility*, Thomas J Dodd Research Centre University of Connecticut, 2007. Available online at: http://doddcenter.uconn.edu/dd/events/sackler/Crawford%20transcript.pdf.

40 Tomuschat, note 31 above, 60.

41 According to the ICJ, 'Such obligations drive, for example, in contemporary international law, from outlawing of acts of aggression, and of genocide, and also from the principles and rules governing basic rights of the human person including protection from slavery and racial discrimination'. *Barcelona Traction, Light and Power Company, Limited (Belgium v. Spain); Preliminary Objections*, International Court of Justice (ICJ), 24 July 1964, I.C.J. Reports 1964, p. 9, 12, para. 34.

42 Linos Scillianos, 'The Classification of Obligations and the Multilateral Dimensions of the Relations of State Responsibility', *European Journal of International Law* 13 (2002): 1139.

But as Meron states, the recognition of the concept of *erga omnes* 'has been largely doctrinal and rhetorical' and that 'it has not spawned, so far, significant practice'.[43] Goodwin-Gill, sharing the foregoing sentiment, also states that in today's migration context obligation *erga omnes parte* 'offers little more than theoretical redress'.[44] Moreover, state responsibility cannot be interpreted in a similar fashion across the wide spectrum of forced displacement. It is also stated that human rights obligations of states with respect to IDPs relate to a variety of legal instruments with respect to which even the Draft Articles prepared by ILC, to borrow Goodwin-Gill's phrase, are 'equivocal'.[45] A doctrine whose major legal consequence heavily hinges upon financial compensation provides little in the way of relief to victims as most of the countries experiencing internal displacement lack the means to provide such a remedy.[46]

State responsibility provides limited tools to third states and the international community to respond to crises of internal displacement of populations, particularly when the state experiencing the displacement is either unwilling or unable to provide protection and relief.[47] The concept, however, engages the role and responsibility of the wider community of states in taking a range of steps to promote compliance by states with internationally recognised norms and standards.[48]

Responsibility to protect

The legality of coercive measures including a possible use of military force by third states and the international community in order to protect IDPs within the territory of another state was sharply debated particularly in the post-Cold War setting, mostly in light of measures taken by the United Nations in countries such as Somalia, Iraq and former Yugoslavia.[49] Though intervention by

43 Theodor Meron, *The Humanisation of International Law* (The Netherlands: Martinus Nijhoff Publishers, 2006), 262.

44 Goodwin-Gill, note 4 above, 81.

45 Ibid.

46 A similar point has also been made by Hathaway as a critique to Garvey's vision of refugee law as 'a system of tort law in which the parties are the States of origin and the States of asylum'. James Hathaway, 'Preconceiving Refugee Law as Human Rights Protection' in *Problems and Prospects of Refugee Law*, eds. Vera Gowlland and Klaus Samson (Geneva: The Graduate Institute of International Studies, 1992), 16.

47 See Daniel Bodnsky and John Crook, 'Symposium: The ILC's Articles: Introduction and Overview', *American Journal of International Law* 96(2002): 790.

48 It was noted that, at least with regard to the implementation of international humanitarian law, 'what other States may or must do when a state violates international humanitarian law' remains to be 'one of the most difficult, delicate and yet rarely analysed questions of international humanitarian law'. Marco Sassoli, 'State Responsibility for Violations of International Law', *International Review of the Red Cross* 84(2002): 421.

49 Roberta Cohen and Francis Deng, *Masses in Flight: The Global Crisis of Internal Displacement* (Washington, DC: Brookings Institution Press, 1998), 4.

the UN is often raised in connection with the most severe cases of human rights violations, the relevance of the doctrine to the protection of IDPs is evident. It is not a coincidence, therefore, that commentators and experts became prominent advocates of concepts such as 'conditional sovereignty' and 'sovereignty as a responsibility'.[50]

The aforementioned concepts were linked with a brief revival of 'humanitarian intervention' in the early 1990s. The latter broadly refers to a situation where a threat of or actual force is used by a state, group of states or Security Council for protecting nationals of a given state from serious violations of human rights.[51] Articles 55 and 56 of the United Nations Charter, where the obligation of states and the United Nations to promote human rights is provided for, is occasionally involved to justify such a measure. Article 1, paragraph 3, of the Charter provides that one of the purposes of the Charter is the promotion of the 'respect for human rights and fundamental freedoms'. Of course, there are numerous actions that can be taken by the United Nations or other States with respect to the protection and promotion of human rights within one state; and not all of these steps raise concerns with similar weight. Robert Jennings and Arthur Watts, for example, note that the prohibition of intervention under the United Nations Charter does not preclude measures by the United Nations to undertake 'study, discussion, investigation and recommendation'.[52]

According to Lauterpacht, certain violations of human rights by the state may legitimatise the use of force.[53] This school of thought argues that human rights violations triggering internal displacement and subsequent breaches may also constitute an *abus de droit* and hence may justify intervention by the UN.[54] Under certain conditions, it is submitted, states and international organisations may even have a duty to intervene when a particular state is unable or unwilling to provide protection for civilians.[55] Reference is made to decisions by the United Nations Security Council in Somalia, former Yugoslavia and Iraq where its resolutions called for the provision of humanitarian assistance irrespective of the availability of the concept by the state.[56]

50 Antonio Cassese, '*Ex Iniuria Ius Oritur:* Are We Moving towards International Legitimation of Forcible Humanitarian Countermeasures in the World Community?', *European Journal of International Law* 10 (2000): 27.

51 Sean Murphy, *Humanitarian Intervention: The United Nations in an Evolving World Order* (Philadelphia: University of Philadelphia Press, 1996), 11, 12.

52 Robert Jennings and Arthur Watts, *Oppenheim's International Law*, Ninth Edition, Vol. I (Harlow: Longman, 1992): 449.

53 Hersch Lauterpacht, 'The Grotian Tradition in International Law', *British Yearbook of International Law* 46(1946): 1.

54 Richard Plender, 'The Legal Basis of International Jurisdiction to Act with regard to the Internally Displaced', *International Journal of Refugee Law* (1994) 6 (3): 356.

55 Roberta Cohen and Francis Deng, *Masses in Flight: The Global Crisis of Internal Displacement* (Washington, DC: Brookings Institution Press, 1998), 276.

56 Note 54 above, 354.

The utility of the doctrine of humanitarian intervention in the protection of human rights in general and in addressing the protection and assistance needs of IDPs in particular however is constrained by numerous factors. The ICJ questioned the legality of the threat or use of force by a state trying to justify its action based on human rights in a territory of another state.[57] The ILC also excludes the use of force from the list of 'counter-measures' permissible under its Draft Articles on State Responsibility (Article 22(2)). This position is also supported by a preponderance of opinion in the international legal community.[58] Brownlie reflects this general sentiment when he states:[59]

> [t]he proponents of humanitarian intervention are distinctly in a minority. More significant, however, is the position in customary international law, which depends upon the practice of states based upon *opinio juris*, that is to say, a belief that the action is in accordance with international law. There can be no doubt that the United Nations Charter can be modified by the congruent practice of the member states crystallizing as a new principle of customary law. But there is a burden of proof upon proponents of a change in the customary law. The central point is the absence of evidence of a change of view by a majority of states.

The practice of the Security Council also does not sufficiently reveal whether its interventionist measures were taken based on broader political and security considerations, or on purely humanitarian grounds. In fact, these measures were consistently couched as responses to threats against international peace and security. Even if a clearer picture on the use of force for humanitarian purposes is garnered, there is no assurance that such measures do not openly conflict with principles of territorial sovereignty and political independence of states as enshrined in the Charter of the United Nations.[60] The UN General Assembly, on numerous occasions, has affirmed simultaneously the importance of humanitarian assistance and the question of sovereignty.[61]

57 *Case Concerning Military and Paramilitary Activities in and Against Nicaragua (Merits) (Nicaragua v. United States)* [1986] ICJ Reports 14 [201–209]. Available online at www.icj-cij.org/docket/index.php?sum=367&code=nus&p1=3&p2=3&case=70&k=66&p3=5.

58 Oscar Schachter, *International Law in Theory and Practice* (The Netherlands: Martius Nijhoff Publisher, 1991), 113.

59 Ian Brownlie, 'Kosovo Crisis Inquiry: Memorandum on the International Law Aspects', *The International and Comparative Law Quarterly* 49 (2000): 894.

60 *Case Concerning Military and Paramilitary Activities in and Against Nicaragua (Merits) (Nicaragua v. United States)* [1986] ICJ Reports 14 [201–209], available online at www.icj-cij.org/docket/index.php?sum=367&code=nus&p1=3&p2=3&case=70&k=66&p3=5, 13.

61 See A/RES/43/131(1988) and A/RES/46/182(1991).

The emergence of 'responsibility to protect' is necessitated partly by the need to address the above mentioned constraints. It was articulated by the report of the International Commission on Intervention and State Sovereignty which was released in 2003.[62] Member states adopted the Outcome Document of the 2005 World Summit which recognised the doctrine of the Responsibility to Protect.[63] Since then, the Secretary General has released three key reports which examined the various aspects of the operationalisation of the doctrine.[64]

The responsibility to protect emphasises the primary responsibility of the state concerned to protect its nationals. It covers a broad range of prevention and rehabilitative steps that can be taken by the state. Each individual state assumes the responsibility to protect its population from genocide, war crimes, ethnic cleansing and crimes against humanity.[65] Other states may, through the Security Council, take collective measures when national authorities manifestly fail to protect their population from these breaches.[66] The relevance of this concept to the protection and assistance of IDPs is notable.[67] The Outcome Document also recognises the Guiding Principles as 'an important international framework for the protection of internally displaced persons'.[68] The direct link between 'responsibility to protect' and protection of IDPs can easily be discerned. Situations which trigger the need to invoke the concept often result in massive and severe forms of civilian displacement. But the linkage between the two does transcend the 'casual connection'. The intellectual history of the doctrine of 'responsibility to protect' is also linked to the debate regarding internal displacement.[69] Advocates for the protection of IDPs

62 See The Responsibility to Protect: The Report of the International Commission on Intervention and State Sovereignty, Canada: International Development Centre, 2001.

63 UN General Assembly, 2005 World Summit Outcome: Resolution, adopted by the General Assembly, on 24 October 2005, A/RES/60/1.

64 See UN General Assembly, *Implementing the Responsibility to Protect: Report of the Secretary-General*, 12 January 2009, A/63/677, *Early Warning, Assessment, and the Responsibility to Protect: Report of the Secretary General*, 17 July 2010, A64/864 and *The Role of Regional and Sub-regional arrangements in Implementing the Responsibility to Protect*, 27 June 2011, A/65/877.

65 Ibid., para. 138.

66 Ibid., para. 139.

67 Similar sentiments were expressed during the international conference organized in Oslo, Norway to mark the 10th anniversary of the UN Guiding Principles. Available online at: www.internal-displacement.org/8025747B0037BAC5/(httpHomepages)/$first?OpenDocument. See also Erin Mooney, 'The Guiding Principles and Responsibility to Protect', *Forced Migration Review* (Special Issue 2008): 11.

68 UN General Assembly, 2005 World Summit Outcome, para. 132.

69 See Roberta Cohen and Francis Deng, 'Normative Framework of Sovereignty', in *Sovereignty as Responsibility: Conflict Management in Africa*, ed. Francis Deng *et al.*, 1–34 (Washington, DC: Brookings Institution, 1996).

were important players in the development of the 'responsibility to protect'.[70] Francis Deng had attempted to ground his mandate on the concept of 'sovereignty as responsibility';[71] and this has also been considered as a key legacy of his role as the Representative of the Secretary General (RSG).[72]

Whereas the report of the International Commission on Intervention and State Sovereignty in effect announced the demise of a narrowly constructed version of humanitarian intervention and replaced it with an expanded notion of responsibility, it reframed the debate with a rather more complex, vague and politically nuanced concept.[73] On its own, the doctrine of 'responsibility to protect, much like that of humanitarian intervention, is not a legal doctrine'.[74] Its content 'leaves considerable doubt concerning whether and to what extent States intended to create a legal norm'.[75] For example, the ILC notes that 'responsibility to protect' is unclear with respect to the responsibilities it creates to third parties, the content of these rights, and how these rights may ultimately be implemented. It is a broad concept involving some elements well-established in international law, at the same time incorporating others requiring further clarification. Associating R2P to internal displacement will generate controversy and weakens the acceptance of standards development over the years to regulate internal displacement.

The role of the Security Council

The issues discussed above came to focus on various measures taken by the Security Council with respect to the protection of civilians including those affected by the problem of internal displacement.[76] The actions of the Security Council in countries such as Iraq, the former Yugoslavia, Haiti and Somalia reveal the Security Council's willingness to broaden factors

70 Note 62 above, 218–219. The report of the International Commission on Intervention and State Sovereignty: Responsibility to Protect makes reference to Francis Deng's concept of 'sovereignty as responsibility'.

71 Francis Deng, *Protecting the Dispossessed: A Challenge for the International Community* (Washington, DC: Brookings Institution, 1993), 135.

72 Note 10 above, 25.

73 Stahn Carsten, 'Responsibility to Protect: Political Rhetoric or Emerging Legal Norm?' *American Journal of International Law* 101(2007): 102.

74 Ibid., 99. See also Noel Dorr, 'The Responsibility to Protect – an Emerging Norm?', *Irish Studies in International Affairs* 19(2008): 189–207.

75 Francis Deng, *Protecting the Dispossessed: A Challenge for the International Community* (Washington, DC: Brookings Institution, 1993), 99, 101.

76 The Security Council has also a power to investigate 'any dispute, or any situation which might lead to international friction or give rise to a dispute' (Article 34). The Security Council exercised such authority which also includes disputes of humanitarian nature in South Africa in the 1960s. Brownlie, *Principles of International Law*, 334.

considered as threats to international peace and security[77] with the view to addressing some serious and massive violations of human rights and humanitarian concerns.[78] Resolution 688 was considered groundbreaking by identifying displacement and human rights violations as 'threats to international peace and security'.[79] The Council also established 'safe areas' which sought to provide protection for civilian populations in Iraq,[80] former Yugoslavia,[81] Iraq[82] and Rwanda.[83]

The implications of interventions by the Security Council received considerable attention.[84] Some defended these measures as falling within the mandate of the Security Council under the United Nations Charter and having the potential to remedy existing shortcomings of international law for the protection of IDPs.[85] However, the legal authority of the United Nations to act with respect to internal displacement also raises certain questions.[86] Freedman states,

> In addition to protecting displaced persons and facilitating their repatriation or resettlement, the Security Council has passed numerous resolutions that expand the notion of state responsibility by calling on specific States to put an end to internal displacement and mass exodus.[87]

Resolution 1296 of 19 April 2000 states that gross and massive violations of human rights and humanitarian law *may constitute* a threat to international peace and security. This resolution seems to suggest that it is the consequence of the violations, rather than the violations themselves, which may be considered as threats to international peace and security. However, it is often difficult to differentiate when internal mass displacement becomes a threat to international peace and security *per se*, or when it commands international attention because it is clearly associated or linked with other egregious forms

77 Article 39 of the UN Charter reads, in part, that 'The Security Council shall determine the existence of any threat to the peace, breach of the peace, or act of aggression and shall decide what measures shall be taken in accordance with Articles 41 and 42'.

78 Martti Koskenniemi, 'The Police in the Temple – Order, Justice, and the UN: A Dialectical View', *European Journal of International Law* 6(1995): 328–345.

79 Paul Freedman, 'International Intervention to Combat the Explosion of Refugees and Internally Displaced Persons', *Georgetown Immigration Law Journal* 9(1995), 581.

80 S.C. Res/688(1999).

81 S.C. Res/787(1992); S.C. Res/770(1992), S.C. Res/820/(1993); S.C. Res/819(1993); S.C. Res/836(1992).

82 Brownlie notes that several of these measures were taken by states who received 'delegated' powers from the Security Council. Brownlie, *Principles of International Law*, 334.

83 S.C. Res/929(1994).

84 Ibid., 573–580.

85 Ibid., 580.

86 Note 54 above, 345.

87 Paul Freedman, 'International Intervention to Combat the Explosion of Refugees and Internally Displaced Persons', *Georgetown Immigration Law Journal* 9(1995), 581, 573.

of human rights violations. At least in the practice of the Security Council, these two issues have not been clearly differentiated. Resolution 1973, adopted on 17 March 2011 by the Security Council concerning the situation in Libya, is significant in the sense that it recognised the responsibility of the government of Libya to protect its nationals, warned that the attacks against the civilian population may amount to crimes against humanity, and authorised 'Member States that have notified the Secretary General, acting nationally or through regional organisations or arrangements, and acting in cooperation with the Secretary General, to take all necessary measures ... to protect civilians and civilian populated areas under threat of attack'.

International humanitarian law as such does not explicitly provide a role for the United Nations in exercising a supervisory role with respect to treaty-based and customary international humanitarian law. However, since 1999 the Security Council has adopted some important resolutions which are directly related to the protection of civilians during armed conflicts. These resolutions reaffirmed prohibition of forced displacement in armed conflicts: the Council highlighted the specific negative impact of wars on forcibly displaced persons, and underscored the need to maintain the civilian character of refugee and IDP camps.[88] These resolutions also recognise the fact that deliberate targeting of civilians during armed conflict and systematic, deliberate and flagrant violations of humanitarian and human rights law may constitute a threat to international peace and security. In these situations, the Council may consider and take the appropriate steps.[89] They also highlight the specific vulnerabilities and protection needs of particularly women and children during armed conflicts and reiterate the obligation of states to ensure protection.[90]

International treaty on internal displacement?

From the start establishing international institutional response to internal displacement has dominated the debate on the crisis of internal displacement.[91] For example, the International Conference on the Plight of Refugees, Returnees and Displaced Persons in Southern Africa (SARRED), held in 1988 in Oslo highlighted, as a principal problem, the lack of an international institution or mechanism to coordinate the provision of assistance to IDPs in the Southern Africa region.[92] Numerous resolutions of the

88 S/RES/1674(2006), paras. 1–14.

89 Ibid., para. 26.

90 Ibid., para. 19.

91 See Roberta Cohen and Jaques Eueno, *Improving Institutional Arrangements for IDPs* (Washington, DC: Brookings Institution–Refugee Policy Project on Internal Displacement, 1995), 20.

92 Oslo Declaration and Plan of Action on the Plight of Refugees, Returnees and Displaced Persons in Southern Africa, SARRED Doc. 88/5(August 24, 1988), para. 21.

General Assembly[93] and the Economic and Social Council (ECOSOC)[94] also focused on the institutional aspects of the global response to internal displacement. Codifying a legal instrument dealing with the internally displaced had not been a dominant element of the work of the RSG.[95]

Fitzpatrick bluntly states that the attempt 'to explicate the rights of the internally displaced persons is plagued by conceptual and practical pitfalls'.[96] As the Comprehensive Study clearly highlighted, opinions were divided on whether a new specific legal instrument for the protection and assistance of IDPs is needed.[97] The resistance by states to the idea of codification of a separate binding international instrument on IDPs encouraged the search for an alternative mechanism. A 'soft-law' approach was adopted through the Guiding Principles.[98] This partly helps circumvent some of the difficulties embedded in the traditional method of developing norms. This new approach to developing norms has on occasion been accepted by states. In the context of disaster response, the General Assembly recognised similarly developed guidelines as 'a flexible and helpful reference tool for disaster preparedness and response efforts'.[99] One can also mention in this context the Principles and Rules for Red Cross and Red Crescent Disaster Relief;[100] the 1969 Red Cross Declaration of Principles for International Humanitarian Relief to the Civilian Population in Disaster Situations;[101] and the more recent Guidelines for the Domestic Facilitation and Regulation of International Disaster Relief and Initial Recovery Assistance, adopted by the Thirtieth International Conference of the Red

93 See GA Res. 43/116(1988).
94 See ECOSOC Res. 1990/78 (1990).
95 Francis Deng, Comprehensive Study on the Human Rights Issues Related to Internally Displaced Persons, E/CN.4/1993/95 (United Nations, Commission on Human Rights, 21 January 1993), para. 55.
96 Joan Fitzpatrick, 'Human Rights and Forced Displacement: Converging Standards', in *Human Rights and Forced Displacement*, eds. Anne Bayefsky and Joan Fitzpatrick. (The Hague, The Netherlands: Martinus Nijhoff Publishers, 2000), 10.
97 Francis Deng, Comprehensive Study on the Human Rights Issues Related to Internally Displaced Persons, E/CN.4/1993/95 (United Nations, Commission on Human Rights, 21 January 1993), 55–88.
98 Kälin argues that though the Guiding Principles do not constitute a typical soft law instruments on account of the process of their drafting, they should be considered as such on the basis of their content. Walter Kälin, 'The Guiding Principles on Internal Displacement as International Minimum Standard and Protection Tool', *Refugee Survey Quarterly* 24 (2005): 29.
99 GA Resolution No. 57/150 (2002).
100 Principles and Rules for Red Cross and Red Crescent Disaster Relief: Annex IV, International Review of the Red Cross, No, 310.
101 Declaration of Principles for International Humanitarian Relief to the Civilian Population in Disaster Situations, *XXIst International Conference of the Red Cross, Istanbul, Resolution XXVI, September 1969*. Available at www.ifrc.org/Docs/idrl/I49EN.pdf.

Cross and Red Crescent in 2007.[102]

The recent work of the ILC concerning the protection of persons in the event of disasters is also intended to further develop the law concerning a subject matter in which the protection of and assistance to IDPs assumes an important place. Since 2007, the Commission has been working on the elaboration of a set of Draft Articles on the protection of persons in the event of disasters. During its 59th meeting in 2008, it appointed Mr Eduardo Valencia-Ospina from Colombia as its Special Rapporteur.[103] The Rapporteur has already presented seven reports which included legal commentary on the subject matter and proposed Draft Articles.[104] Working though a drafting committee, ILC has developed 20 Draft Articles covering a wide spectrum of issues such as the definition of disaster, the role of the affected states, basic principles of humanitarian assistance, the duty to cooperate and the role of the international community.[105] While the relevance of this initiative to the further development of norms relevant to the protection of IDPs is significant, the Commission seems to move very cautiously in setting a broad set of standards that are not necessarily focused on protection of individuals *per se*, but cover issues such as inter-state relations during disaster, assistance delivery and humanitarian access.

Codification of a separate international instrument

The codification of a separate international instrument on internal displacement was advanced by the Association of International Law which even elaborated the Draft Declaration of Principles of International Law on Internally Displaced Persons.[106] The Refugee Policy Group had also proposed a declaration or convention, among others, on access to humanitarian assistance. Proponents of such approaches argue that the existence of

102 Guidelines for the Domestic Facilitation and Regulation of International Disaster Relief and Initial Recovery Assistance, adopted by the Thirtieth International Conference of the Red Cross and Red Crescent in 2007. Available at http://icrc.org/web/eng/siteengO.nsf/htmlall/p1108/$File/ICRC_002_1108.pdf!Open.

103 Official Records of the General Assembly, Sixty-second Session, Supplement No. 10 (A/62/10), para. 375.

104 See Seventh Report on the Protection of Persons in the Events of Disaster, Fourth Report on the Protection of Persons in the Events of Disaster, A/CN.4/643, 11 May 2011; Third Report on the Protection of Persons in the Events of Disasters, A/CN.4/629, 31 March 2010; Second Report on the Protection of Persons in the Events of Disasters, A/CN.4/615, 7 May 2009; Preliminary Report on the Protection of Persons in the Events of Disasters, A/CN.4/598, 5 May 2008.

105 See the Fourth Report on the Protection of Persons in the Events of Disaster, A/CN.4/643, 11 May 2011.

106 Luke Lee, 'The London Declaration of International Law Principles on Internally Displaced Persons: Its Significance and Implications', *Journal of Refugee Studies* 14 (2001): 70–75.

a separate international instrument on IDP makes it easy to ensure state accountability for violations.[107]

Codifying a binding and separate international legal instrument governing IDPs is widely considered as not feasible. It often takes a long time to undertake negotiations on such treaties. A treaty on internal displacement may also allow member states to enter reservations.[108] This approach was considered the most problematic since it constitutes 'a major challenge to the principle of state sovereignty'.[109] But it was also highlighted that the mere codification of legal instruments does not necessarily reflect the dilution of sovereignty, but may even be used by states to reinforce elements of their sovereign powers.[110] International organisations such as ICRC were originally reluctant to support such an approach, insisting that international humanitarian law provides the necessary protection for all civilians at least in the case of armed conflicts, and that the development of a separate international instrument risks further weakening existing international norms and standards by providing states the 'opportunity to redraft existing international law, which they could then weaken and undermine'. Others also held the view that the codification of a separate international instrument may formalise a separate legal status for those who flee their homes; thereby creating a hierarchy among human rights victims.[111] Kälin states:[112]

> The standing of the Guiding Principles is firmly established. However, more must be done to strengthen the normative framework for the protection of the human rights of the displaced. Some have suggested

107 See Luke Lee, 'The Case for an International Convention on Displaced People', in *Invisible Refugees: Internally Displaced Persons and the New Understanding of Protection and Sovereignty*, ed. James H. Williams (Washington, DC: Chicago-Kent College of Law and Pax International, 2003).

108 For an analysis of some of these points, see Walter Kälin, *How Hard Is Soft Law? The Guiding Principle on Internal Displacement and the Need for A Normative Framework* (Washington, DC, Brookings Institute, 2001). See also Douglass Cassel, 'Enhancing Human Rights and Legal Protection', in *Invisible Refugees: Internally Displaced Persons and the New Understanding of Protection and Sovereignty*, 13–19 (Washington, DC: Chicago-Kent College of Law and Pax International, 2003).

109 Phuong, Note 21 above, 27.

110 International Committee of the Red Cross, Internally Displaced Persons, Symposium, Geneva, 23–25 October 1995 (Geneva, ICRC, 1996), 44. For the contribution of ICRC in the development of the Guiding Principles, see Jean Philippe Lavoyer, 'Guiding Principles on Internal Displacement: A Few Comments on the Contributions of International Humanitarian Law', *International Review of the Red Cross* 324(1998): 463–466.

111 As Kälin notes, 'Internally displaced persons need not and cannot be granted a special legal status under international law comparable to refugee status', Walter Kälin, *Guiding Principles on Internal Displacement: Annotations* (Washington, DC: American Society of International Law, 2000), 5.

112 Walter Kälin, 'The Future of the UN Guiding Principles on Internal Displacement', *Forced Migration Review* (Special Edition, 2006), 6.

> that a way to do so is to enshrine the Guiding Principles in a UN treaty. I doubt that this would be the best way to proceed. Such an endeavor would only be successful if there were a worldwide consensus that the Principles should be made legally binding at the universal level. Negotiations on the 2005 World Summit Outcome document have shown that while the Guiding Principles are welcomed by all governments, many among them were not ready to explicitly recognize their legal character. The idea that internal displacement is essentially an 'internal affair' remains strong in many parts of the world. In this political environment it is better to continue to build consensus from the bottom up.

Another difficult challenge to a separate legal instrument is presented by those who contend that any attempt to formalise the protection for IDPs will pose a risk of undermining protection provided for other legally recognised categories of victims. In this context, the example is often made of the institution of asylum regarding which, though the attempt to elaborate a separate legal instrument was aborted, reference has been made in numerous human rights instruments. Some governments, civic society organisations, academics and others view that any attempt to codify a separate instrument will undermine the institution of asylum. As Fitzpatrick aptly puts it:[113]

> Clarification, enhancement and promotion of the rights of IDPs should not undermine the right to seek asylum. But it is doubtful whether these caveats will as a practical matter prevent this consequence, as one obvious impetus for conceptualising standards for internally displaced persons is the desire to prevent trans-boundary flight. A paper set of norms for IDPs would be counterproductive if it failed to result in improved conduct by the state of origin and armed groups while serving as a rationalisation for even less generous treatment of asylum seekers. The danger is that a formal framework for protecting the internally displaced without the resources and political will to implement it will lead asylum adjudicators to order deportation of asylum seekers based on a misleading assessment of their risk and their actual opportunities for relocation.

Codification of a binding legal instrument covering, among others, issues of internal displacement

A variant of this approach calls for a codification of an instrument that will, in addition to issues affecting internally displaced persons, also address other concerns related to the problem of internal displacement. Examples of initiatives falling under this category include the proposal on the Draft

113 Note 2 above, 13.

Convention on Expediting the Delivery of Emergency Assistance. The Draft Convention was annexed to the report of the Secretary General on the activity of what was then known as the Office of the United Nations Disaster Relief Coordinator (UNDRO) and was later submitted to the ECOSOC for an inter-governmental review. Though the ECOSOC referred the matter to the UN General Committee's second committee in 1977, the proposal, which mainly focused on access to relief assistance, did not go very far owing to major objections from some Eastern European member states of the UN.[114]

A proposal had also been forwarded to redefine the refugee concept under the 1951 Convention with the view to incorporate, *albeit* in a limited manner, some displaced persons who do not yet fall within the definition of refugee under the Convention. Shacknove's attempt to define refugees as 'persons whose basic needs are unprotected by their country of origin, who have no remaining recourse other than to seek international restitution of their needs, and who are so situated that international assistance is possible' is one example.[115] Luke Lee also promoted the idea of what he called a 'legal synthesis' which essentially reopens the definitions of the refugee with a view to addressing the protection and assistance needs of the internally displaced.[116] Some also argued that any attempt to make a distinction between refugees and IDPs was considered both impractical and unethical. It has to be noted that even during the drafting of the 1951 Refugee Convention, some had expressed their wish to see the problems faced by internally displaced persons addressed by the Convention.[117] Phuong notes that refugees and IDPs require protection which is different in nature.[118] The protection given to refugees is a surrogate protection by a third state since the relationship between the state of origin and the individual is severed, whereas whatever protection provided to IDPs by a third state or international organisations can only be complementary to measures that should be taken by the state of origin which has the primary responsibility to ensure such assistance and protection.[119]

There was also an attempt to fill the 'normative gap' with respect to IDPs through an elaboration of a Draft Declaration on the Minimum Humanitarian Standards Applicable during Internal Violence and Strife. This Draft Declaration was submitted by the Sub-Commission to the Former

114 The attempt to placate states who felt that their concerns about sovereignty should be seriously considered led even the proponents of the draft to consider emphasising sovereignty entitlement and control by receiving state.

115 Andrew Shacknove, 'Who is a Refugee?' *Ethics* 95(1985): 274–275.

116 Luke Lee, 'Internally Displaced Persons and Refugees: Toward a Legal Synthesis?' *Journal of Refugees Studies* 9(1996): 31.

117 Ibid., 47.

118 Note 21 above, 25.

119 Ibid.

Commission on Human Rights in 1994.[120] Some member states originally expressed interest to see gaps identified by the RSG's Compilation and Legal Analysis to be jointly addressed together with other concerns covered by the Draft Declaration.[121] The area of overlap is understandable given the fact that both the Draft Declaration and the Guiding Principles seek to extend the reach of international humanitarian law into situations of violence. But the difference is also equally evident. The discussion over the Draft Declaration was difficult and no significant progress has been achieved so far. In the meantime, significant developments such as the publication of ICRC's study on customary humanitarian law were underway. In 2005, the former Commission on Human Rights adopted Resolution 2005/63 on the protection of the human rights of civilians in armed conflicts, where the Commission took note with appreciation of Sub-Commission decision 2004/118 and requested the preparation of a working paper on human rights law and international humanitarian law.[122]

The Human Rights Council also adopted in its ninth ordinary session a resolution calling for its special procedures and Advisory Committee and human rights treaty bodies to consider, within their respective mandates, to address relevant aspects of the protection of human rights of civilians during armed conflict.[123] The same resolution also requested the Office of the United Nations High Commissioner for Human Rights (OHCHR) to undertake a consultation on the issue of protecting the human rights of civilians in armed conflict on the basis of which the Council envisaged to request the Advisory Committee to undertake a study with a view to presenting it with recommendations.[124] The resolution notes that the Advisory Committee would have to take into account the work undertaken by the Sub-Commission on the Promotion and Protection of Human Rights.[125] OHCHR organised a series of expert consultations on the protection of human rights of civilians during armed conflicts and has also issued a major report on the topic.[126]

120 Declaration of Minimum Humanitarian Standards, reprinted in the Reports of the Sub-Commission on Prevention of Discrimination and Protection of Minorities on its 46th Session, Commission of Human Rights, E/CN 4/1995.

121 Summary Record of the 39th meeting of the Sub-Commission, Commission on Human Rights, E/CN.4/1996/SR.39 (1996), para. 49.

122 UN Commission on Human Rights, *Resolution 2005/63 on Protection of the Human Rights of Civilians in Armed Conflicts*, 20 April 2005, E/CN.4/RES/2005/63.

123 Human Rights Council Resolution 9/9, Protection of the Human Rights of Civilians during Armed Conflict, 24 September 2008.

124 Ibid., paras. 7–9.

125 Ibid., para. 9.

126 International Legal Protection of Human Rights in Armed Conflicts, Office of the High Commissioner for Human Rights, 2011.

Codification of a comprehensive legal instrument on forced displacement

The possibility of developing a treaty with a broader scope of covering both IDPs and refugees was considered in the past. Freedman, for instance, argued that codification of an international treaty on displacement, which may include both IDPs and refugees, may fill the deficiencies identified under international law concerning protection and assistance of IDPs.[127] A comprehensive approach on codification for the purpose of this section stems from an important assumption that the problems of refugees and IDPs are similar in certain contexts. It also arises from the premise that the international legal system regarding the protection of refugees is also inadequate.[128] A comprehensive approach has an additional added value in helping to address some of the gaps of the existing refugee legal regime.

The RSG did not provide in his recommendation such an option, largely due to the fact that his mandate did not extend to monitoring the implementation of international refugee law. There are also various problems and challenges that the envisaged drafting process may face. Some have argued that the practical and operational impact of any attempt to codify norms regulating concerns of forced displacement will not be meaningful unless it is comprehensive enough to also cover issues of both internal and external displacement. It is specifically argued that this comprehensive approach should not only be able to provide binding legal norms on the protection and assistance of IDPs, but also address some of the gaps in international refugee law, including the narrow definition of who qualifies for a refugee status, the role of UNHCR in the context of returnees and mass influx, and elaboration of the principle of burden-sharing[129] and international solidarity for the continued application of the institution of asylum. This proposal does not necessarily call for a renegotiation of the 1951 Refugee Convention. Even though this partly allays the fear of those who caution regarding the unintended consequences of reopening the said convention, it is not yet clear how the relationship between such a comprehensive and complex legal instrument and the original convention would be defined.

Codification of a regional binding legal instrument

Regional codification in human rights law has been an important aspect of development of human rights law. One can also see the utility of regional

127 Paul Freedman, 'International Intervention to Combat the Explosion of Refugees and Internally Displaced Persons', *Georgetown Immigration Law Journal* 9(1995), 598.

128 David Petrasek, 'New Standards for the Protection of Internally Displaced Persons: A Proposal for a Comprehensive Approach', *Refugee Survey Quarterly* (Spring/Summer, 1995): 289.

129 See Eve Burton, 'Leasing Rights: A New International Instrument for Protecting Refugees and Compensating Host Communities', *Colombia Human Rights Law Review* 19(1987): 307–332.

codified instruments on refugee protection as evidenced by the 1969 Organisation of African Unity (OAU) Refugee Convention and the Cartagena Declaration.[130] The RSG has conducted several workshops and activities with regional organisations such as the OAU/AU, Organisation of American States (OAS), and the European Council, and these activities often highlighted the role and the relevance of regional organisations in promoting and implementing the Guiding Principles.

There are promises and limitations in regional legal instruments concerning internal displacement. Regional norms may easily gain legitimacy among states in the region. They are better placed in providing opportunities to circumvent the oft-difficult treaty-making at the international level. They may also serve as tailor-made tools for addressing distinct regional dynamics in internal displacement. There is also a possibility that gradual regional approaches may encourage the development of new norms at the international level. But experience with regional legal instruments such as the 1969 OAU Refugee Convention clearly shows that these promises are not easily achieved. Almost four decades after its adoption and warm reception by refugee experts and academics, the influence of the OAU Convention in expanding the restrictive definition of a refugee under the 1951 Convention is difficult to assess. It may also be feared that regionalisation of legal instruments on IDPs may undermine existing norms. This uncertainty is accentuated by the fact that internal displacement invites the 'convergence' for numerous legal norms particularly in the fields of human rights law and humanitarian law.

The Guiding Principles on Internal Displacement

The process of codification

Finding long-term solutions to internal displacement including through the development of a framework for the protection and assistance of IDPs has been an important element of the mandate of the RSG.[131] UN's former Human Rights Commission conferred on the RSG the mandate

> to continue his work aimed at a better understanding of the general problems faced by internally displaced persons and their possible long-term solutions, with a view to identifying, where required, ways and means of improving protection for and assistance to internally displaced persons.[132]

130 Convention Governing the Specific Aspects of Refugee Problems in Africa ('OAU Convention'), 10 September 1969, 1001 U.N.T.S. 45, entered into force on 10 June 1974. Cartagena Declaration on Refugees, Colloquium on the International Protection of Refugees in Central America, Mexico and Panama, 22 November 1984.

131 CHR Res. 1992/73.

132 CHR. Res. 1993/95, para. 4.

Human Rights Commission Resolution 1996/52 of 19 April 1996 called, in para. 9, 'upon the Representative of the Secretary General to continue, on the basis of his compilation and analysis of legal norms, to develop an appropriate framework in this regard for the protection of internally displaced persons'. The RSG's comprehensive study outlined both the short-term and long-term undertakings within the context of his mandate. The study states:[133]

> With respect to legal norms and principles, there is a mid- to long-term need to fill gaps in the existing law. As an immediate measure, however, it is essential to compile and consolidate relevant international instruments and standards into comprehensive documents focused on the human rights and humanitarian problems of internal displacement. This would also lay the foundation for the longer term objectives. Among the envisaged documents would be a statement of guiding principles, a code of conduct, a declaration and, as an objective to be achieved through an evolutionary process, a convention.

The Comprehensive Study, among others, specifically noted that any attempt to elaborate a normative basis for protecting and assisting IDPs should be first based on a preparation of comprehensive compilation and analysis of existing legal norms and principles. This suggestion was a 'balancing act' whereby the RSG tip-toed the fine line between the conflicting demands of the advocates of a new legal regime on internal displacement and those who hold that existing norms and principles are sufficient in providing protection.[134] The RSG's Compilation and Analysis of Legal Norms has been an important contribution in assessing the efficacy and limitations of existing legal frameworks, i.e. human rights norms, international humanitarian law and refugee law in protecting IDPs. The RSG's Compilation and Legal Analysis did not rule out the possibility of drafting a distinct international legal instrument that looks at various issues concerning IDPs, including their legal status. His report includes several proposals covering issues which should be incorporated as elements of a future instrument governing internal displacement. The first part of his Compilation and Analysis of Legal Norms provided an assessment of existing international standards and their application for the protection and assistance of IDPs during displacement and following their return. As recommended in his first report, the RSG mandated a separate study on applicable law governing the issue of prohibition of arbitrary displacement. This study, while recognising the absence of

133 Francis Deng, Comprehensive Study on the Human Rights Issues Related to Internally Displaced Persons, E/CN.4/1993/95 (United Nations, Commission on Human Rights, 21 January 1993), para. 270.

134 Simon Bagshaw, *Developing a Normative Framework for the Protection of Internally Displaced Persons* (New York: Transnational Publishers, 2005), 80.

explicit prohibition of arbitrary displacement under international law save for international humanitarian law and laws relating to indigenous peoples, attempted to distil, based on existing norms from international human rights law and international humanitarian law, an international norm on the prohibition of arbitrary displacement.[135]

As a short-term measure, however, it became clear that the RSG and the team of prominent international lawyers supported a soft law approach, convinced that an elaboration of a binding international treaty is neither feasible nor desirable.[136] What has been commonly considered as a 'tactful' decision to privilege 'soft law' over a binding international treaty was informed by a combination of considerations.[137] First, it was thought that treaty-making in the human rights field had become quite complex and time consuming and the urgent nature of the crisis of displacement should not be subject to a long-winded negotiation among government legal experts.[138] Second, even if a convention or a protocol on the protection and assistance of internally displaced persons is adopted, such an instrument may still face problems associated with a slow ratification process and reservations. Third, since the problem of internal displacement involves an application of distinct legal regimes (i.e. human rights and humanitarian law), a comprehensive codification process may lead to a merger of what are otherwise fundamentally separate concepts, not only in one instrument but in a single provision. Fourth, to a limited extent, it is also reckoned that existing international legal instruments provide norms and standards applicable to IDPs.

The output of the mandate, as reflected in the elaboration of a non-binding set of norms, was extraordinarily far-reaching. The Guiding Principles are not even typical soft laws like declarations or resolutions since they did not go through an inter-governmental negotiation process, and as such cannot be said to reflect a general consensus among states. Their authoritative nature stems not from the format of their elaboration, but from their content which is primarily drawn from existing human rights as well as international humanitarian instruments. The exercise was based on a rigorous process of identifying generalised principles from existing branches of international law.[139]

The appropriateness of applying the oft-protracted and long-winded international treaty-making procedures[140] for drafting rules applicable to IDPs was

135 This study was undertaken by Ms Maria Stavropoulou and was reviewed by a panel of international legal experts. See Note 2 above, 65.

136 Walter Kälin, *How Hard is Soft Law?: The Guiding Principles on Internal Displacement and the Need for a Normative Framework*, presentation at Roundtable Meeting, Ralph Bunche Institute for International Studies, CUNY Graduate Centre, 19 December 2001, 4–7, available at: www.brookings.edu/speeches/2001/1219guidingprinciples_kälin.aspx.

137 Ibid.

138 Ibid.

139 Ibid., 29.

140 Reference has often been made to the negotiation over the International Convention on the Protection of the Rights of All Migrant Workers and Members of Their Families that was initiated in 1990, but took more than a decade before it came into force.

seriously questioned. States, invariably envious of their sovereignty, often respond ambivalently to processes whose outcome further entrenches their obligations and internationalise certain matters which they believe to be domestic in nature. This is not to argue that the Guiding Principles fail to recognise state responsibility. On the contrary, though the RSG was acutely aware of the tension between the state-centred principle of sovereignty and the internationalisation of IDP protection and assistance,[141] his approach was intensely informed by the presupposition that states are the bedrocks of the international system, and hence, the responsibility of ensuring adequate institutional and legal protection to IDPs lies with states themselves. But the methods adopted for the formation of the Guiding Principles are considered 'unusual in the history of international standard setting'.[142]

The rationale which so forcefully shaped the argument in favour of a non-binding commitment also strongly informed the model of 'negotiation' on the Guiding Principles. The RSG adopted a method for formulating the Guiding Principles which in effect discouraged an effective participation of states. The process significantly limited the participation of government representatives, and to the chagrin of some government representatives and diplomats, visibly circumvented inter-governmental debate and scrutiny. When a similar position was expressed by some delegations in the General Assembly (GA) in 2001, the RSG argued that given the fact that the development of the Guiding Principles was a response to the requests from the Human Rights Commission and the General Assembly, it would not be accurate to suggest that they were not discussed in pertinent government bodies.[143]

Through the support of a largely western pool of experts and non-governmental organisations, the RSG formulated the Guiding Principles without formal inter-governmental dialogue and approval. Unlike many other human rights special mechanisms, the project run by the Representative was also independently financed and supported.[144] The considerations were straightforward. This approach was defended as a 'new diplomacy' and standard-setting process which transcended traditional multilateralism's boundaries by incorporating non-governmental actors.[145] This even led one commentator to claim that,

141 See Deng, note 11 above, 249–286. See also Francis Deng *et al.*, *Sovereignty as Responsibility: Conflict Management in Africa* (Washington, DC: Brookings Institution Press, 1996).

142 Roberta Cohen, 'The Guiding Principles on Internal Displacement: An Innovation in International Standard Setting', *Global Governance* 10(2004), 460.

143 E/CN.4/2002/95, para. 16.

144 The Brookings Bern Project on Internal Displacement intimately supported the mandate of the UN Secretary General Representatives.

145 Weiss and Korn also state that this model 'shows how individuals and groups working outside of the diplomatic circuit can affect the norms that to a considerable extent shape international action'. Note 15 above, 3. See also Simon Bagshaw, *Developing the Guiding Principles on Internal Displacement: The Role of a Global Public Policy Network* (Italy: European University Institute, 1999).

> the major impetus behind international recognition of the problem of internal displacement lay neither with states nor for that matter with inter-governmental organisations. On the contrary, it lay with a group of NGOs mobilised as a result of problems encountered in gaining access in the field to a large number of so called 'internal refugees' in need of assistance and protection.[146]

Others including the RSG argued that the Guiding Principles only restated, deduced and interpreted existing norms to which states assented. This, however, belies the RSG's own identification of gaps in existing norms and the fact that the Guiding Principles indeed seek to respond to gaps such as those concerning restitution; the duty of states to accept the offer of assistance from international humanitarian organisations; and the obligations of non-state actors regarding protection of IDPs.[147] In a few other cases where norms already exist, such as in the case of the principle of non-refoulement (a norm prohibiting forceful expulsion of refugees to an area where they will be persecuted), they are not well known to be applicable in the context of internal forced displacement.[148]

Owing to the 'considerable enthusiasm' surrounding the mandate of RSG from certain quarters and the noticeable influence civil society organisations brought to bear on the process, an outcome was achieved despite the fact that the process largely circumvented inter-governmental dialogue and negotiation. This process projected the Guiding Principles as constituting a viable normative framework on IDPs. But it has done so by postponing what could have been a timely discussion on important questions involving member states. The fact that Mr Francis Deng visited 21 countries, some of which are from Africa, never meant that countries which were peculiarly affected by the scourge of internal displacement were active participants of the articulation of the Guiding Principles.[149]

Scope of the Guiding Principles

The Guiding Principles rely on an eclectic source, and their provisions are considered to be consistent with the various elements of international law on which they are based.[150] They are the outcome of an exercise of identifying rights and guarantees which are implicitly imbedded in the rich body of existing international law.[151] It is often contended that the Guiding Principles did

146 Note 134 above, 75.

147 Michael Kingsley Nyinah, 'What may be borrowed: What is new?', *Forced Migration Review* 4(1999): 29.

148 Ibid.

149 These African countries include Angola, Burundi, Mozambique, Rwanda, Somalia and Sudan.

150 Rules 3, the Guiding Principles.

151 Kälin, note 136 above, 28.

not break new legal grounds, but rather restated and reaffirmed existing ones. The principles of sovereignty and non-intervention were reflected in a number of provisions. For example, Principles 3 clearly states that national authorities assume the primary responsibility for the protection and assistance of IDPs within their own jurisdiction. While the Principles recognise the rights of IDPs to seek humanitarian assistance (Principles 3(2)), they do not clarify whether such claims can be made against the international community.

It is also reckoned that the Guiding Principles include some innovations. For example, it is noted that the rules relevant to the prevention of displacement are 'one of the more innovative' elements of the Guiding Principles'.[152] It did so by articulating and restating a concept that has not been commonly stated in human rights regimes. The Guiding Principles are a unique normative instrument not just in the manner in which they have been drafted, but also in their format and content. They not only provide 'minimum standards' of protection identifying guarantees for IDPs and obligations owed to them by states and non-state actors, they also seek to provide practical tools for planning, implementing and monitoring activities.[153] The text does not have a preamble but includes an introduction where the concept 'internally displaced persons' is defined. Whereas typical international legal instruments are intended to provide for state responsibilities and guarantees of individuals and groups, it is clearly stated in the Guiding Principles that the latter intend to provide guidance not only to states but also to the RSG, intergovernmental organisations, non-governmental organisations and others.[154] They clarify international obligations of states with respect protection and assistance to IDPs, and also provide 'international and non-international organisations (NGOs) an important tool to use in their advocacy work on behalf of the displaced'.[155]

The Guiding Principles embrace a broad definition of IDPs. Accordingly, internally displaced persons are defined as 'persons or group of persons who have been forced or obliged to flee their homes or habitual places of residences, *in particular* as a result of or in order to avoid the effects of armed conflict, situation of generalised violence, violations of human rights or natural or human made disasters, and who have not crossed an internationally recognised state border'.[156] Two broad observations can be made here. First, it is often emphasised that the Guiding Principles do not seek to provide a

152 Roberta Cohen, 'The Development of International Standards to Protect Internally Displaced Persons', in *Human Rights and Forced Displacement*, eds Anne Bayefsky and Joan Fitzpatrick (The Netherlands: Martinus Nijhoff Publishers, 2000), 79.

153 Walter Kälin, *Guiding Principles on Internal Displacement: Annotations* (Washington, DC: Brookings Institution, 2008).

154 Guiding Principles, Introduction, para. 3.

155 Francis Deng *et al.*, *Sovereignty as Responsibility: Conflict Management in Africa* (Washington, DC: Brookings Institution Press, 1996), 76.

156 Guiding Principles, Introduction, para. 2.

'legal definition', but attempts to give a description of individuals or groups with specific needs. No legal status thus accrues from such definition. It was suggested that by providing the definition of IDPs under the introductory section as opposed to the main section of the text, the RSG wanted to 'downplay the normative significance of the definition'. Second, the causes of displacement are broad and may include, as the phrase 'in particular' indicates, several other additional elements which are not explicitly indicated or listed.

The Guiding Principles are comprehensive in nature. Unlike the 1951 Refugee Convention which deals with rights and protection during 'flight', they identify 'rights and guarantees' relevant to address protection and assistance of IDPs during the whole cycle of displacement: (1) prohibition of arbitrary displacement; (2) protection and assistance during displacement; and (3) protection and assistance during return and integration. The Guiding Principles are structured with a view to sufficiently addressing all three phases of displacement. The first part of the text deals with prevention of displacement. This is followed by provisions dealing with protection and assistance framework during displacement (Principles 10 to 27). The last section of the Guiding Principles covers the aspects of return, integration and resettlement.

The content of the Guiding Principles covers key issues that emerge during the various phases of forced displacement. The first section outlines broad principles such as the primary responsibilities of 'national authorities' to provide assistance and protection to IDPs; equal treatment and protection from discrimination; the rights of IDPs to request assistance and support; the relationship between implementation of obligations under the Guiding Principles and the legal status of 'all authorities, groups and persons' ; the application of the Principles without any discrimination; the relationship between provisions of the Guiding Principles with international obligations of States under international human rights law and humanitarian law in particular as they relate to the right to seek and enjoy asylum. The second edition provides for grounds where forced displacement of persons is prohibited. It prohibits displacement based on apartheid, ethnic cleansing and other major breaches of international law. It also renders unlawful displacement based on 'large-scale development' that is not justified by compelling and overriding public interest.

The Guiding Principles include provisions providing explicit protection to the most vulnerable among the displaced including women, children, unaccompanied minors, female heads of households, persons with disabilities, the elderly and others. Accordingly, these categories of persons 'shall be entitled to protection and assistance required by their condition and to treatment which takes into account their special needs'.[157] Displaced women are protected against rape, gender-based violence and forced prostitution, and it

157 Principle 4.

is provided that their special needs to have access to reproductive health services and counselling for sexual and gender-based violence should be guaranteed.[158] National authorities are requested to involve women in the planning and distribution of basic social services,[159] and ensure the participation of women and girls in educational programmes including by providing educational and training facilities.[160] Displaced persons with disabilities should also have access to medical services 'to the fullest extent practicable and with the least possible delay, the medical care and attention they require, without distinction on any grounds other than medical ones'.[161] The recruitment of displaced children into armed groups or their participation in hostilities is prohibited under any circumstances.[162] The Guiding Principles also note the particular obligation of states to ensure that indigenous people, minorities, peasants, pastoralists and others with special dependency on and attachment to their land are protected from displacement.[163]

Recognition of the Guiding Principles

Remarkably enough, the method adopted to prepare the Guiding Principles does not appear to prevent the Guiding Principles from being largely welcomed both by states and other stakeholders. For instance in Africa, the OAU/AU passed resolutions which acknowledged and recognised the authoritative value of the Guiding Principles.[164] ECOWAS also requested its member states to disseminate and apply the text of the Guiding Principles.[165] A ministerial declaration by Inter-Governmental Authority for Development (IGAD) referred to the Guiding Principles as 'useful tools'.[166] The Organisation for Security and Co-operation in Europe (OSCE) recognised the Principles as 'a useful framework for the work of the OSCE and the endeavour of participating States in dealing with internal

158 Principles 11, paras. 2 and 19.

159 Principle 18.

160 Principle 23.

161 Principle 19, para. 1.

162 Principle 13, para. 1.

163 Principle 9.

164 See Nairobi Declaration: Ministerial Conference on Refugees, Returnees and Internal Displaced Person in the IGAD Region, para. 2, 21 February 2006, available at www.unhcr-rlo.org/Regional Partners/Docs/Nairobi%20Declaration.pdf. See also Khartoum Declaration of the OAU Ministerial Meeting on Refugees and Internally Displaced Person in Africa, 13–14 December 1998, 34. Available at www.issafrica.org/AF/RegOrg/unity_to_union/pdfs/oau/keydocs/KHARTOUM_DECLARSON_REFUGEES.pdf.

165 See the Report of the First Regional Conference on Internal Displacement in West Africa, Abuja, Nigeria, 26–28 April 2006, 5. Available at: www.brookings.edu/fp/projects/idp/conferenceECOWAS_rpt.pdf.

166 Khartoum Declaration: Ministerial Conference on Internally Displaced Persons in the IGAD Sub-Region, adopted on 2 September 2003. Available at www.brookings.edu/fp/projects/idp/conferences/DecKhartoum.pdf.

displacement'.[167] The European Parliament Assembly adopted a recommendation which states that the Guiding Principles 'constitute a standard for governments and other responsible authorities and intergovernmental and non-governmental organisations, and is an important tool in their work for displaced persons'.[168] The Durban Declaration and Programme of Action adopted in September 2001 at the World Conference against Racism in Durban, South Africa encourages the bodies, agencies and relevant programmes of the UN system and states to promote and to make use of the Guiding Principles.[169] The outcome document of the Durban review conference also incorporates provisions which, even if they do not make explicit reference to the Guiding Principles, nonetheless underline the need to protect the human rights of IDPs.

During the 2005 Summit, heads of state and government recognised the Guiding Principles as an 'important international framework for the protection of internally displaced persons'.[170] The Security Council noted the use of the Guiding Principles by states, international organisations and non-governmental organisations.[171] The General Assembly accepted the Guiding Principles as an important framework.[172] The former Human Rights Commission adopted Resolution 1998/50 in which it took note of the progress achieved in the development of a legal framework applicable to IDPs, among others, through the development of the Guiding Principles.[173] The nature of its support for the text improved significantly in the following years. In 2005, the Commission on Human Rights expressed 'its appreciation of the Guiding Principles on Internal Displacement as an important tool for dealing with situations of internal displacement', welcomed 'the dissemination, promotion and application of the Guiding Principles' and encouraged 'the continued dissemination and promotion of the Guiding Principles'.[174]

This, however, does not mean that states did not raise questions on the status and scope of the Guiding Principles, or more generally regarding the mandate of the RSG. To the contrary, states including African countries often emphasised the primary role of the state in providing protection to IDPs; and that international assistance and support should be provided based

167 Ministerial Council Decision No. 4/03; Tolerance and Non-Discrimination. Available online at www.osce.org/cio/37720

168 Recommendation 1631(2003), text adopted by the Standing Committee, acting on behalf of the European Parliament Assembly, on 25 November 2003, para. 11.

169 Durban Declaration and Plan of Action, adopted at the World Conference Against Racism, Racial Discrimination, Xenophobia and Related Violence, 8 September 2001, endorsed by the GA resolution 56/266 of 15 May 2002.

170 UN General Assembly, GA Resolution A/60//L.1 para/132.

171 SC Resolution 1286(2000), para. 6.

172 GA Res. 54/167 9 (1999).

173 E/CN.4/RES/1998/50.

174 CHR Res, 2005/45, paras. 7 and 8.

on the consent of the particular state etc.[175] They also continue to highlight the fact that the Principles were not negotiated in an inter-governmental process.[176]

The reaction from UN humanitarian organisations, international organisations, NGOs and academia to the Guiding Principles has also been considerably positive. The Secretary General of the United Nations has considered the formulation of Guiding Principles as a notable achievement.[177] Their formulation was considered as having the potential to 'fill a major gap in the international protection system for the internally displaced'. There has also been a discussion, though limited, on the role of the Guiding Principles in the development of customary norms. Several states have adopted domestic legislations and policies that seek to implement the Guiding Principles. A review of peace agreements between and among warring parties signed after 1998 clearly indicates a certain willingness to include references to IDPs.[178]

In the last decade, the Guiding Principles have been considered as an important authoritative framework on the protection of IDPs. But they also have their own limitations and shortcomings. Some of these shortcomings are linked to the nature of the Guiding Principles themselves whereas others are related to recent developments which have exposed the limitations of their remit. One should note that from the beginning, the objectives set for the codification of the Guiding Principles were enormous. As one commentator noted, 'the effort to explicate the rights of the internally displaced is plagued by conceptual and practical pitfalls'.[179] It was also noted that it is indeed difficult to bring together in a coherent manner all the relevant rules and principles from the fields of humanitarian law, human rights law and refugee law by analogy. An instrument specifically dedicated to situations of internal displacement risks creating a privileged class of displaced victims over those who decide to remain behind. The Guiding Principles are neither binding nor incorporate mechanisms for monitoring their implementation. Thus, states may not necessarily feel obliged to implement their provisions. Some, therefore, would like to see them as the first step in a process that will ultimately lead to the adoption of a legally binding international instrument. Others find

175 For a summary of states' views regarding the Comprehensive Study by the RSG, see Summary Record of the 40th meeting, E/CN.4/1993/SR.40 (1993), at paras. 82–83.

176 See The Inter-Active Dialogue with Experts on Enforced Disappearances, Arbitrary Detention and Internally Displaced Persons, The Human Rights Council, 16th Session. Available at www.unog.ch/80256EDD006B9C2E/(httpNewsByYear_en)/9A76CC8BC4FF4B47C125784D004078FE?OpenDocument.

177 See Report of the Secretary-General to the Economic and Social Council, Strengthening the Coordination of Humanitarian Assistance, UN Doc. E/1998/67 (12 June 1998).

178 Elizabeth Ferris, 'Assessing the Impact of the Principles: An Unfinished Task', *Forced Migration Review* (Special Edition, 2008): 10.

179 Joan Fitzpatrick, 'Human Rights and Forced Displacement: Converging Standards', in *Human Rights and Forced Displacement*, eds. Anne Bayefsky and Joan Fitzpatrick. (The Hague, The Netherlands: Martinus Nijhoff Publishers, 2000), 10.

this approach problematic and think that the development of the Guiding Principles is already an important achievement and that 'it is the most that can be achieved to improve the legal protection of internally displaced persons'.[180] There have also been criticisms against the Guiding Principle for what they have failed to incorporate. For example, it was pointed out that the Principles do not provide for rights of IDPs against the international community, i.e. no obligation to accept international assistance is mandated.[181] Though the Principles have several provisions dealing with the protection and assistance needs of women, some argue that the question on how harmful traditional practices such as female genital mutilation are related to internal displacement is neglected.

Conclusion

Traditional principles of international law such as sovereignty, non-interference and prohibition of the use of force were effectively used by states to resist the treatment of the subject of internal displacement under international law. This has sustained a belief that international law does not provide relevant protection to victims of displacement who have not yet crossed international boundaries. This chapter attempted to shed light on the status of IDPs under international law, and how its various relevant fields provide protection and assistance to these vulnerable groups. Though, as the Compilation and Legal Analysis undertaken by the RSG clearly establishes, IDPs are not a separately recognised legal entity in international law, there are numerous fields of international law which are still relevant to their protection.

Internal displacement, considered for far too long domestic in nature, is now assuming considerable importance under international law. Since the end of the Cold War, the international response to the plight of IDPs has become significant particularly in strengthening institutional mechanisms for coordinating response and assistance. Since the end of the Cold War, there has been a notable internationalisation of the phenomenon of internal displacement due to, among others, the complex nature of new conflicts that generate a large number of displaced persons, and the relative ability and willingness of principal organs of the United Nations to take action on behalf of IDPs. Whereas the internationalisation of the phenomenon of internal displacement has undoubtedly helped the creation of an environment whereby numerous new international and regional legal instruments have made specific reference to the issue of internal displacement, the role of the Security Council and what sort of international measures can be taken is still shrouded in controversy. This was evident in the too often sterile debates

180 Preliminary Report on the Protection of Persons during Disasters, Mr Eduardo Valencia-Ospina, Special Rapporteur, International Law Commission, 60th Session, A/CN.4/598, paras. 54, 74.

181 Note 2 above, 12.

regarding the concept of humanitarian intervention. It is notable that the problem of internal displacement played a central role in the elaboration of the concept of 'responsibility to protect' which sought to address some of the manifest weaknesses of the doctrine of humanitarian intervention. Ongoing controversy and questions regarding the legal content of these norms and their consequences make the concept far less operationally relevant than originally thought.

The UN Guiding Principles, developed within the mandate of the RSG, remain the key normative framework for protection and assistance. The Guiding Principles have significantly relied on norms drawn from human rights law, international humanitarian law and refugee law. In recent years, there have been further significant developments making international law even more relevant to the topic of internal development. The increased involvement of the UN system, particularly the engagement of the Security Council in human rights issues and in the protection of civilians during armed conflict, has also revived interest to see an increased role and responsibilities of third states and international organisations in orchestrating an effective international response to the crisis of internal displacement. Though these fields of international law were for long considered as 'self-contained' systems, internal displacement has emerged as an important point of convergence and cross-fertilisation. Moreover, norms and standards in these areas continue to evolve and grow. Newer human rights instruments continue to involve direct references to IDPs. There is a trend in international humanitarian law to narrow the gap of coverage in norms applicable to international conflict and non-international conflicts. Though there is a noticeable consensus on postponing the search for a binding international legal instrument on IDPs, the questions cannot be said to be totally ignored. There are a number of reasons for a rather cautious 'soft-law' approach as evidenced by the formulation of the UN Guiding Principles. Long-held principles of international law such as sovereignty, non-interference and non-intervention were used by states to resist any international norm that authorises and legitimises any action on behalf of internally displaced persons. There was also a conviction shared by organisations such as the ICRC and others arguing against the attempt to draft a separate international instrument believing that doing so would further fragment existing international regimes, particularly that of international humanitarian law.

The Guiding Principles have become important benchmarks for the development of domestic, regional and international norm-setting on internal displacement. Though non-binding, the Guiding Principles have now become, as evidenced by the increasing reference to them by national legislations and regional instruments, authoritative sources of legal reform since they are drawn from binding sources of treaty and customary law in various fields. Their formulation was informed by a comprehensive and elaborate analysis of the capacity and limitations of international law to provide protection. They are comprehensive and practical in their content and form.

3 African regional norms, institutions and internal displacement

Introduction

Armed conflicts, inter-communal tensions, organisations, effects of climate change and poverty triggered large-scale displacement across Africa. For decades the sub-Saharan African region topped the list of regions most affected by displacement. The Central African Republic, South Sudan, Nigeria, the Democratic Republic of Congo and Somalia have a significant number of their population internally displaced. According to the 2015 Global Overview of the Internal Displacement Monitoring Centre, there were 11.4 million IDPs across 22 countries. Conflicts and violence remain the most significant triggers of displacement in these countries. Millions across the continent are leaving rural areas to urban centres seeking better opportunities. Major public infrastructure and development projects put pressure on local livelihoods and displace communities. Effects of climate change, urbanisation and competition among communities over resources have also become sources of great concern.

Owing largely to the experience with internal displacement, the African region has been at the epicentre of experiments to find regional normative and institutional solutions for internal displacement. The OAU in its early years grappled with the problem of forced displacement. Though the formative years of the OAU saw legal advances being made in refugee protection including through the adoption of the 1969 OAU Refugee Convention, these measures were considerably limited in reach, thanks in large measure to the dominant doctrines of sovereign equality of states and non-intervention in the internal affairs of member states of the OAU.

Prior to the codification of the Kampala Convention in 2009, there had been attempts to incorporate norms regulating internal displacement in regional treaties and relevant instruments. Some of these instruments provide explicit guarantees for the rights and freedoms of particularly vulnerable populations among displaced persons.[1] Others incorporate provisions clarifying the

1 See Art 11 of the Protocol to the African Charter on Human and Peoples' Rights on the Rights of Women in Africa, adopted by the 2nd Ordinary Session of the Assembly of the Union, Maputo, Mozambique, entered into force on 25 November 2005. See also Art 23

mandates of regional institutions with respect to the protection of IDPs.[2] Institutions such as ACHPR gradually formalised their mandate towards IDPs including by establishing the mandate of the Special Rapporteur who will be monitoring, among others, the implementation of the human rights of IDPs

African regional laws and institutions on human rights including those with direct relevance to internal displacement did not abruptly emerge with the establishment of the African Union in 2002. They evolved over time. The Africa Charter on Human and Peoples' Rights,[3] drafted and negotiated under the auspices of the former OAU, has been the pillar of regional mechanisms on human rights protection. Initially, there were very little linkages to speak of between the African human rights system and internal displacement. This calls for a break from the dominant perspective embedded in the literature on African human rights mechanisms by positioning the regional internal displacement laws and institutions within the framework of human rights mechanisms in Africa.[4]

Several international and regional developments influenced OAU's development of its legal and institutional mechanisms on a myriad of issues including the promotion of human rights and protection of victims of internal displacement. The establishment of the African Union (AU) led to the adoption of several legal instruments including the Constitutive Act[5] and the various protocols establishing the organisation's various bodies. Specialised regional human rights instruments such as the African Charter on the Rights and Welfare of the Child and the Protocol on the Rights of Women in Africa specifically recognise the protection and assistance needs of displaced children and women respectively.[6] For instance, the African Charter on the Rights and Welfare of the Child provides that internally displaced children will benefit from protection and assistance accorded to refugee children under the Charter and other regional and international legal instruments.[7] The Charter also stipulates that refugee children shall 'receive appropriate

of the African Charter on the Rights and Welfare of the Child, adopted on 11 July 1990, entered into force on 29 November 1999.

2 See ACHPR/Res. 116(XXXVI) 04: Resolution on the Mandate of the Special Rapporteur on Refugees, Asylum Seekers, Migrants and Internally Displaced Persons in Africa, 23 November – 7 December 2004. See also ACHPR/Res. 116(XXXXII) 07: Resolution on the Renewal of the Mandate of the Special Rapporteur on Refugees, Asylum Seekers, Migrants and Internally Displaced Persons in Africa, adopted on 28 November 2007.

3 African Charter on Human and Peoples' Rights, adopted on 27 June 1981, OAU Doc. CAB/LEG/67/3 rev.5, 21 I.L.M. 58(1982), entered into force on 21 October 1986.

4 Brian Gorlick, 'Human Rights and Refugees: Enhancing Protection through International Human Rights Law', Working Paper No. 1, New Issues in Refugee Research, Geneva: UNHCR, 2000. See also Rachel Murray, *Human Rights in Africa: From the OAU to the African Union* (Cambridge: Cambridge University Press, 2004), 185.

5 Constitutive Act of the African Union, OUA Doc. CAB/LEG/23.15, adopted on 9 July 2002, entered into force on 26 May 2001.

6 Note 1 above.

7 Art 23.

protection and humanitarian assistance in the enjoyment of the rights set out in the Charter and other international human rights and humanitarian instruments to which the States are Parties'.[8] Moreover, the Charter underscores the principle of equal protection of children whose parents, legal guardians or relatives could not be found with those that have been temporarily or permanently deprived of their family environment, and also recognises the role of international organisations in providing assistance and protection including by facilitating family reunification.[9] The Protocol on the Rights of Women in Africa stipulates several provisions relevant to the protection of internally displaced women. It provides for all the rights of women including freedom from discrimination and entitlement to socio-economic rights such as the right to land and housing;[10] it seeks to protect women from harmful traditional practices;[11] stipulates provisions dealing with protection of women during armed conflicts;[12] calls for special protection of women in distress;[13] and requires states to undertake to protect women including those who are internally displaced,

> against all forms of violence, rape and other forms of sexual exploitation, and to ensure that such acts are considered war crimes, genocide and/or crimes against humanity and that their perpetrators are brought to justice before a competent criminal jurisdiction.[14]

Other African Union's legal instruments such as the Constitutive Act and the Protocol on the Establishment of the African Union Peace and Security Council (herein after referred as the PSC Protocol)[15] further contributed to the strengthening of the legal response to internal displacement. For instance, the Constitutive Act provides that the Council of Ministers and the Peace and Security Council (PSC) shall have the mandate to coordinate policy and practical measures on humanitarian and disaster relief.[16] Some legal instruments of sub-regional organisations have also provided similar or in some circumstances more elaborate legal provisions dealing with internal displacement.[17] Among these instruments, the Protocol on the Protection

8 Art 23(1).
9 Arts 23(2) & (3).
10 Art 16.
11 Art 5.
12 Art 11.
13 Art 24.
14 Art 11(3).
15 The Protocol Concerning the Peace and Security Council of the African Union, adopted on 11 July 2002, entered into force on 26 December 2003.
16 Arts 13(1) and 21 of the Constitutive Act.
17 See Chaloka Beyani, 'Recent Developments: The Elaboration of a Legal Framework for the Protection of Internally Displaced Persons in Africa', *Journal of African Law* 50 (2006): 187–197. See also Allehone Abebe, 'Legal and Institutional Dimensions of Protecting and Assisting IDPs in Africa', *Journal of Refugee Studies* 22(2009): 155–176.

and Assistance of Internally Displaced Persons in the Great Lakes constitutes arguably the first binding sub-regional instrument on internal displacement.[18]

The search for a regional approach on internal displacement

Thomas Franck defines a regional organisation as 'any grouping of states in some defined geographical context with historic, ethnic, or socio-political ties, which habitually acts in concert through permanent institutions to foster unity in a wide range of common concerns'.[19] 'Regionalism' has also often been invoked to explain developments in security, environment, trade and other fields where it is also broadly understood as 'a collective or communal response within a region to a global issue where the parties share a common destiny or purpose'.[20] Chapter VIII of the United Nations Charter explicitly mentions the role of 'regional arrangements and agencies' in the maintenance of peace and security.[21] The Security Council in recent years has also adopted numerous resolutions acknowledging the role of regional organisations such as the OAU/AU.[22] The General Assembly also adopted similar resolutions.[23] The Vienna Declaration and Program of Action acknowledges that 'regional arrangements play a fundamental role in promoting and protecting human rights'.[24]

The significance and utility of regional human rights mechanisms as complementary frameworks to the international system is increasingly acknowledged.[25] Regions which did not have visible regional arrangements

18 Protocol on the Protection and Assistance to Internally Displaced Persons, adopted on 30 November 2006, International Conference on the Great Lakes Region, available online at www.internal-displacement.org/8025708F004BE3B1/(httpInfoFiles)/29D2872A54561F66C12572FB002BC89A/$file/Final%20protocol%20Protection%20IDPs%20-%20En.pdf.

19 Thomas Franck, 'Who killed Article 2(4)? OR: Changing Norms Governing the Use of Force by States', *American Journal of International Law* 64(1970): 809–37.

20 Susan Kneebone and Felicity Rawlings-Sanaei (eds.), *New Regionalism and Asylum Seekers: Challenges Ahead* (New York/Oxford: Berghahn Books, 2007), 2.

21 Arts 51, 52 and 53 of the UN Charter.

22 See SC/RES/251, SC/RES/770, SC/RES/1625, SC/RES/1809, SC/RES/2002 and SC/RES/1973. See also Roberta Cohen, *The Role of Regional Organisations* (Washington, DC: Brookings Institutions, 2000), available online at www.brookings.edu/projects/idp/Article-Index-Pages/regional.aspx.

23 See GA/Resolution 32/127, GA/Resolution 63/170, GA/Resolution 48/42, GA/Resolution 49/57, GA/Resolution 60/1, GA/RES/61/296 and GA/RES/63/310.

24 Vienna Declaration and Programme of Action, UN General Assembly, 12 July 1993, A/CONF.157/23, para. 37.

25 See Bertrand Ramcharan, 'Complementarity between Universal and Regional Human Rights Organizations: Perspectives from the UN High Commissioner for Human Rights', *Human Rights Law Journal* 21(2000): 324–326.

are now taking measures with a view to establishing such mechanisms.[26] The practice of the Human Rights Council also lays bare the resilience of such a trend.[27] Recent resolutions of the United Nations General Assembly on assistance to refugees, returnees and displaced persons in Africa acknowledge the role of the African Union, particularly that of the ACHPR and the Special Rapporteur on Refugees, Asylum Seekers, IDPs and Migrants (ACHPR Special Rapporteur).[28]

The African region is often defined based on its shared historical experience of colonialism, cultural connectedness, geographical affinity and common economic aspirations.[29] Such an approach, however, has been criticised for lacking precise content and thus failing the test for a working definition.[30] The attempt by the OAU/AU to define regional and sub-regional organisations has faced similar challenges. For instance, various legal instruments use 'regional' and 'sub-regional' interchangeably. The Treaty Establishing the African Economic Community defines Africa broadly on a geographical basis stating that it includes five regions constituting of the North, South, East, West and Central parts of the continent.[31] It also states that a 'sub-region' should refer to an inter-relationship among at least three states in one of these geographical areas.[32] Currently, more than fourteen sub-regional organisations exist in Africa out of which eight are formally recognised by the African Union.[33] Enjoying the membership of all states from the African continent except the Kingdom of Morocco, the OAU/AU can be considered as a broadly constituted Pan-African institution.

For the purpose of this research, the African regional human rights system broadly refers to human right treaties, decisions and practices of institutions

26 See Yash Ghai, 'Human Rights Governance: The Asian Debate', *Asia Pacific Journal of Human Rights and Law* (2000): 9–52.

27 See Human Rights Council Resolutions 6/20(2007); Allehone Abebe, 'Shaming and Bargaining: African States and the Universal Periodic Review of the UN Human Rights Council', *Human Rights Law Review* 9 (2009): 1–35.

28 GA Resolution 62/125 and GA Resolution 65/193.

29 OAU's Council of Ministers recognised the division of the African continent into five regions exclusively on the basis of geographical configuration. See Resolution on the Division of Africa into Five Regions, CM.Res 464. (XXVI), adopted during the 26th Ordinary Session of the Council of Ministers, Addis Ababa, 23 February 1967.

30 Paul Taylor, *International Organisations in the Modern World: The Regional and Global Progress* (New York: London, 1993), 7.

31 Art 1(d) of The Treaty Establishing the African Economic Community, adopted on 3 June 1991 and came into force in 1993.

32 Art 1(e), ibid.

33 These sub-regional economic communities include: The Arab Maghreb Union (AMU), the Community of Sahel-Saharan States (CEN-SAD), the Common Market for Eastern and Southern Africa (COMESA), the East African Community (EAC), the Economic Community of Central African States (ECCAS), the Economic Community of West African States (ECOWAS), the Intergovernmental Authority on Development (IGAD), and the Southern African Development Community (SADC).

at the level of the African Union and its sub-regional blocs.[34] The African regional human rights system is one of the principal regional human rights mechanisms in the world.[35] Academic writings on the nature and competence of regional organisations have increasingly examined the role of these organisations in contributing to the development and implementation of international law, particularly with respect to the law regulating the use of force.[36] International human rights text books have increasingly given attention to these organisations.[37]

All members of the African Union have ratified the African Charter on Human and Peoples' Rights which created ACHPR. The Commission together with the newly created African Court of Justice and Human Rights constitutes the chief regional human rights organs.[38] A number of additional human rights instruments have supplemented the African Charter on Human and Peoples' Rights, some of which provide for separate and distinct implementation and monitoring mechanisms.[39]

Many of the conflicts which generated forced population displacement situations in Africa have regional dimensions. This encourages regional and sub-regional organisations to assume important roles in addressing the problem of displacement.[40] The role of regional organisations in the maintenance of peace and security has also expanded their relevance to the protection of human rights and humanitarian law. There is a growing expectation that regional mechanisms for conflict prevention, management and resolution should also integrate protection of victims of displacement in their mandate.[41]

Beyond the issue of addressing conflict-generated displacements, the role of these institutions in dealing with the problems of victims of man-made

34 See Chidi Anselem Odinkalu, 'Back to the Future: The Imperative of Prioritising for the Protection of Human Rights in Africa', *Journal of Africa Law* 47 (2003): 1–37.

35 The others include the European human rights system which was established based on the European Convention on Human Rights of 1950 and the Inter-American Human Rights System which was established based on the adoption of the American Convention on Human Rights in 1967. With the coming into force of the ASEAN Charter in December 2008, a group of South East Asia has become the newest bloc to have a regional human rights system.

36 See Christine Gray, *International Law and Use of Force* (Oxford: Oxford University Press, 2004).

37 See Christof Heyns and Magnus Killander, 'Africa in International Human Rights Text Books', *African Journal of International and Comparative Law* 15 (2007): 130–137.

38 See Protocol on the Statute of the African Court of Justice and Human Rights, adopted on 1 July 2008. This Protocol has not yet entered into force.

39 This is for example the case with the African Charter on the Rights and Welfare of the Child that established the African Committee on the Rights and the Welfare of the Child.

40 See Khartoum Declaration of the OAU Ministerial Meeting on Refugees, Returnees, Internally Displaced Persons in Africa, 13–14 December 1998, para. 11.

41 Recommendations of the OAU/UNHCR Symposium on Refugees and Forced Population Displacements in Africa, 21 September 1994, EC/1994/SCP/CRP.7/Add.1, Recom.1.

and natural disasters has also been under scrutiny.[42] In the realm of refugee protection, regionalism has always received a great deal of attention. For instance, in the African context, the 1969 OAU Convention's extended definition of refugees filled the gaps in the 1951 UN Convention.[43] Coming as it did prior to the African Charter on Human and Peoples' Rights, the Convention signalled an emerging trend of elaborating regional instruments to complement international standards. UNHCR worked closely with organs of the OAU in the drafting of both the 1969 OAU Refugee Convention and the 1987 African Charter on Human and Peoples' Rights.[44] These forms of collaboration also exist in spheres of international humanitarian law.[45]

No formal relationship exists between regional human rights instruments and institutions on the one hand and those that exist at the United Nations on the other. Conflict of norms and institutions are thus often mediated based on a general principle enshrined in Article 103 of the Charter of the United Nations[46] and norms of international human rights that are anchored in the universalism of human rights. Past discussions on the role of regional human rights instruments were too often held within the context of the universalism versus regionalism debate, and analysis of the African Charter on Human and Peoples' Right emphasised the latter's 'unique African conceptualisation of human rights'.[47] Through time, however, this once dominant discourse has given way to a search for an effective response to human rights violations on the ground, and hence the support for these regional systems is grounded on the argument that these organisations are well-positioned to provide the most effective protection for human rights. It is of course expected that increased codification of human rights instruments at the regional level will raise important questions regarding their complementarity and congruence with international standards. In some instances such as the elaboration of the African Protocol on the Rights of Women in Africa, it was argued that some provisions of the protocol are at variance with international principles. A comparative analysis has been made of the African

42 Programme of Action for the Implementation of the African Regional Strategy for Disaster Risk Reduction (2006–2010), EX/CL/228(VIII) Annex II.

43 Ivor Jackson, *The Refugee Concept in Group Situations* (The Hague: The Netherlands: Kluwer Law International, 1999), 177.

44 See Bertrand Ramcharan, 'The Travaux Preparatoires of the African Commission on Human and Peoples' Rights', *Human Rights Law Journal* 13(1992): 307–314.

45 Churchill Ewumbue-Monono and Carlo von Flue, 'Promotion of International Humanitarian Law through Cooperation between the ICRC and the African Union', *International Review of the Red Cross* 85(2003): 749–773.

46 Art 103 of the Charter states: 'In the event of a conflict between the obligations of the Members of the United Nations under the present Charter and their obligations under any other international agreement, their obligations under the present Charter shall prevail'.

47 Makau Mutua, 'The Banjul Charter and African Cultural Fingerprint: An Evaluation of the Language of Duties', *Virginia Journal of International Law* 35(1995): 339–80.

Charter on the Rights and Welfare of the Child with the Convention on the Rights of the Child.[48]

The dominant approach to the African regional human rights system

The 1963 OAU Charter did not envisage the establishment of a regional human rights mechanism. Both the 1969 OAU Refugee Convention and the African Charter on Human and Peoples' Rights were adopted much later. It is notable that concerns regarding population displacement have been a harbinger of regional human rights development as shown by the adoption of the 1969 OAU Refugee Convention which, according to some, is 'the true origin of the pan-continental human rights system in Africa'.[49]

At the heart of the African regional human rights system lays the African Charter on Human and Peoples' Rights which was further strengthened and buttressed by a number of additional protocols and other 'soft-law' human rights instruments. But much of the literature on the African regional human rights system regrettably ignores any serious discussion on the 1969 OAU Convention.[50] Accordingly, the period of the adoption of the African Charter and the subsequent establishment of the Commission were taken as a starting period in the genealogy of the African human rights system.[51] Moreover, the regional human rights system is too often studied in isolation without any consideration of how it relates to the body of other laws and jurisprudence of the OAU/the AU.

The role of regional and sub-regional mechanisms in humanitarian, human rights and displacement issues has been growing.[52] As was already noted, the first important binding sub-regional regional instrument on IDPs has been adopted by the Great Lakes Conference.[53] Others such as Inter-Governmental Authority on Development (IGAD), Economic Communities for West African States (ECOWAS), South African Development

48 See Frans Viljoen, 'Supra-national Human Rights Instruments for the Protection of Children in Africa: The Convention on the Rights of the Child and the African Charter on the Rights and Welfare of the Child', *The Comparative and International Law Journal of Southern Africa* (1998): 99–210.

49 Note 34 above, 19.

50 For example Okafor defines the African regional human rights system as mainly constituting the African Charter, its Protocols and the Commission. See Obiora Chindu Okafor, *The African Human Rights System, Activist Forces and International Institutions* (Cambridge: Cambridge University Press, 2007), 2.

51 Note 34 above, 1.

52 See Frans Viljoen, 'The Realisation of Human Rights in Africa through Sub-regional Institutions', *African Year Book of International Law* 7(1999): 185.

53 These instruments include the Protocol on the Protection and Assistance to Internally Displaced Persons and the Protocol on the Property Rights of Returning Persons.

Community (SADC) and East African Communities (EAC) have also been engaged in issues affecting displaced persons.[54]

The increased convergence of human rights and laws applicable to internal displacement within the African Union and ACHPR encouraged the consideration of 'internal displacement' within the framework of human rights. African Union policy organs and special ministerial conferences on human rights, refugee problems and internal displacement adopted declarations, decisions and other soft-laws that underlined such convergence. The decision of the ACHPR to establish a Special Rapporteur also helped anchor the issue within the works of the Commission. Combinations of these factors have become so visible that recent publications on regional human rights systems provide equal treatment to the protection of refugees and IDPs.[55] Some factors have been cited as justifying the consideration of sub-regional arrangements. First, sub-regional arrangements are considered important 'building blocks' of broader regional arrangements and integration. Second, as the experience of the International Conference of the Great Lakes Region (ICGLR) indicates there is a notable cross-fertilisation of principles and norms. Their experience also shows the relevance of economic integration for human rights in general and migration laws in particular.

Convergence between internal displacement and human rights

Early codification efforts within the African regional human rights system did not result in a legal acknowledgement of internal displacement. Notwithstanding its explicit provisions on asylum and freedom of movement, neither the African Charter on Human and Peoples' Rights nor its early reform debate addressed the specific needs and human rights of IDPs. This is not surprising since, during the same period, there was little recognition of internal displacement even at the international level. Moreover, the discussion within the regional human rights system to a greater extent had been influenced by the rhetoric of sovereignty, non-interference in the internal affairs of OAU member states and the fight against apartheid. The idea of protection of IDPs was hence considered with certain ambivalence and

54 See Report of the First Regional Conference on Internal Displacement in West Africa, Abuja, Nigeria, 26–28 April 2006, Brookings-Bern Project on Internal Displacement. Available online at: www.brookings.edu/fp/projects/idp/conferences/ECOWAS_rpt.pdf; Conference on Internal Displacement in the IGAD Sub-Region, Report of the Experts' Meeting, Khartoum, Sudan, 30 August–2 September 2003, Brookings Institution and SAIS Project on Internal Displacement. Available online at www.brookings.edu/dybdocroot/fp/projects/idp/conferences/IGAD/20030903.pdf; See John Oucho, 'Internal Displacement of Populations in the SADC Region: An Overview', paper presented at the Seminar on Internal Displacement in the SADC Region, 24–25 August 2005, Gaborone, Botswana, available at: www2.warwick.ac.uk/fac/soc/afrobrain/oucho/publications/.

55 See Murray at note 4 above, 185–235.

resistance. But this state of affairs started changing as a result of the development of some key binding and soft-law instruments. Additional protocols concerning women and children were added to the Charter, among others, with specific reference to IDPs.[56] Additional soft laws such as the Kigali Declaration in 2003 and the Grand Bay Plan of Action sought to further ground the protection of IDPs in the regional human rights regime by giving an explicit mandate to the African Commission to monitor forced displacement.[57]

In the wake of the transformation of the OAU into the AU, a new era and opportunity of reforming Africa's regional human rights system emerged where important legal instruments such as the Constitutive Act and some of its supplementary legal instruments have been adopted with notable relevance to internal displacement.[58] According to Levitt, these developments have indeed positioned Africa 'at centre stage in confirming the status and nature of existing norms of international law and at the cutting edge of norm creation'.[59] He further notes:[60]

> Throughout Africa the notions of state sovereignty, democracy and the absolute prohibition on interference in internal affairs of member states accepted throughout the world are now undergoing revolutionary change, as are traditional conceptions of protecting refugees and internally displaced persons who find themselves in harm's way.

Early Pan-African high-level conferences on refugees in Africa did not address the problem of forced displacement in a comprehensive manner. For example, none of the numerous recommendations adopted in the 1979 first ministerial conference to review the application of the 1969 OAU Convention mentioned internal displacement.[61] The two international conferences on assistance to refugees in Africa held in 1981 and 1984 were

56 See Article 11 of the Protocol on the Rights of Woman in Africa and Article 23 of the African Charter on the Rights and Welfare of the Child.

57 Kigali Declaration, adopted at the First African Union Ministerial Conference on Human Rights in Africa on 8 May 2003, MIN/CONF/HRA/Decl. 1(I), 15; Grand Bay Declaration and Plan of Action, adopted at the First OAU Ministerial Conference on Human Rights in Africa on 16 April 1999, CONF/HRA/Decl. (I), 9.

58 Christof Heyns, 'The African Regional Human Rights System: In Need of a Reform?' *The African Human Rights Law Journal* 2(2001): 158. See Article 13(1)e of the Constitutive Act. See also Article 15 of the Protocol Establishing the Peace and Security Council of the African Union.

59 Jeremy Levitt, 'Introduction–Africa: A Maker of International Law', in *Africa: Mapping New Boundaries in International Law*, ed. Jeremy Levitt (Oxford, Portland OR: Hart Publishing, 2008): 6.

60 Ibid.

61 Recommendations from the Pan-African Conference on the Situation of Refugees in Africa, Arusha, Tanzania, adopted on 17 May 1976. Available online at: www.unhcr.org/refworld/category,LEGAL,AFRICA,,,3ae6b37214,0.html.

important in underscoring the linkage between refugee protection and developments in host countries.[62] The Oslo Declaration and Plan of Action recommended, among others, coordinating relief and emergency programmes by the international community to displaced persons in southern African countries.[63] As the title of this important conference clearly suggested the utility of broadening the categories of victims had been understood at the time. The various soft laws adopted by the OAU, particularly its Commission of Fifteen, attempted to articulate the contemporary challenges of the refugee movement including the need to address the root causes of Africa's refugee problems. One example of such an instrument was the Khartoum Declaration on Africa's Refugee Crisis adopted during the 17th Extraordinary Session of the Commission of Fifteen that focused on root causes of the refugee problem.[64]

An explicit acknowledgement of the problem of forced displacement came in 1994 during a major symposium jointly organised by the OAU and UNHCR as a part of commemorating the 25th anniversary of the adoption of the 1969 OAU Convention.[65] The outcome of this symposium incorporated several recommendations which explicitly mention IDPs.[66] The same can be said with respect to the outcomes of the ministerial conference held in Burkina Faso in 2006 which unambiguously endorsed the UN Guiding Principles, and helped the development of what can be considered as a soft law that complements the 1969 OAU Convention.[67] Policies and practices of the OAU and the AU clearly show that the recognition of forced displacement has been an evolutionary process. The series of ministerial conferences on refugees organised by the OAU and the AU were instrumental in this respect. These meetings focused not just on refugees but on a broader concept of 'forced displacement' which also includes returnees and IDPs.

62 Report of the Secretary-General: International Conference on Assistance to Refugees in Africa (ICARA I), 11 June 1981, A/36/316, available at: www.unhcr.org/refworld/docid/3ae68f3f8.html; Second International Conference on Assistance to Refugees in Africa, Geneva, 9–11 July 1984. Available online at http://unhcr.org/3ae69edbf.html.

63 See Oslo Declaration and Plan of Action, adopted 9 June 1999. Available: www.unhcr.org/refworld/docid/3ae68f3d8.html.

64 Khartoum Declaration on Africa's Refugee Crisis, 24 September 1990, BR/COM/XV/55.90. Available at: www.unhcr.org/refworld/docid/3ae6b39524.html.

65 The Addis Ababa Document on Refugees and Forced Population Displacement in Africa, OAU/UNHCR Symposium on Refugees and Forced Populations Displacement in Africa, 8–10 September 1994, available at: www.unhcr.org/refworld/publisher,OAU,3ae68f43c,0.html.

66 Ibid., para. 18.

67 Ouagadougou Declaration on Refugees, Returnees and Internally Displaced Persons, adopted at the Second Ministerial Meeting on Refugees, Returnees and Internally Displaced Persons in Africa, 29–30 May 2006, Burkina Faso. Available online at: www.unhcrrlo.org/Regional_Partners/Docs/Ouagadougou%20Declaration.pdf.

They also highlighted the role of regional and sub-regional institutions in addressing the challenges of forced displacement.

Internal displacement and African regional treaties

The Charter of the Organisation of African Unity

The Charter of the Organisation of African Unity ('the OAU Charter') prioritised decolonisation, the struggle against apartheid and the protection of sovereignty of member states as principal objectives of the OAU.[68] The doctrine of sovereignty and non-interference in the internal affairs of states were enshrined as its underpinning philosophies. The OAU Charter may well be considered as a 'charter for liberation' since it underlines the defence of sovereignty of member states and the fight against colonialism as fundamental objectives of the organisation.[69]

The OAU Charter did not have many references to human rights. Its preamble expressly acknowledged the Charter of the United Nations and the Universal Declaration of Human Rights.[70] Article II provided that the organisation shall have, among others, the purpose of promoting 'international cooperation, having due regard to the Charter of the United Nations and the *Universal Declaration of Human Rights*' (emphasis author's). Though the Charter made a limited reference to human rights, it did not as such proclaim human rights of individuals. Even when a general reference to human rights was made, it was conspicuously broad and a strong emphasis was given to issues which were high in the minds of the drafters of the Charter at the time, which included topics such as racism, people's rights and the right to self-determination.[71] The original specialised commissions or organs envisaged by the Charter did not include institutional mechanisms on human rights issues in general or victims of internal displacement in particular.[72] Thus, the

68 Article III of the Charter of the Organisation of African Unity. The Charter was adopted on 25 May 1963 in Addis Ababa, Ethiopia and entered into force on 25 October 1965.

69 See John Dugard, 'The Organisation of African Unity: An Inquiry into the Plea of Self-Defence as a Justification for the Use of Force in Eradication of Colonialism', *The International and Comparative Law Quarterly* 16(1967): 157–90. See also Gino Naldi, *The Organisation of African Unity: An Analysis of Its Role*, 2nd edition (London: Monsell, 1999), 2–18 and Taslim Elias, *Africa and the Development of International Law*, 2nd edition (Netherlands: Martinus Nijhoff, 1988), 124–29.

70 Article 2(1) of the Charter.

71 Murray, note 4 above, 8.

72 The following institutions have been mentioned in Article XX of the Charter: Economic and Social Commission; Educational, Scientific, Cultural and Health Commission, and Defence Commission. It should be stated that the Charter did not envisage the establishment of the African Commission on Human and Peoples' Rights. But a commentator argued that the establishment of the ACHPR can be considered to emanate from the same article, See, Vincent Nmehielle, *The African Human Rights System: Its Laws, Practices and Institutions* (The Netherlands: Njihoff Publishers, 2001), 171.

Charter's reference to human rights, in general, did not translate into a specific human rights agenda.[73] Even long after the adoption of the Charter, the political environment during the Cold War kept the organisation in similar orientation for several decades to come.

The Convention Governing the Specific Aspects of Refugee Problems in Africa

The 1969 Refugee Convention was adopted as a regional complement to the 1951 UN Convention.[74] It is the only binding regional legal instrument on refugees. Its adoption was grounded on the conviction widely shared among African states that the 1951 Convention does not sufficiently address the peculiar nature of the refugee problem in Africa.[75] But the Convention, whose elaboration the UNHCR supported, was not conceived as a separate or parallel legal arrangement, but rather a regional complementary legal instrument to the 1951 Convention.[76] The instrument's usefulness for the promotion of the mandate of UNHCR is indicated by the fact that it provides cooperation between member states on the one hand and OAU and UNHCR on the other.[77]

The Convention provides rights to refugees and underlines the principles of non-refoulement and asylum. It also provides some novelties. For example, it expands the definition of 'refugee' by covering 'every person who, owing to external aggression, occupation, foreign domination or events seriously disturbing public order in either part or the whole of his country of origin or nationality, is compelled to leave his place of habitual in order to seek refuge in another place outside his country of origin or nationality'.[78] It is often cited as the first legally binding instrument incorporating a detailed provision on voluntary repatriation.[79] The OAU Convention also made key contributions in strengthening the legal basis for burden sharing, non-rejection of refugees at borders and non-refoulement. It provides detailed provisions dealing with the prohibition of subversive activities. It was often argued that these novelties were designed to address the specific problem of African refugees.

Some commentators considered the refugee problem as 'Africa's most

73 Olusola Ojo and Amadu Sesay, 'The OAU and Human Rights: Prospects for the 1980s and Beyond', *Human Rights Quarterly* 86(1986): 96.

74 See Preamble paras. 7 and 10. See also Article VIII (3).

75 See Sam Aiboni, *Protection of Refugees in Africa* (Uppsala: Swedish Institute for International Law, 1978).

76 Note 43 above, 191.

77 See Art VIII.

78 Article 1(2).

79 Marjoleine, Zieck, *UNHCR and Voluntary Repatriation of Refugees: A Legal Analysis* (The Hague: Martinus Nighoff Publisher, 1994), 97.

serious human rights problem'.[80] But it is far less clear whether the Convention was an effective instrument in addressing these human rights challenges. There is no indication that the OAU itself considered the instrument as a human rights legal text. The Convention's relationship with human rights instruments has also not been that strong. On the one hand, the Convention brought to light the question of asylum, which was later entrenched in the African Charter on Human and Peoples' Rights. It has expanded the definition of refugee and also provided a legal shield to those whose flight is triggered by basic violations of their rights within the context of colonialism, foreign aggression, occupation and what is termed as 'serious public disturbances'. But the definition does not sufficiently cover refugee-producing circumstances such as generalised violence and human rights violations as is the case for example in the Cartagena Declaration.[81] Moreover, the problem of mass forced displacement has not fully been taken into account. The Convention also does not incorporate a detailed enumeration of entitlements and rights of refugees. It also fails to address the specific needs of Africa's most vulnerable groups such as women, children and minorities.[82] Critics also pointed out how some of the provisions of the Convention may contravene if not the provisions of the 1951 Convention, at least the international instruments on human rights. For example, Hathaway argued that the Convention's sweeping provisions limiting political rights such as freedom of expression of refugees are inconsistent with international human rights standards.[83] It was also highlighted that the Convention restricts the rights of refugees to freedom of movement and association.[84] Even from a refugee law perspective, a point was made that provisions dealing with the prohibition of subversive activities, the humanitarian and peaceful nature of granting of asylum and the plea that member state should settle refugees at a reasonable distance from frontiers highlight the fact that 'the motive forces of the Convention were essentially political, and then particularly security-driven, even if the animation was to be cast and organised in legal terms'.[85]

Some authors point out that the Convention's broader definition of refugee was meant to include a wide spectrum of victims of forced displacement triggered by wars of national liberation and 'environmental catastrophes such as drought and famine which had given rise to flight en

80 Evelyn Ankumah, *The African Commission on Human and Peoples' Rights: The System in Practice 1986–2000* (Cambridge: Cambridge University Press, 2008), 139.

81 George Okoth-Obbo, 'Thirty Years On: A Legal Review of the 1969 OAU Convention Governing the Specific Aspects of Refugee Problems in Africa', *Refugee Survey Quarterly* 20(2001), 116.

82 Ibid., 10.

83 James Hathaway, *The Rights of Refugees under International Law* (Cambridge: Cambridge University Press, 2005), 894.

84 Ibid., 10.

85 Ibid.

masse and displaced whole populations'.[86] Such interpretation, however, was criticised as an attempt to attribute to the Convention 'purposes and intentions it never pretended to have'.[87] It is perhaps accurate to state that despite its expansive definition of refugee, the 1969 OAU Convention shared the flaws and weaknesses of the 1951 Convention in that it failed to present a comprehensive response to forced displacement. Its definition of refugee still does not sufficiently cover a large number of victims who are displaced by various man-made and natural causes. If the 1951 Convention was elaborated to address the specific nature of Europe's refugee problem in the wake of the Second World War, the 1969 OAU Convention's objective was orientated to the needs of African refugees whose flight and vulnerabilities were marked by challenges such as decolonisation struggles and external aggression. The Convention was thus envisaged as a political tool of expressing African solidarity with the African refugee. This was reinforced with an almost mythical faith in African generosity and an open door policy to refugees and victims of displacement which, for many reasons, waned over the years.[88]

The OAU Convention is not known for being widely implemented and for strongly influencing national policy and legislation. For almost over a decade following the entry into force of the Convention, there was a notable stagnation in refugee legal reform in member states.[89] In 2008, one commentator noted, 'until this decade, it could hardly be affirmed that refugee matters are conducted in conformity with international and regional norms'.[90] The promises of the Convention did not materialise owing to the absence of a consistent regional jurisprudence which is based on the Convention.[91]

This, however, did not hinder some commentators from criticising the OAU Convention for failing to cover IDPs. On the specific question of whether the Convention should have included those displaced internally, opinions were divided. Some readily accept the failure to incorporate IDPs as a major legal lacuna in the Convention. As Oloka Onyango notes, 'a necessity exists to provide a protection mechanism enshrined in the law, to assist internally displaced persons in any way possible, even while clearly recognising the

86 Gino Naldi, *The Organization of African Unity: An Analysis of Its Role*, 2nd edition (London: Monsell, 1999), 79.

87 Note 81 above, 87.

88 See Gaim Kibraeb, Reflections on the African Refugee Problem: A Critical Analysis of Some Basic Assumptions, Research Report No. 67, Uppsala, Scandinavian Institute of African Affairs, 1983.

89 Ibid., 98.

90 Cristiano d'Orsi, 'Sub-Saharan Africa: Is a New Special Regional Refugee Law Regime Emerging?', *Zeitschrift für ausländisches öffentliches Recht und Völkerrecht* 68(2008): 1079.

91 See Ekuru Aukot, 'Refugee Protection in Africa: A Developing Country's Dilemma towards Effective Protection', *East African Journal of Peace and Human Rights* 9(2003): 213–254.

political problems thereby entailed'.[92] A number of legal reform options had been recommended to rectify these gaps. One such proposal refers to an additional protocol to the 1969 OAU Refugee Convention, similar to the protocol to the 1951 Refugee Convention, wherein issues which are not sufficiently discussed under the Convention might be included.[93] For others, however, the development of normative standards on refugees and IDPs should be treated separately.[94] Accordingly, it is argued that any the issue of internal displacement should not appear as a major reform element of the 1969 OAU Convention.[95]

The African Charter on Human and Peoples' Rights

The African Charter on Human and Peoples' Rights explicitly recognises key rights and freedoms including the freedom of movement and the right to asylum.[96] The Charter also prohibits mass expulsion 'aimed at national, racial, ethnic or religious groups'.[97] It guarantees myriads of socio-economic rights including the right to property,[98] best attainable physical and mental health,[99] education,[100] and satisfactory environment,[101] and the freedom to dispose of ones' wealth and natural resources.[102] It protects the right of self-determination,[103] family,[104] and the right to peace and security.[105] The Charter's provision on the right to seek asylum has been considered as constituting a real and practical significance to Africa. The Charter is considered to have reflected the particular human rights features of the region. Some of its unique elements include: its provisions on socio-economic rights that are not encumbered with the condition of 'progressive realisation'; the inclusion not only of rights of individuals but also duties; and the elaborate reference to peoples' rights.

92 Joe Oloka Onyango, 'Human Rights, the OAU Convention and the Refugee Crisis in Africa: Forty Years after Geneva', *International Journal of Refugee Law* 3(1991): 458.
93 Conclusions and Recommendations of the Consultative Meeting between the African Commission on Human and Peoples' Rights and the United Nations High Commissioner for Refugees, Addis Ababa, 20 and 21 March 2003, para. 6.
94 Note 81 above, 136.
95 Okoth-Obbo notes, 'Therefore, there is no support found … for the preposition that IDPs implicitly figure as a key challenge facing the OAU Convention in the next millennium and that, therefore the legal reforms envisaged for the convention in that context must necessarily include IDPs'. Note 81 above 137.
96 Art 12 of the African Charter.
97 Art 12(5).
98 Art 17.
99 Art 16.
100 Art 18.
101 Art 24.
102 Art 21.
103 Art 20.
104 Art 18(1).
105 Art 23(1).

The African Charter enjoys a universal ratification by all members of the African Union. Its entry into force was considered by OAU's Council of Minsters as contributing 'to the eradication of one of the root causes of the refugee problem'.[106] Its provisions such as Article 5 on the right to respect for dignity and protection from all forms of degradation have been invoked to call for the application of the principle of non-refoulement.[107] Yet like the 1969 OAU Refugee Convention, the Charter does not provide any specific mention of IDPs. When the Charter was being drafted and negotiated there was far too little understanding about the nature of displacement, its consequences and the legal responses to its victims. Surprisingly the Charter also does not make reference to the 1969 OAU Refugee Convention. Early on during the negotiation, a draft protocol was prepared for the establishment of an African regional human rights Commission whose mandate would have been based on a substantive body of law including, among others, the 1951 UN Convention and the 1969 Refugee Convention.[108] This proposal, however, did not make it into the final version of the Charter. Under the existing Charter, the Commission has been established with the mandate to promote and protect human rights in the continent. While exercising its mandate, the Commission may draw inspiration from regional and international human rights, many of which are directly or indirectly related to the question of forced displacement.[109] The provisions of the Charter also open the possibility of developing additional protocols or instruments that will further fill some of the normative gaps which may be identified in the Charter.[110] It was on this legal basis, for instance, that the Protocol on the Rights of Women in Africa was drafted.[111] A similar approach could have also been adopted in dealing with the issues of internal displacement. Though ACHPR, particularly its Special Rapporteur on Refugees, Asylum Seekers, IDPs and Migrants, participated in the drafting of the Kampala Convention, the initiative was undertaken outside of the ACHPR.

106 Preamble of Resolution on the Situation of Refugees in Africa, *CM/Res. 1117 (XLVI) 1987*, adopted by the Council of Ministers of the OAU meeting in its 46th Ordinary Session in Addis Ababa, Ethiopia, 20–25 July 1987.

107 Preamble of Resolution on Guidelines and Measures for the Protection and Prevention of Torture, Cruel, Inhuman or Degrading Treatment or Punishment in Africa, ACHPR/Res.61 (XXXII), the Gambia, adopted during the Commission's 32nd Ordinary Session, 17–23 October 2002.

108 Note 44 above, 309.

109 Arts 60 and 61.

110 Art 66 states: 'Special protocols or agreements may, if necessary, supplement the provision of the present Charter'.

111 Note 1 above.

Specific regional human rights treaties

The African Charter on the Rights and Welfare of the Child

The African Charter on the Rights and Welfare of the Child (ACRWC) is the first regional binding instrument in Africa to explicitly recognise the rights of IDPs. This is not entirely surprising since displacement places children in a vulnerable position and displaced children are affected by abduction, forced recruitment into the military and violations of other entitlements.[112] The preamble of the Charter refers to 'the special needs of children in Africa on account of their situations marked by natural disasters, armed conflict, exploitation and hunger'. The overriding objective of the Charter is to provide a specific legal instrument, mainly as a regional complement to the 1989 Convention on the Rights of the Child, by catering to the specific needs of African children.[113] The Charter recognises access to health, education and other social services. It also gives due recognition to children who are separated from their families. It specifically stipulates that, 'where no parents, legal guardians or close relatives can be found the child shall be accorded the same protection as any other child permanently or temporarily deprived of his family environment for any reason'.[114] Unlike its international counterpart wherein children between 15 and 18 can be recruited into the military, the African Charter prohibits the recruitment of children under the age of 18.[115]

Regarding the protection of internally displaced children, Article 23(4) states that provisions of Article 23 shall 'apply *mutatis mutandis* to internally displaced children whether through natural disaster, internal armed conflicts, civil strife, breakdown of economic and social order or howsoever caused'. The Charter's provision on refugee children is similar to those incorporated under the 1989 Convention on the Rights of the Child. Not only does the Charter 'equalise' the protection accorded to refugee and internally displaced children, it also adopts a rather expansive definition of internal displacement including that which is triggered by 'breakdown of economic and social order'. The phrase 'howsoever caused' indicates that the list of causes of displacement covered under the provision is not exhaustive.[116]

Article 23 provides a general description of the obligation of states and the

112 See The Rights and Guarantees of Internally Displaced Children During Armed Conflict, Working Paper No. 2, September 2010, Office of the Special Representative of the United Nations Secretary General on Children and Armed Conflict, www.un.org/children/conflict/_documents/10-08849%20Rights%20Guarantees%20Internally%20Displaced%20Children%20Armed%20Conflict_WP_2.pdf.

113 Note 48 above, 199.

114 Art 23 (3) of ACRWC.

115 Art 22 of ACRWC.

116 Toko Kaime, 'The Protection of Refugee Children under the African Human Rights System: Finding Durable Solution in International Law', in *Children's Rights in Africa: A Legal Perspective*, ed. Julia Sloth Nielsen (Abingdon: Ashgate Publishing Limited, 2008), 184.

rights to which refugees and IDPs are entitled. Accordingly, states are obligated to ensure that refugee and internally displaced children, whether accompanied or not, are provided with protection and assistance in the full enjoyment of rights as stipulated in the Charter itself and other international human rights and humanitarian law. The reference to 'international humanitarian law' is significant since armed conflict affects children in myriad ways including in resulting in their displacement and family separation. The Charter's use as a protective mechanism for war-affected children enhances its particular relevance to internally displaced children. Under Article 22, states are required to respect all rules of international humanitarian law relevant to the child, and protect children from directly participating in armed conflict or from being forcedly recruited into the military. Article 22 stipulates that similar states' obligations shall apply to children affected by internal armed conflict and international armed conflict.[117]

Cooperation between states and international organisations is also clearly provided for in the Charter.[118] This provides the necessary guidance to states in their relationship with institutions such as UNHCR and ICRC which work in assisting children during displacement including by facilitating family reunification.[119] An African Committee of Experts on the Rights and Welfare of the Child has been established with the mandate, among others, to consider communications from individual persons and NGOs.[120] The Charter allows specific tasks to be entrusted to the Committee by the African Union and even by the UN.[121] The Committee is also empowered to consider reports by state parties regarding the implementation of the Charter including those provisions dealing with refugees and IDPs.[122] It has been argued that there is no organic or institutional link between the African Charter on Human and Peoples' Rights and the African Charter on the Rights and Welfare of the Child.[123] Neither is the relationship between the African Commission on Human and Peoples' Rights and that of the Committee well-articulated and defined.[124] More recently, however, the cooperation

117 Art 22(3) of ACRWC.

118 Art 23(4) of ACRWC.

119 Promotion and Protection of the Right of Children: ICRC Statement to the United Nations, General Assembly 65th Session, 18 October 2010, available online at www.icrc.org/eng/resources/documents/statement/united-nations-children-statement-2010-10-18.htm. See also Handbook for the Protection of Women and Girls (Geneva: United Nations High Commissioner for Refugees, 2008).

120 Art 32 of ACRWC.

121 Art 42 of ACRWC.

122 Guidelines for Initial Reports of State Parties, CMTT/ACRWC/2II, adopted at the 2nd Session of ACERWC, 21–23 February 2003, Nairobi, Kenya, para. 21.

123 Amanda Lloyd, 'A Theoretical Analysis of Children's Right in Africa: An Introduction to the Rights and Welfare of the Child in Africa', *African Human Rights Law Journal* 1(2002): 11.

124 Amanda Lloyd and Rachel Murray, 'Institutions with the Responsibility for Human Rights Protection under the African Union', *Journal of African Law* 48(2004): 175.

between the two institutions has improved. The African Union pursued and initiated a dialogue to further rationalise and facilitate cooperation.[125] The Commission justified its interest in forging cooperation with the Committee citing serious violations of rights of children in the continent and the fact that the Protocol on the Rights of Women in Africa does apply to girls. During its 45th Session held in May 2009, ACHPR adopted a resolution designating its Special Rapporteur on the Rights of Women as a focal point for the cooperation and requested the latter to regularly report on the status of its relationship with the Committee.[126]

The Protocol on the Rights of Women in Africa

The Protocol to the African Charter on the Rights of Women in Africa is one of the few regional binding instruments drafted under ACHPR's auspices. Following a recommendation from a regional seminar held during the 17th Ordinary Session of the ACHPR in 1995, the Commission adopted a decision to set up a Working Group tasked with drafting an additional protocol with the purpose of filling some of the gaps identified in the Charter.[127] The Commission's Special Rapporteur on the Rights of Women in Africa joined the Working Group and provided expert advice. The African Union adopted the Draft Protocol in July 2003 which then entered into force in November 2005.[128]

The Protocol addresses the needs of women affected by, among others, discrimination, armed conflicts, traditional harmful practices, environmental degradation, poverty, and developmental projects and policies. It spells out the rights of women to education, health, housing, property and political participation.[129] Moreover, the Protocol also recognises women's right to reproductive health,[130] food security,[131] the right to housing,[132] right to

125 See Concept Note, Brainstorming Consultative Meeting of the AU Organs on their Working Relationship, Ouagadougou, Burkina Faso, from 28 to 30 September 2008. Available online at: www.achpr.org/english/other/Brainstorming%20-%20consultations_AU%20Organs%20burkina%20.pdf.

126 See Resolution on Cooperation between the African Commission on Human and Peoples' Rights and the African Committee of Experts on the Rights and Welfare of the Child in Africa, ACHPR/Res144 (XXXXV) 09, adopted on 27 May 2009.

127 See Martin Nsibirwa, 'A Brief Analysis of the Draft Protocol to the African Charter on Human and Peoples' Rights on the Rights of Women', *African Journal of Human Rights* 1(2001): 40, 41.

128 Kristin Davis, 'Emperor is Still Naked: Why the Protocol on the Rights of Women in Africa Leaves Women Exposed to More Discrimination', *Vanderbilt Journal of Transnational Law* 42(2009), note 62.

129 Art 9.

130 Art 14.

131 Art 15.

132 Art 16.

peace[133] and the right to sustainable development.[134] It prohibits all forms of discrimination and sexual violence.[135] The Protocol also has a number of specific provisions regarding the protection needs of displaced and refugee women. Article 11 in particular, recognises the right of internally displaced women during armed conflicts including the protection from all forms of violence, rape and sexual exploitation.[136] It guarantees protection from gender-based violence and affirms the rights of women including those affected by violence to access compensation and reparations.[137] Article 4, for instance, provides that women should enjoy equal access to asylum determination procedures and be accorded with the full and equal protection available under international law.[138] Moreover, it is provided that states should take appropriate measures with a view to ensuring the participation of women in decision-making processes at all levels set up to provide 'physical, psychological, social and legal' protection to asylum seekers, refugees, returnees and displaced persons.[139] Women's involvement in decision making regarding the management of camps and settlements for displaced women and in the planning, formulation and implementation of post-conflict reconstruction and rehabilitation has also been clearly laid out.[140]

Under the Protocol, states are required to take a wide range of legislative, institutional and other measures to combat discrimination.[141] In some respects, the Protocol may even be considered to have made more major advances than the CEDAW.[142] It has been stated that the Protocol includes a 'substantial array of rights that are not provided for in other human rights treaties'.[143] Unlike the African Charter on the Rights and Welfare of the Child, no treaty-specific monitoring mechanism has been provided for supervising the implementation of the Protocol. ACHPR has filled this lacuna by assuming the role of overseeing the implementation of the

133 Art 10.
134 Art 19.
135 Though the Protocol does not use the term gender-based violence, its definition of sexual violence is broad. According to Article 1(f), sexual violence refers to 'all acts perpetrated against women which cause or could cause them physical, sexual, psychological, and economic harm, including the threat to take such acts; or to undertake the imposition of arbitrary restrictions on or deprivation of fundamental freedoms in private or public life in peace time and during situations of armed conflicts or of war'.
136 Art 11(3).
137 Art 45.
138 Art 4(2)k.
139 Art 10(2)c.
140 Art 10(2)h and g.
141 See Art 2.
142 Fareda, Banda, 'Protocol to the African Charter on the Rights of Women to Africa', in *The African Charter on Human and Peoples' Rights: The System in Practice 1986–2000*, eds. Malcom Evans and Rachel Murray (Cambridge: Cambridge University Press, 2004), 441–475.
143 Curtis, Doebbler, *International Human Rights Law: Cases and Materials* (Washington, DC: CD Publishing, 2004), 181.

Protocol, but also by establishing a Special Rapporteur mandated to promote its implementation.[144]

The birth of the African Union and its Constitutive Act

The Constitutive Act of the African Union was adopted during the OAU's 36th Ordinary Session of the Heads of State and Government on 11 July 2000. It entered into force on 26 May 2002.[145] In many respects, it presents a major departure from the legal and institutional framework of the OAU.[146] Some of its innovative provisions help position the AU to address serious and gross violations of human rights.[147] Though it reaffirms some of the traditional norms that were given much attention during the period of the OAU such as the doctrines of sovereignty, non-interference, *jus possitedis* and the peaceful settlement of disputes, the Act underscores the promotion and protection of human rights.[148] In the preamble, member states expressed their determination, among others, 'to promote and protect human and peoples' rights'.[149]

Article 4 of the Constitutive Act lists some of the fundamental principles the organisation will pursue. These include, among others, the peaceful settlement of disputes, early warning and emergency response, human rights, sanctity of colonial borders, sovereignty and non-intervention.[150] The Act provides for the right of the AU to intervene in a member state to address situations of genocide, war crimes and crimes against humanity.[151] Article 4 thus presents the most far-reaching provisions of the instrument where the possibility of regional punitive measures against violations of human rights is provided for.[152] The Act is the first international legal instrument expressly

144 See Resolution on the Designation of the Special Rapporteur on the Rights of Women in Africa, ACHPR/38(XXV) 99, adopted 5 May 1999.

145 Constitutive Act of the African Union, OAU Doc. CAB/LEG/23.15, entered into force on 26 May 2001.

146 Tiyanjana Maluwa, 'The Constitutive Act of the African Union and Institution-Building in Postcolonial Africa', *Leiden Journal of International Law* 16(2003): 158.

147 Ben Kioko, 'The Right of Intervention under the African Union's Constitutive Act: From Non-Interference to Non-Intervention', *International Review of Red Cross* 85(2003): 814.

148 Jermey Sarkin, 'The Role of the United Nations, the African Union and Africa's Sub-Regional Organisations in Dealing with Africa's Human Rights Problems: Connecting Humanitarian Intervention and the Responsibility to Protect', *Journal of African Law*, 53(2009): 17. See also Kithure Kindiki, 'The Normative and Institutional Framework of the African Union Relating to the Protection of Human Rights and the Maintenance of Peace and Security: A Critical Appraisal', *African Human Rights Law Journal* 3(2003): 98.

149 Para. 9 of the Preamble of the Act.

150 Art 4.

151 Art 4(h) and (i).

152 Note 147 above, 163.

authorising intervention on grounds of certain forms of human rights violations.[153] As such it represents what can be considered as a statutory intervention.[154] In situations where the Union decides to intervene on its own, no consent from the concerned state is required.[155] In addition, the Constitutive Act also guarantees the right of member states to request intervention to restore peace and security.[156] This curtails the principle of non-intervention that had previously been a closely held mantra of the OAU.[157]

The relevance of the foregoing provisions to the protection of IDPs cannot be underestimated. Conditions in which intervention by the AU is envisaged such as situations of genocide, war crimes, crimes against humanity and serious threat to law and order are often accompanied by forced displacement.[158] Though guidance on when and how regional interventions may be authorised has not been stipulated for, the challenges of internal displacement *per se* would not be a sufficient basis for military intervention. Serious human rights and humanitarian developments in Sudan, Cote d'Ivoire and Libya have clearly shown that even when grave violations of human rights and international humanitarian law occur, agreeing on the decision of intervention is far from easy.[159] Even if decisions authorising regional interventions were to be taken, implementing these decisions will be undermined by a lack of enforcement capacity of the Union.[160]

Key principles have been incorporated in the Act, which are directly or indirectly relevant for the protection of civilians both during periods of peacetime and conflicts.[161] The Act provides rules with respect to the peaceful resolutions of disputes and protection of civilians from the impact of armed conflicts. The Act also substantially expands the competence of the

153 Art 4 of the Act.

154 See Dan Kuwali, 'The End of Humanitarian Intervention: Evaluation of the Union's Right of Intervention', *African Journal of Conflict Resolution* 29(2009): 41–61.

155 Note 147 above, 815.

156 Art 4(j) of the Act.

157 This ground of intervention is incorporated based on The Protocol on Amendments to the Constitutive Act, which was adopted in February 2003.

158 Certain specific cases of forced displacement may amount to war crimes and crimes against humanity. See Guido Acquaviva, Forced Displacement and International Crimes, Legal and Protection Policy Research Series, UNHCR, June 2011, 19.

159 Note 147 above, 815.

160 See Jakkie Cilliers and Kathryn Sturman, 'The Right of Intervention: Enforcement Challenges for the African Union', *Africa Security Review* 11(2002): 28–39.

161 These principles include: peaceful resolution of conflicts (Article 4 (e)); the right of the AU to intervene during grave circumstances such as war crimes, crimes against humanity and genocide (Article 4 (h)); the right of member states to request the intervention of the Union to restore peace and security (Article 4 (j)); promotion of human rights, democratic principles and good governance (Article 4 (m)); respect for the sanctity of human life, condemnation and rejection of impunity and political assassination, acts of terrorism and subversive activities (Article 4 (o)); and condemnation and rejection of unconstitutional change of government (Article 4 (p)).

principal organs of the Union such as the Assembly and the Executive Council. For instance, it is provided that the Assembly has, among others, the competence 'to give directives to the Executive Council on the management of conflicts, war and other emergency situations and the restoration of peace'.[162] Likewise, the Executive Council is responsible for coordinating policies and operations in areas including, 'environmental protection, humanitarian action, and disaster relief and response'.[163]

The African Union PSC was set up by a separate legal instrument. The Protocol Relating to the Establishment of the Peace and Security Council of the African Union establishes the PSC as a permanent organ of the African Union for the prevention, management and resolution of conflicts.[164] The Council is also given the mandate to coordinate humanitarian action and disaster management, and support and facilitate humanitarian action in situations of armed conflicts or major natural disasters.[165] In addition to the promotion of peace and security, the Council has the objective of anticipating and preventing conflicts and promoting and implementing peace building and post-conflict reconstruction activities.[166] The Protocol incorporates key provisions with direct and indirect references to the problem of refugees and IDPs. In key paragraphs of the preamble of the Protocol, states express their concern about the fact that conflicts have forced millions of civilians 'into drifting life as refugees, and internally displaced persons, deprived of their means of livelihood, human dignity and hope'.[167] Among some of the objectives of the Council are included the promotion and protection of human rights and humanitarian law.[168] The Protocol provides that the Council, in order to assist member states adversely affected by armed conflicts, shall undertake among others, 'resettlement and reintegration of refugees and internally displaced persons'.[169] In order to realise these objectives, a number of key mechanisms are envisaged. One of these mechanisms is the Continental Early Warning System which, among others, 'shall develop an early warning module based on early defined and accepted political, economic, social, military and humanitarian indicators, which shall be used to analyse developments within the continent and to recommend the best course of action'.[170] The Protocol also provides for the establishment of a regional peace-keeping mechanism whose implication for the protection of

162 Art 9(1)g of the Act.
163 Art 13(1)e.
164 Protocol relating to the Establishment of the Peace and Security Council of the African Union was adopted in Durban on 9 July 2002 (AU 2002). It came into force on 26 December 2003.
165 Arts 6(f), 7(1) p and 15.
166 Art 3(a) and (d).
167 Preamble para. 10.
168 Art 3(f) of the Protocol.
169 Art 14(3)d.
170 Art 12(4).

civilians in situations of armed conflicts is very important. The standby force will have the mandate to undertake humanitarian activities and also facilitate the work of other humanitarian agencies in conflict areas.[171] In order to provide the necessary financial resources for peace support missions and other operational activities, a Peace Fund has also been established.[172]

Other relevant normative developments

Similar to the post-Cold War trend in the promotion of human rights and good governance at the universal level, Africa in the 1990s saw an increased emphasis on the human rights agenda in the region.[173] Binding treaties and soft laws have been utilised by the OAU to develop norms governing several issues falling within its general competence and authority.[174] Soft laws have been particularly important instruments in dealing with issues that were not effectively addressed within the framework of existing binding instruments.[175] The OAU and the AU policy organs often adopted declarations and communiqués which have no binding status. As the adoption of several human rights treaties and soft laws testify, there has been an emphasis on human rights. In 1999 the OAU Ministers of Justice adopted the Grand Bay Declaration and Plan of Action which, among others, considered refugee flows and internal displacement as serious human rights challenges.[176] This declaration broke tradition from the OAU by clearly identifying the obligation of states to ensure the rights and freedoms of persons including those belonging to refugees and displaced persons.[177]

If the Grand Bay Declaration attempted to articulate the role of the OAU in the promotion and protection of human rights, the Kigali Declaration adopted during the first African Union Ministerial Conference on human rights held in Rwanda in 2003 helped to formulate the human rights agenda of the new African Union.[178] The New Partnership for Africa's Development

171 Arts 5 and 15.

172 Art 21.

173 Sakha Mahmud, 'The State and Human Rights in the 1990s: Perspectives and Prospects', *Human Rights Quarterly* 15(1993): 485–498.

174 See Tiyanjana Maluwa, 'International Law-Making in the Organization of African Unity: An Overview', *African Journal of International and Comparative Law* 12(2000): 216–217.

175 Abebe, note 17 above.

176 Grand Bay Declaration and Plan of Action, adopted at the First Ministerial Conference on Human Rights in Africa, 12–16 April 1999, Mauritius, available at www.achpr.org/english/declarations/declaration_grand_bay_en.html (accessed on 13 April 2010).

177 See Kofi Kufour, Human Rights in Africa: Interpreting the Organisations of Africa Unity's Grand Bay Declaration and Plan of Action. Available online at www.uel.ac.uk/law/research/publications/index.htm.

178 Kigali Declaration, MIN/CONF/HRA/Decl.I (I), adopted on 8 May 2003 during the First African Union Ministerial Conference on Human Rights in Africa, 8 May 2003, Kigali, Rwanda. Available online at www.africa-union.org/Structure_of_the_Commission/Political%20Affairs/x/KIGALI%20DECLARATION%20as%20adopted%20in%20Kigali.pdf.

(NEPAD) was launched later in the 1990s as a result of various processes which sought to entrench greater economic integration and human rights development.[179] African Peer Review Mechanism (APRM) emerged as an important component of this process where human rights and good governance of member states are subjected to peer review.[180] The OAU's Conference on Security, Stability, Development and Cooperation in Africa (CSSDCA) was also an important milestone as it positioned and contextualised 'human rights' within elements of other activities undertaken by the organisation. In the Solemn Declaration which came out of the process, member states enhanced the visibility of human rights in the work of the organisation, expressed continued support by states to regional human rights instruments and reiterated their call for the establishment of a new mechanism for protection for human rights. The CSSDCA incorporated Memorandum of Understanding (MOU) which provided indicators for measuring success which include, among others, drafting of new legal instruments and revision of the 1969 OAU Convention on Refugees by 2005.

Regional institutional frameworks for the protection of IDPs

Similar to the situation in the international arena, there has not been any specialised institutional mechanism for the protection and assistance of IDPs in Africa. However, institutions within the framework of refugee protection and human rights have taken steps to address, *albeit* in a fragmented and tentative manner, the issue of protection of IDPs. This section traces the evolution of how both the former OAU and the AU approached the question of protecting and assisting IDPs within their broader response to forced displacement. As will be seen, there has been a conscious attempt to expand the scope of existing mandates and activities with a view to meeting the needs of IDPs.

Organisation of African Unity

Though the role of the policy organs and secretariat of the OAU focused on political and diplomatic activities, the Secretary General regularly presented reports to the organisation's policy organs concerning refugees and those who were forcibly displaced. OAU's Council of Minsters often adopted resolutions and sometimes requested the latter to present reports on the

179 Norbert Funke and Saleh Nsouli, The New Partnership for Africa's Development (NEPAD): Opportunities and Challenges, IMF Working Papers 03/69, 2003.

180 Okezie Chukwumerijie, 'Peer Review and the Promotion of Good Governance in Africa', 32 *North Carolina Journal of International Law and Commercial Regulations* 32(2006–2007): 49–111.

implementation of its resolution.[181] Though these resolutions often made reference to the protection needs of refugees and displaced persons, issues related to refugees and IDPs were not considered within the regional framework of human rights.[182] The 1969 OAU Refugee Convention did not establish any specific institutional mechanism with the mandate to follow-up states' compliance with its provision.[183] Nevertheless, a number of specialised bodies such as the Bureau for Refugees, Displaced Persons and Humanitarian Assistance, the Commission of 15 (later the Commission of 20), and the Coordination Committee on Assistance to Refugees (CCAR) were established to coordinate OAU's activities with respect to refugees.[184] The Commission was OAU's principal decision-making body on all refugee matters.[185] It undertook various activities including on-site missions, reviewed the annual activity and work of the bureau; occasionally provided token financial assistance to affected member states and presented a report to the OAU Council of Ministers. Its reports ordinarily cover not only issues affecting refugees, but also displaced persons in general.

The Bureau for the Placement, Education and Training of Refugees (BPETR), established in 1968, had a rather specific mandate. Its responsibilities included: (a) seeking educational and economic opportunities for refugees in host countries; (b) developing and sharing information with member states and the international community on the patterns, causes and consequences of refugee movement in Africa; (c) providing resources for refugees to enhance their capacity to cope; (d) mediating between refugees and host countries with respect to violations of national legislations by refugees; and (e) cooperating with relevant actors to ensure the realisation of the 1969 OAU Convention.[186] Though this institution was originally established as an independent organisation, it was brought under the OAU secretariat in 1974. Faced with the difficulty of raising the necessary financial support for OAU's programmes on refugees, the Coordinating Committee on Assistance to Refugees was established in 1981.

181 These resolutions have often been titled 'Resolution on the Situation of Refugees in Africa'. See, *CM/Res. 1117 (XLVI) 1987*; CM/Res. 1084 (XLV; CM/939 (XL); Resolution CM/Res. 1022 (XLIII).

182 Murray, note 4 above, 186.

183 Early on during the negotiation on the draft of the 1969 Convention, African governments mulled over the issue of establishing a regional office for refugee affairs with a mandate akin to that of the UNHCR. This proposal, however, was met with resistance including by the UNHCR itself which feared that the establishment of the office will undermine the global mandate of UNHCR and will politicise refugee protection in Africa. Gil Loescher, *The UNHCR and World Politics – A Perilous Path* (Oxford: Oxford University Press, 2001), 125.

184 See Joe Oloka-Onyango, 'The Place and Role of the OAU Bureau for Refugees in the African Refugee Crisis', *International Journal of Refugee Law* 6: (1994): 34–52.

185 It was established at the 2nd Ordinary Session of the OAU Council of Ministers, Problem of a Refugee in Africa, Resolution CM/19(11), adopted during the 2nd Extraordinary Session in Lagos, Nigeria from 24 to 29 February 1964.

186 Note 184 above, 35.

The effectiveness of the aforementioned institutions with respect to displaced persons was considerably limited, if not disappointing.[187] Very little was done with regard to IDPs.[188] For example, CCAR's mandate did not clearly cover the problem of displacement, and the Committee found it extremely difficult to adapt to the changing dynamic, particularly the resurgence of the problem of forced displacement in general.[189] But the traditional resolutions of the Council of Minsters with titles such as 'Situations of Refugees in Africa' were later expanded to include returnees and displaced persons. OAU's resolutions often requested the Secretary General of the organisation to monitor situations of refugees and displaced persons. Even within the context of their mandate to ensure the implementation of the 1969 OAU Convention, both the Commission and the bureau were not able to exercise their mandate independently from the OAU and their activity was also significantly constrained by lack of funding and resources.[190] Moreover, there was no meaningful cooperation with ACHPR.

The decision by the 26th Assembly of heads of state and government to establish the OAU Mechanism on the Prevention, Management and Resolution of Conflicts in 1993 was a significant development from the perspective of protection of civilians displaced by conflicts. The declaration establishing the mechanism states that conflicts have led millions of Africans into 'a drifting life as refugees and internally displaced persons'.[191] It was envisaged that at the heart of this mechanism will be the Central Organ that will have the objective of undertaking preventive diplomacy, peace making and peace building.[192] In the fulfilment of its functions, the Central Organ was empowered to deploy a limited civilian and military observers' team.

Institutional framework of the African Union

The transformation of the OAU into the AU has significantly boosted the capacity of regional institutional response to violations of human rights in general and the problem of internal displacement in particular. This institutional dynamic should be considered at two levels. First, one needs to

187 See Revitalising the African Union Coordinating Mechanism on Assistance to Refugees, Returnees and Internally Displaced Persons, UNHCR, 17 November 2006. Available online at www.unhcrrlo.org/AfricanNews/Press_Release/CCAR.pdf.

188 Some of the resolutions adopted by the Council of Ministers urge the OAU together with organizations such as UNHCR to find durable solutions for refugees and displaced persons. See for example, CM/Res. 1084 (XLV, Op. para. 6).

189 Note 187 above.

190 Note 184 above, 40.

191 Declaration of Heads of State and Government of the Assembly on the Establishment within the OAU of a Mechanism for Conflict Prevention, Management and Resolution, AHG/DEC L.3(XXIX), para. 9. This paragraph was taken up in the preamble of the Protocol on the establishment of the Peace and Security Council of the African Union.

192 Ibid., para. 15.

consider both substantive and procedural developments at the level of decision-making organs of the Union. The institutional evolution associated with the transformation of the former secretariat of the OAU into the Commission of the African Union should also be properly analysed.

The African Union's decision-making organs primarily include the Assembly, the Executive Council and Committee of Permanent Representatives (PRC). The Assembly is the supreme organ of the Union. The Executive Council represents an institutional mechanism where most of the decisions are made and presented to the Assembly for endorsement. The Council has the mandate of coordinating and taking decisions on wide-ranging issues including 'environmental protection, humanitarian action and disaster response and relief'.[193] Its authority and power under the Constitutive Act include, among others, the coordination of measures in areas of immigration, disaster and relief.[194] Based on the considerations of the report of the AU Commission and the PRC sub-committee, the Executive Council often adopts decisions with respect forced displacement. The PRC is chiefly responsible for preparation of the meeting of the Council and acts as the latter's advisory body.[195] The mandate of the PRC includes undertaking missions to member countries; considering reports on forced displacement by the Commissioner for Political Affairs; providing assistance to host countries; and providing recommendations to the Executive Council and through the latter to the Assembly. It is also the first layer of policy deliberation and decision-making process where the reports of the Commission of the African Union and the PRC's sub-committees are deliberated upon. The PRC is also responsible for organising, coordinating and facilitating regional meetings on forced displacement. This body was responsible for preparing the special African Union summit on forced displacement held in October 2009.[196] It may establish sub-committees or working groups as it may deem necessary.[197] Accordingly, a new sub-committee of the Permanent Representative Committee involving all 53 members of the African Union was established with a broader mandate of looking at issues concerning refugees, returnees and IDPs. Discussions on reports of the Commission and the sub-committee are regularly incorporated as the agenda items of the

193 Art 13 (1)e.

194 Art 13(1).

195 Art 4 of Rules of Procedure of the Permanent Representatives' Committee, adopted during the 1st Ordinary Session of the Assembly of the African Union, 9–10 July 2002, Durban, South Africa.

196 Decision on the Situation of Refugees, Returnees and Internally Displaced Persons in Africa, Doc. EX. CL/299/(x), adopted during the 10th Ordinary Session of the Executive Council, 25–26 January 2007.

197 Ibid. In addition to the PRC sub-committee on Refugees, Returnees and Internally Displaced Persons, the following sub-committees have already been established: The Sub-Committee on Multilateral Cooperation; Sub-Committee on Structures; Sub-Committee on Contribution and Sub-Committee on Administrative, Budgetary, Financial Matters; Sub-Committee on Conferences and Programs.

PRC. Among others, the sub-committee undertakes missions to countries, presents reports and provides limited financial assistance.

Forced displacement is now considered as a regular agenda item of the summits of the African Union. Special ministerial meetings are also held where important decisions are often adopted. Two such special sessions have been held so far. Moreover, the first special summit on forced displacement was held in October 2009 in Kampala, Uganda where the Kampala Convention was adopted. During these summits, the Commission and the PRC sub-committee both presented reports on activities undertaken within their mandate with respect to refugees, returnees and IDPs.

The Constitutive Act has also established new institutions such as the Pan-African Parliament, the Economic, Social and Cultural Council[198] and the African Court of Justice.[199] The Parliament, whose members are designated by national legislative assemblies, is established as an advisory and consultative body.[200] But its power with respect to the protection of IDPs is potentially significant given the fact its fundamental instrument provides that the body 'shall be vested with legislative powers to be determined by the Assembly'.[201] The objectives of the Pan-African Parliament include the promotion of peace, democracy, human rights and stability.[202] Some of the specific functions provided for under the Protocol include: (a) providing recommendations with respect to human rights, the rule of law and good governance; (b) facilitating the harmonisation of laws of member states, and (c) promoting the harmonisation and coordination of policies among member states.[203] With a view to undertaking these functions, the Parliament has established various committees including one which specifically deals with human rights and justice. That its mandate is couched in the broadest language possible allowed the organ to undertake a raft of activities including supporting conflict resolutions. It adopted resolutions authorising fact-finding missions to Sudan,[204] Congo[205] and Cote d'Ivoire.[206] For example, both the resolution and the report of the fact-finding mission on

198 Art 22.

199 Art 18.

200 Art 14(1).

201 Art 11 and 2 of the Protocol to the Treaty Establishing the African Economic Community to the Pan-African Parliament, adopted on 2 March 2001. It entered into force on 14 December 2005.

202 Art 3.

203 Art 11.

204 Resolution on Conflict Resolution, PAP. Res. 002/04, adopted during the 2nd Ordinary Session of the Pan-African Parliament, 16 September–1 October 2004.

205 Resolution on the Dispatch of the Pan-African Parliament Peace Mission to the Democratic Republic of Congo during the First Fortnight of May 2005, PAP-Res. 007/05, adopted on 11 April 2005 during the 3rd Session of the Pan-African Parliament.

206 Resolution on the Dispatch of the Pan-African Parliament Peace Mission to Cote d'Ivoire at the Beginning of May 2005, PAP-Res. 06/05, adopted on 11 April 2005 during the 3rd Session of the Pan-African Parliament.

Darfur, provide a number of recommendations to the African Union and the international community including a proposal to establish a trust fund for facilitating the resettlement of refugees and internally displaced persons. These fact-finding missions and resolutions provide insights into the organisations' readiness to take on issues and on the other hand indicate the serious challenges of overlapping mandates of organs of the African Union. The institution is obviously aware of this particular challenge as its 2006–2010 strategic plan identifies overlapping of jurisdictions among AU organs as one of the 'threats'.[207]

The African Union Social, Economic and Cultural Council (ECOSOCC), launched in 2008, was established with a view to enhancing the role of the civic society in the activities of the African Union, particularly in the area of promotion of human rights, democracy, peace and stability.[208] Its specific powers include: (a) undertaking studies and providing recommendations to the African Union, (b) provision of advisory opinions to the various organs of the Union and (c) the promotion of human rights. In accordance with its Statutes, ECOSOC will have a number of sectoral committees working in the areas of peace and security, human rights and social issues including migration.[209] Within the secretariat, the African Union Commission has also created a unit, the African Union Citizens Directorate, with the mandate and responsibility of assisting Civil Society Organisations (CSOs) to be involved in the activities of AU organs.[210] It remains difficult to judge to what extent this organisation has enhanced the role of civic society in addressing the challenges of internal displacement.

Despite the fact that human rights have been important considerations in the transformation of the OAU into the AU, the Constitutive Act and other relevant legal instruments have not clearly delineated the human rights related role to be played by these institutional mechanisms.[211] It was noted that the Constitutive Act provides limited provisions on the 'functional attributes, institutional powers, and inter-relationships between different organs'.[212] At the beginning, this led to a significant confusion on the status and mandate of some of the institutions. This was particularly relevant with

207 '"One Africa-One Voice": Pan-African Parliament Strategic Plan 2006–2010', November 2005, 7. Available online at www.pambazuka.org/aumonitor/images/uploads/PAP_Strategic_Plan_2006_-_2010.pdf.

208 See Art 2, Statutes of the Economic, Social, and Cultural Council of the African Union, adopted during the 3rd Ordinary Session of the African Union held in Addis Ababa, Ethiopia, 6–8 July 2004.

209 Art 11.

210 See Partnership to Protect: CSOs and the AU: An advocacy toolkit for civilian protection, African Humanitarian Action, 2008.

211 Kristin Davis, 'Emperor is Still Naked: Why the Protocol on the Rights of Women in Africa Leaves Women Exposed to More Discrimination', *Vanderbilt Journal of Transnational Law* 42(2009): 165.

212 Note 146 above, 166.

regard to the Central Organ of the former OAU responsible for conflict resolution, the African Commission on Human and Peoples' Rights and the African Court on Human and Peoples' Rights. Later on, the African Union adopted new protocols which sought to clarify the status of these institutions. The establishment of the African Court of Justice under the Constitutive Act was complicated by the fact that there already existed a Protocol establishing the African Court of Human and Peoples' Rights. Following a series of negotiations, a decision was reached[213] by the African Union to merge the African Court of Justice with the African Court on Human and Peoples' Rights.[214] The jurisdiction of this new court has been articulated very broadly and includes the interpretation and application of the Constitutive Act, treaties and agreements of the Union, and regional human rights instruments.[215] Unlike the African Charter on Human and Peoples' Rights, the Protocol provides for a clear language on the provision of reparations for breaches of international obligations.[216] It is notable that whereas the Protocol specifically does cite some regional human rights instrument the 1969 OAU refugee Convention has not been mentioned. The legal consequence of such lacuna may not be significant since the court is also empowered to consider the interpretation and application of 'any other legal instrument relating to human rights ratified by the state parties concerned'.[217] It nonetheless indicates how the traditional resistance to consider the 1969 OAU Convention, as a typical human rights instrument, has been entrenched.

The institutional framework of the African Union on the prevention, management and resolution of conflicts has a direct repercussion on the protection of IDPs. The Constitutive Act did not originally provide clear guidance on the PSC. The elaboration of an additional protocol establishing the African Union PSC as 'a standing decision making organ on the prevention, resolution and management of conflicts' was meant to address such gaps.[218] In the Protocol, member states express their concern about the fact that 'conflicts have forced millions of people, including women and children, into a drifting life as refugees and internally displaced persons, deprived of their means of livelihood, human dignity and hope'. The Protocol gives the member states of the Council a broad mandate and function including facilitating and supporting humanitarian action.[219] The Council's prerogative is

213 See Decision, Assembly AU/Dec. 45(III), adopted during the 3rd Ordinary Session of the Assembly of the African Union held between 6 and 8 July 2004, Addis Ababa, Ethiopia.
214 Ibid.
215 Art 28.
216 Art 28(h).
217 Art 28(c).
218 Note 164 above.
219 See Arts 6(f) & 7(p).

envisaged to be exercised not only within the context of the traditional area of peace and security, but also in the area of natural disasters.[220] A number of other provisions of the Protocol further elaborate the specific functions of the Council with respect to the protection and assistance of the IDPs. Accordingly, the Council will coordinate and conduct humanitarian action.[221] The Council will also be responsible for the operation of the African Standby Force.[222] In situations of peace building, the Council shall assist member states by undertaking 'resettlement and reintegration of refugees and internally displaced persons'[223] and providing assistance to vulnerable groups.[224] In extreme and grave circumstances of genocide, war crimes and crimes against humanity, the Council may recommend intervention and define the modalities of its implementation including the deployment of African Union forces.[225]

The aforementioned responsibilities present challenges rooted in the lack of institutional capacity and potential jurisdictional overlap and contradictions of mandates with other organs of the African Union. The Council aspires to have a full-fledged operational structure for conflict prevention, peace making, peace support operation, intervention and post-conflict reconstruction. The Protocol states that the Council 'shall develop its own capacity to efficiently undertake humanitarian action'.[226] On the question of institutional relationship, however, the Protocol provides little guidance. The Assembly assumes general powers over the Council. But nowhere does the Protocol provide guidance on the relationship the PSC should have with the Executive Council. It is noted that the Executive Council has a coordination role with respect to humanitarian and disaster issues. There are few instances, however, where the Protocol discusses the relationship between the Council and other organs of the African Union. For example, in accordance with Article 19, the Council is required to pursue a 'close cooperation with the African Commission on Human and Peoples' Rights in all matters relevant to its objectives and mandate'. The AU Commission may also bring to the attention of the Council information relevant to the mandate of the Council.

Similarly, at the level of secretariat, a number of structures exist having certain responsibilities and mandates with respect to IDPs. The Constitutive Act does not specify the functions of the Commission of the African Union but generally states that the Assembly shall determine the structure, function and regulation of the Commission.[227] The Commission has eleven Commissioners including the Commissioner for Political Affairs whose office

220 Ibid.
221 Art 15(1).
222 Art 15(4).
223 Art 14(3)d.
224 Art 14(3)e.
225 Art 7(c), (e), (f).
226 Art 15(2).
227 20(3) of the Constitutive Act.

enjoys the mandate of overseeing the activities of the Division for Political and Humanitarian Affairs. The Statutes of the Commission attempt to clarify the mandate and function of the secretariat.[228] Importantly, they state that the Commission shall take action in 'domains of responsibility' including issues of 'populations, migrations, refugees and internally displaced persons', and disaster management.[229] Under the Statutes, the Commission enjoys a wide spectrum of authority which includes: (a) assisting member countries to implement policies and programmes of the Union, (b) coordinating and monitoring the implementation of decisions of organs of the Union, (c) preparing strategic plans, and (d) presenting and submitting annual reports to the Assembly, the Executive Council and the Parliament.[230] The powers granted to the Commission by far exceed those normally enjoyed by the secretariats of international organisations. The Statutes authorise the Commission to initiate proposals for consideration by other groups.[231]

There are considerable cross-linkages among the mandates of the various portfolio of the Commission. Issues of internal displacement touch upon questions that fall within the respective mandates of the Commissioner for Peace and Security and the Commissioner for Political Affairs. Under the current arrangement, activities on refugees and IDPs fall within the portfolio of the Commissioner for Political Affairs whereas migration issues are handled by the Commissioner for Labour Affairs.[232] Moreover, the issues of displaced women are addressed by the special unit on gender established under the office of the chairperson of the African Union.[233] For example, the drafting of the Kampala Convention has been overseen by the political directorate. It was argued that the Political Affairs Department focuses on policy and legislative advancements whereas the Social Department focuses on specific programmes and forging partnerships. In addition, OAU's institutions dealing with the issue of forced displacement such as the Bureau and CCAR continued under the African Union, and recently there have been attempts to revitalise them as a part of the portfolio of the Political Affairs Department.

The regional human rights framework and the role of the ACHPR

The African Commission on Human and Peoples' Rights

The African Commission on Human and Peoples' Rights is established as a regional human rights institution under the African Charter on Human and

228 See Statutes of the Commission of the African Union, ASS/AU/2(1), adopted at the 1st Ordinary Session of the African Union, 9–10 July 2002.
229 Art 2(2).
230 Art 2.
231 Art 2(2)b.
232 Art 12(2).
233 Art 12(3).

Peoples' Rights with protective, promotional and advisory functions.[234] The Charter provides an expansive and broad mandate to the Commission which includes examining reports by state parties, receiving and considering communications, and undertaking promotional activities.[235] Article 45(1)b states that the Commission may also formulate 'principles and rules aimed at solving legal problems relating to human and peoples' rights and fundamental freedoms upon which African Governments may base their legislations'. In situations of 'serious and massive violations of human rights', the Commission also enjoys an investigative power where it may undertake studies based on a request by the Assembly of the African Union.[236] Though the Charter does not explicitly use the phrase 'advisory opinion', the Commission, citing its general competence under Article 45 of the Charter, often provides an advisory opinion.[237] Despite criticisms against the Commission on certain aspects of its works, its record on interpreting the Charter, often drawing on the jurisprudence of other regional human rights mechanisms, has been positively reviewed.[238] Since 1994, the Commission has broadly interpreted the Charter and pursued the supervision of its implementation by establishing special mechanisms to complement its promotional and protective mandate. In 2004, it established the mandate of the Special Rapporteur on Refugees, Asylum Seekers, Migrant Workers and Internally Displaced Persons.[239] The Commission's jurisprudence includes the consideration of reports by states, the examination of communication brought against states and adoption of resolutions, communiqués, decisions, recommendations and advisory opinions.

Consideration of state reports

In accordance with Article 62 of the African Charter, member states are required to submit a national report on the implementation of the provisions of the Charter once every two years. Following extensive examination of these reports, the Commission often draws a set of conclusions and recommendations. The Commission uses these recommendations to encourage states to undertake specific measures with a view to implementing the provisions of the

234 Art 45.

235 Chapter II of the Charter.

236 Art 58(1)–(3).

237 Art 45(3) states that the functions of the Commission should include the interpretation of 'all provisions of the present Charter at the request of a state party, and institution of the OAU or an African organization recognized by the OAU'.

238 Chidi Odinkalu, 'The Individual Complaint Procedures of the African Union on Human and Peoples' Rights: A Preliminary Assessment', *Transitional Law & Contemporary Problems* 8(1998): 414.

239 Resolution on the Mandate of the Special Rapporteur on the Refugees, Asylum Seekers, Migrants and Internally Displaced Persons in Africa, adopted at the 36th Ordinary Session of the African Commission on Human and Peoples' Rights in Dakar, Senegal, ACHPR/Res. 116(XXXVI) 04, 4th December 2004.

Charter; requests states to provide the Commission with specific and detailed data including on IDPs;[240] encourages states to implement its decisions on communications concerning the country under review; and urges states to undertake dialogue and cooperate with its special mechanisms.[241] These recommendations often incorporate issues which touch on the protection of people who are forcibly displaced. For example, in its concluding observations on the report of Uganda, the Commission called for enhanced implementation of the national IDPs policy through rehabilitation of social and infrastructural development which will make return and resettlement viable and sustainable.[242]

Communications under the Commission's protective mandate

Communications involving human rights violations of individuals and groups may be brought to ACHPR by victims, states[243] or by others including non-governmental organisations.[244] Prior to their consideration by the Commission, these communications must pass the admissibility test provided for under the Charter and the Commission's Rules of Procedure. The complainant is expected to exhaust local remedies unless the procedure provided for under domestic jurisdiction is deemed 'unduly prolonged'.[245] In *Constitutional Rights Project* in respect of *Zamani Lekot & 6 others v. Nigeria,* the Commission noted that a complainant's plea for a hearing before the Commission shall not be judged inadmissible for lack of exhaustion of local remedies if such remedies are *unavailable, inadequate and ineffective.*[246] In another communication involving the mass expulsion of several hundred West African nationals from Zambia, the Commission reasoned that the criteria of exhaustion of local remedies as standard under the Charter does not mean that 'complainants are required to exhaust any remedy which is found to be, as a practical matter, unavailable or ineffective'.[247] In a communication concerning a complaint regarding a widespread practice of slavery in Mauritania, the Commission noted that it

240 Concluding Observation of the 3rd Report of Uganda, para. 35. Available at www.achpr.org/english/other/Con_Oberservations/uganda_3rd_rpt.pdf.

241 See Concluding Observation of ACHPR on the 3rd and 4th combined Periodic Reports of Algeria, presented at the 42nd Ordinary Session of the African Commission on Human and Peoples Rights held from 14 to 28 November 2007 para. 21. Available online at www.achpr.org/english/other/Con_Oberservations/Algeria-3rd_rept.pdf.

242 Note 240 para. 27.

243 Art 47–54 of the Charter.

244 Art 55–57 of the Charter.

245 Art 56(5) of the Charter.

246 Communication 87/93, *Constitutional Rights Project* (in respect of *Zamani Lekot & 6 others v. Nigeria),* in Eight Annual Activity Report of the African Commission on Human and Peoples' Rights 1994–95, 18th Ordinary Session, 2–11 October 1995, ACHPR/AHG/201/XXXI, Annex VI, 16, 18, para. 6.

247 Communication 71/92, *Recontre Africane poure la Defence des Droits de l'Homme (RADDHO) v. Zambia,* in Tenth Annual Activity Report of the African Commission on Human and Peoples' Rights 1996–97, para. 12.

> cannot hold the requirement of exhaustion of local remedies to apply literally in cases where it is impractical or undesirable for the complainant to seize the domestic courts in the case of each individual complaint. This is the case where there is a large number of individual victims. Due to the seriousness of the human rights situations as well as the number of people involved, such remedies as might theoretically exist in the domestic courts are as a practical matter unavailable or are unduly prolonged.[248]

In a widely discussed case, *SERAC and CESR v. Nigeria*, the Commission further elaborated its important jurisprudence yet on the right to property and prohibition of eviction, by deciding that the right to housing may be read into the Charter's provisions on the right to health, family, and right to property.[249] The communication covers claims arising from the practice by Nigerian military of 'ruthless military operations' and 'wasting operations coupled with psychological tactics of displacement' against the Ogoni people.[250] It also further alleges that Nigerian troops destroyed villages including vital resources on which local populations rely on as sources of food.[251] The Communication also covers violations committed by non-state actors such as rebel groups and oil companies. The Commission, by citing the UN Human Rights Committee's General Comment No. 7 (1997) on the right to adequate housing (Article 11.1), determined that actions taken by Nigeria's government amount to forced eviction.[252] It adopted the definition of forced eviction used by the Committee as 'the permanent removal against their will of individuals, families and/or communities from the homes and/or which they occupy, without the provision of, and access to, appropriate forms of legal or other protection'.[253] Accordingly, the Commission requested the Nigerian government to: (a) stop the attacks by its military troops against the Ogoni people, (b) investigate alleged human rights violations and prosecute those responsible for these violations; and (c) ensure provision of compensation including relief and resettlement assistance.[254]

In another important communication involving the government of Mauritania, the Commission held that the forced displacement of black Mauritanians from their lands and homes by government troops and rebel

248 See also Communications 25/89, 47/90, 56–91, 100/93, *World Organization against Torture et al. v. Zaire*, in Ninth Annual Activity Report of the African Commission on Human and Peoples' Rights 1995–96, 32nd Ordinary Session, 7–10 July 1996, AHG/207(XXXII), 2. 6, para. 37.

249 Communication No. 155/96, The Social and Economic Rights Action Centre and the Centre for Economic and. Social Rights v. Nigeria, Fifteenth Activity Report, para. 60.

250 Ibid., 8.

251 Ibid., para. 9.

252 Ibid., para. 63.

253 Ibid.

254 Ibid., para. 69.

groups constituted a violation of the Charter's provisions on freedom of movement, equality and non-discrimination.[255] Though the submissions largely dealt with those who were expelled to Senegal, they also include those 'who were on the run to escape the massacre'.[256] It also held that the confiscation, looting and destruction of property of black Mauritanians before forcing them to leave constituted a contravention of Article 14 of the Charter which guarantees the right to property.[257] The decision particularly highlighted the fact that 'many Mauritanians were forced to flee or were detained, tortured or killed because of the colour of their skin'[258] and that for

> a country to subject its own indigenes to discriminatory treatment only because of the colour of their skin is unacceptable discriminatory attitude and a violation of the very spirit of the African Charter and the letter of its Article 2.[259]

Even if some of the attacks against villagers were perpetrated by rebels, the state is responsible for ensuring that civilians are duly protected against attack by such forces.[260] The Commission recommended that the government of Mauritania, among others, take diligent measure to reinstate the nationality of those expelled; provide restitution to property lost and ensure their return to Mauritania, and provide compensation to victims including widows.[261]

The Commission, through a couple of important cases, has also elaborated the provision of the Charter on nationality. In the *Legal Resource Foundation v. Zambia,* it considered a complaint brought on behalf of the former president of the Republic, President Kenneth Kaunda, and many other citizens of the country, alleging that a constitutional amendment passed by the Zambian Parliament in 1996 requiring that contestants to the office of the president should prove that both of their parents were Zambian by birth or decent is discriminatory and disfranchises many individuals from participating in politics.[262] Article 2 of the Charter dealing with non-discrimination does not make an 'explicit' reference to 'place of birth' as a ground of prohibited non-discrimination. The Commission, however, read

255 Communications 54/91, 61/91, 98/93, 164/97, 196/97, & 210/98, Malawi African Association, Amnesty International, Ms Sarr Diop, *Union Inter Africaine des Droits de Inhume v. Mauritania (Merits) in Thirteenth Annual Activity Report of the African Commission on Human and Peoples' Rights 1999–2000*, ACHPR/AHG/222 (XXXVI) Add. 136, 158 (2000).

256 Ibid., para. 13.

257 Ibid., para. 128.

258 Ibid., para. 130.

259 Ibid., para. 131.

260 Ibid., para. 140.

261 Ibid., para 142.

262 Communication 211/1998, *Legal Resources Foundation v. Zambia*, 14th Annual Activity Report of the African Commission on Human and Peoples' Rights, AHG/229(XXXVIII), 86–97.

into this provision a prohibition of such discrimination. In so doing it made reference to General Comment No. 25 of the Human Rights Committee which states 'persons who are otherwise eligible to stand for election should not be excluded by unreasonable or discriminatory requirements such as education, residences, or descent, or by reason of political affiliation'.[263] It underscored the particular significance of this issue to many situations in Africa where 'these forms of discrimination have caused violence and social and economic instability'.[264] It noted the historical fact that prior to Zambian independence in 1994, there had been a free movement of people in what had been the Central African Federation (now Malawi, Zambia and Zimbabwe).[265] Accordingly it held that the constitutional amendment disfranchises numerous Zambian citizens whose parents were freely moving within the federation. It stated, 'one who bears the burden of disadvantage because of one's place of birth or social origin suffers indignity as a human being and as an equal and proud citizen'.[266]

In a recent landmark case inspired by the jurisprudence of the European Court of Human Rights and the Inter-American Court of Human Rights and which involved indigenous peoples in Kenya, the Commission held that the displacement of the Endorois peoples by the Kenyan government from their traditional land violated the Charter.[267] The case covers measures taken by the Kenyan government as far back as the 1970s which resulted in the eviction of these pastoralist communities from their land around Lake Bagoria in the Rift Valley Province to make way for the construction of national parks. The Commission held that the Kenyan government's actions violated provisions of the Charter dealing with the right to practise religion, property, culture, free dispossession of natural resources, and the right to development. Accordingly, the Commission ordered the government to reinstate the group to their traditional land and provide them with compensation.[268] By recognising the Endorois people as an indigenous group with a special dependence on the land, it determined measures to evict them from it as a violation of not only the right to property but also the right to development. Citing the work of its own Working Group on Indigenous Populations/Communities, it stated that special measures are required to

263 General Comment No. 25: The Right to Participate in Public Affairs, Voting Rights and the Right to Equal Access to Public Services (Art 25), CCPR/C/21/Rev.1/Add, 07 December 1996, para. 16.

264 Ibid., para. 63.

265 Ibid., para. 71.

266 Ibid., para. 63.

267 *Centre for Minority Rights Development (Kenya) and Minority Rights Group International on Behalf of Endorois Welfare Council v. Kenya,* 276/2003, 27th Activity Report of the African Commission on Human and Peoples' Rights, 109–178.

268 The Commission states: 'Members of indigenous peoples who have unwillingly lost possession of their lands, when those lands have been lawfully transferred to innocent third parties, are entitled to restitution thereof or to obtain other lands of equal extension and quality'. Ibid., para. 209.

protect the group from displacement from their traditional land.[269] The Commission further stated that the forced removal of people from their land also constitutes a violation of the right to housing which, though not expressly recognised under the Charter, is guaranteed within the framework of the right to property.[270]

Despite the absence of a clear reference under the Charter on awarding remedies including compensation to victims, the Commission was able to adopt decisions granting compensations to victims.[271] Early in its history, the Commission hesitated to award compensation for violations but left it to the judicial organs of the state party implicated in the complaint to determine the compensation. But some of its decisions included orders involving specific measures to be taken by the offending state such as legislation to be annulled,[272] or an individual to be freed.[273]

The Commission, often citing broad principles of non-discrimination and equality enshrined in Articles 2 and 3 of the Charter respectively, showed commitment to the protection of not only national but also other *categories of persons* including refugees and stateless persons.[274] For example, the Charter's provision on non-refoulement, according to the Commission, means that the state should ensure due process of law before returning asylum seekers to their country.[275] Since the displacement of populations often occurs during events of emergencies, the Commission's approach on the application of human rights in the context of emergencies is also quite important. In a communication involving the Republic of Chad, the Commission held that derogation under the Charter is not allowed even during a lawfully and properly declared emergency.[276] Considering how derogation from human rights treaties undermines the relevance of human rights to situations of emergency which too often generate forced displacement,

269 Ibid., 200.

270 Ibid., 191.

271 See Gino Naldi, 'Reparations in the Practice of the African Commission on Human and Peoples' Rights', *Leiden Journal of International Law* 14(2001): 681–693. The Protocol establishing the African Court on Human and Peoples' Rights, however, specifically grants the latter the authority to decide on damages.

272 Communication No. 101/93, *Civil Liberties Organization in respect of the Nigeria Bar Association v. Nigeria*, para. 16, 8th Annual Activity Report of the African Commission on Human and Peoples' Rights 1994–1995.

273 Communication No. 60/91, *Constitutional Rights Project v. Nigeria*, 8th Annual Activity Report of the African Commission on Human and Peoples' Rights 1994–1995; see also Communication No. 87/93, *Constitutional Rights Project v. Nigeria*, 8th Annual Activity Report of the African Commission on Human and Peoples' Rights 1994–1995.

274 Communications 27/89, 49/91, 99/93, *Organisation Mondiale Contre la Torture v. Rwanda*, Tenth Activity Report, (2000) AHRLR 282 (ACHPR 1996).

275 Ibid.

276 Communication 74/92, *Commission Nationale des Droits de l'Homme et des Libertes v. Chad*, Ninth Annual Activity Report of the African Commission on Human and Peoples Right, AHG/2007 (XXXII), para. 21.

some may see such interpretation as positive. Others, however, argue that lack of procedure on derogation is an anomaly that creates legal uncertainty on how lawfully declared states of emergency put constraints on the implementation of human rights during an emergency.[277]

In *Recontre Africaine pour la Defence des Droits de l'Homme v. Zambia*, the Commission held that mass deportation of mainly West African nationals by the Zambian government was a violation of the Charter.[278] In *Union Inter Africaine des Droits de l'Homme, Organisation Nationale des Droits de l'Homme au Sénégal, and Association Malienne des Droits de l'Homme au Angola v. Angola*, the Commission also made a similar ruling.[279] In *John D. Ouko v. Kenya,* the complainant, a student organiser from Nairobi, was arrested and detained for ten months without trial prior to his flight to the Democratic Republic of Congo (DRC) where he was admitted by the UNHCR as a refugee.[280] When the war broke out in DRC in 1998, the UNHCR evacuated, thus putting Mr Ouko in an even more precarious condition. He then lodged a complaint alleging that his arrest, detention, treatment and then flight from Kenya constituted a violation of rights recognised under the Charter. The Commission found the government of Kenya in violation of provisions of the Charter dealing with dignity, freedom of expression, freedom of association and freedom of movement. By considering the documentary evidence from UNHCR establishing the status of the complainant as a refugee in the DRC, the Commission seemed to accept the presumption that refugees may not be able to take advantage of domestic remedies in another country. It appears that no other evidence other than the attestation establishing the fact that Mr Ouko is a refugee was required to relax the criteria of exhaustion of domestic remedies.[281]

277 See Murray, note 4 above, 126; Makau Mutua, 'The African Human Rights Court: A Two-Legged Stool', *Human Rights Quarterly* 21(1999): 358; Thedor Meron, 'Internal Strife: Applicable Norms and a Proposed Instrument', in *Humanitarian Law of Armed Conflict: Challenges Ahead,* eds Astrid Delissen and Gerard Tanja (The Hague: T.M.C. Asser Institute, 1991), 257, 258.

278 Communication 71/92, Tenth Annual Activity Report of the African Commission on Human and Peoples' Rights 1996/97, paras. 60–63.

279 *Communication 159/96, Union Interafricaine des Droits de l'Homme, Fédération Internationale des Ligues des Droits de l'Homme, Rencontre Africaine des Droits de l'Homme, Organisation Nationale des Droits de l'Homme au Sénégal and Association Malienne des Droits de l'Homme v. Angola, Nov. 1997,* 11th Annual Activity Report of the African Commission on Human and Peoples' Rights, 1997/1998, 22nd and 23rd Sessions, 2–11 November 1997 and 25–29 April 1998, Annex II.

280 Communication No. 232/99 (2000), *John D. Ouko v. Kenya,* 14th Annual Activity Report of the African Commission on Human and Peoples' Rights, 2000–2001, AHG/229(XXXVII), pp. 73–77.

281 Ibid., paras. 18–19.

The Commission's fact-finding missions

The Commission's competence to undertake investigations into human rights situations within member states stems from its promotional and protection mandate under the African Charter.[282] Article 46 of the Charter states that the Commission 'may resort to any appropriate method of investigation'. Moreover, according to Article 58, the Assembly of the African Union may also request the Commission 'to undertake an in-depth study of these cases and make a factual report, accompanied by its findings and recommendations'. Members of the Commission often undertake promotional visits to various member states and present their reports. The promotional missions of the special rapporteurs however, are much focused on the protection and assistance to groups falling under her or his mandate including refugees, migrant workers and IDPs. These missions are undertaken by members of the Commission with the assistance of the secretariat and based on the consent and invitation of the state concerned. The foregoing provisions do not define what constitutes 'serious and massive' violations of human rights which will trigger the Commission's investigative power. Neither the Charter nor the Rules of Procedure provide norms governing fact-finding missions. But the Commission previously has conducted fact-finding missions involving allegations of massive violations of human rights in countries such as Sudan, Zimbabwe and Mauritania. Since these missions often look at human rights developments within the context of 'serious and massive' human rights violations, their relevance in examining the particular issue of internal displacement cannot be underestimated. This section, by looking at the case study of the crisis in the Darfur region of Sudan, attempts to look at the contributions by the Commission's investigative mandate to address the problem of internal displacement.

The Commission's fact-finding mission to Sudan, undertaken between 8 and 18 July 2009, is arguably one of its most important missions relevant to the protection and promotion of the rights of IDPs.[283] Under pressure from NGOs and human rights activists, the Commission adopted, during its 35th Ordinary Session in 2004, a resolution authorising a mission to Sudan with a view to verifying 'allegations/facts relating to the human rights situation in the Darfur and consider with all actors, possible medium and long-term solutions for arresting the situation'. The conflict in Darfur, as the report of the mission indicates, resulted in the displacement of over a million people, most of whom are black African farmers forced to flee their homes by the war between government forces and rebels, and by constant attack of armed *Janjaweed* militia.[284] The mission was led by Mr Bahame Tom Nyandunga

282 Art 45 of the African Charter.

283 The Commission undertook similar missions in Senegal and Mauritania.

284 See Report of the African Commission on Human and Peoples' Rights' Fact-Finding Mission to the Republic of Sudan in the Darfur Region, EX. CL/364(XI), Annex III.

who was serving as ACHPR's Special Rapporteur. The team undertook visits to a number of IDP camps for IDPs located in different parts of Darfur including in Dali, Ardamata, Drothi and Deribeiri. Its members met and held discussions with IDPs, organisations working with victims and authorities. Stark human rights violations such as massive displacement of civilians, sexual violence against women in and around IDP camps and severe restrictions on access to IDPs were reported by humanitarian organisations working on the ground.

Based on its visits to these camps and meeting with IDPs themselves, the mission concluded that 'the fundamental freedoms of refugees and IDPs have been greatly curtailed'.[285] IDPs often did not enjoy sufficient access to basic services and were victims of direct military attacks. There were many reports of rape and other forms of sexual violence especially when women ventured outside of the camps to collect firewood or fetch water. Women IDPs provided accounts of these violations and also informed the mission that though victims routinely reported these violations to local government officials, no follow-up measure had been taken. Government institutions set up to verify violations did not have an impact. Most of these IDPs did not want to return to their villages since they believe their safety was not guaranteed.[286] The mission also observed first hand the presence of 'an undetermined' number of IDPs who were not located in any camp and hence were not reachable by humanitarian organisations. The mission concluded that all parties particularly the *Janjaweed* militia committed atrocities, but also categorically stated that the Sudanese government failed to provide protection to women IDPs.[287] It recommended the establishment of an international Commission of Inquiry. It requested the government to halt bombardment of civilian areas and ensure protection of civilians from attacks by the *Janjaweed* fighters; investigate accounts of rape and other forms of sexual violence; facilitate access by humanitarian organisations to IDPs; and ensure through the cooperation of the international community that repatriation of IDPs is conducted on a voluntary basis.

Pending the examination and the adoption of the report, and in line with Rule 111(3) of the Commission's Rules of Procedure, the chairperson of the Commission sent a letter to the Republic of Sudan requesting the latter to take certain provisional measures.[288] The provisional measures incorporated a request to improve access to IDPs; halt of involuntary repatriation of IDPs; and strengthening national institutions vested with the power to investigate human rights violations particularly against women. The finding of the report was presented during the 3rd extraordinary session of the Commission. The Commission's work on Darfur uncovered the delicate

285 Ibid., para. 113.
286 Ibid., para. 126.
287 Ibid., para. 128.
288 Ibid., para. 15.

relationship between the Commission and policy organs of the African Union. The Commission's decision to publish its report was thwarted by the Sudanese delegation's effective complaint that it was not given sufficient time to reply to the report. The Assembly made a decision suspending the publication of the Commission's report pending the official reaction by the Sudanese government, and requesting that the ultimate publication of the report should include the reaction of the Sudanese government. The work of the Commission on Darfur also enjoyed very little link with the African Union, particularly that of the PSC which at the time was running an AU peace keeping mission in Sudan.

The Commission's standard-setting work

The Charter mandates the Commission to 'formulate and lay down principles aimed at solving legal problems relating to human and peoples' rights and fundamental freedoms upon which African Governments may base their legislations'.[289] The Commission also adopts resolutions which are either country-specific in which case they refer to a human rights situation in a particular country, or are thematic in nature where certain legal principles are elaborated. Its country resolutions, particularly those concerning conflict situations, often deal with protection issues affecting IDPs. Several of the Commission's resolutions addressing a number of thematic issues such as the establishment of a Special Rapporteur or commemoration of the anniversary of the OAU Convention on Refugees relate directly to internal displacement. The Commission holds seminars and workshops which result in concluding recommendations and resolutions. Such efforts had been encouraged by the adoption of the Grand Bay and Kigali declarations in which the Commission's role in monitoring the implementation of the OAU Convention has been recognised.[290] For example, during the 30th anniversary of the 1969 OAU Convention, the Commission adopted a resolution in which it expressed concerns about the plight of refugees and displaced persons in Africa; underscored the inadequate nature of the existing mechanisms for the protection of refugees and IDPs; decided to forge closer cooperation with the OAU Refugee Bureau; and importantly decided to maintain the issue of refugees, IDPs and other groups as an agenda item in its ordinary sessions.[291]

The Commission's Guidelines which seek to provide guidance for states in the implementation of human rights are key aspects of the Commission's

289 Art 45(1)b.

290 Thirtieth Annual Activity Report of the African Commission on Human and Peoples' Rights, AHG/222/(XXXVI), Annex IV, page 47.

291 Resolution on the Occasion of the 30th Anniversary of the OAU Convention on the Specific Aspects of Refugee Problem in Africa, ACHPR/43/XXVI (99), adopted during the 26th Ordinary Session of the African Commission on Human and Peoples' Rights, 1–15 November 1999.

contribution to the development of legal norms.[292] ACHPR's Draft Guidelines on Socio-economic Rights is perhaps one of the most detailed normative standards of its kind with direct relevance to the protection of displaced persons.[293] It provides for provisions recognising the justiciablity of social, economic and cultural rights; recognises IDPs as vulnerable groups;[294] contains a detailed provision on the protection of rights of those who are forcefully evicted from their homes, obligates states, through legislations, to provide remedies and compensations; and underlines the need to pay particular attention to the needs of women and children during evictions.

Designating the Commission's resolutions as being either country-specific or thematic may not always be appropriate. For example, the Commission's resolutions with respect to humanitarian law are often based on country-specific situations. There are numerous resolutions and communiqués which indicate this approach.[295] Though specific in its geographical application, the Commission's resolutions on the human rights violations in Darfur contained detailed reference to the human rights situations of IDPs.[296] In Resolution 117 adopted during its 42nd Ordinary Session and titled 'Strengthening Responsibility to Protect in Africa', the Commission reaffirmed the United Nations Summit Declaration in 2002 on responsibility to protect and urged conflicting parties in the Democratic Republic of Congo (DRC), Central African Republic (CAR) and Somalia to 'respect the fundamental rights of the civilian populations, in particular the right of women, children, and internally displaced persons'. In an important resolution on issues of reparation and compensation for victims of sexual violence, the

292 See the Guidelines and Measures for the Prohibition of Torture, Cruel, Inhuman and Degrading Treatment or Punishment in Africa, adopted during the 32nd Ordinary Session of the African Commission on Human and Peoples' Rights, 7–23 October 2002; Declaration of Principles on Freedom of Expression in Africa, October 2002; and Principles and Guidelines on the Right to a Fair Trial and Legal Assistance in Africa, adopted during the 33rd Ordinary Session of the African Commission on Human and Peoples' Rights, 29 May 2003. Available at www.achpr.org/english/_info/index_declarations_en.htm.

293 Draft Principles and Guidelines on Economic, Social and Cultural Rights in the African Charter on Human and Peoples' Rights, available at www.communitylawcentre.org.za/achpr/files-for-achpr/draft-pcpl-guidelines.pdf (accessed on 13 December 2010).

294 Other groups which are considered vulnerable include victims of natural disasters and indigenous peoples.

295 See Resolution on Situation in Rwanda, Seventh Annual Activity Report of the African Commission on Human and Peoples' Rights, 1993–94, ACHPR/APT/7th, Annex II; Resolution on Burundi, Ninth Annual Activity Report of the African Commission on Human and Peoples' Rights, 1995–96, ACHPR/APT/9th, Annex VII; Resolution on Sudan, Eighth Annual Activity Report of the African Commission on Human and Peoples' Rights, 1994–95, ACHPR/APT/8th, Annex VII; Resolution on Liberia, Eighth Annual Activity Report of the African Commission on Human and Peoples' Rights, 1994–95, ACHPR/APT/8th, Annex VII.

296 See ACHPR/Res.68 (XXXV) 04, ACHPR/Res.74 (XXXVII) 05 and ACHPR/Res.93 (XXXVIII) 05, and ACHPR/Res.102 (XXXX) 06.

Commission called states to ensure the availability of compensation and reparation for victims of sexual violence during armed conflicts.[297]

The Commission's Resolution on Migration and Human Rights adopted during its 42nd Ordinary Session in November 2007 reflects the growing recognition by the Commission of the subject of migration. Recalling the fact that about half of the world's IDP population are from Africa, and that more than 70 per cent of the refugees and IDPs are women, the resolution recognises that a number of provisions of the Charter are important in addressing the challenges of migration in general.[298] The resolution provides that states should (a) ensure conformity between national and international norms on migration, (b) fund and support the activities of the Special Rapporteur and (c) incorporate issues affecting migrants including IDPs in their periodic reports.[299]

The Commission's work on the promotion and protection of indigenous populations in Africa also played an important role in expanding the reach of the Charter to protect communities who have a special attachment to the land. Its major achievement so far has been the publication of its major study on indigenous peoples; a study that was later adopted by the Assembly of the African Union.[300] The Working Group undertook missions to a number of countries. Though the Working Group holds the view that the ACHPR's Special Rapporteur is the principal mechanism to deal with the issue of displacement, some of the issues incorporated in its study are relevant to clarifying the Commission's view with respect to the relationship between indigenous people's rights and internal displacement. The Commission identifies 'subjugation, marginalization, dispossession, exclusion or discrimination' as elements of indigenousness. The experience of displacement often involves dispossession of land and discrimination, and severely affects those with a special attachment to the land. Thus, one should not be hard pressed to see the relevance and utility of this definition in recognising groups that are displaced from areas of their ancestral lands and other resources on which their livelihood depend.

297 Resolution on the Right to Remedy and Reparation for Women and Girl Victims of Sexual Violence, ACHPR/Res.111/07, adopted on 28 November 2007 during the 42nd Session of the African Commission on Human and Peoples' Rights.

298 See Resolution on Migration and Human Rights, ACHPR/Res. 114/2007, adopted on 28 November 2007 during the 42nd Session of the African Commission on Human and Peoples' Rights.

299 Ibid.

300 Report of the African Commission's Working Group of Experts on Indigenous Populations/Communities, adopted at the 34th Ordinary Session in November 2003; the 17th Annual Activity Report of the African Commission later noted and authorized for publication by the 4th Ordinary Session of the AHSG of the AU held in January 2005 in Abuja, Nigeria (Assembly/AU/Dec.56 (IV)).

The Special Rapporteur on refugees, asylum seekers, migrants and internally displaced persons

The Commission's promotional and protection mandate has been a particular source of innovation that helped the Commission address some of the imperfections of the Charter. Currently, the Commission has several special mechanisms, and their mandate is generally similar to the special procedures of the UN.[301] Though no country-specific mandate has so far been established, the Commission's thematic procedures were able to consider a set of human rights issues in different countries. The Charter does not explicitly recognise the mandate of the Commission to establish these mechanisms and the legal basis has been suggested to be tenuous. But these mechanisms have been an important basis for the Commission's protection work and serve as sources of legal developments.

ACHPR's Special Rapporteur made significant contributions to the promotion of the rights of IDPs. The need to establish a 'focal point' with a mandate of monitoring the implementation of states' obligations to refugees and other vulnerable groups and people of concern was identified in the MOU signed between UNHCR and the Commission during the 34th Ordinary Session of the Commission in November 2003.[302] During the same session, the Commission appointed Commissioner Bahame Tom Mukirya Nyandunga as a focal point. But the elements of the mandate were defined only during the Commission's 35th Session when he was named a Special Rapporteur and the Commission adopted a resolution outlining elements of his mandate during its 36th Session.[303] Accordingly, the mandate of the Special Rapporteur includes undertaking field missions to member states, conducting researches, undertaking awareness-raising activities (participating in seminars and meetings); cooperating with member states in designating appropriate policies and legislations; presenting inter-session activity reports and cooperating with African Union organs and other partners. The mandate was reviewed in November 2007.[304] Following the completion of the terms of mandate by Commissioner Nyandunga, the Commission appointed Ms Kayitesi Zainabou Sylvie from Rwanda who was then replaced by Ms Maya Sahli-Fadel in November 2011.

The Special Rapporteur often relies on international frameworks and norms such as the UN Guiding Principles in the implementation of his

301 Unlike UN special mechanism, ACHPR procedures are established directly by the members of the Commission, not through an inter-governmental negotiation process.

302 Resolution on the Adoption of the Memorandum of Understanding between the African Commission on Human and Peoples' Rights and the United Nations High Commissioner for Refugees, 33rd Ordinary Session, Niamey, Niger, 15–29 May 2003.

303 Resolution on the Mandate of the Special Rapporteur on Refugees, Asylum Seekers and Internally Displaced Persons in Africa, 23 November-7 December 2004, ACHPR/Res. 72/(XXXVI)04.

304 Final Communiqué of the 42nd Ordinary Session of the African Commission on Human and Peoples' Rights, Brazzaville, Republic of Congo, 15 to 28 November 2007, para. 31.

activities. The Special Rapporteur's inter-sessional reports provide an overview of situations of refugees, asylum seekers and IDPs. Often brief and condensed, these reports cannot be said to provide detailed information and data on the plight of the displaced across the continent. They are, however, instrumental in creating awareness regarding the plight of the displaced. They also occasionally identify states in whose territories violations of human rights of people under his mandate occur and call the Commission to take measures. He has also conducted few missions in member states. Moreover, the Special Rapporteur also sent direct communications in countries to address human rights situations with respect to individuals under his mandate. For example, he has done so in respect to the Zimbabwean government's slum clean-up operation called Murambatsvina.[305] In his communication, the Rapporteur requested the government of Zimbabwe to halt the operation, assist IDPs, provide victims with basic social and humanitarian assistance and design means and ways of finding amicable solutions to the problem of illegal settlement and squatting.[306] The Special Rapporteur also issued a press release condemning the expulsion of humanitarian agencies from Sudan and requesting the later to rescind its decision.[307]

In principle, the Special Rapporteur receives individual communications from victims and their representatives. Sometimes, these requests are for material assistance to which both the Commission and the Special Rapporteur are ill-equipped. But even when the applications relate to concerns about human rights conditions, there is no procedure allowing the transfer of such requests into the proper procedure for communication under the Commission's protective mandate.[308] It should be noted that the Special Rapporteur was also intimately involved in the drafting the Kampala Convention.

The African Court on Human Rights and Justice

The African Court on Human and Peoples' Rights was originally envisaged by a protocol adopted in 1998 by the OAU Summit.[309] The adoption of the AU Constitutive Act in 2003 brought to the fore the idea of a regional court

305 The 19th Annual Activity Report of the African Commission on Human and Peoples' Rights, EX/CL/236(VIII), para. 37.

306 Ibid.

307 Press Release, 13 March 2009. Available online at www.achpr.org/english/Special%20Mechanisms/IDP's/Press%20releases%20or%20statements/PRESS%20RELEASE%20DARFUR%20IDPS%202009.pdf.

308 Bahame Tom Nyandunga, 'Working Groups of the African Commission and their Role in the Development of the African Commission on Human and Peoples' Rights', in Malcolm and Murray, *African Charter on Human and Peoples' Rights*, 368.

309 The Protocol to the African Charter on Human and Peoples' Rights on the Establishment of the African Court on Human and Peoples' Rights, adopted in Sham El-Sheikh, Egypt, on 1 July 2008. The Protocol and Statute annexed to it shall enter into force thirty days after the deposit of the instrument of ratification by fifteen states.

of justice.[310] Following a series of consultative meeting, a decision was reached to merge the two protocols and enact a legal instrument which established the African Union Court on Human Rights and Justice.[311] This Protocol establishes a judicial chamber with the mandate of overseeing the interpretation of AU's Constructive Act, the African Charter, regional human rights protocols, AU treaties, decisions of the African Union and any other human rights instrument ratified by the country concerned.[312] The potential of the African Court in implementing binding instruments and decisions of the African Union regarding forced displacement is considerable in the future. The evaluation can be made about the efficacy of the court since it was only able to consider a couple of cases.[313]

Sub-regional legal developments: Great Lakes Protocols relating to internal displacement

In addition to developments at the level of the African Union, sub-regional legal frameworks and institutional arrangements have been key instruments of addressing the protection needs of IDPs. The first-ever sub-regional binding legal instrument concerning IDPs was adopted during the second ICGLR that took place in Nairobi, Kenya between 14 and 15 December 2006.[314] The Great Lakes region covers a wide geographic area involving Angola, Burundi, Central African Republic, Republic of Congo, DRC, Kenya, Rwanda, Sudan, Tanzania, Uganda and Zambia. Many of these countries experience some of the worst forms of internal displacement and are hosts of large numbers of IDPs.[315] It is, therefore, not surprising that the continent's most blighted areas by the problem of forced displacement hosted the international conference and adopted the Pact on Security, Stability and Development, which among others, seeks to provide a legal framework governing forced displacement.[316] The severity and dramatic nature of forced population movement in the area has been marked by the 1994 Rwanda genocide, the continuing crisis in Sudan, the conflict in northern Uganda, the post-election displacement in Kenya and the continuing

310 Art 18 of the Act.

311 Protocol on the Statute of the African Court on Human Rights and Justice, available at www.african-court.org/fileadmin/documents/Court/Statute%20ACJHR/ACJHR_Protocol.pdf.

312 Art 28.

313 *The Matter of Michelot Yogogobaye v. the Republic of Senegal:* Judgment, Application No. 001/2008. Available at: www1.umn.edu/humanrts/africa/comcases/1-2008.pdf.

314 The outcome of the conference and texts of official documents including the Protocol on the Protection and Assistance of IDPs can be accessed at ICGLR's official website at www.icglr.org.

315 See *Internal Displacement: Global Overview of Trends and Developments in 2008* (Geneva: Internal Displacement Monitoring Center, 2009), 13.

316 Ibid., 29.

conflict in the Democratic Republic of Congo. A significant number of Africa's displaced persons are located in the Great Lakes region.[317]

During the first ICGLR held in 2004, leaders from 11 states in the Great Lakes region negotiated and agreed upon the Dar Salaam Declaration.[318] In the instrument, member states agreed to incorporate 'selected, concrete, achievable and measurable draft protocols and programmes of action together with specific short, medium and long-term objectives'.[319] The Declaration outlines four main priority areas: peace and security; democracy and good governance; economic development and regional integration; and humanitarian and social affairs. It establishes a regional follow-up mechanism regarding the implementation of the Declaration; promotes the implementation of humanitarian norms and principles; and tasks a regional inter-ministerial committee to prepare specific protocols and a plan of action.[320] The Declaration provides for the protection of vulnerable groups of refugees and displaced populations such as children, women and other marginalised groups. It underlines the commitment of member states 'to adopt and implement the UN Guiding Principles on Internally Displaced Persons, harmonise all the relevant human rights legislations, define a national and regional framework for the monitoring and follow-up of the standard contained therein, and which relates to the access, protection of disaster victims, internally displaced persons, refugees, women and children who are victims'.[321]

The Pact involves ten protocols and four programs of action covering a wide range of issues.[322] Two of the protocols relate to the protection and assistance of IDPs and the property rights of IDPs and returnee populations.[323] Another relevant protocol deals with the prohibition of sexual and

317 Ibid., 29, 37.

318 See Dar es Salaam Declaration on Peace, Security, Development in the Great Lakes Region, International Conference on Peace, Security and Development in the Great Lakes Region, First Summit of Heads of State and Government, Dar es Salaam, 19–20 November 2004. Available at: www.icglr.org/key-documents/declarations-pacts/Dar%20Es%20Salaam%20Declaration%20on%20Peace%20Security%20Democracy%20and%20Development.pdf.

319 Art 67.

320 See Section IV.

321 Art 58.

322 These instruments include the Protocol on Non-aggression and Mutual Defense in the Great Lakes Region, the Protocol on Democracy and Good Governance, the Protocol on Judicial Cooperation, the Protocol for the Prevention and the Punishment of the Crime of Genocide, War Crimes and Crimes against Humanity and all forms of Discrimination, the Protocol against the Illegal Exploitation of Natural Resources, the Protocol on the Specific Reconstruction and Development Zone, the Protocol on the Prevention and Suppression of Sexual Violence Against Women and Children, the Protocol on the Protection and Assistance to Internally Displaced Persons, the Protocol on the Property Rights of Returning Persons and the Protocol on the Management of Information and Communication. These texts are available at: www.icglr.org/spip.php?article2.

323 See the Protocol on the Protection and Assistance to Internally Displaced Persons and the Protocol on the Property Rights of Returning Persons.

gender-based violence against women including those who are displaced.[324] These instruments are considered as an integral part of the Pact and notably do not require separate ratifications by the member states. The Pact entered into force in 2008 upon the deposition of the necessary number of ratifications. In 2009, the United Nations General Assembly noted the Pact and its protocols 'with appreciation'.[325] Two important assumptions can be discerned from the ICGLR process. First, it was considered that the causes and manifestations of internal displacement are too often regional in dimension and nature, and hence require regional responses. Second, the issue of internal displacement should not be considered in isolation but together with other security and development issues. The legal instruments that emerged out of this process are also unique in the sense that they are supplemented with action plans involving specific projects to be implemented both at the regional and national levels. A regional secretariat has also been established as a mechanism with a view to spurring the implementation of these instruments.

The Protocol on the Protection of and Assistance to Internally Displaced Persons

The Great Lakes Protocol on the Protection of and Assistance to the Internally Displaced Persons is the first binding international instrument which exclusively deals with the issues of internal displacement. It acknowledges the fact that 'there is no specific coherent international or regional legal regime and institution mandated to provide protection and assistance to internally displaced persons'.[326] Article 6 provides that members of the ICGLR process recognise the Guiding Principles as 'regional framework' and perhaps remarkably the Annotations as 'an authoritative source for interpreting the application of the Guiding Principles'. Not only does the Protocol uncover a rather striking similarity with the Guiding Principles, Article 6 of the Protocol obliges states specifically to adopt and implement the Guiding Principles.[327] It requires states to take steps in domesticating provisions of the Guiding Principles by adopting legislations incorporating these standards.[328] The Protocol offers an explicitly broad definition of internally displaced persons to include those who are affected by large development projects and

324 The Protocol on the Prevention and Suppression of Sexual Violence against Women and Children.

325 A/RES/63/149 (2009), preamble para. 6.

326 Preamble of the Protocol.

327 Walter Kälin, The Great Lakes Protocol on Internally Displaced Persons: Response and Challenges, paper presented at International Law Project Symposium on International Law in Post Conflict Situations: The Great Lakes Process, 27 September 2007, at 3. Available at www.brookings.edu/projects/idp/Article-Index-Pages/country.aspx.

328 Art 2(3).

natural disasters.[329] Both the texts of the Guiding Principles and model legislation on internally displaced persons are annexed to the Protocol. The Protocol also envisages a number of projects that could be incorporated into a regional program of action.

The Protocol recognises the special needs of vulnerable groups such as women, children and communities with special dependence on land.[330] It calls for member states to undertake national assessments of forced displacement within their borders and keep data on IDPs, and put in place and designate government organs with specific responsibilities in meeting the protection and assistance needs of IDPs. Specific rules are included in the protocol regulating humanitarian access to affected populations. Member states are obligated to 'facilitate rapid and unimpeded humanitarian access and assistance to internally displaced persons' and 'ensure the safety and security of humanitarian personnel in the areas of displacement'. It also establishes a sub-regional supervisory mechanism for monitoring the protection of internally displaced persons. Domestication of the protocol and the Guiding Principle through the adoption of a national legislation is given a great importance. To that effect, the Protocol outlines the following as critical elements of a national legislation on internal displacement: (a) definition of IDPs in accordance with the provision of the Protocol, (b) procedure of addressing the impact of development-induced displacement; (c) identification of a national body with the mandate to protect and provide assistance to internally displaced persons, (d) establishment of rules of cooperation and engagement with international organs and civic society organisation.[331] It also underscores the primary responsibility of the state for the protection of IDPs.

The Protocol on the Property Rights of Returning Persons

The Protocol on the Property Rights of Returning Persons deals with the protection of the right of property of refugees, IDPs and other resettled persons, and stipulates provisions for recovery of lost property or compensation. It seeks to facilitate the restitution of property of refugees and IDPs upon their return to their area of origin.[332] Returnees are defined as 'Internally Displaced Persons and refugees who return to their original places or residence in their country of origin'.[333] As is the case with the Protocol on the Protection and Assistance to IDPs, the Protocol adopts a rather broad definition of 'internally displaced persons' which includes among others those who are affected by development projects. It is mentioned in the text

329 Art 1(5).
330 Art 4.
331 Art 6(4).
332 Preamble.
333 Art 1(8).

that one of the objectives of the Protocol is to ensure availability of legal remedies to IDPs who lost their property due to large-scale development projects.[334]

The Protocol underlines the right of property and obligation of states to protect such a right as enshrined under the African Charter on Human and Peoples' Rights and under international human rights instruments. By invoking well-known principles of international humanitarian law, it also recognises the obligation of states to protect the property of civilians from pillage, direct or indiscriminate attack or any other violence, reprisal, from military attack and collective punishment.[335] The Protocol incorporates specific provisions dealing with the property interests of marginalised groups such as women,[336] children[337] and communities with a special attachment to the land.[338] The Protocol recognises the special needs of 'communities, pastoralists and other groups' which have a special attachment to the land. After their displacement, states are required to ensure proper integration of these groups to areas previously occupied by them, or provide alternative land with equal value when such reintegration is not possible.[339] When such options are not possible, then compensation should be paid as provided by national legislations. States may expropriate land or property abandoned by displaced persons, but such authority is constrained by a number of conditions. It is particularly stated that acquisition or expropriation of property belonging to IDPs and refugees may only be exercised 'in compelling and overwhelming circumstances which are justified in the general interest of the public or community, provided that such acquisition or expropriation shall be carried out under procedures prescribed by law'.[340] Moreover, the state that undertakes the expropriation is obligated to undertake to maintain 'a fair balance' between the objectives of the expropriation and the interest and right of IDPs, particularly by ensuring that such expropriation does not put unreasonable and disproportionate burden on them without being restituted or compensated for such a loss, and that such measures do not undermine other entitlements and rights.

By requiring that states' measures should comply with the UN Principles on Housing and Property Restitution, it provides legal recognition to the latter.[341] The Protocol recognises right to land both under statutory and customary legal systems, and stipulates that states establish an 'affordable registration scheme'. It recognises the important role which traditional and customary authorities play in the administration of land, and requires states to

334 Art 2(5).
335 Art 3(2).
336 Art 5.
337 Art 6.
338 Art 7.
339 Art 7(1)–(3).
340 Art 4(5).
341 Art 3(3).

adopt legislations in which the role of traditional authorities in assisting the recovery of property displaced persons left behind or were dispossessed of during their displacement, may be recognised. When recovery is not feasible, states are responsible for paying compensation 'in situations where they are directly responsible'. In situations where the responsibility of the state is not so direct, they are responsible 'to establish a framework for enabling the compensation of internally displaced persons and refugees by those responsible for the loss of the property'.[342] Regarding the terms and nature of the compensation, the Protocol leaves the issue to be determined by national legislations. States are also required to adopt 'simplified procedures' which allows IDPs and refugees to lodge complaints for recovery of property.

The Protocol does not establish a judicial or quasi-judicial organ to monitor the implementation of its provisions. However, it establishes a sub-committee of experts under the Coordination Committee of Humanitarian and Social Issues which will assume responsibility for monitoring the implementation of the Protocol. Domestic and regional mechanisms are envisaged as institutional platforms where remedies for breaches of the Protocol may be sought. It indirectly acknowledges the right of individual victims to bring their case to national and regional human rights bodies when it states that, 'Nothing in this protocol shall affect the rights of internally displaced persons and refugees to take legal action aimed at recovering their properties through national courts and/or the African Commission or the African Court on Human and Peoples' Rights'.

Protocol on the Prevention and Suppression of Sexual Violence against Women and Children

The Protocol on the Prevention and Suppression of Sexual Violence against Women and Children in the Great Lakes region of Africa guarantees the rights of women to be protected from sexual violence; obligates states to criminalise and prosecute a range of sexual and gender-based violations against women and children, and provides for compensation for victims. Provisions of the Protocol are important in the light of the prevalence of sexual violence during conflict-generated displacement. The Protocol as such takes into account developments at the international level such as criminalisation of certain forms of sexual violence as war crimes.[343] Thus, it represents an ambitious attempt to 'rationalise' recent developments in international criminal law. It is provided that the principles prohibiting and criminalising sexual violence will derive from 'contemporary developments … under international criminal law'.[344] It defines sexual violence as 'any act which violates

342 Art 8(2).

343 The Great Lakes Pact and the Right of Displaced Persons: A Guide for Civic Society (Geneva: Internal Displacement Monitoring Centre (IDMC), 2008), 25.

344 Art 3(1) of the Protocol.

the sexual autonomy and bodily integrity of women and children under international criminal law'.[345] The Protocol provides a non-exhaustive list of acts constituting sexual violence both during peace time and conflict. These include: rape, sexual assault, grievous bodily harm, assault or mutilation of reproductive organs, sexual slavery, enforced prostitution, forced pregnancy, enforced sterilisation, harmful traditional practice, sexual exploitations, trafficking and enslavement.[346]

The Protocol transcends the traditional focus of similar legal instruments on protection by incorporating principles and implementable provisions on assistance. Accordingly, it provides for the establishment of a regional mechanism or facility for the provision of medical, material and social assistance to victims and survivors of sexual violence.[347] Addressing the problem of impunity is incorporated as a core element of the Protocol. As such it is provided that the prosecution of sexual crimes shall not be subjected to a statute of limitation. It obligates states to cooperate and provide assistance to each other to facilitate the arrest and trial of persons involved in the commission of such crimes. The Protocol also calls for the establishment of a regional mechanism for assisting and compensating victims of sexual violence.[348] Such compensation may be determined at the national level.

Challenges to ICGLR's sub-regional approach

The Great Lakes Pact and its protocols address internal displacement in a holistic and comprehensive manner. These legal instruments have received wide international praise including by the former RSG who noted that the initiative is 'a very promising way to build consensus on the need to legally protect IDPs and on the content of such protection bottom-up; it could serve as an example for other regions'.[349] The most visible impact of the ICGLR yet has been the influence it has on the elaboration of the Kampala Convention itself. The involvement of the AU in the ICGLR process, the role of some key drafters in both the ICGLR and AU processes and the similarity between the Protocol and the Kampala Convention signals a strong link between the ICGLR and the AU initiative to elaborate a legal framework for the protection of IDPs.[350]

Effective implementation of the ICGLR protocols, however, faces some key challenges. The protocols provide that specific elements and terms of compensation for victims of human rights violations should be determined at the national level.[351] In principle, such a position is not objectionable. The

345 Arts 1(5) of the Protocol.
346 Ibid.
347 Art 2(2) of the Protocol.
348 Art 2 of the Protocol.
349 Ibid., 4.
350 Note 17 above.
351 For example, see Art 8 of the Protocol on the Protection of the Property of Returning Persons.

Protocol, however, does not provide guidance on how to address a situation when specific national legislations on compensation do not exist. The Pact establishes various levels of institutional oversight and monitoring mechanism for the implementation of the various protocols. At ICGLR, the secretariat's work will be scrutinised at technical, ministerial and summit levels. The establishment of a separate institutional mechanism for monitoring the implementation of the Protocol might be justified in light of the specific circumstance of the Great Lakes region. It nevertheless creates an additional layer of institutional mechanisms on top of what already exists. Many ICGLR member states are also member states of other sub-regional institutions such as East Africa Community, Intergovernmental Authority for Development, Common Marker for Eastern and Southern African and Southern African Development Community. One can envisage potential conflicts and overlap among these mechanisms. At the national level, national coordination mechanisms are identified. The establishment of specific dedicated national authorities is where stiff resistance by member states is observed. In some instances, national authorities accredited to the process or identified as national focal points are from ministries of foreign affairs, suggesting the absence of the articulation of the process as human rights agenda.

Conclusion

Though OAU's involvement early on has been focused on refugees, its activities had gradually evolved with respect to victims of forced displacement in general. The creation of the African Union was a milestone both from the perspective of normative development and the transformation of regional institutions. Now both the African Union and its sub-regional mechanisms such as the International Conference on the Great Lakes Region are important players in the promotion and protection of human rights in general and in meeting the protection and assistance needs of vulnerable groups such as IDPs. As was the case at the international level, there has been a growing convergence between human rights law and norms regulating internal displacement. This convergence has both normative and institutional dimensions. Newer regional human rights instruments and ACHPR's cases have increasingly made reference to displaced persons.

It has been shown that the Kampala Convention on IDPs has indeed been preceded by the codification of regional binding and soft-law instruments touching upon a wide variety of issues. These regional instruments provide explicit *de jure* recognition to IDPs. There are also a number of regional human rights instruments which explicitly recognise the rights of vulnerable groups of displaced persons such as women and children. The growing codification of regional law of internal displacement received a significant boost by the establishment of the African Union and particularly by the adoption of its Constitutive Act and other binding legal instruments. These instruments not only acknowledge the problem of displacement but also grant an explicit mandate to the African Union's organs with respect to coordinating response to humanitarian and human rights issues relevant to IDPs. In addition to these legal instruments, numerous other relevant 'soft laws' have also been elaborated. What one then finds is a growing, complex and progressive, if incomplete, regional approach towards internal displacement.

The elaboration of the Kampala Convention is a milestone for this regionalist approach on a host of humanitarian and human rights. It particularly strengthens the convergence between human rights and displaced persons. From the perspective of legal development, however, the regional codification, which defies long-held assumptions about states' reaction to proposals of international codification of norms regulating internal displacement, will undoubtedly represent a landmark in the legal protection of IDPs. It looks ironic that a regional mechanism whose approach towards human rights in general and forced displacement in particular had been so deeply influenced by the doctrines and rhetoric of state sovereignty and non-interference in the domestic affairs of states, is now at the forefront of legal developments dealing with a problem with regards to which normative developments have been constrained by similar considerations. However, this legal development should in no way be considered in isolation. Rather, the African Union's effort to codify a legally binding legal instrument should be analysed within the broader evolution of a regional human rights standards and institutions that has received a limited but consistent international support. Moreover, it should also be underscored that following the establishment of the African Union, newer regional instruments such as the Constitutive Act and the Protocol on the establishment of the African Union PSC incorporated quite innovative doctrines of regional intervention and state responsibility towards human rights protection.

In addition to regional normative developments, the role of existing regional institutions has been important. The ACHPR has made rulings on several communications touching upon issues such as evictions, deportations, dispossession of nationality, prohibition of discrimination, violations of socio-economic rights and others. In cases where the country concerned is under significant crisis, which is often the case in the context of internal displacement, the Commission's flexible standards on exhaustion of local remedies has helped simplify the possibility of submitting communications. Moreover, the Commission has adopted thematic and country-specific resolutions which make specific reference to the protection of and assistance to IDPs. The Commission's decisions on communications and its resolutions are not binding on their own but are suggestive of the willingness of the Commission to consider the plight of displaced persons. The Commission has also undertaken several missions to countries such as Sudan where significant numbers of people are displaced as a result of armed conflicts. The reports of these missions incorporate important recommendations including specific measures to be taken with respect to IDPs.

As has been shown by ACHPR's decision to establish the Special Rapporteur on Refugees, Asylum Seekers, Migrant Workers and IDPs, the African regional human rights system sought to institutionalise its work with respect to IDPs. The actual impact of this on the transformation of a regional human rights system which had in the past considered the protection of refugees and displaced persons more as a humanitarian issue than an agenda for human rights shall not be overstated. The regional approach has often considered norms and institutions on refugees as separate and distinct regimes. ACHPR's role in the protection of IDPs should also be considered within the broader context of African regional response to the problem of displacement. While the transformation of the OAU into the African Union has led to a reorientation and revitalisation of existing institutions and the creation of new ones, there remains a clear coordination gap among these institutions. It is widely considered that the establishment of the African Court for Human Rights and Justice will further reinforce the decisions of the ACHPR. The clearer mandate given to the African Union's policy organs in humanitarian issues under the Constitutive Act will also revitalise their engagement and role. It is, however, a point of great concern that there is, a gap in the coordination between the African human rights mechanisms and the African Union policy organs and its secretariat.

In addition to significant legal development at the level of the African Union, sub-regional institutions have also played proactive roles in promoting development of new legal instruments and establishment of institutions that cater for the protection and assistance needs of IDPs. By all counts, the initiative spurred by the ICGLR represents a comprehensive and innovative legal and institutional response at the sub-regional level.

4 Preparatory work and legal source of the Kampala Convention

Introduction

This chapter discusses the legislative history of the African Union Convention on the Protection and Assistance of IDPs (the Kampala Convention), and identifies, by examining the preparatory work with respect to the drafting of the Convention, its genesis, rationale and legal sources.[1] The Executive Council of the African Union adopted a landmark decision in 2004 requesting the 'the Commission to collaborate with relevant cooperating partners and other stakeholders to ensure that internally displaced persons are provided with an appropriate legal framework to ensure their adequate protection and assistance'.[2] Two ministerial meetings involving high-level government officials in charge of forced displacement were held in 2006 and 2008.[3] A series of legal experts' meetings and consultations among partner organisations of the African Union has also been held. The Convention was finally signed at the first AU Special Summit of heads of state and government hosted by the government of Uganda in October 2009. The summit also endorsed a declaration.[4]

The drafting of the Kampala Convention can be considered as the most

1 The Kampala Convention was adopted by the African Union Special Summit on Refugees, Returnees and Internally Displaced Persons in Africa held in Kampala, Uganda between 19 and 23 October 2009.

2 Decision on Refugees, Returnees and Displaced Persons, EX.CL. Dec 127(V), adopted during the 5th Ordinary Session of the Executive Council of the African Union, 30 June-3 July 2004, Addis Ababa, Ethiopia, para. 8.

3 See Report of the Ministerial Conference on Refugees, Returnees and Displaced Persons in Africa, EX/CL/259(IX). The third ministerial was held in November 2008 where the draft Convention was discussed and adopted at the ministerial level. See Explanatory Note on the African Convention on the Protection of and Assistance to Internally Displaced Persons in Africa. Available at: www.unhcrrlo.org/Conference_Special_Events/Docs/Explanatory%20note_Eng.pdf.

4 Kampala Declaration on Refugees, Returnees and Internally Displaced Persons in Africa, Ext/Assembly/AU/PA/Draft/Decl.(I) Rev.1, adopted on 23 October 2009. Available at: www.unhcr.org/refworld/docid/4af0623d2.html.

significant regional treaty making which reinforced the status of the UN Guiding Principles. The Convention was born within the framework of the continent's overarching quest for solutions to the challenges of forced displacement. Regional engagements on the problem of forced displacement in Africa, as was described in detail in Chapter 3, have a long pedigree. The OAU/AU held a series of ministerial meetings on refugees, returnees and displaced persons which served as important platforms for dialogue and policy making on forced displacement. The first special ministerial meeting was held in 1998 in Khartoum, Sudan where a key outcome was adopted.[5] The second ministerial meeting was held in 2006 in Burkina Faso which, among others, discussed the elaboration of a legal framework on the protection and assistance of IDPs.[6] That states were ready to accept a decision to grant the African Union the authority to stir a process for the development of a legal framework on IDP is indeed remarkable. During the first ministerial meeting on forced displacement in Khartoum, some delegates held the view that the meeting should not discuss issues relating to internal displacement since the latter, it was argued, involves matters representing internal affairs of the state concerned.[7]

The transformation of the OAU into the African Union boosted the development of norms and institutions which have both indirect and direct relevance to the protection of the human rights of IDPs.[8] Thanks to the close partnership between the AU and UNHCR, and the strengthening of African Union institutions such as the Permanent Representatives Sub-Committee on Refugees, Returnees and Displaced Persons (PRC sub-committee); the Coordination Committee on Refugees, Returnees and Displaced Persons (the Coordination Committee); and the Humanitarian Affairs, Refugees and Displaced Persons Division (HARPD), the ground for elaboration of a binding treaty increasingly became fertile. The adoption of the Great Lakes Protocol in 2006 was also a significant milestone which

5 See Recommendations of the OAU Ministerial Meeting on Refugees, Returnees and Internally Displaced Persons in Africa, adopted during a meeting held in 10–14 December 1998, Khartoum, Sudan, BR/COM/Rec.I (I).

6 Report of the Ministerial Conference on Refugees, Returnees and Displaced Persons in Africa, 1–2 June 2006, AU/MIN/HARDP/Rpt.

7 OAU Experts and Ministerial Meetings on Refugees, Returnees and Internally Displaced Persons in Africa, 10–14 December 1998, Khartoum, Sudan. UNHCR Report. Available online at: www.unhcrrlo.org/Regional_Partners/Docs/OAU%20Experts%20and%20Ministerial%20Meetings%20on%20Refuges%20and%20Returnees.pdf.

8 See Patrick Tigere and Rita Amukhobu, 'The African Union's Institutional Framework for responding to Forced Displacement in Africa: Policy Review', *Conflict Trends* 3(2005): 48–55; Allehone Abebe 'Legal and Institutional Dimensions of Protecting and Assisting Internally Displaced Persons', *Journal of Refugee Studies* 22(2009): 155–176; and Rachel Murray, 'Refugees and Internally Displaced Persons and Human Rights: The African System', *Refugee Survey Quarterly* 34(2005): 56–66.

boosted the consideration of a similar approach at the continental level.[9] In addition to these regional developments, there was a much broader trend at the international level where, as discussed in greater detail in Chapter 2, normative and institutional dimensions of the protection and assistance to IDPs were increasingly refined.[10]

Numerous treaties have been negotiated and adopted under the auspices of the OAU/AU.[11] The Kampala Convention is the latest addition to the growing body of African Union law.[12] It exemplifies both the features and shortcomings of regional treaty making in Africa. One hardly finds systematically arranged *travaux preparatoires* for a great many of these legal instruments. The absence of what is an important source of information on the history of regional treaties undoubtedly presents a serious setback for both the development of jurisprudence and for research undertakings on the nature and scope of these treaties.[13] It was, for example, noted that the absence of *travaux preparatoires* for the 1969 OAU Refugee Convention led subsequent discussions on the Convention to rely on research materials published early during the adoption and coming into force of the Convention, which encouraged 'perceptions to ossify about the Convention that are not correct'.[14] The study of the Kampala Convention has to deal with similar constraints. The AU did not elaborate norms and principles governing the drafting and negotiation of regional treaties. Until recently, there has also not been any specific organisation tasked with the responsibility of

9 The process of drafting the Kampala Convention had been influenced by the elaboration of the Great Lakes Protocols. See Bhame Tom Nyandunga, 'The African Union IDP Declaration, The Kampala Convention and Recommendation: The Challenges Faced and Strategies Needed to Ensure Speedy Signature, Ratification and Implementation', p. 8. Available at: www.unhcrrlo.org/Conference_Special_Events/Docs/AU%20IDP%20 Convention_Advocate%20Bahame%20Tom%20Nyanduga.pdf.

10 See Catherine Phuong, *The International Protection of Internally Displaced Persons* (Cambridge: Cambridge University Press, 2005), 39–75.

11 For a comprehensive list of legal instruments adopted under the auspices of the OAU/AU. See the African Union's website at www.africa-union.org/root/AU/Documents/ Treaties/treaties.htm.

12 The African Union established the African Union Commission on International Law with the mandate 'to undertake activities relating to codification and progressive development of international law in the African continent with particular attention to the laws of the Union as embodied in the treaties of the Union'. Art 4(a), The Statute of the African Union Commission on International Law, EX.CL/478(XIV), adopted on 4 February 2009.

13 Article 32 of the Vienna Convention on the Law of Treaties (1969) recognises the role of 'travaux preparatoires' as supplementary means of interpreting texts of a treaty. It is very much hoped that the recent establishment of the African Union International Law Commission will partly address this shortcoming at least with respect to legal instruments elaborated within the mandate of the African Union.

14 George Okoth-Obbo, 'Thirty Years On: A Legal Review of the 1969 OAU Convention Governing the Specific Aspects of Refugee Problems in Africa', *Refugee Survey Quarterly* 20(2001): 11.

undertaking codification or progressive development of regional treaties and legal instruments.[15]

The drafting process pursued by the African Union to elaborate the Kampala Convention lays bare certain differences from the procedures used to formulate the UN Guiding Principles.[16] The drafting of the Kampala Convention was not preceded by any preliminary study whether on procedural or substantive issues. The Comprehensive Study and the legal analysis undertaken within the framework of the mandate of the RSG were instrumental in the elaboration of the UN Guiding Principles.[17] A similar exercise in the context of the Kampala Convention would have: (a) allowed an assessment to be made on existing regional jurisprudence on forced displacement and scrutinise the advisability of adopting a binding legal instrument on internal displacement; (b) addressed the issue on whether the new legal instrument should be made a part of an existing legal instrument or form a separate one; (c) set out working methods and negotiation forum that ensure inclusiveness, efficiency and transparency; (d) identified the specific gaps the new legal framework intends to fill; (e) addressed numerous general procedural and substantive issues which would have otherwise consumed the time and resources of the drafting organ; (f) identified some of the essential elements of the new framework; (g) provided a survey of national legal frameworks and institutional mechanisms; and (h) indicated the perception particularly among member states about the initiative in general and some of the specific issues incorporated in particular. The African Union could also have considered a range of options to assign the responsibility for undertaking such a study. The task of preparing the study could have been given to a group of independent experts, to ACHPR Special Rapporteur, to the African Commission on Human and Peoples' Rights; or to an inter-governmental working group or panel.

The AU Commission prepared reports on the meetings of government officials and legal experts held for the purpose of negotiating the text of the

15 During its 12th Ordinary Session held in February 2008, the Assembly of the African Union adopted the Statute of the African Union Commission on International Law. According to Article 4 of the Statute, the Commission has the mandate to: 'undertake activities relating to the codification and progressive development of international law in the African Continent with particular attention to the law of the Union as embodied in the treaties of the Union, in the decisions of the policy organs of the Union and in the African Customary international law arising from the practice of member states'.

16 For a comprehensive review of the treaty-making processes of the United Nations, see Review of the Multilateral Treaty Making Process, 21 UN Legislative Series (ST/LEG/SER.B/21, 1985).

17 See Report of the Representative of the Secretary General, Mr Francis Deng, submitted pursuant to Commission on Human Rights Resolution 1997/39, Compilation and Analysis of Legal Norms, Part II, E/CN.4/1998/53/Add.1 (1998) and the Report of the Representative of the Secretary General, Mr Francis Deng, submitted pursuant to Commission on Human Rights Resolution 1995/57, Compilation and Analysis of Legal Norms, E/CN.4/1996/52/Add.2 (1995).

draft Convention. These reports, however, are often very brief accounts of the proceeding of the meetings, and thus they do not present comprehensive and detailed information. For instance, they do not provide detailed descriptions of statements made and positions held by various delegations on the Convention's specific provisions.

Unlike some other AU legal instruments – such as the Protocol to the African Charter on Human and Peoples' Rights of Women in Africa whose legislative history was marred by complex, uncoordinated and often competing initiatives by ACHPR and AU bodies – the drafting and negotiation of the Kampala Convention – though it involved the participation of the AU's office of the legal counsel and the ACHPR Special Rapporteur – had been undertaken under the auspices of the secretariat of the AU, particularly its HARPD.[18]

The Annotated Outline of the legal framework

The first important step in the drafting process was the preparation of the Annotated Outline, which presented a draft Outline incorporating key elements of the future Convention.[19] It presented some of the most important issues which were clustered under twelve topics, namely: (1) definitions; (2) objectives; (3) principles; (4) prohibition of arbitrary displacement; (5) responsibility for protection, assistance and solutions; (6) protection during displacement; (7) protection and assistance in areas of displacement; (8) development-induced displacement and displacement induced by lack of development; (9) provision of humanitarian assistance; (10) promotion of return; (11) reparations; and (12) monitoring and enforcing mechanism. As the final Convention more or less followed the structure presented in the Annotated Outline, it is important first to discuss in detail the content of the Annotated Outline.

Legal form and background

The Annotated Outline for the first time gave an indication that the outcome of the drafting process should be a Convention.[20] At the international level 'legal framework' as a reference to the UN Guiding Principle signified a compromise between those who advocated for a binding legal instrument to

18 Gino Naldi, 'The African Union and the Regional Human Rights System', in *The African Charter on Human and Peoples Rights: The System in Practice 1986–2000* in Malcolm Evans and Rachel Murray, 2nd edition, 20–48 (Cambridge: Cambridge University Press, 2008): 31.

19 Annotated Outline of a Draft Legal Framework for the Protection and Assistance of Internally Displaced Persons in Africa, AU/EXP/HARDP/2(V-ii), Ministerial Conference on Refugees, Returnees and Displaced Persons in Africa, 2 June 2006, Ouagadougou, Burkina Faso, p.1.

20 Ibid.

the protection of IDPs and others who preferred a soft-law approach in addressing the challenges of internal displacement.[21] It is rather clear even from the decision of the Executive Council that what was envisaged under the AU's initiative was a binding legal instrument. Both the Ouagadougou Declaration and the decisions of the AU Executive Council clearly stipulated that what was being envisaged is an elaboration of a legal instrument that would have the objective of filling a 'legal vacuum'.[22]

The Outline stipulated that the purpose of the annotation was 'to set out the proposed structure and content of an African Union Legal Framework on internally displaced persons'.[23] It provided a list of thematic issues to be covered under the legal framework and incorporates explanations and background to some of these concepts. Beyond drawing the structure of a legal framework, for example, it covered numerous substantive issues to be addressed in the provisions of the future legal instrument. Here it is important to raise one notable difference between the preparation of the UN Guiding Principles and the Kampala Convention. Whereas the former benefited from an extensive work on a legal analysis of existing norms, such work was not envisaged within the context of the Kampala Convention. It may be argued that sufficient work has been done within the context of the preparation of the Guiding Principles. But this ignores the fact that the two-volume legal analysis prepared prior to the drafting of the Guiding Principles largely focused on international human rights and humanitarian law and thus could not possibly undermine the need for a legal analysis of regional human rights norms which could have benefited the drafting of the Kampala Convention. But this is not to suggest that the consultant should have undertaken such a task himself. Understandably, the consultant could only perform a task specifically asked of him under the terms of reference agreed with the African Union. But surely such a task could have easily been performed within the mandate of the ACHPR Special Rapporteur whose mandate includes, among others, to: (a) undertake studies, research and other related activities to examine appropriate ways to enhance the protection of refugees, asylum seekers and internally displaced persons in Africa; (b) develop and recommend effective strategies to better protect the rights of refugees, asylum seekers and internally displaced persons in Africa and to follow up on his recommendations; and (c) to assist Member States of the African Union to

21 Both the General Assembly (GA Res50/195 of 22 December 1996) and the Human Rights Commission (Resolution 1996/52) use the phrase 'appropriate framework'. This was reiterated by the 2005 General Assembly Outcome which gave the highest possible political endorsement to the Guiding Principles. See UN General Assembly, 2005 World Summit Outcome: resolution/adopted by the General Assembly, 24 October 2005, A/RES/60/1.

22 Decision on the Situation of Refugees, Returnees and Displaced Persons, EX., CL/Dec. 254 (VIII), adopted during the 8th Ordinary Session of the Executive Council of the African Union, 16–21 January 2006, Khartoum, Sudan, preamble.

23 Note 19 above, 1.

develop appropriate policies, regulations and laws for the effective protection of refugees, asylum seekers and internally displaced persons in Africa.[24]

The impact of the absence of such analysis of existing regional human rights norms relevant to the protection of IDPs cannot be understated. First, as has already been noted, there is a lack of clarity with respect to the extent to which the Kampala Convention has taken into account these norms, and whether an appropriate legal framework that facilitates a coherent implementation of the Convention in conjunction with other relevant regional human rights instruments has been formulated. The implications of the Convention on regional human rights including the provisions of the African Charter on Human and Peoples' Rights is not also properly explored. Any analysis of the relationship between the regional mechanism on human rights and the emerging regime on IDPs would have been illuminating and helpful. This issue, however, was not lost to the drafter who suggested, in his Annotated Outline, the inclusion, in the future instrument, of a principle that the Convention shall implement 'the rights and duties of internally displaced persons'.[25] It specifically stated that the rights of IDPs to lodge their complaint either in the African Commission on Human and Peoples' Rights or the African Court of Human Rights and Justice should be guaranteed. Second, as the proceedings of the negotiations on the Kampala Convention shows, participants sometimes had differing understandings of regional human rights instruments. Thus, a background document on existing human rights instrument would have facilitated the negotiation process. Third, an approach that took into account regional human rights issues would have appropriately placed the drafting process in the context of regional human rights developments. This would have been most relevant to the problem of displacement which is too often discussed outside of the human rights regime. Whether the new instrument should be appended to the African Charter on Human and Peoples' Rights would have been addressed. The role of the regional human rights mechanisms such as the African Commission on Human and Peoples' Rights, the ACHPR Special Rapporteur, the African Court on Human Rights and Justice, the Committee of Experts on the Rights and Welfare of the Child would have also been streamlined. Here, care should be taken not to give an impression that the Annotated Outline did not consider regional human rights instruments to be applicable to IDPs. On the contrary, the Annotated Outline clearly relied on the notion of the continuing protection of internally displaced persons as nationals of states in which they are displaced. The Outline also suggested that the preamble

24 Resolution on the Mandate of the Special Rapporteur on Refugees, Asylum Seekers and Internally Displaced Persons, ACHPR/Res 72(XXXVII) 04, adopted at the 36th Ordinary Session of the African Commission on Human and Peoples' Rights on 7 December 2004, para. 1.

25 Note 19 above, 3.

of the future Convention should make reference to regional human rights instruments.[26]

The Annotated Outline provides important insights with respect to the general approach the legal framework took, at least at the early stage of the drafting process. It reinforced state responsibility for the protection and assistance of internally displaced persons. It also notes that the content of the legal framework will draw from existing international and regional African human rights law, international humanitarian law and of course the Guiding Principles. It is also stated that the legal, political and philosophical basis of the Convention would be based on the African Union's Constitutive Act and relevant Security Council resolutions. The explicit endorsement of 'relevant AU and UN human rights instruments' notwithstanding, the text underscores the 'lack of an African legal and institutional framework for protection and assistance of IDPs'.[27] Even so, it is striking that there has been no reference to the provisions in some regional human rights instruments which, as we saw, explicitly provide for the protection of IDPs. For example, it is not clear how the proposal to establish the African High Commissioner for Internally Displaced Persons which the Annotated Outline called 'the High Level Office' is related to existing institutions.

In the introductory part of the drafter's Annotated Outline, it is stated that the content of the text draws on existing international and human rights norms and principles while 'seeking to incorporate directly, where relevant, aspects of the Guiding Principles on Internal Displacement'. This represents a direct endorsement of the Guiding Principles. The drafter's Annotated Outline even went beyond the reference to the Guiding Principles by directly endorsing the Annotations to the Guiding Principles[28] as sources for some of the ideas contained in the draft.[29] OAU/AU and the regional ministerial conferences had already endorsed the Guiding Principles as an important framework for the protection and assistance of IDPs.[30] Moreover, both nationally and regionally, the Guiding Principles and their Annotations have increasingly become acknowledged sources of legal reform. The Great Lakes Pact in which the drafter had closely been associated with in fact made a much stronger endorsement of the Guiding Principles.[31] Moreover, the

26 Ibid., 3.

27 Ibid., 1.

28 Walter Kälin, *The Guiding Principles on Internal Displacement, Annotations*, 2nd edition (Washington, DC: The American Society of International Law, 2008).

29 Note 19 above.

30 See Khartoum Declaration: Ministerial Conference on Internally Displaced Persons in the IGAD Sub-region, adopted on 2 September 2003, available at: www.brookings.edu/fp/projects/idp/conferences/DecKhartoum.pdf.

31 Article 2 of the Protocol on the Protection and Assistance of IDPs states that one of the objectives of the Protocol is to 'establish a legal framework in the Great Lakes region for ensuring the adoption and implementation by member states of the Guiding Principles on Internal Displacement'.

constructive participation of the RSG including in the meetings of independent experts and Consultative Group also provided additional support for such an approach.

Objectives of the legal framework

The drafter indicated that the objective of the outcome of his mandate was to 'establish a legal framework for protecting and assisting internally displaced persons in Africa'.[32] Dr Beyani also stipulated that one of the main objectives of the process should be the establishment of a legal framework for protecting and assisting IDPs and an appropriate institutional mechanism for its implementation. He noted that the legal framework seeks to 'prevent arbitrary displacement and eliminate the root causes of displacement, as well as searching for durable solutions to the problem of displaced persons'.[33] Moreover, the drafter proposed to provide both for the responsibilities of states and for 'armed groups' and other non-state actors. By covering problems of displacement associated with the role of non-state actors including armed groups, companies, private military structures, the drafter proposed to go beyond the scope of the Guiding Principles.

On the question of institutional framework for the new instrument, the Annotated Outline endorsed the proposal that a new AU portfolio on IDP should be established. The Annotated Outline seems to create a niche for this new office and suggests some mechanisms on how it may cooperate with existing mechanisms. Among the objectives of the new legal framework is the establishment of a model of 'solidarity, cooperation, promotion of durable solutions and sharing of responsibilities between the AU states to combat displacement'. Though the presentation of these general objectives is a welcome development, the meaning and implication of the concept of 'sharing of responsibilities' has not been clarified by the drafter. But the Annotated Outline discusses the role of the African Union, establishment of the High Level Office on IDPs and the creation of a special fund on internal displacement. In addition to the creation of a framework for cooperation among member states of the African Union, the legal framework was also intended to have the objective of providing 'a framework for international humanitarian assistance to internally displaced persons'.[34] The Annotated Outline stated that the preamble of the legal framework should reinforce the mandate of existing international organisations with respect to IDPs and that the Annotated Outline included additional substantive provisions on the role of international organisations. It also stipulated for the obligation of states and other actors in facilitating such a role.

32 Note 19 above, 2.
33 Ibid.
34 Note 19 above, 2.

General principles

Part Three of the Annotated Outline describes some of the legal principles which would shape the evolution of the future Convention. It underlined the principle of the obligation of states to prevent and prohibit displacement. The obligation and accountability of 'non-state actors, including multinational companies, and private military and security companies, for acts of displacement or complicity in such acts' was also covered.[35] The Outline also suggested that the legal framework should incorporate the principle of individual criminal responsibility 'for unlawful acts of displacement by members of armed groups or armed forces in accordance with existing international criminal law'.[36]

The Annotated Outline stressed human rights as an important principle of the framework. Some of its components included non-discrimination, equality, human dignity, freedom of movement, protection from 'political and economic exclusion and marginalisation'. Importantly also, the draft Outline stipulated 'reparations or adequate and just compensation for violations of the rights of internally displaced persons'. It also mentioned 'the rights and duties of internally displaced persons'. Other important normative principles incorporated in the Annotated Outline include: (a) the civilian and humanitarian character of protection of and assistance to IDPs; (b) African traditional hospitality to victims of displacement; (c) rapid and unimpeded access to IDPs; and (d) the promotion of self-reliance and sustainable livelihood for IDPs.

Definition

The Annotated Outline did not provide any specific definition of IDPs. The objective of the Outline, it was stated, is rather to highlight some of the issues that may be raised with respect to IDP definition. But it simply endorses the definition given to IDPs as provided for under the UN Guiding Principles.[37] It reinforces the principle that any definition given to IDPs should not be construed as warranting a distinctive legal status. It underlines the need to ensure that definition given under the Guiding Principles is attuned to 'the special circumstances of the phenomenon of internal displacement in Africa'.[38]

Arbitrary displacement

The Annotated Outline underscored that displacement is generally prohibited under international human rights and humanitarian law. It states that

35 Ibid., 3.
36 Ibid.
37 Note 19 above.
38 Ibid.

prohibition of displacement by states and non-state actors is 'a corollary to the rights not to be displaced'. It states that 'the rights of individuals not to be displaced' is violated when they are displaced by: (a) armed conflict; (b) generalised violence; (c) violations, denial, neglect of human rights; (d) development projects and lack of development; and (e) natural or man-made disasters. It provides states have a responsibility to prevent and prohibit arbitrary displacement. The ambit of the Outline is more expansive and hence includes issues that were not explicitly mentioned in the Guiding Principles. For example, whereas the Guiding Principles generally provide situations where arbitrary displacement might have occurred, the Outline specifies the bearers of the obligation. Accordingly, both states and non-state actors have the responsibility for prohibiting and preventing arbitrary displacement. The situation in which arbitrary displacement is prohibited is also much broader in the Annotated Outline. Accordingly prohibition is discussed not only within the context of grave breaches of humanitarian law violations but also with regard to: (a) violations of human rights; (b) generalised violence; (c) violations of land rights of communities with special entitlement and attachment to land, and (d) even more broadly 'any act, event, or factors, or phenomenon of comparable gravity'.

The responsibility of states and non-state actors

The responsibility of states has been incorporated as an overarching conceptual framework. The drafter stated that under international law, states have the obligation not to displace persons within the territories. But the drafter also found it very important to 'delineate the quantum of the responsibilities for providing protection and assistance' and to state that some of the responsibilities are 'owed jointly between states and non-state actors'.[39] All actors have the responsibility to provide protection and assistance to displaced populations in areas under their control; to provide unimpeded access to these IDPs, and to fully respect international humanitarian law and human rights law applicable to displaced persons. These obligations and responsibilities are applicable during all phases of displacement. The Annotated Outline cites armed groups, private military and security companies and multinational enterprises as a few examples of non-state actors.

Durable solutions for internal displacement

The promotion of return is presented as an important aspect of a durable solution to IDPs. The Annotated Outline also suggests that other solutions such as relocation and reintegration should be considered. The state is under

39 Note 19 above, 4.

an obligation to promote return, reintegration or relocation and ensure that the process of implementing such conditions is implemented in 'dignity and safety'. The Outline does not talk about 'returnees' as categories of people, but stipulates that the state assumes the responsibility of ensuring 'the return, reintegration or relocation and insertion in safety and dignity'.[40] The search for different kinds of durable solutions, according to the Annotated Outline, should be based on consultation and should respect the free consent and will of people concerned. With respect to 'communities with special attachment to land', the state should ensure that these communities are restored to their land.

The Annotated Outline considers 'reparation, restitution or compensation' for loss of property and violations of human rights of IDPs as a critical aspect of the legal framework. States have the responsibility for 'the recovery and restoration of property belonging to persons returning from situation of displacement'.[41] It specifically stipulates that the state has the obligation to ensure just and fair compensation. The Outline also requires states to ensure that appropriate domestic legislations are put in place with a view to ensuring that modalities exist at the national level for reparation and compensation. The remedies envisaged are broad and include specific compensation, restitution in kind, apologies, public acknowledgement of wrongs and guarantees of non-repetition. It is stated that these interventions would bring about 'reconciliation between returning persons and those who caused their flight in the first place'.

Monitoring mechanism

The Annotated Outline envisages the establishment of 'a High Level Office with the gravity and weight of the High Commissioner for Refugees' – an idea first suggested by the group of AU independent experts.[42] Endorsing such a proposal, the Outline suggested that the High Level Office should have the following mandate: (a) monitoring compliance; (b) publicising and disseminating information, and (c) collaborating with the African Commission on Human and Peoples' Rights and the latter's Special Rapporteur. Some of these responsibilities overlap with the mandate and responsibility of existing regional mechanisms. Taking into account this dilemma, the Annotated Outline provides that the Office should report to the ACHPR and the Special Rapporteur. This proposal, as will be shown, did not get sufficient support from member states.

40 Ibid.
41 Note 19 above, 10.
42 Ibid., 9.

Preparatory process and negotiation

The African Union requested 'the Commission to finalize the review of all OAU Treaties and Conventions, to determine their relevance to the African Union, and to convene a meeting of experts, to consider the review'.[43] A group of experts submitted its report with some recommendations in May 2004.[44] Not only did the experts recommend the drafting of new treaties including one on the topic of internal displacement, they also suggested the establishment of an African Commission on International Law that would address some of the shortcomings identified regarding the development of human rights instruments. The 5th Ordinary Session of the Executive Council endorsed these recommendations in July 2004 stating that, 'the specific needs of IDPs such as protection and assistance should be addressed through a separate legal instrument'.[45] According to the AU Commission, the idea of drafting a separate binding legal instrument on internal displacement had an earlier pedigree as reflected in a report on the joint visit by the OAU secretariat and the PRC sub-committee to refugee and IDP camps in Sierra Leone in early 2000.[46]

The recommendation or proposal to hold the special meeting originally emerged in one of the special ministerial meetings on displacement which the OAU/AU is increasingly relying on as a forum for undertaking serious deliberations on the challenges of forced displacement.[47] Moreover, the objective of the special summit was broader than developing a legal framework for the protection and assistance of IDPs. It was expected to provide 'strategic guidance' not only to the problem of IDPs but also to challenges faced by refugees and returnees.

The AU Executive Council, in its meetings in 2006, requested 'the Commission to collaborate with relevant cooperating partners and other stakeholders to ensure internally displaced persons are provided with an appropriate legal framework to ensure their adequate protection and assistance'.[48] As previous treaty-making efforts had not been as conspicuous with

43 Decision on the Status of Signature and Ratification of AU Treaties, DOC. EX/CL/36(III), adopted during the 3rd Ordinary Session of the Executive Council of the African Union, 4–8 July 2003, para. 3.

44 Decision on the Meeting of Experts on the Review of OAU/AU Treaties, DOC.EX/CL/95 (V), adopted during the 5th Ordinary Session of the Executive Council, 25 June–3 July 2004, Addis Ababa, Ethiopia, p. 2.

45 See Decision on the Meeting of Experts on the Review of OAU/AU Treaties, EX.CL/Dec. 129(V), adopted during the 5th Ordinary Session of the Executive Council of the African Union, 25 June–3 July 2004, Addis Ababa, Ethiopia.

46 Interview with an official of the African Union, 22 January 2008.

47 See Decision on the Situation of Refugees, Returnees and Displaced Persons, EX., CL/Dec. 254 (VIII), adopted during the 8th Ordinary Session of the Executive Council of the African Union, 16–21 January 2006, Khartoum, Sudan, para. 9, 11.

48 Ibid.

regard to the participation of other actors, the decision to invite non-AU bodies to participate in the drafting process was remarkable indeed.

The decisions of the Assembly, the Executive Council and the Ouagadougou Ministerial Meeting invoked the word 'legal framework' as opposed to a 'Convention', a 'treaty' or a 'Protocol'.[49] Was this an indication that precaution was being taken not to prejudge the nature and form of the future instrument? Would a possible development of 'soft law' have been acceptable as 'appropriate legal framework'? As discussed in Chapter 3, the term 'legal framework' has often been used in the context of the international debate with respect to IDPs to avoid any specific reference to a binding instrument on IDPs. Deliberations within the African Union indicate that there has been a keen awareness of the legal vacuum in the protection of IDPs and a desire to fill such gaps.[50]

The Executive Council together with the special ministerial meetings on forced displacement has served as an important forum for providing political direction and oversight to the drafting process which took a period of four years and involved a number of important stages.

The process of drafting the Annotated Outline of the Legal Framework (the Annotated Outline) that would become the initial basis for drafting a Convention then commenced. Based on this decision, the African Union requested Dr Chaloka Beyani, a lecturer at London School of Economics and a well-known African expert in international law, to assume the role of a drafter of the initial text.[51] He was tasked with drafting a preliminary text which would then be considered by a series of meetings involving independent experts, legal officers representing governments and representatives of African Union's partners. Dr Beyani previously played a crucial role in drafting the Great Lakes Protocols.[52] It is often stated, including during the drafting of the Kampala Convention, that the Great Lakes Protocols served as inspiration and source for the drafting of the Convention. Both during this stage and after, no competing draft legal instruments were put forward by a member state or group of states, an international organisation or a civil society organisation. Therefore, the draft text produced by the independent

49 See for example the Report of the Ministerial Conference on Refugees, Returnees and IDPs in Africa, EX/CL/259(IX)Rev 1.

50 Note 47 above, 1.

51 Chaloka Beyani, 'Recent Development: The Elaboration of a Legal Framework for the Protection of Internally Displaced Persons in Africa', *Journal of African Law* 50(2006): 187–197.

52 See the Protocol on the Protection and Assistance to Internally Displaced Persons, the Protocol on the Property of Returning Persons, and the Protocol on the Prevention and Suppression of Violence against Women and Children. The Great Lakes Pact of which these protocols form a part entered into force on 21 June 2008. The texts of these legal instruments are available online at the website of the secretariat of the International Conference on the Great Lakes Region at www.icglr.org.

consultant under the auspices of the African Union Commission was the sole basis of the future negotiation.

A group of independent legal experts, which included ACHPR's Special Rapporteur, reviewed the Annotated Agenda in 2006. A Consultative Group composed of representatives from UN agencies, international organisations and civil society institutions provided its inputs. As has been stated already, those organisations had been invited by the African Union to participate in the process. A series of legal experts' meetings involving member states of the African Union were held, ushering in an important aspect of the preparatory work where each provision of the draft Convention was meticulously negotiated. Not all regional treaties in Africa have been negotiated by legal experts; a phenomenon which presented in the past a significant shortcoming both in the preparation of the legal instrument and the quality of its outcome.[53] That a series of meetings of legal experts were held in addition to a meeting of experts and minsters in charge of forced displacement issues had indeed been of a considerable significance to the drafting process. By the time the draft text was presented to the ministerial meeting in November 2008, almost all the provisions of the Kampala Convention, except very few bracketed articles, were agreed upon by the legal experts. Only a few provisions of the Convention were revised at the meeting of the African Union's Executive Council.[54]

Contributions by the Consultative Group

The Annotated Outline was submitted for endorsement by a ministerial meeting on refugees, returnees and displaced persons held in Ouagadougou, Burkina Faso in June 2006. Considering the Annotated Outline submitted by the consultant, a meeting of experts, which was held prior to the meeting of ministers, recommended to the ministerial conference that it takes note of the report and encourage the Commission to further develop the instrument with a view to submitting it to the AU summit in January 2007. The ministerial meeting endorsed the recommendation of the experts and decided that the draft legal framework should be shared with African Union partners for their contributions.[55] The Consultative Group sought to channel the contributions of these organisations. This group included organisations such as the

53 For a comment on the preparation of the AU Protocol on the Establishment of the African Union Peace and Security Council, see Jeremy Levitt, 'The Peace and Security Council of the African Union: The Known Unknowns', *Transnational Law and Contemporary Problems* 13(2003): 109–137.

54 Allehone Abebe, 'The African Union Convention on Internal Displacement: Its Codification Background, Its Scope and Enforcement Challenges', *Refugee Survey Quarterly* 29(2010): 41.

55 Report of the Ministerial Conference on Refugees, Returnees and Displaced Persons in Africa, AU/MIN/HARDP/Rpt, 1–2 June 2006, Ouagadougou, Burkina Faso, 7.

International Committee of the Red Cross (ICRC) and the UNHCR. The group held several meetings. Some of these meetings involved the participation of the former UN Secretary General's Representative on the Human Rights of Internally Displaced Persons and by the Special Rapporteur on Refugees, Returnees, Asylum Seekers, Migrant Workers and Internally Displaced Persons (ACHPR).[56]

That the process of drafting the Convention was well publicised within the UN system is partly attributable to the close involvement of these organisations in the process.[57] For example, two well-attended side events were jointly organised by UNHCR and the African Union during the 59th and 60th sessions of the Executive Committee in Geneva. In addition to holding a seminar on international law and internal displacement, on 27 May 2007, the ICRC also publicised its contribution and role in supporting the draft.[58]

The inputs by the Consultative Group to the drafting process of the Kampala Convention revealed the changing international context. It also exemplifies a regional ramification of an international support, and the impact UN agencies and international organisations can have on legal reform at regional levels.[59] The active involvement of UN agencies and international organisations in the drafting of the Convention was made possible through existing institutional mechanisms which were initially established with a view to forging a partnership between these organisations and the African Union. This was further facilitated by bilateral legal arrangements between the African Union and these organisations to cooperate on a range of issues.[60]

56 Activity Report of the Special Rapporteur on Refugees, Asylum Seekers, Migrants and IDPs in Africa, presented during the 4th Ordinary Session of the African Commission on Human and Peoples' Rights, 16–30 May 2007, 5. The text of this report can be located at: www.achpr.org/english/Special%20Mechanisms/IDP's/41st%20activity%20report_rdp.pdf. Report submitted by the Representative of the Secretary-General on the human rights of internally displaced persons, Walter Kälin, A/HRC/8/6, 24 April 2008, para. 61.

57 The United Nations General Assembly expressed its appreciation 'for the decision of the African Union to convene the Special Summit of Heads of State and Government of the African Union on Refugees, Returnees and Internally Displaced Persons in Africa, and welcoming the ongoing process to elaborate a draft African Union convention for the protection and assistance of internally displaced persons in Africa'. See General Assembly Resolution 63/149(27 January 2009), preamble.

58 See information on the regional seminar and ICRC's recommendations at: www.icrc.org/eng/resources/documents/misc/internal-displacement-africa-0407008.htm.

59 Paragraph 8 of the Statute of UNHCR provides that the High Commissioner shall provide for the protection of refugees falling under the competence of his office including by 'promoting the conclusion and ratification of international conventions for the protection of refugees, supervising their applications and proposing amendment thereto'.

60 See the Cooperation Agreement between the Organization of African Unity and the International Committee of the Red Cross, signed on 4 May 1992, 104–10. Available online at: www.icrc.org/eng/resources/documents/misc/57jn8e.ht. See also Cooperation Agreement between the Office of the United Nations High Commissioner for Refugees and the Organization of African Unity, signed on 9 April 2001, available online at http://untreaty.un.org/unts/144078_158780/12/3/4502.pdf.

The participation of international organisations in the Consultative Group was just one aspect of a much broader partnership developed throughout the years. Policy organs of the OAU and the AU adopted decisions which acknowledged and reinforced the role of these organisations in the protection of IDPs in particular. A number of UN agencies and NGOs were already members of the Coordinating Committee on Assistance to Refugees, established in 1981. Under the recent attempt to revitalise the Committee, the role of AU partners has been further enhanced.[61] Under its expanded mandate, the Committee will include, among others, the promotion of positive policies on refugees, returnees and IDPs. Moreover, they are also members of the technical Task Force set by the Commission to: (a) mobilise resources for the financing of the meeting, and (b) prepare the various background papers discussed during the meetings. This, of course, made available an extraordinary array of opportunities for these organisation to influence developments on the protection of IDPs including the drafting of the Kampala Convention.

NGOs participated in the drafting process, sometimes providing written submissions to the group.[62] Overall, however, the role of NGOs was considerably limited.[63] Even though the mandate of the AU ECOSCC was to facilitate the role of CSOs in the deliberation and policy-making processes of the African Union, this particular body was not able to meaningfully mobilise NGOs to participate in the drafting process. There were very few African NGOs which have sufficient expertise in humanitarian and forced displacement issues. Far fewer are located in Addis Ababa, Ethiopia where much of the negotiation took place. Even those that are operational have limited financial and institutional capacity to engage in the process.[64] For example, only four NGOs participated in the African Union consultative meeting of civil society held prior to the ministerial meeting undertaken in November 2008 in Addis Ababa, Ethiopia.[65] However, both prior and during the Kampala summit, NGOs held their own meetings with the purpose of providing inputs to the organisation of the meeting and the development of its important outcome. The discussion of this meeting did not focus on the draft Convention. Neither did its outcome provide a list of recommendations that one could consider as

61 See Revitalizing the African Union Coordinating Mechanism on Assistance to Refugees, Returnees and Internally Displaced Persons, UNHCR, 17 November 2006.

62 Internally Displaced Persons in Africa Need a Strong Convention, joint submission by Amnesty International, IDP Action, and International Federation for Human Rights and Refugee Rights, 6 June 2008, available at: www.fidh.org/IMG/pdf/IDPconventionAUngoComments.pdf.

63 Interview with African Union official, 22 January 2009, Addis Ababa.

64 Interview with Mr Dawit Zewde, President of the African Humanitarian Action, Addis Ababa, January 2008.

65 Report of the African Union Consultative Meeting of Civic Society for Experts and Ministerial Meetings on Refugees, Returnees and Internally Displaced Persons in Africa, African Center for Humanitarian Action, 4 November 2008.

inputs to a further development of the Convention. Rather, the aim of the meeting was conceived as enabling 'the inclusion of the views of civil society actors engaged with the issues of the special summit and to contribute, from their experiences, towards the successful outcome of the summit's deliberations by presenting their observations and recommendations on the draft Conference Paper'.[66] Some of the topics that were extensively discussed included implementation of domestic refugees' legislations, the need to enhance the capacity of indigenous CSOs with respect to the protection and assistance of IDPs; ensuring an effective regional mechanism for response and oversight; and the implication of humanitarian intervention for the protection of civilians. Obviously, some of the issues discussed such as the protection of refugees and the role of NGOs were not necessarily connected to themes covered under the Kampala Convention. But others clearly were. For example, participant discussed ways and means of ensuring the implementation of principles of civilian protections embedded in AU's Constitutive Act. Though there was no direct recommendation that the doctrine of 'responsibility to protect' be incorporated in the future Convention on IDPs, participants were clearly open to the idea of operationalising this doctrine in peace agreements negotiated under the auspices of the African Union.[67]

Comprehensive approach

Members of the Consultative Group generally supported a comprehensive scope for the Convention. They suggested that any approach to the problem of internal displacement in Africa should: (a) adopt a broad definition of IDPs; (b) cover issues relevant to all phases of internal displacement such as prevention of displacement, protection during displacement and the search for durable solutions; (c) incorporate detailed provisions on the human rights of IDPs and ensure their protection and assistance; and (d) also include provisions dealing with the protection of communities hosting IDPs. Members of the group also highlighted the potential risk associated with a rather broad definition to IDPs, particularly one that includes reference to displacement triggered by 'the effect of large scale development projects or lack of development'.

Compatibility with international norms and standards

It was clearly stated, particularly by the RSG and ACHPR's Special Rapporteur, that effort should be made to ensure the complementarily of the Kampala Convention with international norms and standards. This approach was consistent, as is indicated previously, with the stance taken by the

66 Ibid., para. 2.
67 Ibid., para. 4(e).

independent consultant who, in his draft Annotated Outline, noted that the legal framework should reinforce the UN Guiding Principles. The group, however, suggested additional provisions which specifically spell out in greater details human rights norms and corresponding responsibilities of states. In an attempt to ground the protection and assistance efforts towards IDPs within a 'human rights framework', the group also submitted that the principle of non-discrimination should be an overarching doctrine being inscribed both within the preamble and the main text of the Convention.

State responsibility and the role of non-state actors

The group also recommended that obligations of the state be incorporated into the Convention.[68] But this raised two related issues. First, while noting the relevance of identifying the role of non-state actors such as armed groups and companies, participants stated that the terminology to 'armed groups' and 'non-state actors' should clearly be defined in the text.[69] The group also discussed the question of when and how intervention from outside may be justified when the state becomes unable or unwilling to address the problem. While there was a general acceptance and support for international assistance including the role that may be played by CSOs, the group held that the principle of 'humanitarian intervention' would be quite sensitive among member states of the African Union, and hence recommended that the incorporation of 'provocative language' be avoided.[70]

Institutional mechanism

The Consultative Group supported the principle that states shall assume the primary responsibility for protecting and assisting IDPs including through the establishment of an appropriate national institutional framework. The meeting of the group also held a detailed discussion as to the role of African Union institutions in overseeing the implementation of the Convention. While underscoring the need for all relevant institutions of the African Union to play their role in the implementation of the Convention, the group supported the proposed establishment of the African Union High Commissioner. It further recommended that this organ should be given enhanced responsibilities including advocacy and mobilisation of resources to ensure an effective protection of and assistance to IDPs in affected countries. While the group clearly wanted to strengthen the Convention by recommending additional elements, it was very careful not to overburden the text with radical proposals that would have created obstacles to

68 Mebrat Senui, Brief Report on AU Consultative Meeting, 16 May 2007, African Humanitarian Action, 2.

69 Ibid.

70 Ibid.

ratification. During the meeting, the RSG stressed that 'the AU instrument must be drafted in the way that would encourage member states to adopt and implement'.[71] Both African Union officials and state representatives also supported similar approaches.

Meetings of legal experts

The Department for Political Affairs of the African Commission facilitated the preparatory and drafting work on the Convention. A series of meetings involving legal experts were held between 2007 and 2009. The mandate of these meetings was to commence and finalise negotiation on the provision of the draft Convention. It should be highlighted that there was also a number of other meetings involving experts on forced displacement. The latter involved the participation of representatives of member states representing various governmental agencies working on issues relating to refugees and IDPs. It was during these meetings that working documents for AU sessions at the ministerial and heads of state levels were prepared. And yet, the contribution of these meetings specifically to the draft Convention has not been straightforward. On the one hand, these experts had not been specifically involved in the drafting and negotiation of the text of the Convention. However, they created an opportunity for member states and other stakeholders to deliberate on wider problems of forced displacement. Recommendations adopted at the conclusions of these meetings indicate the valuable contributions these meetings were able to make. The expert meeting held prior to the November 2008 ministerial meeting in Addis Ababa can be cited as an example. Moreover, through a series of these meetings, a wider network of participants including member states, the AU Commission, UN agencies, ICRC and civil society organisations participated in the preparation of the working paper that was considered and deliberated upon during the Executive Council and the Assembly.[72] Though this paper did not specifically address the substance of the draft Convention, the fact that consultations on the document were held parallel to the drafting process was generally positive. First, it created an opportunity to sensitise the various actors about the challenges of forced displacement. Second, it allowed negotiators to consider the drafting process within the broader context of the problem of displacement. Whether this working paper has specifically influenced the drafting of the Convention is difficult to ascertain. The working document, though an official conference paper of the ministerial and Assembly meeting, had not been formally introduced to the meeting of legal experts negotiating the Convention. Neither can it be said that the document contained well-formulated legal concepts and issues that can easily be adapted into legal forms.

71 Ibid.

72 Evolution and Current Situation of Forced Displacement in Africa, African Union Ministerial Conference on Forced Displacement, 10–11 November 2008.

The first legal experts' meeting

The meetings of legal experts represented perhaps the most important forum wherein states reviewed and negotiated the Convention. The first meeting was held from 15 to 17 December 2007. This was followed by the second one which was held from 2 to 6 June 2008. A third meeting was held on 9 November 2009. All these meetings took place in Addis Ababa. The African Union Directorate for Political Affairs, particularly its Division on Humanitarian Affairs, was instrumental in providing the necessary technical and secretariat assistance. The participation of the PRC sub-committee was also notable. Because of the experience of some of the members of this sub-committee, the value of their participation cannot be undermined.

The announcement of the venue and time of the first meeting was issued by the Commission on 2 August 2007. Annexed to the letter of invitation to member states was the first official draft copy of the Convention. The draft text of the Convention represented the evolution of the Annotated Outline into a full-fledged Convention. The draft Convention at this stage possessed a structure and substance of a formal treaty with an elaborate preamble, sixteen systematically arranged substantive provisions, and a final provision covering procedural issues, namely ratification, entry into force and deposition. Its preamble made explicit reference to a long list of regional and international human rights instruments and recognised the UN Guiding Principles as 'an important international framework for the protection of internally displaced persons'. It recognised 'the inherent rights of internally displaced persons' and affirmed the responsibility of states to 'respect, protect and fulfil the human rights' of IDPs. It embraced a broad and comprehensive definition of IDPs. Accordingly, IDPs were defined as:[73]

> Persons or group of persons who are inside internationally recognised state borders of their country but who have been forced or obliged to flee or to leave their homes or places of habitual residence, in particular as a result of or in order to avoid (i) the effects of armed conflict, situations of generalised violence, violations of human rights and/or natural or human made disasters, and (ii) the effects of large scale development projects or lack of development.

The substance and format of the draft Convention was broadly consistent with the raft of issues outlined in the Annotated Outline. It stipulated norms and principles regulating the responsibility of states and non-state actors (Article 6). States are obligated to respect their responsibilities under existing international law, cooperate with all relevant organisations and institutions, ensure the implementation of prohibition of arbitrary displacement, facilitate

73 Art 1(1) I, Draft AU Convention for the Protection and Assistance of Internally Displaced Persons (August 2007).

unimpeded access to IDPs, promote durable solutions (Article 12), and provide national framework for compensation and reparation for victims of internal displacement (Article 13). With respect to the role of non-state actors, the draft Convention reaffirmed the obligation of armed groups to: (a) provide protection and assistance to IDPs in the territories under their control, (b) grant rapid and unimpeded access to IDPs, and (c) protect humanitarian personnel and resources used for humanitarian cause (Article 6). The draft Convention also provided for rules governing the actions of private institutions. It obliged state parties to ensure that not only both public and government institutions refrain from causing the displacement of populations as a result of a particular project, but also guarantee the protection of 'the social and cultural rights' of IDPs displaced by 'lack of development' (Article 10).

The draft Convention included a provision establishing a compliance and monitoring mechanism through a body referred to as the High Commissioner of the African Union for Internally Displaced Persons (Article 15). It stated that the mandate of this body would include monitoring compliance, liaising with organisations and institutions, sharing of information on internal displacement in Africa, and undertaking capacity-building programmes for national organisations and institutions. The role and responsibility of the African Union was also recognised (Article 7). The draft Convention went beyond the scope of the provision of the Constitutive Act by stating that states shall respect the right of the African Union to 'intervene, under the Constitutive Act, in the territory of a member state in order to protect and assist internally displaced persons'. It also provided that 'state parties shall request the African Union to intervene, under the Constitutive Act, to protect and assist internally displaced persons during displacement when such state parties are unable or unwilling to do so'. The draft also stipulated that the implementation of the Convention would be without prejudice to the right of IDPs to seek protection under regional human rights mechanisms and asylum under the 1969 OAU Convention Governing the Specific Aspect of Refugees Problem in Africa (Article 16).

The negotiation during the first meeting of legal experts can hardly be considered even a modest success as delegates were able to review only four articles. Representatives of delegations spent a considerable amount of time discussing the text of the Convention in broad and general terms. A considerable amount of time, therefore, was spent on providing briefings and background information to participants. As some of the representatives did not possess expertise in the area of forced displacement, the usefulness of these briefings cannot really be questioned. But this did not stop some participants from complaining that the meeting resembled more a seminar than a drafting meeting.[74] The price of this approach became apparent when

74 Interview with a diplomat who attended the meeting, 25 January 2009.

the conclusion of the meeting neared without it being able to cover any significant portion of the Convention. An attempt was made to address the problem by putting in place an inter-sessional process in accordance to which states wishing to submit their written comments were encouraged to do so prior to the second expert meeting. These considerations notwithstanding, the first draft Convention that was brought to the attention of member states was considered as too ambitious and far reaching, going well beyond existing international legal frameworks such as the UN Guiding Principles.[75]

The second legal experts' meeting

During its twelfth meeting held in January 2008, the Executive Council of the African Union took note of the outcome of the first meeting of legal experts and requested the African Union Commission to convene a second meeting to finalise the document before the special summit in 2008. The second meeting of legal experts was held from 2 to 6 June 2008 which was attended by the RSG, the ACHPR Special Rapporteur, representative of UN Offices and the ICRC.[76] Though the expectation was to finalise the negotiations by the legal experts during this meeting, achieving this turned out to be impossible. But the meeting succeeded in reviewing all articles of the Convention. The version of the draft Convention discussed during the first meeting of experts also served as a basis for negotiation and discussion during the second meeting. This is indeed hardly surprising. As has been noted, the first meeting was able to cover only four out of a total of 16 articles. Moreover, the discussion on these first set of provisions was couched in a general language.

Though the meeting was influenced by AU's very informal procedures, much of the discussion over the text was held in plenary. The meeting commenced with the review of what had been achieved during the first meeting and a presentation of a summary of written contributions from very few individual delegations. Few countries had made written submissions as per the request made during the first meeting, thus giving little material for the drafter to further improve the text during the inter-session period. The independent consultant presented a review of these contributions made by delegations. Some delegates complained that the summary did not indicate their written contributions. This did not become a significant hurdle, since the meeting decided to review the text article by article, offering delegations an opportunity to present their comments and proposals orally.

It did not take long before the meeting encountered a major problem regarding translations. Differences in terminologies and meaning among the

75 Ibid.

76 Report of the Second Meeting of Legal Experts of member states of the AU on the Draft AU Convention for the Protection and Assistance of Internally Displaced Persons in Africa, Addis Ababa, Ethiopia, 2–6 June 2008.

four official languages (mainly French and Arabic) became such a critical problem that a decision was made to set up a small group representing the various linguistic groups with the responsibility of harmonising the text. Delegations disagreed about definitions of terminologies in the different language versions of the text. There was a view that even the title of the French version of the Convention did not correspond with the English text. It was also pointed out by Arabic-speaking participants that the Arabic word used in the text as a translation for Internally Displaced Person had a pejorative connotation associating IDPs with the homeless and beggars.[77] African Union treaties often suffer from serious inconsistences among the various versions of the text, even well after the particular treaty came into force.[78]

It was, therefore, agreed that an amendment be made with respect to the title. There were also some specific decisions taken by the expert meeting on revising the format of the text by rearranging some articles; merging or splitting others or reorganising paragraphs. In some few instances, legal experts felt that certain articles of the draft Convention included concepts or issues that were already covered by other articles. Under these circumstances, the meeting generally agreed to synthesise or merge articles. Article 11, for instance, incorporated numerous issues with respect to humanitarian assistance that were relevant to situations of durable solutions. The meeting, therefore, agreed to delete these provisions and merge them with Article 12 of the draft Convention on the issue of 'promotion of durable solution'. Some of the major substantive issues which received considerable attention included: (1) definition of IDPs and the cessation clause; (2) the issue of displacement induced by development; (3) the relationship between doctrines of intervention and sovereignty of states; (4) the role and responsibilities of non-state actors particularly that of armed groups; (5) the establishment of the Office of AU High Commissioner on Internally Displaced Persons; and (6) intervention and the role of international organisations and NGOs. There were, of course, many other issues that have also undergone serious scrutiny. For example, the draft Convention's reference to reparation injected a debate whether the latter can be considered as an effective remedy for violations of rights of IDPs in the African context.

Concerning definition, experts generally accepted definitions provided for under the UN Guiding Principles and the Great Lakes Protocol. However, this, as has been clearly pointed out in the Annotated Outline, did not result in granting any form of status to IDPs. Two important issues with respect to what we may call the 'status problem' of IDPs were raised. The first one relates to the question of whether one needs to have a cessation clause regarding IDPs. Because IDPs do not possess a distinctive legal status, it was

77 Interview with the Head of delegation of Sudan, October 2009, Geneva, Switzerland.

78 For a discussion of similar problems regarding the AU Convention relating to corruption, see Peter Schroth, 'The African Union Convention on Preventing and Combating Corruption', *Journal of Africa Law* 49(2005): 24–38.

argued that, unlike in the context of refugee status determination, the issue of application of a cessation clause would not arise. This was raised particularly in connection with Article 12 of the Convention dealing with durable solutions. However, some experts argued that it would perhaps be important to at least mention the cessation of 'situation of internal displacement'. Accordingly, it is suggested that that situation of displacement would come to an end 'when there is effective state control, re-establishment of law and order and provision of basic services'.[79] According to proponents of this proposal, a link should be created between durable solution with 'long term development and post-conflict and post natural disaster reconstruction'.[80] Another related problem concerned registration and documentation. It was noted, including in Article 14 of the draft Convention, that 'identity documents are necessary for the exercise and enjoyment of human rights of IDPs'. Registration and issuance of identity documents, however, present certain problems, in particular whether formal registration of IDPs does not risk creating a distinction between those internally displaced persons who are registered and possess identification cards and those who do not. The draft Convention attempted to address this particular challenge by stating that 'the failure to issue internally displaced persons with such documents shall not in any way impair the exercise or enjoyment of their human rights'. But some participants including the RSG warned that the failure of complying with mandatory registration may pose the risk of depriving IDPs of their rights.[81] They also raised the particular challenge faced in numerous African countries where availability of resources and institutional capacity to implement such a monumental task under complex emergencies is often strained. A provision, therefore, was included in the text that stipulated that states while undertaking registration of IDPs, may cooperate with international organisations and NGOs.

There is often a tension between the principles of sovereignty and the need to provide effective provision of protection and assistance including through international intervention. This was first raised in connection with the role of the African Union under the Constitutive Act, to take intervention measures with a view to preventing genocide, crimes against humanity and war crimes.[82] A discussion on intervention *vis-a-vis* the sovereignty of states also arose with respect to the role of humanitarian organisations (Article 5). Though intervention may take several forms and thus present several questions under international law, the discussion appeared to suggest that all forms of intervention may present identical legal challenges. The discussion on intervention did not clarify what kinds of intervention were being discussed. With respect to measures taken by UN organisations,

79 Note 76 above, 8.
80 Ibid.
81 Ibid., 9.
82 Art 4.

delegates called for a firm procedure regarding the accountability of UN agencies.[83] The RSG made a case for finding a balance between national sovereignty and humanitarian assistance. With respect to accountability of UN agencies, he highlighted the existence of such mechanisms within the UN system itself.[84] Legal experts from the ICRC also defended the principle of humanitarian assistance, arguing that international law stipulates for access to civilians, the right of international organisations to provide assistance and the responsibility of the state to provide unhindered access to IDPs.[85]

Provisions of the draft Convention on the role of the responsibility of armed groups (Article 6) were a subject of considerable scrutiny. The article included three paragraphs providing for the responsibility of armed groups to: (a) ensure respect for the protection and assistance of IDPs without any discrimination; (b) grant rapid and unimpeded access to IDPs; and (c) protect humanitarian personnel and resources deployed for the assistance of IDPs. A number of delegates expressed their fear that the provisions dealing with the responsibility of armed groups presented a risk of legitimatising and conferring legal status to these groups, and 'equalise the status of states and armed groups'. Similar to the views expressed regarding the language of 'responsibility of states', experts argued that the word 'responsibility of armed groups' as it appears in the title of the draft resolution ought to be changed into 'obligation'.[86] It was also suggested that the provision be further expanded with a view to including additional elements such as 'individual criminal responsibility'. These discussions led to the inclusion of an additional five new paragraphs on top of the original three. It was agreed to include a paragraph constraining the legal status of armed groups and incorporating the principle of criminal responsibility for crimes committed by these groups. No reference was made with respect to 'criminal responsibility' for breaches committed by states. The relevant paragraph read:

> Nothing in this Convention shall be construed as affording legal status or legitimatising or recognising armed groups and its provisions are without prejudice to the individual criminal responsibility of their members under domestic or international criminal law.

Also included in Article 6 was a new paragraph dealing with the responsibility of protecting the humanitarian and civilian character of places where IDPs are sheltered. A related paragraph was also incorporated which proscribed the recruitment of children by these groups. Though the paragraphs visibly avoided the use of the term 'camps', it was unmistakably a reaction to a prominent problem in Africa where armed groups often attack IDPs

83 Note 76 above, 9.
84 Ibid.
85 Ibid., 6.
86 Ibid.

sheltered in camps and forcefully recruit them into their military activities. The revised text also stated that armed groups must refrain from restricting the freedom of movement of IDPs, within and outside of the area under their effective control. Additional paragraphs were included which required armed groups 'to ensure that internally displaced persons are received without discrimination of any kind and live in satisfactory conditions of dignity, security, sanitation, food, water, health, and shelters and that members of the same family are not separated'.

Article 10 contained a detailed and comprehensive list of obligations owed to IDPs during displacement. True to its broad and forward-looking reach, the title of the article was coined as 'protection during displacement'. This drafting was unusual in that it sought to expand the application of 'obligations' too often ascribed to states under international humanitarian and human rights law to armed groups and other relevant actors. Accordingly, 'states parties, armed groups and other relevant actors' were obligated to: (a) respect and ensure the respect for international human rights law; (b) protect IDPs from discrimination; (c) provide protection for, and refrain from committing genocide, war crimes, crimes against humanity, arbitrary killing, summary execution, abduction, arbitrary detention, enforced disappearance, torture, gender-based violence, forced labour, human trafficking and other human rights and humanitarian violations; and (d) provide special protection for those with special needs, namely children, female heads of households, expectant mothers, people living with HIV/AIDS, people with disabilities and the elderly. The article also provided that states parties, where appropriate and in cooperation with other relevant actors, should: (a) guarantee that IDPs are received without any forms of discrimination; (b) provide and ensure the provision of humanitarian assistance; (c) ensure the provision of essential social services, and provide special protective and assistance services to those with special needs, including the provision of reproductive and sexual health services for displaced women as well as provision of counselling for victims of sexual and other abuses; (d) protect IDPs from forced return and ensure the protection of the rights of IDPs to seek safety in other part of the country or seek asylum abroad; (e) ensure the protection of the right to movement and choice of residence; (f) maintain the civilian and humanitarian character of places of location for IDPs; (g) take specific measures to reunite those who are separated with their families; (h) protect cultural property of both host communities and IDPs; (i) take specific measures to safeguard against environmental degradation; and (j) ensure the protection of civil and political rights of IDPs and their participation in issues that affect them. Though the negotiation explored whether these obligations owed to IDPs by states should be expanded to non-state actors, the meeting agreed to limit the focus to the obligation of states.

While the meeting acknowledged the importance and relevance of an effective monitoring mechanism, the proposal to create the Office of High Commissioner of the African Union for Internally Displaced Persons faced stiff objections. Two arguments were particularly put forward against this proposal. First, some experts, citing the existence of mechanisms within the AU, recommended that the most reasonable course of action to be taken would be to strengthen existing mechanisms of the African Union. On the part of many of the experts who propounded this particular line, the most obvious and visible example of such mechanisms was the AU Division of Humanitarian Affairs, Refugees and Displaced Persons. Second, experts also raised the resource, particularly the financial implications of creating a new institution on top of already hugely underfunded institutional mechanisms within the AU. They warned against the proliferation of institutions, which, in their view, would have encumbered the AU Commission financially as well as structurally.

The meeting also debated the draft resolution on development-induced displacement (Article 9) and what was termed 'displacement induced by lack of development' (Article 10). These two provisions became one of the most controversial articles of the draft Convention. Article 9 sought to prevent displacement induced by development projects unless these specific projects are justified by compelling and overriding public interests. The draft Convention had incorporated two elements for determining whether certain public or private development projects could be justified by compelling and overriding public interests. These included the requirement: (a) that these projects should contribute to the economic or social development of the country, and (b) that the projects should be in the interest of the people including persons or communities displaced by such projects. Experts recommended that the word 'sustainable' be added in order to strengthen the link between the project and that of a sustainable development. Experts held divergent views with regard to the definition of the term; the objective of the provision; the issue of compensation for victims of displacement generated by development projects; protection of property; and the procedure for an impact assessment and evaluation. The article's specific reference to the responsibility of 'private actors' and states to ensure prevention of displacement by development projects was not controversial. Delegates discussed in detail the conceptual and practical relationship between development and displacement. First, it was recommended that the title of Article 9 be changed from 'development induced displacement' into 'displacement caused by development projects'. This stemmed from the fear that the original title created an impression that there is a necessary relationship between development and displacement.[87] Several delegates, insisting that the issue of compensation and reparation have been covered under their national legislations, suggested that the issue be left to domestic legislations. The question thus was not whether compensation should be provided to victims of development-induced displacement, but whether compensation should be provided for under the Convention or be left to domestic rules. Though

87 Note 76 above, 7.

access to remedies is stipulated for under the African Charter on Human and Peoples' Rights, the specific type and value of compensation is left for national courts to be determined based on domestic regulations. One was therefore not necessarily a substitute for the other. The original reference of the draft to the issue of compensation was later taken out of the text. With respect to impact assessment, based on recommendations by experts, it was agreed to include a new paragraph which required states to carry out a socio-economic and environmental impact assessment of a proposed development project prior to undertaking such a project.

The proposal to include in the Kampala Convention a reference to 'displacement generated by a lack of development' did not receive any significant support from delegations. First, many of them argued that the concept is extremely vague, ambiguous and 'is incapable of legal definition'.[88] Second, it was also argued that provisions related to 'displacement generated by lack of development' would introduce concepts that were included neither in the UN Guiding Principles nor in the Great Lakes Protocols. Third, it was feared that the consequences of such provisions would further broaden the obligation of states. A few supporters of the text however, pointed to Africa's own experience with displacement as a result of 'hunger, famine and underdevelopment' to support the Convention's coverage of the issue. The meeting could not reach any consensus on the issues, and hence simply agreed to bracket the article for further discussion and consideration.

Following the meeting the independent consultant together with the AU Commission and a team of resource persons took the responsibility of amending and revising the draft Convention based on comments and proposals put forward during the meeting. Little time and resource was available to the African Union to translate the newly revised text into all the AU's working languages. In light of the considerable disagreement seen with respect to translation, the experts were keen in ensuring the compatibility of the translated version with what was agreed upon. The meeting, therefore, decided to establish a small drafting team responsible for reviewing and harmonising the draft text in the various AU languages.

Meeting of the drafting Committee

Contrary to what its name suggests, the mandate of the drafting Committee was rather specific, i.e. to review and harmonise the draft Convention in all the four languages of the African Union. Since the work of the Committee was mainly focused on ensuring the harmonisation of the different versions of the draft Convention, the composition of the members was made to reflect the representation of the various linguistic regions of the continent. Thus, the Committee included Egypt and Saharawi Republic from the

88 Ibid., 8.

Arabic-speaking region; Benin and Gabon from the French-speaking area; Angola and Mozambique from the Portuguese-speaking region; and Uganda and Namibia from the English-speaking areas. Egypt was elected to chair the meeting. Both the drafter and other resource persons participated in the meeting.

The experts, in four separate groups, then reviewed the text in all four working languages and compared them with the provisions of the English text. They were not mandated to raise and discuss 'issues of substance'. Nor were they expected to resort to amending the text unless there was a consensus among members of the group.[89] The meeting of the drafting group then reconvened on the fourth day in a plenary with a view to adopting the various texts. The report of the drafting Committee indicated that the group not only did some editorial work but in few instances incorporated some changes in the text. It agreed, for example, to provide definitions for some phrases. Under Article 3(3)a, the Committee suggested a reference to 'international law' in order to ensure that states' obligation to domesticate the Convention is in conformity with international law. It was also suggested and agreed upon by the Committee that the responsibility to 'incorporate the relevant principles contained in this Convention into peace negotiation and agreements' should be replaced with another provision requesting states simply to 'endeavour to incorporate'.

Under Article 4, which dealt with the obligation of state parties relating to the protection from internal displacement, the meeting revised four subparagraphs with a view to ensuring 'greater clarity'. The new Article 4(2) read: 'State parties shall provide persons affected by such displacement with effective remedies'. This wording was much shorter than the previous text that required states to 'ensure respect and protection of the right of everyone against arbitrary displacement from his or her home or place of habitual residence by providing them with effective remedies against violation of such right'. In the same article, another revised paragraph was also included. Article 4(3) stipulated that: 'states parties shall devise early warning systems in areas of potential displacement, take disaster risk strategies, emergency and disaster management measures and, where necessary, provide immediate protection and assistance to internally displaced persons'. This improved the earlier text by requiring states: (a) to take disaster risk reduction strategies, and (b) to provide immediate protection and assistance to IDPs where necessary during emergency and natural disaster. The meeting also agreed to create a separate paragraph covering states' cooperation with international organisations. Earlier the issue was considered jointly with the aspect of emergency and disaster management. But now a decision was made to have a new and separate paragraph altogether. Accordingly, the new paragraph

89 See Report of the Meeting of the Drafting Committee of the African Union Member States Legal Experts on the Draft AU Convention for the Protection and Assistance of Internally Displaced Persons in Africa, Addis Ababa, Ethiopia, 25–29 July 2008.

read: 'States Parties may seek the cooperation of international organisation, humanitarian agencies, non-governmental organisations, civil society and other relevant actors'. Two points need to be stated here. First, though the list of institutions with which states are required to cooperate with was not made to be exhaustive, members of the drafting Committee were unable to agree whether to specifically mention 'civil society' or not. It was therefore decided that the word 'civil society' should be bracketed. Second, the original text incorporated the word 'shall', signifying a stricter obligation on the part of states to cooperate with forgoing institutions. The meeting later changed it into 'may'.

The Committee also suggested the addition of one new paragraph under Article 5 which gives guidance as to when states should seek the assistance of international organisations; and whether such organisations can also provide assistance to populations other than those who are displaced. The new paragraph stated that: 'States Parties shall provide sufficient protection and assistance to internally displaced persons, and where maximum available resources are inadequate to enable them to do so, they shall seek the assistance of international organisations and humanitarian agencies, non-governmental organisations, civil society and other relevant actors. Such organisations may offer their services unconditionally to all those in need'.

It is difficult to argue that this addition brought any new element. The draft Convention included numerous articles which require the state concerned to seek international assistance where and when it is unable to provide assistance. Moreover, the approach generally taken by the Annotated Outline and the text of the Convention itself is that communities that are not necessarily displaced such as host communities should be provided assistance and protection, too. The implication of the new amendment, however, is that government may not complain if international organisations seek access or provide assistance for others who are in need.

Article 6 covered the controversial topic of the role of armed groups in protection and assistance to IDPs. This was also an area, as can be seen from the report of the meeting of the drafting Committee, where a substantive amendment was incorporated in the text. The third paragraph of the previous text stipulated that armed groups shall ensure that IDPs are received without any forms of discrimination and in satisfactory conditions. It was agreed that a new reference to the obligation not to separate families should be provided for.

With respect to the role of the African Union (Article 7), three new amendments were made which were intended to harmonise the draft with the Constitutive Act. The original text required states to respect the authority of the African Union to intervene in a member state with a view to protecting and assisting IDPs (Article 7(1)). The same article also provided for the responsibility of states to request the African Union for an intervention when they are unable to do so (Article 7(2)). These provisions raised more questions than answers. The scope and nature of 'intervention' was far from clear. The Constitutive Act, as discussed in detail in Chapter 3, empowers the African Union to intervene in a limited number of circumstances, namely, genocide, war crimes, crimes against humanity and disruption of legitimate order. Nowhere is it mentioned that similar interventions can be envisaged to situations of internal displacement. In the same token, the Constitutive Act only talks about 'the right of member states to request intervention from the Union in order to restore peace and security' (Article 4(j)). The Act does not stipulate that states have the obligation to request intervention. Nor does it provide that such request be made with respect to situations of displacement. It is therefore not surprising that the drafting Committee picked up the variance between the Act and the draft Convention. The Committee, thus, introduced the following paragraphs:

> Article 7(1): The African Union shall have the right to intervene in a state party in accordance with Article 4(h) of the Constitutive Act in respect of grave circumstances, namely: war crimes, genocide, and crimes against humanity.

> Article 7(2): The African Union shall respect the right of states parties to request intervention from the Union in order to restore peace and security in accordance with Article 4(j) of the Constitutive Act and thus contribute to the creation of favourable conditions for finding durable solutions to the problem of internal displacement.

The Committee also agreed to introduce a new part in the chapeau of the provision enumerating the various activities of the Union. Accordingly, a new sentence has been inserted which states that 'the African Union shall support efforts of the state parties to protect and assist internally displaced persons under the Convention'.

The Committee revised three paragraphs of Article 8 dealing with the obligation of state parties. The first amendment reinforced the obligation of states to protect the cultural property of Article 8(2) I. The second revision suggested the incorporation of similar language to the paragraph dealing with the obligation of the state to 'take necessary measures to safeguard against environmental degradation in areas where internally displaced persons are located'. The third amendment related to paragraph I of Article 8 according to which states were required to 'take necessary measures to ensure that internally displaced persons who are citizens in their country of nationality cam enjoy their civil and political rights, public participation, the right to vote and be elected to public office'. The Committee agreed to include a phrase 'in their country of nationality' in the forgoing paragraph. The revision aimed at making a distinction between IDPs who are citizens and those who are not. But in the light of the existence of the phrase 'who are citizens', the new revision looks quite redundant.

During previous expert meetings, considerable amount of time was spent on Articles 9 and 10 which covered the topic of displacement induced by development projects and lack of development respectively. The only change introduced to Article 9 by the drafting Committee related to the title of the article where 'displacement by development projects' was changed into 'displacement induced by development projects'. These revisions reflected the position expressed during previous meetings that language which creates the impression that development projects necessarily produce displacement of people should be avoided. This was consistent with the title of Article 10 ('Displacement induced by lack of development'). No change or revision was introduced to Article 10 which the second legal expert meeting decided to bracket for the ministerial meeting. The plenary meeting also adopted without any revision Articles 11 and 12 dealing with issues of durable solutions and compensation respectively.

As has been noted earlier, the draft Convention's provisions on registration and personal documentation (Article 12) triggered a debate particularly within the context of the practicality of keeping comprehensive data on IDPs. The Committee seemed to articulate those concerns when it suggested a new language requiring states to create and maintain a register of all IDPs. The newly added wording read: 'In doing so, states Parties may collaborate with international organisations or humanitarian agencies, or non-governmental agencies'.

Regarding the procedural articles of the draft Convention, namely, ratification, deposition, amendment and entry to force, the Committee decided to follow the practice of African Union treaty making. It decided to include provisions for dealing with 'accession' to the Convention. After going through the draft Convention, the Committee decided to adopt the revised draft Convention in the four languages of the African Union. At the conclusion of their meeting, the representatives of the drafting Committee adopted a statement which read as follows:

> That the representatives of drafting Committee of the member states legal experts on the African Union Convention for the protection and assistance of internally displaced persons in Africa as recommended by the second meeting of the member states legal expert meeting held from 2 to 6 June 2008 have examined the copies of the draft Convention in our respective languages and that it confirms to the technical and legal requirement and it also compatible with the English language.[90]

The third legal experts' meeting

The third and last meeting of legal experts took place on 9 November

90 Ibid., 8.

2009.[91] Its objective was to continue negotiation on the provisions of the Convention and adopt it by reviewing the progress achieved during the second meeting of the legal experts and that of the drafting Committee.[92] That the meeting was held only for one day was indicative of the conviction of its organisers that most provisions of the draft Convention were sufficiently discussed and hence may not present a problem.

Unlike previous meetings, the third meeting of legal experts took place within a framework of an expert and ministerial meeting held in November 2009 to discuss the problem of forced displacement generally. The meeting of experts in charge of forced displacement took place between 5 and 7 November 2008. In addition to discussing the draft Convention, this meeting also considered a background paper prepared by the African Union.[93] The meeting of ministers in charge of forced displacement in Africa was then held between 10 and 11 November 2008. The ministerial meeting deliberated upon and finalised the draft Convention that had been negotiated at the level of experts.[94] Though the major highlight of the agenda of this meeting chaired by a Ugandan representative was the discussion and finalisation of the Convention, this ministerial meeting, like its predecessors, discussed topics which also included and were relevant to forced displacement. The meeting, for example, considered a report of the PRC sub-committee on refugees, returnees and IDPs.

Much like participants in the third meetings, the expert meeting decided to go through the text of the draft Convention article by article. The meeting adopted a working method which pretty much resembled those adopted at its earlier two meetings. Gabon was elected as a chair of the meeting whereas Egypt, Uganda and Liberia were elected as the first, second and third vice-chairs. Namibia was elected to serve as rapporteur. Despite the presence of this rapporteur, it was the independent consultant who often summarised the outcomes of previous meetings. He also introduced the summary of the second legal experts' meeting and that of the drafting Committee.

A number of suggestions were incorporated in the preamble. The meeting, for example, agreed to incorporate a paragraph in the preamble where the role of UNHCR and ICRC in the protection and assistance of IDPs is recognised. Achieving this agreement among state representative was quite

91 Report on 3rd Meeting of AU Member States Legal Experts on the Draft AU Convention for the Protection and Assistance of Internally Displaced Persons in Africa, Addis Ababa, 9 November 2008.

92 Draft Programme, Legal Experts meeting on the draft AU Convention for the Protection and Assistance of Internally Displaced Persons in Africa, Addis Ababa, Ethiopia, 9 November 2008.

93 Evolution and current situation of forced displacement in Africa, Background Paper, Expert Meeting, Special Summit on Refugees, Returnees and Displaced Persons in Africa, Addis Ababa, Ethiopia, 5–7 November 2008.

94 AUC News, African Commission Newsletter, Issue 36, December 2008, 5.

notable given the fact that states were in the past critical of the mandate creep of the UNHCR with respect to IDPs. Equally important was the consensus on the need to mention the participation and role of civil society organisations. During the meeting, it was suggested that the word 'NGOs' should be replaced with 'civil society organisations'. It was also further suggested that while exercising such a role, CSOs should respect the laws of the county in which they work. It was also during this meeting that member states suggested that a reference to the devastating impact of man-made and natural disasters should be included.

As expected, experts disagreed on the issue of internal displacement related to development. The draft Convention had expanded the definition given to displacement by the Guiding Principles by including the concept of 'lack of development as a cause for displacement'. This, however, generated impassioned arguments among member states. While accepting the idea of engaging in further negotiation and discussion over development-induced displacement, the meeting, however, proposed that provisions dealing with 'lack of development related displacement' be deleted altogether. Disagreement over reference to the role of armed groups continued during the meeting. Some delegations resisted the broad objectives of the Convention constructed in a manner that they felt was legitimising armed groups. Experts agreed that the reference to 'armed group' would be applicable only within the context of ensuring their accountability under international humanitarian law.

On the question of compensation and reparation, the discussion focused on the question of remedies. It was recommended that the Convention should adopt a narrow conception of remedies only by focusing on compensation. There were a number of provisions that were agreed upon during this meeting without much discussion. These include articles dealing with documentations (Article 14); return and durable solutions (Article 11); and obligation of state parties (Article 8). The meeting also adopted without discussion a number of procedural provisions.

General observations on legal experts' meetings

The three consecutive meetings of legal experts facilitated the negotiation of the draft Convention. Despite its aura of formality, the drafting process exhibited an informal approach where revisions to the text were made outside of formal settings. Even at an advanced stage of the negotiation, it was the secretariat together with the draftsman which single-handedly assumed the responsibility of reviewing the text based on comments and proposals put forward by member states. When a drafting Committee constituting member states was established, its mandate was ostensibly limited. This drafting Committee to a certain extent exceeded its original mandate by considering some substantive elements of the draft Convention. Its responsibilities were intended only to focus on 'harmonising' the text of the Convention in the four working languages of the African Union. As was seen during the second legal expert meetings, there were times where member states complained that such working method was not sufficiently transparent and that their views were not properly taken on board. The time allocated to the meetings was also considerably short. The first legal expert meeting was held only for three days. Only a day was allocated for the third meeting. Both the second meeting and the drafting Committee session were held during a period of five working days each. Time pressure on negotiators of the Convention was, therefore, evident.[95]

No minutes were taken during these meetings by the AU secretariat.[96] Even member states find it difficult to have access to these records as the secretariat does not keep records.[97] As has been mentioned in the introductory part of this chapter, *travaux preparatoires* could have been significantly helpful to understand the negotiation process. No documents of a similar nature exist with regard to the Kampala Convention. However, official reports of these meetings are available and the researcher has been privileged to have access to these reports. These reports, however, are imbued with glaring shortcomings and limitations. They are cursory and brief. They do not, for example, succinctly explain positions expressed by individual delegations. Other than summarising a general subject of agreement or disagreement among participants, the reports often do not show specific proposals or amendments agreed upon during the negotiations. References are plenty in the reports wherein it is indicated that the meeting agreed to amend or reformulate a certain article without saying much about how the same article will be amended or reformulated. These regrettable shortcomings would have been avoided if the African Union kept minutes of official meetings.

Except in a few cases, the contributions of member states during the meetings were made orally. Though a decision was made to introduce a procedure by which contributions by member states on the draft text will be considered and processed during the inter-sessional period, few experts took advantage of such opportunity.[98] Though the meetings saw an informal way of conducting business, it was during the plenary of the meetings that actual negotiations were often held. The initial phase of the negotiations was extremely slow as significant time was spent on presentations of concepts and background information to participants. Participants in these legal experts'

95 Interview with a counsellor at the Embassy of Congo, Addis Ababa, Ethiopia (10 February 2009).

96 It should also be stated that the African Union secretariat does not prepare reports for the meetings of the Executive Council and the Assembly.

97 Discussion with a legal advisor to one of the members states of the African Union (23 December 2009).

98 Interview with a counsellor at the Embassy in Congo, Addis Ababa, Ethiopia (10 February 2009).

meetings were not necessarily experts in the area of forced displacement. This would have required a certain level of information to be provided to participants prior to the commencement of the negotiations. While the usefulness of the information session cannot be understated, it was noted that that some of the meetings were organised more like workshops than negotiation forums.[99]

States pursued different styles and approaches in determining the level and composition of their representation in the meeting. Whereas some member states designated experts from their capitals, others chose to second an expert from their permanent missions to the African Union based in Addis Ababa.[100] Except on the occasion where the meeting established a small drafting Committee to sort out the inconsistencies between the translated versions of selected provisions of the draft Convention, all three meetings were held in plenary. The drafter of the Convention participated in all these meetings often acting as a resource person, providing an introduction to the text, explaining the legal basis and consideration behind certain provisions and reflecting the consensus reached at the meeting. In a few instances, West African and Southern African states sought to coordinate their positions through ECOWAS and SADC consultations.[101] In terms of the logistical arrangements made for organising the expert meetings, the African Union was expected to cover the organisational and administrative costs of these meetings by allocating the necessary resources from its regular budget. This money went into covering the costs of organising ordinary meetings such as preparation of necessary documents; paying for translation and interpretation; and in this case even paying for travel, accommodation and per diem of participants. The average cost of organising an African Union expert meeting is between 100,000 to 200,000 USD.[102] But such budgetary allocation was often insufficient and the situation during the organisation of the forgoing meetings has not been an exception. The financial support from international organisations and other partners of the African Union should thus not be understated.

Both the RSG and ACHPR Special Rapporteur actively participated in the negotiation process, often acting as resource persons.[103] But equally visible was the involvement and participation of UN agencies, international organisations such as ICRC and civil society organisations. It was thus clear that

99 Interview with a diplomat from South Africa.
100 Ibid.
101 Ibid.
102 Interview with an official of the African Union, 22 January 2009.
103 Report of Activities by Commissioner Bahame Tom Nyandunga, Special Rapporteur for Refugees, Asylum Seekers, Migrants and IDPs during the Inter-Session Period November 2007 to May 2008. Available at: www.achpr.org/english/Commissioner%27s%20Activity/43rd%20OS/Special%20Rapporteurs/refugees%20and%20IDPs.pdf. Report submitted by the Representative of the Secretary-General on the human rights of internally displaced persons, Walter Kälin, A/HRC/8/6, 24 April 2008, para. 61.

the participation and contributions of these organisations through the Consultative Group was a channel for these organisations to influence the evolution of the draft Convention. As was seen, the representative of the ICRC even participated as an active member of a small drafting Committee. Some member states harboured uneasiness regarding a very active involvement of these organisations, particularly during the negotiation process.[104] The significance of these criticisms, however, should not be exaggerated. The various decisions of the Executive Council of the African Union specifically requested the Commission of the African Union to facilitate the involvement of these organisations in the process.

AU special summit on refugees, returnees and displaced persons

Procedural issues and objectives of the special summit

Early on during the drafting process, the Assembly, a summit of heads of state and government of the African Union, was designated as a forum for the adoption of the Convention. Whether the Assembly retains the ultimate authority to adopt regional legal instruments has not been expressly provided for under the Constitutive Act. But it can safely be stated that such an authority resides within the overall competence of the Assembly which, under the Constitutive Act, is the supreme body of the African Union.[105] In the past, the Assembly consistently adopted legal instruments, often at the recommendation of the Executive Council.[106] The Constitutive Act provides far more detailed provisions with respect to the function and authority of the Executive Council. Accordingly, it states that the Council shall coordinate and take decisions on issues such as humanitarian action, disaster response, relief and immigration.[107] It is, therefore, natural that the draft Convention was finally considered by the Executive Council and the Assembly. Never before had the African Union held an Assembly-level meeting specifically for the purpose of discussing the problem of forced displacement. More importantly, it was the first time that the African Union held a meeting of the Executive Council and the Assembly with a specific aim of considering and adopting a regional treaty. Previously, regional treaties were invariably adopted during the ordinary sessions of the Assembly.

The role of international organisations in treaty making is often provided for expressly or implicitly under the constitution of the specific

104 Note 99 above.
105 Art 6(2) of the Act.
106 See Decision on the Draft Protocol to the African Charter on Human and Peoples' Rights Relating to the Rights of Women (Assembly/AU/Dec.19(II)); Decision on the Draft Protocol of the Court of Justice of the African Union (Assembly/AU/Dec.25(II)); and Decision on the Draft Convention on the Prevention and Combating of Corruption (Assembly/AU/Dec.27(II)).
107 Art 13 of the Act.

organisation.[108] As has already been noted, it is important to note that the Constitutive Act does not have provisions on treaty making. Neither does the Constitutive Act expressly grant the African Union the power to make treaties. The African Union often exercised a very broad mandate covering security, political, economic and social issues. The AU has initiated or facilitated the development of legal instruments governing issues ranging from election monitoring, conflict resolution to migration. The policy organs of the African Union, particularly the Executive Council, considered issues pertinent to the ratification, status and reform of treaties. An agenda item titled 'the status of AU treaties' is regularly included in the agenda of the Executive Council. Under this, the Council deliberates upon the report of the secretariat on issues including the ratification status of treaties and steps taken by the Commission to undertake a review of existing treaties or codification of new ones. It is also often the case that the Council instructs the Commission to convene a series of government expert meetings with the explicit mandate of drafting a particular protocol, convention or treaty. These procedures were used in the drafting of recent African Union treaties such as the Charter on Elections, Democracy and Governance in Africa, and the additional Protocol to the OAU Convention on the Prevention of Combating and Preventing Terrorism. Thus, it can safely be maintained that the AU has an implied power to elaborate and adopt treaties on issues covered under its mandate, including on IDPs.

That the Kampala meeting of heads of state and government was referred to as 'a special summit' may create certain confusion. Neither the Constitutive Act nor the rules of procedure[109] provide for holding 'special meetings'. Within the framework of these legal instruments, only two types of meetings are expressly provided for: ordinary and extraordinary meetings. It is provided that both the Assembly and the Council may hold extraordinary sessions at the request of any member state and on approval by a two-third majority of members.[110] It should be stated that it is not the first time the Assembly designated one of its meetings as 'special'. For instance, it has done so when it decided to hold a special session in 2009 to consider the situation of conflicts in Africa.[111] This decision was based on a request made by Libya which had invited the Assembly to hold a meeting in Sirte, Libya. The Assembly overwhelmingly supported the request and held the meeting in Libya. The use of the term 'special' to refer to meetings which can otherwise be considered as 'extraordinary' is rather unnecessary. At worst, it may create confusion as to whether the meeting is a formal

108 For a discussion on this topic, see Alvarez Josee, *International Organizations as Treaty Makers* (Oxford Scholarship Monograph, 2006).

109 See Rules of Procedure of the Assembly of the African Union, 1st Ordinary Session, 9–10 July 2002, Durban, South Africa.

110 Arts 6 and 10.

111 See Decision on the Holding of a Special Session on a Consideration and Resolution of Conflicts in Africa, Assembly/AU/Dec.266(XIII), adopted during the 13th Ordinary Session of the Assembly held 1–3 July 2009.

sitting of the policy organ of the African Union, or if it is a meeting of state parties to the Convention. The practical implication of this distinction, however, should not be exaggerated. The Kampala special summit held at the level of heads of state and government represents an extraordinary session of the Council of Ministers and that of the Assembly respectively within the meaning of the Constitutive Act. Some of the official documents adopted a similar description.[112] One major difference between the meeting in Libya and the one held in Uganda on forced displacement is that the former was held based on a request by one member state, in this case Libya, whereas the latter was held based on the recommendation of a ministerial meeting. Of course, one may argue that neither the Constitutive Act nor the rules of procedure provides for holding an extraordinary session other than through the procedure provided for under the Constitutive Act, i.e. the request by member states. The interest expressed by the government of Uganda to host the special summit was not an initiative requesting the Assembly to agree on holding an extraordinary session. The question of whether to have a session on the topic of forced displacement had already been decided upon. The government of Uganda requested to host an already scheduled meeting. Uganda's gesture, therefore, cannot be considered as an official request to organise the session. This said, however, it is very difficult to hold that such a procedural anomaly in any way affects the nature of the meeting or its outcome. Such frequent idiosyncrasies are indicative of how, unlike at the UN level, little attention is being given to procedural issues at the level of the African Union.

Originally, the special summit was scheduled to be held in April 2009. The meeting, however, was postponed a number of times before it finally took place in October 2009. The session of the Executive Council was held from 19 to 20 October 2009 whereas the meeting of the Assembly was held from 22 to 23 October 2009.[113] That the summit was held in Uganda was important.[114] Owing to the unfortunate and on-going conflict in the northern part of the country, Uganda has been one of the hotspots of internal displacement in the continent.[115] Many of the top civilian and military leaders were themselves active participants in Uganda's previous civil wars and hence have a personal experience with displacement and dislocation.[116] Owing to these

112 Press Release No. 9, Member States Sign AU Convention for the Protection and Assistance of Internally Displaced Persons, Press Release, 23 October 2009.

113 See Report on the Extraordinary Session of the Executive Council on Refugees, Returnees and Internally Displaced Persons held in Kampala, Uganda, 19–20 October 2009, Ext. EX.CL/PA/Rpt.(1).

114 See Speech by Prime Minster of Uganda to the Extraordinary Session of the AU Executive Council, 19 October 2009. Available online at: www.auspecialsummitkampala.ug.

115 At the peak of the fighting between the Lord's Resistance Army and the Ugandan government in 2002, the number of IDPs in Uganda was estimated to be over 2.5 million people.

116 Professor Tarsis Bazana Kabwegyere, Ugandan Minster for Disaster Preparedness, Relief and Refugees and the focal person for the summit, often refers to his own personal experience with displacement. During the debate on the Convention's provision on the role of armed groups, President Yoweri Museveni talked of his own previous role as a rebel fighter.

factors, Uganda has also been very active, both at national and regional levels, in standards setting with respect to the protection and assistance of IDPs. It is one of the few African countries which adopted a national policy on internal displacement.[117] It is also a signatory to the two Great Lakes Protocols.

The objective of the 'special meeting' was couched in the broadest possible language. According to the Ouagadougou Declaration, the summit was to 'address forced displacement issues on the continent and allow opportunity for consideration for member states to tackle the root causes of the problem of forced displacement'.[118] It, however, reaffirmed the Executive Council's decision EX/CL/Dec.127 (v), which had called for an elaboration of a legal framework for the protection of IDPs. Moreover, by incorporating in its preamble a reference to a 'legal vacuum' for the protection and assistance of IDPs, the Declaration also undoubtedly gave an indirect recognition that the elaboration and finalisation of a legal instrument constitutes an important outcome of the summit. The 9th Ordinary Session of the Executive Council, noting the progress made by the AU Commission in developing a legal framework, further requested the Commission to 'expedite such efforts in collaboration with the PRC sub-committee on Refugees, Returnees and Internally Displaced Persons and with the participation of relevant partners at the appropriate instance'.[119]

As was previously noted, the purpose and objective of the special summit was not exclusively focused on the deliberation and adoption of the Kampala Convention. Decisions of the Assembly and the Council indicate that in addition to the consideration of the draft Convention, the summit would also deliberate upon various other aspects of forced displacement.[120] The Technical Task Force, which was established to help prepare the meeting, drew a list of thematic issues that would be discussed during the summit. Accordingly, the Task Force determined that the special summit's deliberation would focus on the following thematic areas: (a) prevention of forced displacement; (b) protection of refugees, IDPs and stateless persons; (c) meeting the specific needs of displaced women and children; (d) addressing the problem of displaced persons victimised by natural disaster; (e) post-conflict and disaster reconstruction; and (f) building partnership in addressing forced displacement in Africa. Accordingly, the agenda was

117 The National Policy for Internally Displaced Persons, Office of the Prime Minster Department of Preparedness and Refugees, August 2004. Available at: www.brookings.edu/aboutprojects/idp/laws-and-policies/~/media/Projects/idp/uganda_IDPpolicy_2004.pdf.

118 Note 22 above, 10.

119 Decision on the Situation of Refugees, Returnees and Displaced Persons, Doc. EX.CL/254(IX), adopted during the 9th Ordinary Session of the Executive Council of the African Union, 25–29 June 2006.

120 See Information Note on African Union Special Summit of Heads of State and Government on Refugees, Returnees and Internally Displaced Persons, October 2009.

broadly formulated and not only covered IDPs but also other affected groups such as refugees, stateless persons and host communities. The selected themes also systematically addressed the various phases of displacement and issues that are critical for building an effective regional response to the problem of displacement. In a background paper prepared by the African Union, it was stated that the summit would 'generate recommendations to reinforce and bolster existing structures and, where possible, create other requisite capabilities that will enable the continent to confront the various challenges related to forced displacement'.[121]

The Assembly also considered both the draft Kampala Declaration and the Convention. The African Union invited some delegations to use their statements and interventions to share information or experiences in one of the areas identified as a priority, a request with which a number of countries complied.[122] Heads of all major agencies such as UNHCR, IOM and ICRC were present in an apparent show of their recognition of the importance of the meeting.

At the end of the meeting, the Convention was signed by 17 countries, namely, Burundi, Central Africa Republic, Republic of Congo, Djibouti, Ethiopia, Equatorial Guinea, Gambia, Liberia, Namibia, Nigeria, Saharawi Arab Democratic Republic, Rwanda, Sierra Leone, Somalia, Uganda, Zambia and Zimbabwe. The summit was attended by five heads of state and other high-ranking government officials representing the African continent. But only 17 member states of the African Union out of the 53 member states of the organisation signed the instrument. The African Union downplayed the significance of the level of signature stating that it did not reflect the level of participation and engagement by many states in the drafting process. It also stated that some government officials did not sign since they did not have the required authorisation to sign the instrument.[123]

The extraordinary meeting of the Executive Council

The extraordinary meeting of the Executive Council was held on 19 and 20 October 2009. Its agenda included: (a) consideration of the report and recommendations of the meeting of minsters in charge of forced displacement that took place from 10–11 November 2008; and (b) the consideration of the draft Kampala Convention and the declaration.[124] As is customary, the Executive Council also prepared the draft agenda and programme of work

121 Evolution and Current Situation of Forced Displacement in Africa, Conference Background Paper, Expert Meeting of the Special Summit on Refugees, Returnees and Internally Displaced Persons, Addis Ababa, Ethiopia, 5–11 November 2008, 4.

122 For example, South Africa was invited to make a presentation on the topic of 'Reconciliation and post conflict reconstruction and development'. See the statement of South African Deputy Minister of Home Affairs, Mr M Gigeba. Available at: www.info.gov.za/speeches.

123 Africa: IDP Convention–Now the Hard Work Begins, *IRIN*, 26 October 2009.

for the Assembly. It was decided that the deliberations of the Assembly would focus on the draft Kampala Convention on IDPs and the draft Kampala Declaration.[125] While the Convention is exclusively focused on IDPs, the Declaration covers additional categories of people of concern – refugees and returnees.

Given that the forgoing documents have all been discussed and adopted at a ministerial meeting in November 2008, it was natural to question the appropriateness of any further substantive discussion on the content of the Convention. Citing the fact that extensive discussions were held on the draft Convention both at the expert and ministerial levels, some were of the opinion that the meeting of the Executive Council should not engage in substantive negotiation over the text. Others, however, noted that the draft Convention may benefit from further and additional comments and proposals and that such opportunity should be allowed. The Council then agreed to exchange views on the texts without going into details.[126]

A significant part of the first day of the meeting was spent on discussing thematic areas already identified: (a) prevention and root causes; (b) burden sharing and protracted situations; (c) reconciliation and post-conflict reconstruction; (d) natural disaster, climate change and food security. The Council held a debate on the content of the draft Declaration on the second day. This discussion was far from detailed. The topics that were discussed and the subject matter on which amendments were introduced were very few. These included: definition and obligations of civil society organisations; the role and status of armed groups; issues related to environment and meetings of the oversight mechanism. The delegation of Congo expressed concern about the role of NGOs with respect to forced displacement and suggested that a provision which underlines their responsibility be included.[127] On the question of the role of armed groups, concerns that were expressed during much of the negotiation including in meetings of the experts were raised by Nigeria. Perhaps fuelled by its concern on the operation of armed groups in the Niger Delta, Nigeria asked whether providing for provisions regulating the activities of armed groups does not legitimatise status for these groups. It was argued that Article 6 which provided for the obligation of armed groups gave unwarranted legal status to armed groups which are not party to the Convention. The explanation was offered that legal provisions regulating armed groups exist both in Africa and at the international level, as evidenced through the various instruments regulating mercenaries and the

124 Draft Agenda, Extraordinary Session of the Executive Council, Kampala, Uganda, 19–20 October 2009.

125 Draft Agenda, Meeting of the Assembly of the Heads of State and Government, Kampala, Uganda, 22–23 October 2009.

126 See Ext. EX.CL/PA/Rpt(1), adopted at the Extraordinary Session of the Executive Council of the African Union, 19–20 October 2009, Kampala, Uganda, para. 8.

127 Interview with an Ethiopian delegate who participated in the meeting, 11 January 2008.

UN Guiding Principles. The meeting then agreed that though armed groups are not parties to the Convention, the rules including Article 6 would be applicable to them.[128] With respect to the meeting of the Conference of Parties (COP), it was agreed to retain the proposed provision which provided for the holding of a regular meeting.

During the Council's meeting certain general observations were also made which were, in the author's view, indicative of the prevailing mood that guided the drafting and the conclusion of the process. Member states expressed their interest in seeing a text agreed by consensus. It was argued that this is very important to facilitate a speedy ratification of the Convention. Delegates also saw the draft Convention not in isolation but within the context of the draft Declaration that was being negotiated. It was pointed out that all these documents, i.e. the draft Convention, the draft Declaration and the ministerial recommendations, are interrelated. In a manner that put into context the international environment in which the drafting process was taking place, it was also suggested that the reference in the Convention to environmental protection should further be strengthened and enhanced. After incorporating the necessary amendments, the Executive Council recommended the Convention for adoption to the Assembly.[129]

The extraordinary meeting of the Assembly

The Assembly also considered both the texts of the draft Kampala Declaration and the Convention. The Convention's provisions dealing with the responsibility of armed groups (Article 7) drew particular criticism from some heads of state who felt that such provisions of the Convention may be used to legitimise members of armed groups.

It is stated that the provision shall not be 'construed as affording legal status or legitimizing or recognizing armed groups and are without prejudice to the individual criminal responsibility of the members of such groups under domestic or international criminal law'.

The Declaration

The rationale for the adoption of a separate declaration accompanying the draft Convention was occasioned by the desire to lay out normative guidelines for a number of issues that are not necessarily covered under the draft Convention. More importantly, the declaration offered an opportunity to cover issues relating to refugees and returnees. The African Union also reasoned that it may also help provide guidance especially to the African

128 Note 113 above, para. 11.

129 Executive Council recommends adoption of the Draft Convention and of the Kampala Declaration on Forced Displacement, Uganda, 20 October 2009. Available at: http://reliefweb.int/sites/reliefweb.int/files/reliefweb_pdf/node-330064.pdf.

Union during the period between the adoption and entry into force of the Convention.[130] This soft law was therefore considered as a 'stop gap' measure. It should be noted that previous ministerial meetings on refugees, returnees and displaced persons also resulted in the adoption of similar declarations which are now a part of a growing normative set of regional standards on the protection of IDPs.

The Declaration has both a preamble and operative sections. The latter, which covers a total of 28 sections, is divided into five sections: (a) prevention of forced displacement; (b) effective protection of victims; (c) meeting the specific needs of women, children and vulnerable groups; (d) post-conflict and natural disaster reconstruction; (e) international cooperation and partnerships; and finally (f) the adoption of the Kampala Convention.

Accordingly, states commit themselves to take concrete measures with a view to preventing or eliminating forced displacement, namely, establishing or strengthening national mechanisms; addressing underdevelopment and unemployment which are identified as major causes of forced displacement; and signing, ratifying and implementing relevant international and regional human rights instruments (Articles 1–4). The Declaration also provides the specific measures states are required to take in order to ensure effective protection and assistance mechanisms. These include: (a) respecting the principle of non-refoulement; (b) promoting durable solutions both for refugees and IDPs; (c) ensuring the humanitarian character of camps and centres; (d) encouraging the creation of an enabling environment including by promoting self-reliance programmes particularly for vulnerable groups; and (e) supporting UNHCR and other international organisations to deal with the problem of mixed migration flows and irregular secondary movement. Addressing the specific needs of certain vulnerable groups such as women, children, persons living with disabilities and others was given particular attention. A number of areas were identified as critical in meeting these specific needs, namely the promotion of protection of women, children and other vulnerable groups during armed conflict including the prohibition of recruitment of children into the armed forces; prohibition of gender-based violence against refugees and provision of services for their victims; and provision of education and training programmes.

The Declaration deals at great length with the issue of post-conflict and post-disaster reconstruction. This is important in light of the fact that this phase represents a 'transition from humanitarian response to development assistance'. States commit themselves to take myriad measures both at the national and regional level often in cooperation with international institutions and civil society organisations. Accordingly, states declare that they will ensure that sufficient attention is given in their national development

130 Interview with Ms Dolly Joiner, African Union Commissioner for Political Affairs, 27 January 2009.

programmes to the recovery and reconstruction needs of communities emerging from conflict. With a view to promoting durable solutions, states also commit themselves particularly in the context of post-conflict situations to undertake mine clearance as well as disarmament, demobilisation and reintegration as a method of encouraging durable and safe return. Similarly, addressing the challenges of climate change and the use and management of natural resources is identified as vital in ensuring durable and suitable return. At the regional level, states reiterated their commitment to the speedy implementation of the African Union Policy Framework on Post-conflict Reconstruction and Development and request the African Union to support countries emerging out of conflicts and natural disaster including by expediting the establishment of its volunteer's programme and database.

Promoting partnership and cooperation is considered as a key aspect of implementing the Declaration.[131] States call on the international community, particularly donors, to support measures taken by governments including by dedicating a portion of development assistance to projects assisting displaced populations and host communities. The declaration also highlights the positive role civil society organisations can play, and urges states to create an enabling environment to facilitate their contribution and role. The Declaration calls upon institutions such as the African Development Bank, the World Bank, the International Monetary Fund, as well as other bilateral and multilateral donors to design policies and programmes that assist states and communities emerging from conflicts and natural disasters. Welcoming the UN humanitarian reform programmes, the Declaration also calls upon the United Nations system, international organisations as well as NGOs to coordinate their efforts.

Rationale of the Kampala Convention

Why did the AU and its member states decide to go for and succeed in adopting a binding instrument at a time when this seemed to be impossible at the international level? There are some overriding and overarching objectives that are articulated in the text of the Kampala Convention. Two of these objectives emerge from these lists enumerated under Article 2 of the Convention. They include:

(a) the promotion and strengthening of regional and national measures in addressing the root causes of internal displacement, as well as provide durable solutions,
(b) the establishment of a legal framework for the protection and assistance of IDPs, and the prevention of internal displacement including, among others by providing for the obligations and responsibilities of states and non-state actors.

131 Note 4 above, 20.

As we have previously seen, both the text of the Convention and the preparatory texts refer to 'the absence of binding legal instruments' regarding the protection and assistance of IDPs. ACHPR's Special Rapporteur succinctly captured this when he stated in his activity report as a rapporteur that:[132]

> Apart from the conflict related displacement, which is being addressed by AU political organs, displacement caused by development projects, the natural resources extractive industry, and the worsening climatic and weather conditions, such as witnessed recently in Southern Africa, and elsewhere on the continent, due to heavy rains and drought continues to cause suffering to millions at a time of lack of capacity by the states and decreasing international humanitarian assistance. The legal framework in many African countries, i.e. compensation for development induced displacement, is inadequate in as far as addressing long term concerns of the livelihood of populations, which are uprooted by mining companies and foreign investors, notwithstanding their contributions to our economies.

The African region has witnessed some developments in the codification of norms applicable to the protection of IDPs. The Constitutive Act, the Protocol establishing the African Union Peace and Security Council, the Additional Protocol on the Rights of Women in Africa, the African Charter on the Rights and Welfare of Children are some of the few examples signalling such a shift. A number of developments in regional human rights institutions, as discussed in Chapter 3, also supplement this trend. Hence, one can argue that the Convention has been used as an instrument to consolidate these binding norms applicable to internally displaced persons scattered in the various binding regional instruments, and consolidate other relevant 'soft-law' norms including by giving them enforceable expression. Codification experience from the Great Lakes served as an inspiration. A significant codification milestone has already been achieved by the adoption of the first binding Protocol on the protection of and assistance to IDPs for the Great Lakes in 2006. The African Union and many others saw the opportunity to expand this sub-regional experience into a broader African Union initiative.

Applicable international and regional human rights norms in Africa are also relevant in addressing the human rights concerns of IDPs. Both the African Union and the former OAU facilitated the codification of regional human rights instruments even coverings topics and issues with respect to which enforceable international legal instruments exist. Some of these legal instruments include: the 1969 OAU Convention Governing the Specific Aspects of Refugee Problems in Africa which complements the 1951 United

132 Note 103 above, paras. 3–4.

Nations Convention Relating to the Status of Refugees; the African Convention on the Ban on the Import into and the Control of Trans Boundary Movement of Hazardous Waste within Africa (the Bamako Convention) which corresponds to the Basel Convention on the Control of Trans Boundary Movements of Hazardous Waste and their Disposal; the Protocol on the African Charter on the Rights of Women which corresponds with the Convention on Elimination of All Forms of Discrimination Against Women (CEDAW); and the African Charter on the Rights and Welfare of the Child which is based on the UN Convention on the Rights of the Child. It is totally unsurprising, therefore, that the problem of displacement, one of Africa's most significant human rights issues, sees the emergence of a treaty which seeks to provide protection, assistance and durable solutions to victims.

There is a noticeable borrowing and exchange of concepts between the forgoing African treaties and their international 'counterparts'. Unlike the case of the Convention which does not enjoy corresponding international 'hard law', other regional human rights instruments do compliment binding international standards. The content and nature of these regional treaties can, therefore, be scrutinised based on these binding international standards. It is notable that the objectives of these regional instruments were largely fuelled by dissatisfaction either with the process of treaty negotiation and drafting at the international level, or imagined or real gaps embedded in the instruments in addressing African concerns.[133] The situation with respect to the AU IDP Convention exhibits a certain similarity in that there was a noticeable uneasiness with the state of affairs with respect to international protection regime. The preamble bemoans the lack of binding international legal standards for IDPs. What was an issue is not the sufficiency of the Guiding Principles which were robustly endorsed both by the African Union and its sub-regional blocs. The concern with respect to the Guiding Principles mainly related to the fact that they are not legally enforceable. Thus, one of the principal objectives of the AU Convention has been crafting a protection and assistance regime that is largely based on the Guiding Principles. The negotiation and preparatory work vividly show that this vision was widely shared by those who participated in the negotiation. Though the Convention recognises the 1998 UN Guiding Principles as 'an important legal framework', there was a widely shared view that these principles need to be supplemented with binding legal principles.

During the negotiations, 'experts and state representatives were often reminded that they should attempt to reconcile the national interests of their respective countries with those of Africa, and to promote the

133 Fatsah Ouguergouz, 'The Bamako Convention on Hazardous Waste: A New Step in the Development of the African International Environmental Law', *African Yearbook of International Law* 1(1993): 196.

Convention in all circumstances'.[134] The first paragraph of the Convention's preamble states that the signatories to the Convention are 'conscious of the gravity of the situation of internally displaced persons as a source of continuing instability and tension'. Behind this rhetoric, however, was a vivid interest of the African Union Commission and its international partners to have a framework that will provide an aura of authority for activities they have been undertaking with respect to the protection and assistance of IDPs. From the beginning, the AU secretariat played an active role in stirring the preparatory work on the Convention and it will have an important role in the future implementation of the Convention. Officials of the African Union are pleased with this outcome.[135] When the idea of the establishment of the Office of High Commissioner for Protection and Assistance of IDPs was proposed, it was not only rejected by states but also resisted by African Union officials who thought that such an institution would overlap with existing mechanisms within the African Union secretariat.[136] Similarly, in the view of international organisations such as the ICRC and UNHCR, the Convention will in the long run dampen charges that by actively working on IDP issues these organisations are touching upon sensitive domestic issues.

In addition to some of the objectives described in the draft treaty, other considerations might have weighed in the mind of those who argued for a treaty. The instrument may well create a situation whereby action on behalf of IDPs will not be considered as a purely internal domestic matter. Few have expected the Convention to be an instrument of settling the tension between the sovereignty of states on the one hand and the necessity of international intervention and assistance that may be required when states become unable or unwilling to provide protection and assistance to IDPs within their own national boundaries. Neither can one easily suggest that this would easily be achieved. It is also not clear whether the Convention was originally considered to be an instrument of consolidation and systematically rearranging already existing guarantees and protection, or was envisaged as a mechanism of creating new rights for IDPs or implementing better protection and assistance benchmarks. During the drafting process, the RSG suggested that though current guarantees for IDPs are clearly provided for under binding international treaties and the UN Guiding Principles, it is conceivable that the Convention may incorporate norms whose quality of guaranteeing protection and assistance is 'equal to or even higher' than these standards.[137] But he also cautioned that the objectives of

134 Note 77 above, 2. Similar sentiment has consistently been expressed by the drafter himself who suggested that experts and delegates should 'give precedence to regional over national interests'.

135 Interview with an African Union official, 22 January 2009.

136 Ibid.

137 Note 76 above, 2.

the Convention should also incorporate the element of laying out not just 'grand and ambitious goals' but also those which are 'realistic and could be implemented in practice'.[138] It was reported that during the second meeting of legal experts, Mr Emmanuel Issoze Ngondet, ambassador and permanent representative of Gabon to Ethiopia and the African Union, told the participants 'to discuss and adopt a document, which promotes a non-discriminatory legal regime, a document which should be neither too constraining nor one which would make its ratification problematic'.[139]

Legal sources of the Convention

The Kampala Convention has been described as a ground-breaking,[140] significant and landmark legal instrument.[141] It is also touted as an important African contribution to the growing law of internal displacement.[142] As has been stated on several occasions, the Convention covers an area with respect to which a binding legal instrument has been conspicuously lacking. This, however, does not mean that no binding instrument has served as inspiration for its development. As the codification of the UN Guiding Principles vividly indicates, numerous binding international instruments from fields of international human rights law and humanitarian law can be relied upon to elaborate a set of relevant rules for the protection and assistance of IDPs. It is not the intention of the author to compare and contrast the content of the Convention with these international standards here. This can await the next chapter where an attempt will be made to provide a detailed analysis of the content of the Convention in the light of existing international standards. This section mainly seeks to uncover the various international and regional standards that shaped and influenced the drafting of the Convention. Thus, the purpose is not to provide analysis of the various instruments that might have inspired the Convention, but to identify them.

The drafter of the Convention stated that 'attempts at filling the lacunae in Africa must draw on wider aspects of the efforts made so far'.[143] The Annotated Outline indeed indicated that some general sources of law may be taken into account while codifying the Convention. These include: (a) African regional human rights instruments, and decisions of the African Union; (b) the United Nations Charter, international human rights

138 Ibid.

139 Ibid.

140 New Treaty for Internally Displaced Persons in Africa, *News and Media*, United Nations Office in Geneva, 22 October 2009.

141 New African Union Convention Protects Internally Displaced Persons, 26 October 2009, Refugee International.

142 See An African Solution to Internal Displacement: AU Leaders Agree to Landmark Convention, Brookings-Bern Project on Internal Displacement, 23 October 2009. Available online at: www.brookings.edu/papers/2009.

143 Ibid.

instruments and resolutions of the United Nations Security Council; (c) international humanitarian law; and (d) the UN Guiding Principles on Internal Displacement. The preamble of the Convention lists some of the specific regional and international legal instruments that have been used as sources of inspiration for the codification of the Convention. The following sections highlight some of the principal sources for the codification of the Convention.

The UN Guiding Principles

Perhaps the most important legal development which had occurred prior to the codification of the Kampala Convention at the international level has of course been the elaboration of the UN Guiding Principles. During the negotiation of the Convention, the UN Guiding Principles and the Annotations prepared by the RSG have been extensively cited. The participation of the RSG on the Human Rights of IDPs, Professor Walter Kälin, in the preparation of the drafting process has not only assisted African experts to benefit from the expertise of the world's renowned expert on the subject of internal displacement, but also helped them grasp the state of play as far as international standard setting with respect to the protection and assistance of IDPs is concerned.

The influence of the Guiding Principles on the text of the Convention has been direct. To a certain extent, it can be argued that the drafting of the Convention has been an attempt to transform the UN Guiding Principles into a binding instrument that is relevant in the African context.[144] Even the RSG expressed his hope that the Convention would provide 'better protection and assistance' than the Guiding Principles.[145]

International humanitarian law and human rights law

The reliance on the Guiding Principles means a strong, albeit indirect, reference both to international human rights law and international humanitarian law. As captured in the Annotations by the RSG, some major developments within these discrete international law fields have emerged since 1998 when the Guiding Principles were elaborated. The drafting of the AU Convention took into account both the Guiding Principles and the Annotations. Since the adoption of the UN Guiding Principles, there has also been a phenomenal development of international criminal law. This is reflected not only in the jurisprudence of international criminal courts such as ICTY and ICTR, but also in the coming into force of the Rome Statute, and consequently the establishment and operationalisation of the International Criminal Court. The growing attention given to the relationship between environmental

144 Note 130 above.
145 Note 76 above, 2.

issues such as climate change with displacement has underlined the need to take into account international environmental law while codifying the new AU Convention. While the preamble of the Convention makes explicit references to international human rights and humanitarian law instruments, no similar reference has been made to fields of international criminal law and environmental law. However, as we shall see in Chapter 5, the content of the AU Convention has drawn some normative elements from these areas of international law.

African regional human rights instruments

The Annotated Outline indicated that the AU Convention would take into consideration African regional human rights instruments. The Convention explicitly refers to a number of regional human rights instruments, namely, the African Charter on Human and Peoples' Rights, the Protocol on the Rights of Women in Africa, and the African Charter on the Rights and Welfare of the Child. A detailed analysis and commentary on the relevance of international law for the protection of IDPs informed the elaboration of the UN Guiding Principles. A similar initiative which seeks to analyse the relevant regional human rights instruments has not been undertaken in the context of the development of the Kampala Convention. But the participation of ACHPR's Special Rapporteur on refugees, asylum seekers, migrants and IDPs helped create awareness about the African Commission on Human and Peoples' Rights, and the mandate of its Special Rapporteur. He played an important role in ensuring that the Convention acknowledges and recognised the role these mechanisms play in the promotion and protection of human rights.[146] Following the adoption of the Convention, the ACHPR quickly endorsed the instrument calling it 'one of an impressive body of African human rights instruments',[147] giving a clear signal that it considers the new Convention as one of the region's principal human rights instruments.

The Great Lakes Protocols preceded the African Union IDP Convention as the first binding regional instruments with direct relevance to internal displacement. They were also important legal sources which influenced the drafting of the African Union's Convention.[148] The principal draftsperson of

146 In his 44th Activity Report to the Commission, the Special Rapporteur notes: 'with regard to the draft IDP convention, my participation throughout the process, which started in April 2006, was instrumental in ensuring that the protocol reflects the role of the Special Reporteur, and the African Commission, in the implementation of the convention, and the protection of IDPs'. Note 124 above, 3.

147 Press Release, African Commission on Human and Peoples' Rights. Undated, available at www.achpr.org/english/Press%20Release KAMPALA%20CONVENTION_IDPs.pdf (accessed on 15 June 2010).

148 Macrine Mayanja, 'The Guiding Principles and the Challenges of Forced Displacement in Africa: The Response of the African Union', The Conference on Ten Years of the UN Guiding Principles on Internal Displacement: Achievements and Future Challenges, Oslo, Norway, 16–17 October 2008, 5.

the original text of the AU Convention, Dr Chaloka Beyani, has also been responsible for the drafting of the Great Lakes IDP Protocol. Moreover, eleven African countries have subscribed to these protocols making it easy for them to express support to legislative reforms with a similar scope and objective.

Conclusion

The birth of the AU Convention can only be appreciated if it is considered within the framework of Africa's traditional regional engagement with the challenges of forced displacement. An opportunity to address 'the legal gap' emerged when, following the transformation of the OAU into the AU, the continental body established a committee of experts to review existing treaties and propose new areas where treaty making was required. Rejecting the view that the 1969 OAU Refugee Convention be reopened to cover the protection problems of IDPs, the Executive Council of the African Union in 2004 endorsed the proposal that a new and separate treaty be negotiated to specifically address the protection and assistance concerns relating to IDPs. This chapter sought to discuss the genesis, the procedure of negotiation and the evolution of the Kampala Convention since 2004.

Despite the absence of any formal treaty-making procedure at the level of the African Union, the formulation of the draft Convention was undertaken on the basis of 'procedures' that had been traditionally followed by the Commission of the African Union. Following the decision by the Executive Council to adopt a separate regional Convention on internal displacement and its specific request to the African Union's Commission to convene consultative and negotiation meetings among member states and other stakeholders, the African Union Commission convened a series of legal experts which allowed member states to negotiate on a draft prepared by an independent consultant and further improved through consultation with a group of African legal experts, UN partners, the UN RSG on human rights of IDPs and others.

As the process of drafting the Convention shows, the Commission played an important role in advocating for the Convention. The pro-active role of the Commission became so visible that an imagery of a 'progressive AU Commission' and 'reluctant member states' was created.[149] There has also been remarkably active participation by international organisations in support of the drafting process. That the process was considerably influenced by international organisations such as UNHCR and ICRC should be looked at in the light of past treaty-making experiences in Africa where international organisations were also actively involved. The participation of these organisations in the drafting process helped the text incorporate provisions that

149 'African IDP Convention Fills a Void in Humanitarian Law', *IRIN*, 27 October 2009.

advanced and acknowledged their role in the protection and assistance of IDPs.

The elaboration of the Kampala Convention has not been as controversial as one might have expected before the process commenced. Generally, delegations embraced the agenda of codification and actively participated in the process. If there were some controversial issues, these were associated with specific issues such as development-induced displacement and the role and status of armed groups. As the Chapter attempted to show, the initiative of drafting the Convention did not emerge suddenly or in isolation. Rather the Convention resulted from long-standing efforts within the OAU/AU to address issues affecting refugees and internally displaced persons. Even though a binding regional instrument existed only with respect to the protection of refugees, the discussion by the OAU/AU with respect to the protection and assistance concerns of IDPs has not been challenged. This contrasts with the situation at the international level where many often questioned the legal authority of the UNHCR in providing protection and assistance to IDPs. In codifying the Kampala Convention, however, African states not only showed a different attitude with respect to regional codification as opposed to an international one, but they also accommodated a pronounced and active role by UNHCR at the regional level.

The drafting process also avoided making explicit references to and legal characterisations of concepts such as 'humanitarian intervention' and the 'responsibility to protect' mainly out of fear that such references might have 'radicalised' the text, thus making any future adoption of the Convention difficult. The process attempted to avoid issues that were found to be controversial. This fear was indeed justified when one looks at the concerns delegations expressed regarding how the Convention's provision on regional intervention has been drafted. But the original text of the Convention was indeed broad. It endorsed a much broader role of the African Union with respect to the protection of victims of displacement than is envisaged under the Constitutive Act.

Though the Convention has been considered within the context of the African Union's processes with respect to refugees, it is a significant shortcoming that it has not sufficiently addressed regional human rights instruments and the role of African human rights mechanisms. Except for the participation of ACHPR's Special Rapporteur, the Gambian-based Commission and its other members played no significant role. It is to the credit of the Special Rapporteur that the final text of the Convention included a reference to the role of the African Commission and its special mechanisms.

The regional codification initiative has received a significant boost from enhanced credibility and acceptance of the Guiding Principles. Legal reforms at the national and sub-regional level facilitated the acceptance of some of the concepts. The Convention has taken inspiration, among others, both from the UN Guiding Principles and the Great Lakes Protocols. That some African countries have already laid out national policies and programmes on

IDPs even prior to the adoption of the Convention can surely be considered as a positive outcome. But these national policies are greatly influenced by the Guiding Principles themselves.

5 Scope, innovation and limitations

Introduction

The Kampala Convention contains 23 articles. The first three articles deal with definitions of terms, objectives of the Convention and state obligations respectively. Article 4 stipulates for protection from internal displacement. Article 5 deals with obligations of state parties with respect to protection and assistance. Article 9 discusses the obligation of states during displacement. States' responsibility in the context of seeking durable solutions is elaborated under Article 11. Specific issues involving compensation, reparations, documentation and registration of IDPs are covered under Articles 12 and 13. Though almost the majority of articles are applicable to all forms of displacement irrespective of their causes, Articles 7 and 10 deal with the specific challenges of displacement generated by armed conflicts and projects respectively.

The provisions of the 1998 UN Guiding Principles on Internal Displacement are organised around the needs and vulnerabilities of IDPs. The Kampala Convention, however, takes the obligation of states as a fundamental starting point. It expands this principle to encompass the roles and responsibilities of non-state actors. The Convention's scope is broad and covers all phases of displacement. It thus addresses protection against displacement, protection and assistance during displacement and durable solutions through return, integration and relocation.

Sources of the Convention

The drafters of the Kampala Convention relied on the Guiding Principles as an important source of inspiration. It is from the Guiding Principles that numerous elements of the Convention are drawn. The Preamble recognises the rights of IDPs as set out in the Guiding Principles.[1] It also recognises the Guiding Principles as an international framework for the protection and promotion of rights of IDPs. The drafters have also taken inspiration from

1 Preamble, para. 11.

regional legal instruments such as the Constitutive Act of the AU, the African Charter on Human and Peoples' Rights and the 1994 Addis Ababa Document on Refugees and Forced Displacement of Populations in Africa. The Kampala Convention was developed as a standalone convention rather than, for instance, as an additional protocol either to the 1969 OAU Refugee Convention or the African Charter on Human and Peoples' Rights. This approach was considered as presenting a risk of reopening and weakening the regional refugee protection regime. This said it must be stated that the transplantation of some concepts from the OAU Refugee Convention to the Kampala Convention is quite evident. For instance, the latter invokes Africa's generosity and hospitality in hosting displaced persons – a concept that is well-incorporated in the OAU Refugee Convention.[2] It also incorporates norms including the protection of IDPs from involuntary return to the area of their original displacement where their safety and security is not guaranteed. Both legal instruments broadly deal with persons uprooted from their homes and livelihoods.

The Kampala Convention lays bare certain similarities to key regional human rights instruments in Africa. It reaffirms the rights and freedoms of displaced individuals and groups. The right to equality and freedom from discrimination permeates its provisions (Preamble, para. 12). In addition, the Convention stipulates for obligations of states and recognises the role of Africa's regional human rights mechanisms in monitoring the realisation of such obligation.[3] Beyond human rights protection, the Convention also deals with the prevention of displacement, early warning and disaster response mechanisms – issues that are not fully recognised in human rights instruments. In the Preamble, member states reaffirm their commitment to the prevention of forced displacement of populations and addressing root causes (Preamble, para. 5). This reflects the growing focus in international law on questions of disaster risk management and early warning systems as an important aspect of the protection of the human rights of persons including those who are displaced.[4]

Several provisions of the Kampala Convention are drawn from international humanitarian law as well. The importance of this could not be underestimated as armed conflicts remain prevalent causes of population displacement. States are obligated to 'respect and ensure respect for international humanitarian law regarding the protection of internally displaced persons' (Article 3(1)e). Drawing inspiration from the 1949 Geneva Conventions, the Kampala Convention prohibits arbitrary displacement of civilians during armed conflicts (Article 4(4)b). The role of

2 Preamble, para. 4.
3 Arts 8(3) e & f and 20(3).
4 Allehone Abebe, The African Union Convention on the Protection and Assistance of Internally Displaced Persons as an emerging regional legal regime for humanitarian assistance during natural disaster, paper presented during the 15th Humanitarian Conference, 18–19 February 2010, Webster University, Geneva (unpublished).

non-state actors is duly recognised. The Convention aims to 'provide for the respective obligations, responsibilities and roles of armed groups, non-state actors and other relevant actors, including civil-society organizations, with respect to the prevention of internal displacement and protection of, and assistance to, internally displaced persons' (Article 2). The drafters, some member states and even the ICRC were initially unenthusiastic about the extensive borrowing of norms from international humanitarian law.[5] It was feared that this transplantation may lead to a renegotiation of accepted standards, thereby further weakening existing international humanitarian normative norms. This cautious approach explains the inclusion of a provision which stipulates: 'The protection and assistance to internally displaced persons under this Article shall be governed by international law and in particular international humanitarian law' (Article 7(3)). It was felt that this allows the implementation of the Convention to benefit from an evolving international humanitarian law.

Scope and objectives

The Kampala Convention is a binding legal instrument applicable to all situations of internal displacement in African Union member states.[6] It is comprehensive in its scope, content and objectives. As such it is far more extensive than the Great Lakes Protocol.[7] The initial text of the Convention went through a significant evolution during the drafting process. For example, a reference in the earlier draft of the Convention mandating the AU to take coercive actions against member states to address internal displacement was watered down. A proposal to establish a regional office – 'the High Commissioner for IDPs' – was also later abandoned. However, the Convention covers all forms of displacement, regardless of their causes (Article 15(1)). It incorporates key issues relevant to prevention, response and durable solutions. Its scope also extends beyond the protection and assistance of IDPs and to host communities.

The Convention seeks to reinforce African states' 'common vision of providing durable solutions to situations of internally displaced persons by establishing an appropriate legal framework for their protection and assistance' (Preamble, para. 5). Factors generating internal displacement often have regional resonance in Africa. Putting in place effective normative and institutional responses to these challenges thus requires a regional approach.

5 See Chapter 3.

6 Art 16(1). The first binding regional instrument concerning IDPs, the Protocol on the Protection and Assistance to Internally Displaced Persons, adopted by the International Conference on the Great Lakes Region (ICGLR) in 2006, is applicable only to the 11 states from the Great Lakes region.

7 Protocol on the Protection and Assistance to Internally Displaced Persons, entered into force in June 2008.

In this context, the innovative provisions of the African Union Constitutive Act should be acknowledged. The doctrine of regional 'humanitarian intervention' would otherwise have been quite controversial and unthinkable to include in any legally binding instrument (Article 8(1)). The Convention's provision on regional intervention in a member state to address internal displacement, at least in situations of grave crisis of internal displacement associated with genocide, war crimes and crimes against humanity is, therefore, a significant normative development.

The Convention broadly lays out the normative and institutional dimensions of protecting and assisting IDPs. In particular, it: (a) addresses the root causes of internal displacement and promotes durable solutions; (b) establishes a legal framework dealing with internal displacement; (c) promotes cooperation among states; and (d) stipulates the obligation of states and non-state actors. By adopting the treaty, member states wanted to address problems associated with 'the lack of a binding African and international legal and institutional framework specifically, for the prevention of internal displacement and the protection of and assistance to internally displaced persons' (Preamble, para. 14).

In addition to elaborating the obligation of states, the Convention also examines norms applicable to non-state actors. Moreover, Article 6 addresses obligations relating to international organisations and humanitarian agencies. The roles of the African Union are covered under Article 8. Article 14 covers mechanisms and procedures for monitoring the implementation of the Convention. Articles 15 to 23 cover a panoply of procedural issues including ratification, entry into force, denunciation, amendment, interpretation, reservation, settlement of disputes and deposition.

Definitions and concepts

The Convention provides for definitions of key concepts. These include internally displaced persons, the arbitrariness of displacement, armed groups, traditional harmful practices and non-state actors (Article 1).

Who are internally displaced persons?

The Kampala Convention defines IDPs as

> persons or group of persons who have been forced or obliged to flee or leave their homes or places of habitual residence, in particular as a result of or in order to avoid the effects of armed conflict, situations of generalised violence, violations of human rights or natural or human made disasters, and who have not crossed an internationally recognised state border.
>
> (Article 19(k))

This endorses the widely used definition provided by the Guiding Principles and transforms the latter into a binding legal standard. The definition incorporates all 'causes' of displacement. IDPs can be either individuals or groups. To be considered as IDPs, persons need not directly experience the causes of their flight. It is sufficient that their displacement is triggered by the desire to avoid 'the effects of armed conflict, situations of generalized violence, violations of human rights or natural or human-made disasters' (Article 1 (k)). The word 'in particular' signals that the causes of displacement are not exhaustive. Even persons displaced as a result of factors other than those expressly mentioned may be considered as IDPs. This applies, for example, to persons who are displaced as a result of development projects. While the issue of 'projects' is dealt with both under the Guiding Principles and the Convention, neither of these instruments explicitly includes victims of development projects as a part of the definition for IDPs. The Great Lakes Protocol, on the other hand, adopts a slightly different approach by including in its definition those who are forced to flee 'in order to avoid the *effects of large scale development projects*, and who have not crossed an internationally recognized state border' (Article 1(5)).

The involuntariness of the displacement assumes an important role in determining whether a person can be considered as an IDP or not. This is reinforced by paragraph 1 of Article 1 which states that internal displacement shall mean 'the involuntary or forced movement, evacuation or relocation of persons or groups of persons within internationally recognized State borders'. No separate definition for 'internal displacement' is provided for under the Guiding Principles. The Convention principally deals with persons who are directly coerced to leave their homes as in cases where they are ordered by armed groups or government authorities to flee their areas of residence. There are, of course, cases where persons are 'forced' to flee not necessarily by direct instructions or actions of others. IDPs may flee because of fear for their security linked to ongoing fighting, natural disaster and human rights violations.

Whether an individual has crossed an internationally recognised boundary is also an important element of the IDP definition. As observed in operational environments such as in Afghanistan, Iran and Somalia and stated by the Annotations to the Guiding Principles, situations may emerge where some individuals might cross international boundaries of a third state to get to another part of their own country, or may return to their home country from a third country but find it difficult to return to their homes or residences.[8] Returning refugees may find themselves losing their property or having difficulty in effectively integrating with the local community, exposing them into becoming IDPs. A situation may also arise whereby *de facto*

8 Walter Kälin, *Guiding Principles on International Law: Annotations*. Washington, DC: Brookings Institution, 2008, 3–4.

state boundaries or territories which have declared independence may refuse to consider persons fleeing from 'the mother' territory as IDPs. It is noted that 'international boundaries' should be broadly understood so that the aforementioned individuals are sufficiently covered.[9] This is consistent with the Kampala Convention's purpose and objective and, more specifically, to its reference to 'internationally recognised state borders'. This is also consistent with the practice of the African Union where returnees are often considered alongside IDPs.

When does displacement become arbitrary?

The Kampala Convention stipulates the rights of persons to be protected from arbitrary displacement. It prohibits arbitrary displacement resulting from: (a) policies of racial discrimination or other similar practices aimed at, or resulting in, altering the ethnic, religious or racial composition of the population; (b) armed conflicts; (c) intentional use of displacement as a method of warfare or due to other violations of international humanitarian law in situations of armed conflict; (d) generalised violence or violations of human rights; (e) harmful practices; (f) forced evacuation in the context of natural or human-made disasters or other causes if the evacuations are not required by the safety and health of those affected; and (g) practices of collective punishment. The inclusion, in the chapeau of Article 4(4), of the phrase 'includes but is not limited to' reveals the non-exhaustive nature of the situations that might be considered as arbitrary. It is also stated that any forms of 'displacement caused by any act, event, factor, or phenomenon of comparable gravity … and which is not justified under international law, including human rights and international humanitarian law' will be considered as arbitrary (Article 4(4)h).

How does one determine the arbitrariness of a displacement? The arbitrariness of civilian evacuations in armed conflicts, for instance, will be assessed based on a determination of whether evacuation of civilians is necessary to fulfil military objectives or to ensure the safety of civilians. Such determination shall be made in accordance with international humanitarian law (Article 4(4)b). The explicit recognition of human rights norms under Article 4(4) underlines the relevance of human rights considerations in situations where international humanitarian law is not applicable. In non-conflict situations, arbitrariness of an evacuation will be examined by closely examining whether the measure has been ordered with the view to guaranteeing the safety or health of civilians concerned.

By explicitly listing situations that may constitute arbitrary displacement, Article 4(4) of the Convention adopts a similar approach taken by the Guiding Principles (Principle 6). The Convention appears to be more expansive than the Guiding Principles. The recognition of displacement triggered

9 Ibid.

by harmful practices as arbitrary forms of displacement is one example of its broader scope. Despite the Convention's recognition of displacement associated with development projects, it does not clarify under what circumstances development projects may generate arbitrary displacement. This contrasts with Principle 6 of the Guiding Principles wherein displacement caused by development projects 'not justified by compelling and overriding public interest' is considered as arbitrary. Article 4 of the Convention does not mention concepts including 'ethnic cleansing' and 'apartheid'. The practical significance of this, however, should not be overstated. As mentioned above, any 'act, event, factor, or phenomenon of comparable gravity' not justified including under human rights law may be considered as arbitrary (Article 4(4)).

Displacement caused by harmful practices

The Kampala Convention states that any displacement caused by harmful practices is arbitrary. Harmful practices include 'all behaviour, attitudes and/or practices which negatively affect the fundamental rights of persons, such as but not limited to their right to life, health, dignity, education, mental and physical integrity and education' (Article 1(j)). This definition seems to have been drawn from the Protocol on the Rights of Women in Africa.[10] Its aim is to address the unique vulnerabilities of women and children in several countries where harmful traditional practices are widely practised.[11] Displacement situations that might be caused by harmful practices present complex questions. Harmful practices hardly present situations similar to those triggered by armed conflicts, generalised violence, massive human rights violations or disasters. 'Perpetrators' of these practices are often private actors, namely, individuals, clan groups and religious communities. Under the Convention, it is provided that the state assumes the obligation to 'ensure the accountability of non-state actors concerned … for acts of arbitrary displacement or complicity in such acts' (Article 3(1) I). Enforcing this provision will present a significant challenge. This represents an aspirational aspect of the Convention.

Responsibility of armed groups and non-state actors

The scope of the Kampala Convention extends both to armed groups and non-state actors. It aims to 'provide for the respective obligations,

10 Art 1, African Union, Protocol to the African Charter on Human and Peoples' Rights on the Rights of Women in Africa, 11 July 2003. Available at: www.unhcr.org/refworld/docid/3f4b139d4.html. See also Art 5(i) of the Protocol of the Great Lakes region on the Prevention and Suppression of Sexual Violence against Women and Children.

11 See Audrey Macklin, 'Legal Aspect of Conflict Induced Migration by Women', in Susan Forbes Martin and John Tirman, *Women, Migration and Conflict: Breaking a Deadly Cycle* (Dordrecht, Heidelberg, New York, London: Springer, 2009), p. 25.

responsibilities and roles of armed groups, non-state actors and other relevant actors' (Article 2(e)). Armed groups are defined as 'dissident armed forces or other organized armed groups that are distinct from the armed forces of the state' (Article 1(e)). This definition is similar to that which was adopted under the Optional Protocol on the Involvement of Children in Armed Conflicts.[12] It may be argued that the definition does not sufficiently identify conditions that must be satisfied before a particular group is categorised as an armed group. Armed groups need to satisfy the requirements of organisation, command and territorial possession.[13] Notwithstanding its broad scope, there is little to suggest that Article 1(e) intends to cover all groups. Article 1(n) defines non-state actors as 'private actors who are not public officials of the State, including other armed groups not referred to in Article 1(d) above, and whose acts cannot be officially attributed to the State'. This definition embodies two important elements: (a) that non-state actors are not public officials of state; and that (b) their actions are not imputable to the state. The inclusion of non-state actors in the Convention was controversial during the negotiation on the text of the Convention. This explains the stipulation that that the treatment of armed groups in the Convention shall not be understood as granting such groups any legal status.[14]

Do IDPs have status?

The Kampala Convention does not seek to confer on IDPs a distinct legal status. Its definition of IDPs should thus be understood as a factual description of persons with specific needs. As highlighted in its Preamble, the overriding objective of the Convention is to address 'the suffering and specific vulnerability of internally displaced persons' (Preamble, paragraph 3). No proof of status is required for individuals to access protection and assistance. States are in fact expected to institute a system of registration and documentation (Articles 13(1) and (2)). States should also issue IDPs with 'relevant documents necessary for the enjoyment and exercise of their rights, such as passports, personal identification documents, civil certificates, birth certificates and marriage certificates'.[15] Procedures should, therefore, be put in place to ensure replacement of lost or destroyed documentation. IDPs

12 Art 4 states that the responsibility of not recruiting children into armed conflict is also applicable to armed groups which are distinct from state armed forces.

13 According to Article 1(1) of Protocol II, armed groups must be 'under responsible command, exercise such control over [a High Contracting Party's] territory as to enable [it] to carry out sustained and concerted military operations and to implement this Protocol'.

14 Art 7(1) states: 'The provisions of this Article shall not, in any way whatsoever, be construed as affording legal status or legitimizing or recognizing armed groups and are without prejudice to the individual criminal responsibility of the members of such groups under domestic or international criminal law'.

15 Ibid.

should be protected from denial of access to documentation on the ground that they are no more in the place of their habitual residence. Provision of registration should be considered as mainly an administrative measure aimed at identifying those who require specific protection and assistance.[16]

Causes of internal displacement

States assume the primary responsibility for the assistance and protection of IDPs regardless of the causes of displacement. The Convention covers all forms of displacement including those that might result from violations of international humanitarian law or human rights law (Article 4(4)). The latter refers to displacement situations resulting from actions of states and other actors that violate the right of individuals to be protected from arbitrary displacement. In all forms of displacement, the rights and freedoms of IDPs and their entitlement to access assistance should be fully respected.

Armed conflicts

The Kampala Convention recognises conflicts as important causes of displacement. The Convention significantly draws upon principles enshrined in international humanitarian law. Its Preamble recognises the 1949 Geneva Conventions and the 1977 additional protocols. 'International humanitarian law' is cited several times throughout the text of the Convention. Similar to the Guiding Principles, the Kampala Convention incorporates norms applicable to different types of conflicts: (a) international armed conflicts, (b) non-international armed conflicts, and (c) other situations which may not be defined as conflicts such as tensions and public disturbances. States commit themselves to 'adopt measures aimed at preventing and putting an end to the phenomenon of internal displacement by eradicating the root causes, especially persistent and recurrent conflicts' (Preamble). The Convention urges both states and non-state actors to take steps to address the various underlining causes of displacement including armed conflicts. It also calls on states to 'endeavour to incorporate the relevant principles contained in this Convention into peace negotiations and agreements for the purpose of finding sustainable solutions to the problem of internal displacement' (Article 3(2)e).

Several provisions of the Convention reinforce states' responsibility under international humanitarian law. Any displacement of population during armed conflicts will be considered arbitrary unless it is justified by 'security of the civilians involved or imperative military reasons'.[17] The Convention prohibits displacement used as a weapon of warfare or that which results from violations of international humanitarian law (Article 4(4)c). It gives

16 Note 8 above, 3.

17 Art 4(4) b. See also Principle 6(2).

particular emphasis on the prevention of the most atrocious violations of human rights including genocide, war crimes and murder. It provides special protection for the most vulnerable among the displaced population particularly to women, children and other groups.

As stipulated under Article 2(e), the Convention aims to regulate the obligation of armed groups. Accordingly, these groups are prohibited from committing: (a) arbitrary displacement, (b) hampering assistance and protection to IDPs, (c) denying IDPs access to basic social services, (d) restricting the movement of IDPs, (e) recruiting and forcing children to participate in armed hostilities, (f) forcibly recruiting persons, kidnapping, abduction or hostage taking, engaging in sexual slavery and trafficking in persons especially women and children, (g) attacking and harming of humanitarian assistance, and (h) violating the civilian and humanitarian character of areas where IDPs are located.[18] In reaction to concerns expressed by states during the drafting process that such a detailed treatment of responsibilities of armed groups may give rise to legal status, it is provided that the Convention's provisions shall not 'be construed as affording legal status or legitimizing or recognizing armed groups' (Article 7(1)). It is also stipulated that they should also be applicable without any prejudice to the individual criminal responsibilities of members of the armed groups under international and domestic criminal law.

The Convention's provisions concerning armed conflicts situations are not necessarily complete. For instance, the Convention does not deal with the threat emanating from the use of IDPs as human shields. The prohibition of the use of civilians as human shields, as provided for under Articles 51(7) and 28 of Protocol I and Convention IV respectively, are applicable to situations emerging from international armed conflicts. The ICRC Study on Customary International Law, however, states that the prohibition of the use of human shields has developed into a norm of customary international law applicable in both international and non-international armed conflicts.[19] The Guiding Principles expands the application of this prohibition even to situations of non-international armed conflicts (Principle 10(2)c). Unlike the Guiding Principles, the Convention also does directly address the problems associated with anti-personnel mines.[20] It should be pointed out that the

18 Arts 7(1) & 7(5). See also Art 15(2) which states that 'States Parties agree that nothing in this Convention shall be construed as affording legal status or legitimizing or recognizing armed groups and that its provisions are without prejudice to the individual criminal responsibility of their members under domestic or international criminal law'.

19 Jean-Marie Henckaerts and Louise Doswald-Beck, *Customary International Humanitarian Law, Volume I: Rules* (Cambridge: Cambridge University Press, 2005), Rule 129(B).

20 It should however be stated that the Kampala Declaration on Refugees, Returnees and Displaced Persons identifies the clearance of land mines and other unexploded ordinance as an important prerequisite for sustainable return and safety of IDPs. African Union, Kampala Declaration on Refugees, Returnees and Internally Displaced Persons in Africa, 23 October 2009, Ext/Assembly/AU/PA/Draft/Decl.(I) Rev.1, available at: www.unhcr.org/refworld/docid/4af0623d2.html.

Convention does not cover issues such as missing persons, handling of remains and protection of grave sites.[21]

During the drafting of the Convention, the relationship between the Convention and international humanitarian law attracted a considerable attention. Some feared that these provisions might dilute or weaken the application of existing international humanitarian law. States were also more interested in prescribing restrictions on the actions of armed groups than reaching an agreement on a principle that might be applicable to them. It is stipulated that the application of the provision shall not be 'invoked for the purpose of affecting the sovereignty of a State or the responsibility of the government, by all legitimate means, to maintain or re-establish law and order' (Article 7(2)).

It may be asked whether the absence of detailed provisions on the obligation of all parties is a 'missed opportunity'. This is particularly relevant in light of the fact that observers often highlighted the incongruence of the IHL's treatment of civilians during international armed conflicts on the other hand and non-international armed conflicts on the other. This approach may also reinforce existing ambivalence of African regional human rights mechanism in monitoring the implementation of international humanitarian law. It is important however to note that the Convention was not intended to provide a comprehensive treatment of international humanitarian law. As is clearly provided in Article 7 the Convention will be applied based on international humanitarian law.

Natural disasters

The frequency and gravity of natural disasters due to factors including climate change reveal the protection concerns faced by persons displaced by such phenomenon.[22] The Kampala Convention underlies the severe impacts of natural disasters on 'human life, peace, stability, security, and development' (Preamble, para. 6). The Convention covers the protection and assistance of those who are forced to flee their homes or habitual residence by natural and human made disasters (Article 1(k)). It is also stated that states assume obligations to provide assistance and protection to those displaced by natural disasters.[23] They are expected, among others, to establish disaster risk reduction strategies and preparedness mechanisms. Not only are they required to take steps to prevent the consequences of disasters but also are required to provide, where necessary, assistance and protection to

21 Note 8 above, 71–75.

22 Fourth Report on the Protection of Persons in the Events of Disaster, Mr Eduardo Valencia-Ospina, Special Rapporteur, International Law Commission, A/CN.4/643, 11 May 2011.

23 Art 5(4). See also Preamble, para. 6.

IDPs (Article 4(2)). These early warning and risk reduction strategies and techniques will enhance the capacity of the state to provide immediate protection and assistance. Authorities should also take steps including by establishing specialised national mechanisms in order to 'trace and reunify families separated during displacement and otherwise facilitate the re-establishment of family ties' (Article 9(2)h). Any forced relocation of persons that is not justified by requirements of the health and safety of the persons concerned will be arbitrary.[24] Persons are protected from 'resettlement in any place where their life, safety, liberty and/or health would be at risk' (Article 9(2)e). Authorities may be allowed to restrict the movement of persons. These restrictions, however, ought to be 'necessary, justified and proportionate to the requirements of ensuring security for internally displaced persons or maintaining public security, public order and public health' (Article 9(2)f).

Provisions of the Convention dealing with natural disasters are not presented in an organised fashion. Relevant norms are scattered throughout the Convention. It has to be stated, however, that some key general provisions of the Convention are relevant to displacement caused by disasters as well. Provisions dealing with prevention of arbitrary displacement and protection from discrimination in accessing humanitarian assistance are particularly important.[25] The same could be said regarding provisions dealing with durable solutions. When designing and implementing durable solution strategies to address disaster-induced displacement, states are required to fully involve victims and implement solutions based on the latter's informed consent. They also assume the responsibility of ensuring the provision of compensation and redress in situations when state agents cause harm by refraining from 'protecting and assisting internally displaced persons in the event of natural disasters' (Article 12(3)).

'Development' projects

Displacement of populations by development projects was one of the most contentious topics during the negotiation of the Convention. Irrespective of their size, projects may result in displacement. The drafters had also proposed to include articles dealing with not only displacement resulting from 'large scale development projects' but also displacement triggered by 'absence of development'.[26] This proposal, however, did not receive support from state parties. The final text acknowledged the obligation of states to 'prevent displacement caused by projects carried out by public or private actors' (Article 10(1)). It is also stated that authorities have the responsibilities to ensure the accountability of non-state actors including multinational

24 Art 4(4)f. See also Principle 6(2)d.
25 These include Arts 3, 4, 5 and 9.
26 Choloka Beyani, Annotated Outline, AU/EXP/HARPD/2(v), 7–8.

companies and those who are involved in the exploration of natural resources (Articles 3(1)h & I). Concerning private projects, it is provided that states, in particular, should avail opportunities to all stakeholders to explore all feasible alternatives by fully informing and securing the consent of IDPs. Whenever states are engaged in public projects, they are expected to undertake socio-economic and environmental impact assessment prior to undertaking projects (Article 10(3)). Descriptions including 'large' and 'development' were dropped from the draft Convention. The consideration is rather straightforward – development *per se* does not displace people.

The Convention provides for a specific provision dealing with project-induced displacement. It, however, does not proffer any explanation as to what constitute forms of development-induced displacement. Neither does it provide detailed procedural guarantees as is the case with the Guiding Principles. The scope of the Convention's provision is far less detailed compared to what was envisaged under the Annotated Outline and the draft Convention. For example, draft texts of the Convention distributed to states in August 2007 and July 2008 included provisions which, among others provided that: (a) the only exception to development-induced displacement are those justified by compelling and overriding public interest; (b) that the states shall seek the participation of women and people with special attachment to their lands; (c) states shall, where no alternatives exist, take all measures necessary to minimise and mitigate the adverse effects of displacement; (d) both states and private actors shall provide persons with alternative and habitable areas of relocation and residence where they have access to appropriate services, infrastructure and livelihood or fully compensate them.[27]

Principle 7 of the Guiding Principles stipulates the following guarantees that must be fulfilled when carrying out evacuation measures. When displacement occurs in situations other than during the emergency phases of conflict and disasters: (a) a specific decision shall be taken by a state authority empowered by law to order such measures; (b) adequate measures shall be taken to provide information to victims on the reasons and procedures for their displacement and, where applicable, on compensation and relocation; (c) free and informed consent of those to be displaced shall be sought; (d) the authority concerned shall endeavour to involve those affected, particularly women, in the planning and management of their relocation; (e) law enforcement measures, where required, shall be carried out by competent legal authorities, and (f) the right to an effective remedy, including the review of such decisions by appropriate judicial authorities, shall be respected. As noted earlier, however, Article 10 of the Convention provides far fewer procedural guarantees, i.e. consultation with victims of

27 Art 10, AU Convention for the Protection and Assistance of Internally Displaced Persons in Africa (Draft), POL/DIR/114(1114). An almost identical provision exists under Article 9 of the draft Convention distributed to member states on 2 August 2007.

displacement, and search for alternative solutions and carrying out of prior impact assessment (Article 10(3)).

In contrast to the Guiding Principles, it can be observed that the Convention does not explicitly list development-induced displacement as a form of arbitrary displacement.[28] However, as the list of situations constituting forms of arbitrary displacement is non-exhaustive, some aspects of displacement induced by projects may well be considered as arbitrary. This approach is supported by the Annotated Outline which suggests contexts where development-induced displacement may well be arbitrary.[29] As provided under Article 4, 'displacement caused by any act, event, factor, or phenomenon of comparable gravity ... which is not justified under international law, including human rights and international humanitarian law' should be considered as arbitrary (Article 4(3) h).

Though Article 10 does not identify the entity responsible for undertaking assessment with respect to development projects carried out by private entities, it is sensible to suggest that companies and entities involved in development projects should carry out the assessment themselves. This may involve exploring all feasible alternatives to displacement, providing full information to those who may be affected by the project and carrying out appropriate consultations with affected communities (Article 10(4)). Should such projects affect the interests of indigenous or pastoral groups, relevant provisions of the Convention touching on the specific protection of communities with special attachment to the land should be used. For example, it is stipulated that that 'State Parties shall endeavour to protect communities with special attachment to, and dependency, on land due to their particular culture and spiritual values from being displaced from such lands, except for *compelling and overriding public interests*' (Article 4(5)).

Compensation and relocation, though important in the context of displacement caused by projects, have not been explicitly incorporated under Article 10. It may thus be argued that Article 12, which deals with compensation and relocation, shall apply.

Generalised violence and human rights violations

The Convention provides a list of grave and systematic human rights violations that may cause arbitrary displacement, including genocide, war crimes, and crimes against humanity, racial discrimination and forced evacuation. States are required to 'prevent political, social, cultural and economic exclusion and marginalisation that are likely to cause displacement of populations or persons by virtue of their social identity, religion or political opinion' (Article 3(1)b). That violations of human rights are expressly indicated as root causes of displacement reinforces the nature of the Convention as a

28 See Principle 6(2).
29 Note 8 above, 3–4.

human rights instrument. The Convention does not define what constitutes 'general violence'. The Convention's definition of IDPs covers those who are forced or obliged to flee their homes or habitual residences due to generalised violence and human rights violations. Accordingly any displacement of population triggered by factors including general violence will be considered arbitrary (Article 4(4)).

National framework for the protection and assistance of IDPs

If the Guiding Principles approach the problem of internal displacement from the perspective of the needs and vulnerabilities of IDPs, the Convention examines the same from the vantage point of state responsibility. It takes the primary obligation of the state as the dominant and overarching doctrine. As the drafters of the Convention explain, the legal instrument is based on the principle of state obligation, which it sought to clarify through its multiple layers, i.e. the obligation to respect, protect, and fulfil.[30] This obligation is applicable to all phases of displacement. Accordingly Article 4 deals with the obligation of the state in preventing displacement. Articles 5 and 9 cover states' obligation regarding protection and assistance. Article 11 stipulates for obligations of states in the context of return, integration or relocation.

The 'state obligation' model adopted by the Convention complements the Guiding Principles. It attempts to marry the doctrine of sovereignty with that of the obligation to respect and ensure the respect of human rights of IDPs. So much as the Convention's provisions stipulate for state obligation, it must be stated that few of its provisions also seek to reinforce the principle of states' sovereignty. The Preamble, for instance, reaffirms the principles of sovereign equality of states, political independence and non-interference. It also prescribes that state obligation towards IDPs shall be enforced without prejudice to the sovereignty of the state concerned (Article 5(12)).

Preventing arbitrary displacement

No working definition has been provided for the concept of prevention of displacement. Within the framework of the obligation of states, however, a raft of activities is envisaged. States can prevent displacement primarily by respecting their obligation under international humanitarian and human rights law (Article 4(1)). They are required to refrain from committing certain actions that may result in arbitrary displacement. The Convention provides a non-exhaustive list of forms of arbitrary displacement. These include any forced movement of populations based on: (a) racial discrimination or other similar practices aimed at/or resulting in altering the ethnic, religious or racial composition of the population; (b) armed conflicts in

30 See note 26 above.

contravention of international humanitarian law; (c) use of displacement as method of warfare; (d) generalised violence or violations of human rights; (e) harmful practices; (f) forced evacuations in cases of natural or human made disasters or other causes not justified by the concerns of safety and health of those affected; and (g) displacement used as a collective punishment (Article 4(4)). Internal displacement of persons triggered by crimes of genocide, war crimes and crimes against humanity are also considered as arbitrary displacement (Article 4(6)).

The protection of communities with a special attachment to and dependency on land from displacement is also guaranteed. In these situations states' action causing displacement is unlawful unless their actions are justified by 'compelling and overriding public interests' (Article 4(5)). Though not specifically stated, it seems rather clear that any incident of displacement of these communities which is not justified by 'compelling and overriding public interests' amounts to a form of arbitrary displacement. States are also required to 'prevent political, social, cultural and economic exclusion and marginalisation that are likely to cause displacement of populations or persons by virtue of their social identity, religion or political opinion' (Article 3(1) b).

In addition to states' negative obligations in preventing arbitrary displacement; they are also required to take certain positive measures in fulfilling the rights and freedoms of IDPs. The broadest articulation of such state obligation is reflected in the requirement that states adopt measures to eradicate or prevent displacement by addressing its root causes (Preamble, para. 6). States may also take steps by establishing a national legal framework which could contribute towards the prevention of displacement (Article 2). They may also take additional steps towards mitigating factors or conditions which may lead to arbitrary displacement (Article 4(1)). Compared to the concept of prevention through the prism of the prohibition of arbitrary displacement, this appears to be a much broader concept which looks at prevention whether the displacement in question is linked with lawful or unlawful acts. In this respect, states' responsibility in enacting national legislation; establishing a national focal point on internal displacement; provision of resources and funds for national programmes; institutionalisation of early warning and disaster prevention and response mechanisms; operationalisation of specialised mechanisms to address the unique needs of vulnerable groups, fall within the responsibility of the state to prevent or mitigate the consequences of internal displacement. Specifically, states are also required to prevent, as much as possible, displacement caused by private and public projects (Article 10(1)). In particular, they shall take a number of steps prior to the launching of projects, including socio-economic and environmental assessment studies (Article 10(3)). It is also stipulated that states are required to institute, in their national legislation, individual criminal responsibility for offences relating to arbitrary displacement.[31]

31 Arts 3(1)g and 7(4).

There are of course several challenges that states in the African continent ought to address if they are to successfully realise their obligation in the prevention of displacement. Promotion of democracy, peaceful settlements of disputes, reversing environmental degradation and tackling social ills such as harmful traditional practices, all play important contributions towards the prevention of displacement. In this respect, the Kampala Convention recognises the crucial role of the prevention, management and resolution of conflicts (Preamble, para. 6). It also makes reference to democracy and rule of law. The Preamble recalls the adoption by members of the AU of democratic practice as provided for under the African Charter on Human and Peoples' Rights as well as under other regional and international human rights instruments (Preamble, para. 9). This establishes linkage between the legal regime regulating internal displacement and the regional legal framework to promote democracy and combat unconstitutional change of government.

Developing national legislations and policies

Countries including Angola, Uganda, Liberia, Sierra Leone and Sudan had enacted national legislative and policy frameworks prior to the adoption of the Kampala Convention. The latter will accelerate this trend as it requires states to domesticate the Convention into the national legal system either by adopting new legislation or amending existing laws (Article 3(2) a). Existing laws may pose unintended obstacles to IDPs or fail to provide effective regulatory frameworks to realise the rights and meet the needs of IDPs.[32] This said any type of legislation a state chooses to adopt must conform to its obligations under international law.[33] These obligations are reflected in commitments states have entered into under the Kampala Convention. Notwithstanding the fact that the Convention principally deals with the enactment or amendment of a national legislation specifically dealing with internal displacement, a number of other national legislations also have direct relevance to address the problem of internal displacement. Some of these domestic legislations may include basic laws or constitutional provisions while others relate to ordinary legislations dealing with topics including the powers and authorities of government institutions both at the national and sub-national level, state of emergency and registration and regulation of humanitarian organisations. Neither should the importance of criminal law be underestimated. States are required among others to punish, by law, acts of arbitrary displacement that amount to genocide, war crimes or crimes against humanity (Article 4(6)). The domestic criminalisation of offences is not necessarily limited to the aforementioned grave crimes; it may also expand into other prohibited forms of arbitrary displacement.

32 Protecting Internally Displaced Persons: A Manual for Law and Policymakers, Brookings Institution, October 2008, p. 27.

33 Ibid.

Beyond the adoption of domestic legislations, states must also enact 'other measures as appropriate, including strategies and policies on internal displacement at national and local levels, taking into account the needs of host communities' (Article 3(2) c). The phrase 'at national and local levels' has been incorporated with the view to addressing the challenges of coordination and harmonisation of state response to internal displacement in decentralised contexts. In principle, it is required that IDPs directly participate in the drafting and preparation of these national laws and policies. For example, the Great Lakes Protocol stipulates that states shall 'enact national legislation to domesticate the Guiding Principles fully' but also to 'ensure the effective participation of internally displaced persons in the preparation and design of the said legislation' (Article 6 of the Protocol). The Kampala Convention also calls for the participation of IDPs in decision-making processes.[34]

Establishing institutional mechanisms

Laws and policies are not ends in themselves. States need to establish a national mechanism that will ensure the implementation of these frameworks and coordinate protection and assistance activities. These activities may include conducting registration of IDPs, tracing and unifying IDP families, carrying out an assessment of the need of IDPs, establishing a simplified procedure to settle property-related disputes and coordinating with humanitarian organisations (Article 3(2) b). The Convention does not promote any typology of a national mechanism on internal displacement. If an existing institutional arrangement is sufficient, establishing a new one may not be required. The Convention allows the possibility of assigning to an existing institutional entity certain responsibilities including coordination with international organisations and CSOs (Article 3(2) b).

A national implementation mechanism on internal displacement plays an important role in bringing together key actors, i.e. relevant line ministries, national human rights institutions, humanitarian organisations, civil society groups and sub-national entities. Though not expressly mentioned in the Convention, the role of national human rights institutions in the protection of IDPs is quite important. National human rights institutions may participate in the elaboration of domestic policies and legislations, investigate alleged violations of human rights of IDPs, promote human rights education and awareness creation and monitor the implementation of relevant laws and policies. Some problems faced by IDPs may also require specific response modalities. For instance, the Convention provides for the establishment of 'specialized mechanisms, to trace and reunify families separated during displacement and otherwise facilitate the re-establishment of family ties'

34 Art 9(2) k states: 'States Parties shall consult internally displaced persons and allow them to participate in decisions relating to their protection and assistance'.

(Article 9(2)h). As has already been mentioned, the state must create national early warning systems and 'establish and implement disaster risk reduction strategies, emergency and disaster preparedness and management measures' (Article 4(2)). They should also 'put in place measures for monitoring and evaluating the effectiveness and impact of the humanitarian assistance delivered to internally displaced persons in accordance with relevant practice, including the Sphere Standards' (Article 9(2)m).

Allocating sufficient resources

Building effective national response to internal displacement and providing humanitarian relief for the displaced, of course, demand the allocation of sufficient human and material resources. Recruitment and retention of specialised experts is also a prerequisite for operationalising a system of early warning, disaster prevention and response envisaged by the Convention. These measures are expectedly expensive, to whose fulfilment states need to contribute within the extent of their available resources (Article 5(6)). Should states be unable to provide the appropriate level of resources, they are required to seek international support and assistance.[35]

The Kampala Convention does not define the concept of humanitarian assistance. However, it incorporates several relevant provisions. Humanitarian assistance, in general, refers to the provision of basic services including food, health, education and sanitation.[36] The concept also applies to the regulation of 'relief consignment, equipment and personnel' (Article 5(7)). Related provisions also deal with topics including, among others, principles of humanitarian assistance, responsibilities of the state, roles of international organisations, modalities of providing humanitarian assistance and the involvement and participation of displaced persons in decision making.

Providing and facilitating humanitarian assistance constitutes one of the fundamental responsibilities of the state. Applicable international framework on humanitarian assistance dictates that states assume the primary role in the 'initiation, organization, coordination and implementation' of humanitarian assistance.[37] Member states shall ensure, to the fullest extent possible and practicable, and with the least possible delay, the provision of material assistance and basic services for those who are in need, by taking the necessary steps in effectively organising relief action that is impartial in character (Article 5(7)). Whenever the state is unable to provide such assistance, it can and it should request international assistance or agree to an offer that may be

35 Arts 3(2) d., 4(3), 5(6), 8(3), 9(3) and 10(3).

36 Art 9(2)b. The Annotation states that humanitarian assistance shall include 'material and services that are essential for the survival of internally displaced persons, such as food, water, medical supplies, shelter and clothing'. Note 8 above, 115.

37 GA Resolution 46/182.

made by humanitarian organisations. Assessment of the need and vulnerabilities of IDPs should be undertaken prior to the initiation of humanitarian assistance by the state itself. When the state is not in a position to undertake the necessary assessment, it should facilitate the involvement of international organisations to support such activities (Article 5(5)).

Humanitarian assistance should be 'adequate', and need be provided with the least possible delay and without 'discrimination of any kind' (Article 5(1)). States shall 'take necessary measures to ensure that IDPs are received, without discrimination of any kind and live in satisfactory conditions of safety, dignity and security' (Article 9(2)). The adequateness of humanitarian assistance should be examined, as the phrase 'to the fullest extent practicable' suggests, on the basis of a number of factors including the resources available to the government. While states may institute a system of registering IDPs, registration should not always be a requirement for delivering or receiving assistance. Authorities are also obliged to 'uphold and ensure respect for the humanitarian principles of humanity, neutrality, impartiality and independence of humanitarian actors' (Article 5(8)). During displacement, IDPs should be protected against human rights violations, and that their right to freedom of movement and choice of residence should also be guaranteed.[38]

Special assistance should be provided to the most vulnerable among the displaced, namely, women, children, persons with disabilities, individuals affected by communicable illness, female-headed households, and communities which have special attachment or dependency to land. Humanitarian assistance provided to IDPs should also include, where appropriate, meeting the assistance needs of local and host communities (Article 5(1)). The phrase 'where appropriate' indicates that the decision to provide assistance to host communities shall be made on a case-by-case assessment of the actual needs of host communities.

Humanitarian assistance can be provided both within and outside of camps. The Convention does not present 'encampment' as the preferred method of providing protection and assistance. Though putting IDPs in a visible location may help publicise existing humanitarian challenges and facilitate the provision of assistance, experience including in the African continent has shown that 'encampment' policy has too often undermined the safety and security of the displaced. The Kampala Convention, however, acknowledges that under certain circumstances, states may find it appropriate and necessary to establish such settlements (Article 9(2)g). In general, however, states should 'respect and ensure the right to seek safety in another part of the state and to be protected against forcible return to or resettlement in any place where their life, safety, liberty and/or health would be at risk' (Article

38 In certain circumstances the freedom of movement and residence of IDPs may be restricted or limited Art 9(2)f.

9(2)e). In situations where camps exist, states shall maintain the civilian and humanitarian character of these areas. They are also required to prevent infiltrations of IDPs settlements or camps by armed groups, and ensure that the latter are disarmed and are separated from IDPs (Article 9(2) g). It is also stipulated that states take measures to ensure that IDPs are not engaged in any subversive activities.

Last but not least, humanitarian assistance needs to be conducted in a transparent manner with full compliance with humanitarian principles. IDPs should fully participate in decision-making processes regarding the regulation of humanitarian assistance (Article 9(2)k). In situations of displacement caused by projects, governments are required to seek alternative and feasible solutions by fully informing and engaging persons likely be affected by displacement (Article 10(2)). The suddenness of disasters may not provide time to undertake the requisite consultations with IDPs and relevant stakeholders. In principle even in disaster situations, governments are expected to inform and consult affected communities about their relocation (Article 11(2)).

Designing and implementing durable solutions

The Kampala Convention recognises all the three potential solutions for displacement – voluntary return, local integration and relocation.[39] Article 11 outlines broad principles which will guide the designing and implementing of durable solutions. These include free and informed decision making by IDPs, participation and consultation, safety and dignity of IDPs, sustainability of measures and international cooperation.

The Convention places the responsibility of states in a broader context. Beyond taking measures to ensure the dignity and safety of IDPs during durable solution process, authorities are required to promote and create satisfactory conditions for the achievement of durable solution (Article 11(1)). Several measures contribute to the achievement of this objective. One important step in this regard is the adoption of an effective national policy or legal framework (Preamble, para. 4). States are also responsible for promoting livelihoods programmes for IDPs (Article 3(1)k). Access to property is a crucial perquisite to promote durable solutions (Article 11(4)). As underscored under the Kampala Convention, governments need to facilitate the return of land belonging to IDPs. This will involve, among others, the establishment of 'mechanisms providing for simplified procedures where necessary, for resolving disputes relating to the property of internally displaced persons'. The words 'where necessary' underscore the constraints authorities often face as they facilitate IDPs' access to their property. When

39 See Brookings-Bern Project on Internal Displacement, When Displacement Ends: A Framework for Durable Solutions, June 2007.

return of property could not be achieved, IDPs should have access to fair compensation and other forms of reparations (Article 12(2)).

The Convention does not explicitly state whether 'communities with special attachment to land'[40] are entitled to compensation. It can safely be suggested however that Article 12, involving general procedures on compensation, will be applicable. There is no denying that determining the monetary value of a piece of land with cultural significance is complex. Disputes among communities may be triggered by ethnic tensions associated with contestation over land and other resources. When displaced populations particularly minorities, pastoralists and indigenous groups return to their original areas, they may find their property already occupied by others. They may also be subject to discrimination. Establishing culturally sensitive dispute settlement mechanisms will play a crucial role in ensuring a durable solution. Authorities are thus called upon to 'establish appropriate mechanisms providing for simplified procedures where necessary, for resolving disputes relating to the property of internally displaced persons'.[41] It goes without saying that dispute settlement mechanisms ought to take into account the unique challenges presented by ethnic conflicts.

Guaranteeing physical security is among the initial steps to be taken in order to ensure sustainability of co-existence between returnees and host communities. IDPs should be protected from violence. They should also be protected from land mines and other dangerous materials that pose a significant threat to their life and physical security. Unlike the Guiding Principles which specifically refer to the protection of IDPs from anti-personnel mines (Principle 10), similar provisions have not been incorporated in the Kampala Convention. Nevertheless, the importance of mine clearance and other unexploded ordinance has been recognised in other regional standards.[42] Underscoring the importance of post-conflict political processes for a durable solution, Article 3(2) e obliges states to 'endeavour to incorporate the relevant principles contained in this Convention into peace negotiations and agreements for the purpose of finding sustainable solutions to the problem of internal displacement'.

Facilitating international cooperation

International cooperation and assistance complement the roles and responsibilities of the state. It builds states' institutional capacity and normative standards in preventing forced displacement, addressing the challenges of

40 This concept generally refers to groups including pastoralists, minorities and indigenous communities whose relationship with nature in general and land in particular has significant cultural and historical resonance.

41 Art 11(4).

42 Kampala Declaration on Refugees, Returnees and Internally Displaced Persons in Africa, 23 October 2009, Ext/Assembly/AU/PA/Draft/Decl.(I) Rev.1. Available at: www.unhcr.org/refworld/docid/4af0623d2.html.

displacement and finding solutions (Article 4(3)). Some humanitarian goods may not be available domestically in sufficient quantity or authorities may lack sufficient technical expertise in certain areas for example in the development of national law and policies, registration and 'profiling' of IDPs, needs assessment, family tracing and reunification programmes and designing and monitoring services for populations affected by displacement.

An effective response to internal displacement evidently demands the involvement of other actors.[43] The Kampala Convention acknowledges the roles of actors such as the AU, international organisations and civil society organisations. The Convention itself is intended to serve as 'a legal framework for solidarity, cooperation, promotion of durable solutions and mutual support between the States Parties in order to combat displacement and address its consequences'. When a government lacks sufficient capacity to respond to internal displacement, it may request assistance and support from the international community. It shall establish an enabling environment and cooperate 'where appropriate, with ... international organizations and humanitarian agencies, civil society organizations, and other relevant actors'.[44] The responsibilities of government include facilitating unhindered and unimpeded passage of all relief consignments, and respecting humanitarian principles relating to the work of humanitarian organisations (Article 5). Governments are also obliged to 'respect, protect and not attack or otherwise harm humanitarian personnel and resources or other materials deployed for the assistance or benefit of IDPs' (Article 5(10)). This also includes the responsibility to refrain from diverting humanitarian material and use the same for any other purpose than what it was intended for.[45]

A request for international assistance can also be made, pursuant to Article 5(2) of the Convention, by the Conference of State Parties. IDPs have the right to request and receive humanitarian assistance from others (Article 5(9)). IDPs should achieve this without any fear of reprisal, prosecution or punishment.[46] International organisations, humanitarian agencies, civil society organisations and other relevant actors 'may offer their services to all those in need'.[47] The Convention does not expressly mention the 'rights' of

43 See Preamble. See also Arts 3, 5, 6 and 9.

44 Arts 5(7) & 9(3).

45 ICRC Commentary states: '[t]he obligation to protect relief consignments means, on the part of the Party concerned, that it must do its utmost to prevent such relief from being diverted from its legitimate destination, particularly by strictly punishing looting and any other diversion of relief and by providing clear and strict directives to the armed forces' (p. 828). See Art 7(5)h where it is provided that armed groups shall refrain from 'attacking or otherwise harming humanitarian personnel and resources or other materials deployed for the assistance or benefit of internally displaced persons and shall not destroy, confiscate or divert such materials'.

46 Article 5(9). Principle 3(2) of the UN Guiding Principles. See also Article 23 of the African Charter on the Rights and Welfare of the Child.

47 Ibid.

humanitarian organisations to offer support.[48] It falls short of specifying the formality any offer and acceptance of humanitarian assistance might take. This may raise some questions. Will denial by the state to provide access to these organisations amount to a violation of the Convention? States may prescribe technical arrangements under which humanitarian passage may be allowed (Article 5(7)). As the nature and type of assistance by international organisations will ultimately depend on prevailing circumstances on the ground, including the magnitude of the needs of the displaced population and the capacity of the state and other local actors, it is only reasonable that the state prescribes the types of assistance it requires from international organisations. It must be stated, however, that an unjustified denial of access may amount to a violation of the Convention. As is already stated, governments have the obligation to take positive measures 'to enable and facilitate the role of local and international organisations' (Article 5(7)).

It is certainly useful to examine the roles of monitoring mechanisms as an aspect of international cooperation. Unlike the Guiding Principles which do not sufficiently address how the various provisions would be implemented, the Kampala Convention incorporates specific provisions concerning the roles of relevant monitoring mechanisms. Of particular relevance are the roles of the Conference of Parties, the African Peer Review Mechanism and the African Commission on Human and Peoples' Rights. The roles of some of these institutions will be discussed in greater detail in the following sections. It suffices here to state that the Convention underscores the importance of these monitoring mechanisms. The Conference of Parties, for instance, is envisaged to have a very broad responsibility to 'monitor and review' implementation (Article 14(1)). The Convention, however, does not require a detailed reporting by member states to the Conference of Parties. Regarding regional human rights mechanisms, it is also stated that authorities should incorporate information in their initial and periodic reports under the African Charter on Human and Peoples' Rights, to the African Human and Peoples' Rights. Information on progress achieved and challenges faced in implementing the Convention need to be incorporated in reports submitted by governments under the African Peer Review Mechanism (Article 14(4)). Remarkably, the Convention does not identify the roles of the United Nations mechanisms, among which, include the United Nations Human Rights Council, treaty bodies and the Special Rapporteur on the Human Rights of Internally Displaced Persons. This may be considered as a limitation of the Convention in bridging the interaction between international-level mechanisms with regional processes. As will be shown in the following sections and the subsequent chapters, the

48 Principle 25 of the United Nations Guiding Principles however states that 'international humanitarian organizations and other appropriate actors have the right to offer their services in support of the internally displaced'.

importance of international mechanisms in supporting the implementation of the Convention cannot be undermined.

The human rights of internally displaced persons

The Kampala Convention conceives states' obligation as an overarching principle. It invokes the human rights of internally displaced persons through the prism of state obligation. It explicitly recognises key typologies of obligation well-recognised under international and regional human rights treaties.[49] Accordingly, it is stated that states have the obligation to *respect, protect and fulfil* the human rights of IDPs.[50] What this means is that, first, states should refrain from interfering in the exercise by IDPs of their rights and freedoms. Second, as will be shown in the following sections states assume the responsibility to guarantee that non-state actors do not interfere with the human rights of IDPs. In particular authorities have the responsibility to bring those who commit such violations into account (Article 3(1)g and h). The Convention prohibits arbitrary displacement (Article 4(4)). It declares that forced movement of populations by 'any act, event, or phenomenon' not justified under international law including human rights law is arbitrary (Article 4(4)h). Third, states are required to take active steps, such as developing national laws, allocating adequate resources and providing services, to enable IDPs to enjoy their full human rights.

The Convention – while underscoring the general framework of State obligation – recognises 'the inherent rights of internally displaced persons' (Preamble, para. 10). IDPs are entitled to the protection of all human rights enjoyed by nationals or habitual residents of the country in which they are displaced. They have the right to humane treatment, equality before the law and protection from discrimination, to freely move and choose their residence, access their individual and collective property, and to seek asylum in third countries.[51] The right of IDPs to peacefully request assistance and protection is also recognised.[52] The Convention recognises the rights of IDPs who are displaced in their country of nationality, to vote and participate in public affairs.[53] Though the Convention does not declare IDPs' right to the

49 General Comments of the Committee on Economic, Social and Cultural Rights and, for example, *Social and Economic Rights Action Centre and Centre for Economic and Social Rights v. Nigeria*, African Commission on Human and Peoples' Rights, Communication No. 155/96, October 2001.

50 Arts 4(1) and 3(1)d.

51 Art 20(1) states: 'No provision in this Convention shall be interpreted as affecting or undermining the right of internally displaced persons to seek and be granted asylum within the framework of the African Charter on Human and Peoples' Rights'. See also Art 3(1)d, Art 9(2)f and Art 9(2)i.

52 Art 5(9).

53 Art 9(2)l. citing the lack of reference under international humanitarian law to the right of public participation and the right to vote, the explicit incorporation of these rights in the Guiding Principles has been considered an important development. See Note 24 above, 57.

family, it stipulates for the obligation of the state to 'take necessary measures, including the establishment of specialized mechanisms, to trace and reunify families separated during displacement and otherwise facilitate the re-establishment of family ties'.[54] It guarantees IDPs' right to seek safety in another part of the state and to be protected against forcible return or resettlement in any place where their life, safety, liberty and/or health will be at risk (Article 9(2)e). It should be noted that the latter, considered as corollary to the principle of voluntary return, does not have any explicit precedent in international human rights law or refugee law.[55]

As is provided under Article 3(1) authorities shall prevent political, economic, social and cultural exclusion of persons, based on social identity, religion or political opinion, which may lead to their displacement. Preventive measures to address the threats of social, economic and cultural exclusion of populations are called for (Article 3(1)b). During displacement, IDPs' access to basic services requires concrete actions by authorities (Article 3(1) b). These 'basic needs' include access to social services, education, sanitation, shelter, health and food which states should provide 'to the fullest extent practicable and with the least possible delay' (Article 9(2)b).

Discrimination against IDPs based on their status is also prohibited.[56] In its General Comment No. 20, issued on 2 July 2009, the United Nations Committee on Social, Economic and Cultural Rights states that the fulfilment of rights under the International Covenant on Social, Economic and Cultural Rights should not be determined based on, among others, whether a person is internally displaced or not.[57] This non-discrimination principle is relevant not only with respect to treatment of displaced persons *vis-a-vis* other groups but also in relation to how the various groups within the displaced population are treated. Authorities are, therefore, obliged to respect, protect and fulfil the human rights of IDPs without any forms of discrimination (Preamble, para. 12). This is of a particular importance to the protection of vulnerable groups including women, children, the elderly, persons with disabilities and other vulnerable groups (Article 13(4)). The right of women to have access to documentation in their own names is recognised, for instance (Article 13(4)).

Several of the key international and regional human rights instruments relevant to the protection of and assistance to IDPs have been recognised.[58]

54 Art 9(2)h. A comparison can be made with Principle 17 of the Guiding Principles where a detailed provision on the right to the family and the responsibility of the state is provided for.

55 Note 8 above, 66.

56 Art 9(1)a. See Principle 1(1).

57 Committee on Social, Economic and Cultural Rights, General Comment No. 20, 2 July 2009, E/C. 12/GC/12.

58 These include: the 1948 Universal Declaration on Human Rights, the 1948 Convention on the Prevention and Punishment of the Crimes of Genocide, the 1949 Geneva Conventions and the 1977 Additional Protocols, the 1951 United Nations Convention

These instruments can certainly be used as a tool for interpreting the Convention.[59] It must be noted that the Convention itself notes that its provisions should not be interpreted as affecting the right to seek asylum as provided for under the African Charter on Human and Peoples' Rights and the 1951 Refugee Convention (Article 20(1)). It also means that though some aspects of human rights have not been specifically mentioned in the Convention,[60] their application can still be invoked. For instance, despite the lack of reference to the right to employment in the Convention,[61] IDPs and their representatives can invoke the right to exercise a freely chosen economic activity requesting the state concerned to fulfil conditions required for their gainful employment. At the minimum, IDPs shall not be discriminated against while seeking access to a just and favourable condition of work.[62]

One significant problem facing the implementation of human rights in the context of internal displacement has been that, in certain situations of internal displacement, a number of human rights principles are either derogable or can be limited or restricted. In relation to the latter, it is provided that no reservation that is incompatible with the purpose and object of the Convention can be entered into by States (Article 21). The Convention does not have a specific provision dealing with how member states can derogate from human rights principles. Neither does the African Charter on Human and Peoples' Rights incorporate a derogation clause.[63] This may raise the

Relating to the Status of Refugees, the 1949 Convention Relating to the Specific Problem of Refugee Protection in Africa, the 1979 Convention on the Elimination of All Forms of Discrimination against Women, the 1981 African Charter on Human and Peoples Rights and the 2003 Protocol to the African Charter on Human and Peoples' Rights on the Rights of Women in Africa, and the 1990 African Charter on the Rights and Welfare of the Child.

59 See Art 20(2). It is further stated that 'it shall in no way be understood, construed or interpreted as restricting, modifying or impeding existing protection under any of the instruments mentioned herein'.

60 See Andrew Solomon, Reintroducing the African Union Convention on the Protection and Assistance of Internally Displaced Persons, 17 February 2010. Available at: www.brookings.edu/articles/2010/0217_african_union_solomon.aspx?rssid=solomona.

61 In contrast, the Guiding Principles states that IDPs shall enjoy, without any discrimination on the basis of their being displaced, 'the right to seek freely opportunities for employment and to participate equally in economic activities' (Principle 22(2)b).

62 See Art 23 of UDHR, 5(e) I of CERD, 6 & 7 of CESCR and 15 of ACHPR.

63 The ACHPR held in a number of occasions that the African Charter does not allow states to derogate from human rights obligations incorporated under the instrument. See *Commission Nationale des Droits de l'Homme et des Libertes v. Chad*, The African Commission, Comm. No. 74/92 (1995), para. 21; *Amnesty International and Others v. Sudan*, The African Commission, Comm. No; 48/90, 50/91, 52/91, 89/93 (1999), para. 42; *Media Rights Agenda and Others v. Nigeria*, The African Commission, Comm. Nos. 105/93, 128/94, 130/94 and 152/96 (1998), para. 67. For criticisms of the exclusion of derogation clause from the Charter, see Rachel Murray, *The African Commission on Human and Peoples' Rights and International Law* (Oxford-Portland Oregon: 2000), p.123.

question of whether a member state can lawfully derogate from their obligation. The answer to this question is in the affirmative. Even in the absence of a derogation clause, international law permits states to derogate from human rights obligation under certain conditions. More specifically it is suggested that principles of necessity, forced majeure, fundamental changes in circumstances may justify derogations. The Convention itself, under Article 7(2), clearly states: 'nothing in this Convention shall be invoked for the purpose of affecting the sovereignty of a State or the responsibility of the government, by all legitimate means, to maintain or re-establish law and order in the State or to defend the national unity and territorial integrity of the State'.

Generally speaking, international human rights treaties require the declaration of public emergency and notification to other member states as procedural requirements for derogation.[64] The Human Rights Committee has further elaborated the procedures applicable with respect to derogability in its General Comment No. 29 dealing with Article 4. Accordingly, it was stated by the Committee that derogation measures: (a) should be proportional, exceptional and temporary, (b) should not involve discrimination on prohibited grounds, (c) should not justify international crimes, (d) be consistent with the obligation of the state, (d) be consistent with the fundamental principle of legality and due process, and (e) should not result in violations of those rights identified as non-derogable or are reflections of peremptory norms.[65] It is also stated that derogation measures shall not undermine the obligation of states under other legal instruments and should take into account legal developments, particularly those relating to emergency situations.[66] In this respect, it is interesting to note that General Comment No. 29 cites the Guiding Principles as one element of these developments.[67]

The Kampala Convention's provision on arbitrary displacement gives an indication of which state's measures cannot be justified as derogation measures. These include international crimes such as genocide, war crimes and crimes against humanity; racial discrimination; mass displacement of individuals during armed conflicts which are not justified by the security of civilians involved or by the imperative of military necessity; and intentional use of displacement as a means of warfare; collective punishment (Article 3).

That some rights are non-derogable does not mean that no limitation or restriction is ever justified. To the contrary, both under international and regional human rights law, restrictions on the exercise of certain rights and freedoms may be justified on certain grounds such as public order, public health, public morals and the rights and reputation of others.[68] Such

64 See Art 4 of ICCPR.

65 See Human Rights Committee, General Comment No. 29 on Article 4 (States of Emergency), CCPR/21/Rev.1/Add.11, 31 August 2001.

66 Ibid., para. 10.

67 Ibid., note 6.

68 See Art 18(3) of ICSECR; Arts 18 & 19 of ICCP; and Art 27(2) of the African Charter.

restrictions, however, shall be provided for by law and be proportional and necessary in nature (Article 19(3)). The much-criticised limitation clause of the African Charter on Human and Peoples' Rights not only recognises that many of the rights and freedoms incorporated in the Charter can be limited based on domestic law, but also declares that 'the rights and freedoms of each individual shall be exercised with due regard to the rights of others, collective security, morality and common interest' (Article 27(2)). In the same manner the Kampala Convention states, for example, that exception to the right to freedom of movement and choice of residence of IDPs should be 'necessary, justified and proportionate to the requirements of ensuring security for internally displaced persons or maintaining public security, public order and public health' (Article 9(2) f). In the context of forced evacuation which may be carried out during an emergency, the Convention stipulates that state measures shall be considered as arbitrary unless the latter is required in the context of 'the health and safety of those affected' (Article 4(4) f). It is also stated that states' measures which result in the displacement of these populations may only be justified by a compelling and overriding public interest (Article 4(5)).

Some of the African regional instruments are unique in their recognition of duties of individuals. The African Charter on Human and Peoples' Rights provides for 'duties' which individuals owe to the 'family and society, the state and other legally recognised communities' (Article 27(1)). These duties are recognised in the Kampala Convention which, in its Article 20(4), stipulates that its provisions shall be without prejudice to the duties of IDPs under the Charter. These provisions were fiercely criticised for introducing a new and impractical concept to the regional discourse of human rights.[69] It was also argued that the concept of duties may be used to reinforce the power of the state against individual citizens and encourage oppressive family values which undermine the rights and freedoms of women. It can safely be stated that the realisation of human rights of IDPs is also very vague.

Protection of vulnerable groups

The Kampala Convention provides specific treatment for vulnerable groups. It covers persons such as displaced women, victims of sexual violence and other abuses, separated and unaccompanied children, the elderly, female heads of household, persons with disabilities, expectant women, mothers with young children, communities with special attachment to land and persons with communicable diseases.[70] This is not an exhaustive list but only an indication of the types of persons with specific vulnerabilities. Compared

69 Makau Mutua, 'The Banjul Charter and African Cultural Fingerprint: An Evaluation of the Language of Duties', *Virginia Journal of International Law* 35(1995): 339–80.

70 Arts 9, 4(5) and 11(5).

to the Guiding Principles, the Kampala Convention appears to be more elaborate.[71] Beyond general rules applicable to all vulnerable groups, the Convention provides detailed norms applicable to persons with vulnerabilities. For example, it incorporates provisions on the protection of women from discrimination and sexual violence (Article 9(2)a). It commits states to refrain from any form of gender-based violence, namely, rape, enforced prostitution, sexual exploitation, harmful practices, slavery, recruitment of children, forced labour and human trafficking and smuggling (Article 9(2) d). Authorities are required to provide sexual reproductive services and psychosocial support for survivors (Article 9(2)c). The Convention acknowledges the impact of harmful practices on displaced women and girls. IDP women and girls are often affected by these practices, particularly FGM (Article 4(4)e). As has been underlined on several occasions the responsibility towards the displaced and the most vulnerable is not limited to states. The Convention, thus, prohibits forcible recruitment, kidnapping, abduction, hostage taking, sexual slavery and trafficking of women by armed groups (Article 7(5)f). Armed groups, which have committed the aforementioned violations, should be criminally liable (Article 7(4)).

The Kampala Convention proffers special protection to vulnerable children including orphans, unaccompanied minors and those affected by armed conflicts.[72] It provides that 'separated and unaccompanied children shall have equal rights to obtain such necessary identity documents and shall have the right to have such documentation issued in their own names' (Article 13(h)). Re-establishing links with family members is often an urgent need. States, therefore, need to establish special mechanisms in order to facilitate the reunification of children with their families (Article 9(2) h). Armed groups are prohibited from 'recruiting children or requiring or permitting them to take part in hostilities under any circumstances' (Article 7(5) e). The Convention reaffirms the 1990 African Charter on the Rights and Welfare of the Child.[73] It is provided that the implementation of the Convention shall not restrict, modify or impede the Charter and any other international or regional human rights instruments (Article 20(2)). This means that, for example, IDPs are entitled to lodge their complaints with the African Commission on Human and Peoples' Rights or the African Court of Justice and Human Rights, or any other competent international body (Article 20(3)). Relevant provisions of the Convention do not expressly mention the role of the African Committee on the Rights and Welfare of the Child. The word 'international' underscores a broader reach of the provision including the roles of regional human rights mechanisms on the right of the child. It

71 Principle 4 makes an explicit reference only to the following categories of vulnerable persons: children especially unaccompanied minors, expectant mothers, mothers with young children, female heads of household, persons with disabilities and the elderly.

72 See Arts 7(5)e and 9(2)c.

73 OAU Doc. CAB/LEC/24.9 (1990), entered into force, 29 November 1999.

can be submitted that the Convention's reference to the Charter is a sufficient legal basis for this interpretation. The Committee is established by the same Charter and its mandate includes consideration of communications based on the Charter and inspiration from international human rights law (Article 46). It must be highlighted that the Charter stipulates several provisions which are particularly relevant to the protection of children affected by armed conflicts (Article 11(3)).

As has already been noted the Convention guarantees the specific protection of those who are known as 'communities with special attachment to and dependency on land' – a category of persons which includes, among others, indigenous and pastoral groups. States have the primary responsibility to prevent the displacement of these groups (Article 4(5)). While designing and implementing durable solutions, states are obligated to take measures in order to restore the land of these communities. It should be underlined that the concept of 'indigeneity' often evokes intense emotions among diplomats and government representatives in many African countries. This was, for instance, prominently expressed during the negotiation of the UN Declaration on the Rights of Indigenous Groups where diplomats from these countries attempted to block consensus on several occasions.[74] Despite the controversy often associated with the concept, however, the African Commission on Human and Peoples' Rights is making headway in its jurisprudence. In the *Endrois's* decision, for example, the Commission creatively interpreted the African Charter with the aim of expanding the application of its provisions regarding indigenous groups in Kenya.[75] The Commission has also established the Expert Working Group on the Rights of Indigenous Populations in Africa tasked with the responsibility to monitor and study progress in this area.[76]

The roles of non-state actors

Several articles in the Convention provide for 'the respective obligations, responsibilities and roles of armed groups, non-state actors and other relevant actors including civil society organizations' (Article 2(e)).[77] Non-state actors are broadly defined as 'private actors who are not public officials of the

74 See the Advisory Opinion on the African Commission on Human and Peoples' Rights on the UN Declaration on the Rights of Indigenous Peoples, adopted during the 41st Session of the African Commission on Human and Peoples' Rights, May 2007.

75 See Communication 276/2003 – Centre for Minority Rights Development (Kenya) and Minority Rights Group International on behalf of *Endorois Welfare Council v. Kenya*.

76 Report of the African Commission's Working Group of Experts, submitted in accordance with the Resolution on the Rights of Indigenous Populations/Communities in Africa, adopted by the African Commission on Human and Peoples' Rights at its 28th Ordinary Session (2003). Resolution on the Composition and Renewal of the Mandate of the Working Group on Indigenous Populations/Communities in Africa, December 2005.

77 See Articles 2(e). See Principle 2(2).

State, including other armed groups not referred to in Article 1(d) above, and whose acts cannot be officially attributed to the state'. The Convention proffers a specific definition for armed groups. Accordingly armed groups are defined as 'dissident armed forces or other organized armed groups that are distinct from the armed forces of the state' (Article 1(d)). Article 3 also mentions 'the accountability' of multinational companies and private military or security companies.

The Convention examines the responsibility of non-state actors within the framework of states' responsibility. The framework of states' obligation cannot be isolated from the roles and responsibilities of non-state actors.[78] This means that, among others, states assume the responsibility of ensuring the accountability of non-state actors in protecting IDPs. However, it should be underscored that non-state actors do assume their own obligations towards IDPs. They are also obligated to refrain from hampering a neutral and impartial provision of humanitarian assistance (Article 7) and are required to cooperate with international humanitarian organisations.

The Convention's provisions covering individual criminal responsibility are relevant in ensuring accountability for unlawful actions taken by individuals. Certain situations where actions taken by non-state actors may result in legal consequences for which the state assumes responsibility have also been covered. The Convention also clarifies the application of state responsibility in situations such as climate change, natural disasters and the practise of harmful traditional practices where linking state responsibility to any clear element of state action or omission is evidently complex.

The Kampala Convention incorporates several provisions dealing with the obligation of armed groups. Article 7 prohibits armed groups from carrying out arbitrary displacement; denying IDPs' access to basic services; restricting the freedom of movement of IDPs; separating family members; recruiting children or requiring or permitting them to take part in hostilities; kidnapping, abducting or taking hostage; engaging in sexual slavery and trafficking in persons especially women and children; impeding humanitarian assistance and passage of relief consignments, equipment and personnel to IDPs; and attacking or otherwise harming humanitarian personnel and resources or other materials deployed for the assistance or benefit of IDPs and destroying, confiscating or diverting such materials; and undermining the civilian and humanitarian character of the places where IDPs are located. Armed groups will be held criminally liable for their acts which violate the rights of IDPs both under national and international law (Article 7(3)).

The Convention also deals with the accountability of private military and security companies. States assume the responsibility of ensuring 'the accountability of non-State actors concerned, including multinational companies and

78 Principles 2 and 5 of the UN Guiding Principles make reference to *de facto* authorities, groups and individuals.

private military or security companies, for acts of arbitrary displacement or complicity in such acts' (Article 3(1) h). Whereas the reference to the role of private military or security actors is innovative, the roles of these actors in forced displacement and their specific responsibilities has not been fully elaborated under the Convention.

Negotiators expressed concern that regulating the roles and responsibilities of armed groups may imply a granting of a distinct legal status to these groups. This led to the inclusion of Article 7(1) which stipulates:

> that relevant article in the Convention should not be interpreted in giving or legitimizing the status of armed groups. Furthermore it is stated that the application of the Convention should not be prejudicial to the criminal responsibility of armed group members.
>
> (Article 7(1))

Humanitarian organisations

Notwithstanding the long-standing debate concerning the respective roles of international organisations, the Kampala Convention proffers 'legitimacy' to their roles in the context of internal displacement. It explicitly acknowledges the responsibilities of the United Nations as well as other international humanitarian organisations (Article 5(3)). It recognises both the inter-agency activities undertaken by the UN on behalf of IDPs and the particular protection expertise of individual organisations, particularly the Office of the United Nations High Commissioner for Refugees and that of the International Committee of the Red Cross (Preamble, para. 12). As was discussed in previous chapters, both organisations provided crucial support to the African Union regarding the development of the Convention. What is provided under the Convention is evidently a much stronger endorsement of the roles of the aforementioned organisations than what was incorporated under Principle 27 of the Guiding Principles. It is also stated that international organisations should, while implementing their activities, respect international law and the human rights of IDPs. States are responsible for putting into place mechanisms which will monitor or help determine the effectiveness of humanitarian assistance provided to IDPs (Article 9(2) m). Such monitoring and evaluation mechanisms need to take into account existing tools and established practices including the Sphere Standards.[79]

79 Ibid., Art 1(q) defines 'Sphere standards' as 'standards for monitoring and evaluating the impact and effectiveness of humanitarian assistance'. The Sphere Standards (The Sphere Handbook: Humanitarian Charter and Minimum Standards in Humanitarian Response, 2011 edition) are available at: www.sphereproject.org/handbook/.

Civil society organisations (CSOs)

One of the innovations of the Kampala Convention is the extent to which it vividly outlines the roles and responsibilities of CSOs. Several provisions explicitly mention the role of CSOs.[80] States may seek the cooperation of civil society actors and they shall cooperate with them when state resources are inadequate. Governments are required to designate an authority which will cooperate with relevant actors including civil society organisations. CSOs on their part are required to respect the Convention. These obligations include respecting the human rights of IDPs,[81] conducting their activities in full compliance with international law and the law of the country concerned, and complying with humanitarian principles such as impartiality, neutrality, impartiality and independence.

The African Union

The African Union plays crucial roles in implementing regional 'measures to prevent or mitigate, prohibit and eliminate root causes of internal displacement as well as provide for durable solutions' (Article 2(a)). Several provisions provide for respect for the mandate and the responsibility of the African Union (Article 5(3)). The Kampala Convention also stipulates that the AU shall: (a) cooperate with States, international organisations, humanitarian organisations and civic society organisations and others with respect to the protection and assistance of internally displaced persons; (b) coordinate the mobilisation of resources; (c) collaborate and share information with the African Commission on Human and Peoples' Rights and specifically the Special Rapporteur on the Rights of Refugees, Returnees, IDPs and Asylum Seekers; and (d) strengthen its institutional framework and capacity to deal with the protection and assistance of IDPs.

During the drafting stage, the draft Convention had included provisions authorising the AU to carry out certain specific interventions in order to address the crisis of internal displacement within a member state. This would have significantly expanded the authority of the AU to undertake intervention to deal with the problem of internal displacement. This approach, however, was challenged by those who argued that the Convention cannot amend or revise the Constitutive Act where interventions, particularly those related to enforcement actions by the African Union, are restricted to massive and systematic violations of human rights violations which are linked to 'genocide, war crimes and crimes against humanity'. Accordingly, it is now stated in Article 8(1) that the AU shall have the right to intervene in a member state pursuant to a decision by the Assembly of the African Union

80 Preamble and Arts 2(e), 3(2) b, 4(3), 5(6), 5(7), 8(3)c, 8(3)d, 9(3) and 11(3).

81 Principle 27(1) stipulates that humanitarian organisations and agencies shall give due regard to the human rights of IDPs.

in the context of 'war crimes, genocide and crimes against humanity'. Member states can also request the intervention of the African Union in line with relevant provisions of the African Union and, thus, contribute to the creation of favourable conditions for finding durable solutions for the problem of internal displacement (Article 8(2)).

Private and multinational companies

The activities of private companies and their impact on forced displacement cannot be underestimated. Some projects run by these institutions may generate displacement. Moreover, Article 4(4)h states that land encroachment by companies could also hinder durable solutions. The Kampala Convention innovatively attempts to address this by providing for state regulation and accountability. According to Article 3(1) states have a responsibility to ensure the accountability, among others, of private and multinational companies 'for acts of arbitrary displacement or complicity in such acts'. The Convention pays particular attention to the roles of private actors involved in certain investments; for instance, in 'the exploration and exploitation of economic and natural resources leading to displacement' (Article 3(1)i). The strong approach on accountability endorsed above contrasts with Article 10 – dealing specifically with project-induced displacement – where states' responsibility is limited to taking measures that are intended to ensure that 'stakeholders' explore feasible alternatives, inform and consult IDPs in decision-making processes and carry out impact assessment.

Accountability for crimes

Two important issues need to be raised with respect to the Convention's provisions concerning accountability to violations. The first relates to the obligations of the states to ensure the criminalisation of certain acts committed against IDPs in violation of the Convention. The second pertains to IDPs themselves where any attempt to manipulate 'one's status of being an IDP' as a shield against criminal prosecution is prohibited. With respect to criminalisation, the state is required to 'ensure individual responsibility for acts of arbitrary displacement, in accordance with applicable domestic and international criminal law' (Article 3(1)g). States will do so principally through the function of their national criminal law system. They shall punish by law acts arising in situations of internal displacement, particularly those that may amount to grave violations such as genocide, war crimes and crimes against humanity (Article 4(4)h).

Despite its reference to international criminal law, the Convention cites neither the statute of the ICC nor any other specific legal instrument which may be considered as forming the corpus of international criminal law. However, the Convention on numerous occasions refers to 'international law'. It is, therefore, legitimate to take inspiration from the broader spectrum of international law to determine when arbitrary displacement is linked with these grave crimes. In this respect, it should be noted that the Genocide Convention's scope of genocide may involve any act of forcible 'transfer of children of the group to another group' committed with the intent to 'destroy, in whole or in part, a national, ethnical, racial or religious group'.[82] According to Article 7(1) of the Statute of the International Criminal Courts, crimes against humanity will include deportation or forcible transfer of population 'when committed as part of a widespread or systematic attack directed against any civilian population, with knowledge of the attack'. For the purpose of the relevant provision of the ICC statute, 'deportation or forced transfer of population' is defined as 'forced displacement of the persons concerned by expulsion or other coercive acts from the area in which they are lawfully present, without grounds permitted under international law' (Article 4(4)h). A similar provision has been provided for under Article 5 of the ICTY Statute. The ICC statute also defines war crimes as constituting violations considered grave breaches of the 1949 Geneva Conventions including unlawful deportations (Article 8(2)(a) vii). On the other hand 'displacement of civilian population in non-international armed conflicts may amount to war crimes' (Article 8(2)(e) viii).

Remedies and compensation

Persons affected by internal displacement should have access to remedies (Article 12(1)). The Convention does not define remedies but provides some examples (Article 12). The responsibility of states to provide reparation or compensation is not necessarily linked to their involvement or that of their agents in any wrongful or unlawful acts. For instance, 'a State Party shall be liable to make reparation to internally displaced persons for damage when such a State Party refrains from protecting and assisting internally displaced persons in the event of natural disasters'. It is also important to underscore that beneficiaries of remedies under Article 12 are not just IDPs but 'persons affected by displacement'. We know too well that populations might be 'affected' by displacement in different ways. Not all displaced persons are, thus, directly affected by the conflict or suffer similar harm. Some may choose to flee in anticipation of effects of their displacement. One will, however, be hard pressed to think of situations where IDPs do not experience one form of harm or another.

States can promote IDPs' access to remedies through their national or legal frameworks. These frameworks help 'establish an effective legal framework to provide just and fair compensation and other forms of reparations, where appropriate, to internally displaced persons for damage incurred as a result of displacement, in accordance with international standards' (Article

82 Art II. See also Art 4(2)e of the Statute of ICTY.

12(2)). Any forms of remedy provided to IDPs and 'persons affected by internal displacement' should be 'fair and just' and should comply with international standards. The phrase 'where appropriate' underlines that the state may determine the scope and nature of the remedies available to IDPs. Some individuals may flee their homes or habitual residences as a result of or in order to avoid the effects of factors causing the displacement.

National legal and policy frameworks on remedies need to take into account regional human rights jurisprudence. For instance, key African regional human rights instruments guarantee remedies for violations of human rights.[83] IDPs can avail themselves of existing regional human rights mechanisms such as the African Commission on Human and Peoples' Rights to remedies (Article 20(2)). It is, however, important to restate that the Kampala Convention casts the issue of remedies in a broader objective of achieving durable solutions. Moreover, remedies are provided 'where appropriate' (Article 12(2)). During their experience of displacement, IDPs lose their land, cattle, crops and other movable property. They might have experienced the destruction of their property or, discovered upon their return that their house or land has been occupied by other people. The question of compensation arises in situations when original property is lost, or resituating the property to its original owner becomes impossible. In this context, the reference to the right to property in the African Charter on Human and Peoples' Rights is crucial (Article 14).

Conclusion

The Kampala Convention is a pioneering treaty which transforms existing international soft law concerning internal displacement (i.e. the UN Guiding Principles) into a set of binding norms. This is clearly seen in the Convention's extensive borrowing of norms from the Guiding Principles. But the Convention also exhibits innovations. The 'state responsibility' model followed by the Kampala Convention differs from the 'needs-based' approach pursued by the Guiding Principles. It could be argued that this difference in approaches may reinforce the complementarity between the UN Guiding Principles. The content of the Convention lays bare remarkable resemblance with existing norms found in international human rights, international humanitarian and refugee law. As a regional human rights instrument, it also widely borrows concepts from the AU's regional treaties and human rights instruments. Its provision on 'regional humanitarian intervention' and the responsibility of the African Union, for example, are drawn from AU's Constitutive Act. Though prominent 'new' doctrines such as the

83 See Art 25 of the Protocol on the Rights of Women in Africa. It is provided that states shall undertake to provide appropriate remedies to any women whose rights and freedoms are violated based on determination to be made by competent judicial, administrative or legislative authorities.

responsibility to protect did not secure any explicit recognition in the treaty, it may be argued that it addresses some of the elements of the concept. Specific provisions exclusively dealing with the problem of displacement arising in the context of armed conflict and development projects have also been incorporated. Article 7, dealing with the protection of displaced persons during armed conflicts, is instructive in that, among others, it provides for the primacy of international humanitarian law for the interpretation of the Convention's provisions relating to armed conflicts. This is designed to specifically address the fear expressed by some that regional codification of international humanitarian law may dilute or weaken international protection as provided for under international human rights law.

The Kampala Convention is comprehensive in its objectives, scope and substance. In a total of 23 articles, it covers all protection and assistance issues arising prior to displacement, during displacement and in the context of durable solutions. It deals with internal displacement caused by various well-known factors, namely, conflicts, natural and man-made disasters including climate change, human rights violations, and generalised violence. The Convention deals with provisions of humanitarian and material assistance to victims of displacement. It also provides for an unimpeded and unrestricted passage of humanitarian goods, assistance and consignments.

The Convention's definition of IDPs is consistent with that which is proffered by the UN Guiding Principles. It also provides for a broad definition movement of populations which may be considered as arbitrary. Accordingly arbitrary displacement includes: (a) displacement caused by human rights violations and generalised violence, racial discrimination or other similar practices aimed at/or resulting in altering the ethnic, religious or racial composition of the population; (b) mass displacement of civilians not justified by the security of civilian populations or imperatives of military necessity; (c) the use of displacement as a method of warfare; (d) forced evacuation not required for the safety or health of individuals concerned; and (e) using displacement as collective punishment. The Convention also considers as arbitrary any forms of 'displacement caused by any act, event, factor, or phenomenon of comparable gravity to all of the above and which is not justified under international law, including human rights and international humanitarian law' (Article 4(4)h).

Though the Convention's conceptualisation of arbitrary displacement is considerably broad, it recognises that under certain circumstances displacement may become unavoidable. In certain contexts, be it during the construction of development projects, conduct of armed conflicts or disaster response, the action of the state may result in some forms of permissible displacement. In these circumstances, however, states should take reasonable and proportional measures which take into account the rights and interests of those who are displaced. Numerous provisions of the Convention stipulate for conditions under which these measures can legitimately be undertaken. In the same token, they also provide conditions in which states' measures may amount to unlawful actions resulting in individual criminal liability and responsibility to indemnify.

In a direct shift in approach from the Guiding Principles which focuses on identifying the entitlements and rights of internally displaced persons, the Convention gives considerable attention to the elaboration of the obligations of states. This emphasis positions the Convention well among traditional human rights instruments wherein the responsibility of implementing obligation is primarily owed by the state. One possible advantage of this approach is that it complements the Guiding Principles. It also allays the fear that specialised legal instruments on IDPs run a risk of granting a distinct and separate legal status. Rather than creating new rights, 'the responsibility of states' model simply clarifies the application of obligations under existing international and regional human rights instrument. Several of the Convention's provisions outline the obligation and responsibility of the state in preventing displacement, providing protection and assistance to IDPs during displacement and ensuring durable solutions. Its scope and reach is further expanded in two directions. First, it seeks to strike a balance between its emphasis on state responsibility on the one hand and the entitlements and rights of IDPs on the other. This means that the protection and assistance needs of IDPs and their rights in having these needs met ought to be covered. A number of provisions elaborating on the rights of IDPs particularly those most vulnerable, namely, women, children, the elderly and communities with special attachment to land are therefore incorporated. The Convention guarantees that its application shall be non-prejudicial to the fulfilment of the human rights of persons incorporated under other regional and international human rights instrument including the right of IDPs to access effective remedies.

The Kampala Convention acknowledges the tension between the right to seek asylum on the one hand, and the protection of IDPs on the other. It provides that the enforcement and application of the Convention shall not be prejudicial to the right of individuals to seek asylum abroad as stipulated for under the African Charter on Human and Peoples' Rights, the 1951 Refugee Convention and the 1969 OAU Convention. While this approach creates the impression that a separate and distinct legal category is being created and established, the Convention is emphatic in that its aim is not to create or establish a separate and distinct legal status. The Convention's attempt to expand protection and assistance given to IDPs also to what are considered as 'host communities' can be cited as an example of this approach.

The Convention also goes beyond state responsibility by outlining the responsibility of non-state actors including international organisations, humanitarian agencies, regional organisations and civil society. Its provisions expressly recognise the role and responsibility of international organisations such as UNHCR and ICRC. This recognition will be instrumental in fostering a smooth relationship between affected states from the African continent and relevant international organisations in their responsibility towards the protection and assistance of displaced persons. This is important in light of reservations often invoked by states including those from the African region with respect to the mandate of these organisations concerning internal displacement.

6 Implementation and its challenges

Introduction

More than half a decade has passed since the African region firmly positioned itself as a pioneer in the protection of IDPs by adopting the first ever binding regional treaty on internal displacement. As of January 2016, 25 states have ratified the instrument while 40 states have become signatories.[1] Manifesting the mismatch between good intentions by governments on the one hand and the situation of IDPs on the other, African countries witnessed a significant surge in the number of those uprooted from their homes and livelihoods, mainly as a result of armed conflicts and violence. As of the end of 2015, there were 40.8 million IDPs worldwide, out of which 11.9 million are in Sub-Sahara Africa. This gives the continent the unenviable position of being a host to the largest number of IDPs.[2] Nigeria, the Democratic Republic of Congo and South Sudan host some of the largest numbers of IDPs in Africa. Achieving durable solutions for many displacement situations in several countries remains elusive due to the absence of stability, social services, compensation schemes, livelihood opportunities and resources.

National authorities have the primary responsibility to provide protection of and assistance to IDPs. However, governments are either the cause of displacement in the first place or lack the capacity and resources to effectively respond to internal displacement. In many African countries access to IDPs is significantly hampered due to either government's restrictive measures, such as in the case of Eritrea and Sudan or to insecurity and deliberate attack

1 The following countries have deposited their ratification at the AU Commission in Addis Ababa: Angola, Benin, Burkina Faso, Central African Republic, Chad, Congo, Cote d'Ivoire, Djibouti, Gabon, Gambia, Guinea Bissau, Lesotho, Malawi, Mali, Mauritania, Niger, Nigeria, Rwanda, Sahrawi Arab Democratic Republic, Sierra Leone, Swaziland, Togo, Uganda, Zambia and Zimbabwe. The latest information on the status of ratification is available at: http://au.int/en/sites/default/files/Convention_on_IDPs.pdf.

2 Internal Displacement Monitoring Centre, 2015, Global Report on Internal Displacement 2016. Available at www.internal-displacement.org/assets/publications/2016/2016-global-report-internal-displacement-IDMC.pdf.'

against humanitarian actors in Somalia, DRC and Sudan.[3] The Special Rapporteur of the African Commission on Human and Peoples' Rights notes 'unless African States address the gap between the assumption of international legal obligations, their implementation and domestication, the adoption of additional instruments will not alleviate human rights violations, including those affecting internally displaced persons'.[4] The role of regional and international actors is particularly important in situations where authorities lack the necessary capacity or fail to muster the political will required to respond effectively.

This chapter tackles the question of how national authorities may effectively fulfil their obligation under the Kampala Convention by incorporating the Convention into national law and taking concrete steps to implement such a national framework. It discusses the roles and limitations of non-state actors including regional and international institutions, particularly in situations when the state lacks the capacity and the political will to carry out decisive action on behalf of IDPs. Legal reform and policy development and institutional coordination often present complex challenges.

Ratification

The Convention entered into force on 6 December 2012, 30 days after Swaziland deposited its instrument of ratification on 6 November 2014 as provided in Article 17(1). The ratification of the Convention took off with a slow start. Only 17 states signed the Convention at the Special Summit held in Kampala, Uganda in 2009; a mere 32 per cent of the total members of the African Union. By July 2012, 36 states had become signatories to the Convention, 18 of them doing so in the period after the Summit. What explains the overall low level of signature during the Summit? Organisers of the Summit had pointed out that several participating delegations did not join the meeting having the required 'full powers'.[5] However, this explanation appears hardly convincing. Governments were fully aware that the meeting represented the culmination of years of tough and lengthy negotiations. Given the meticulous preparation underway prior to the meeting and

3 See also Antonio Guterres, Current Trends in Forced Displacement and Humanitarian Action, 2010 Harrell-Bond Human Rights Lecture, Refugee Studies Centre, University of Oxford, 13 October 2010. Available online at: www.unhcr.org/4cb6f83d9.html.

4 Quoted in Erin Mooney, 'Developing National Law, Policy and Strategies around the African Union Convention for the Protection and Assistance of Internally Displaced Persons in Africa', African Union–Civil Society Organizations Pre-Summit on Internally Displaced Persons in Africa Kampala, Uganda, 13–15 October 2009, 5. Available at: www.internaldisplacement.org/8025708F004BE3B1/(httpInfoFiles)/2D4B21BAB5E0BEC8C12576B8005E79CA/$file/AU-CSO%20Pre-Summit%20IDP_Mooney%20statement%20_2009-10_%20FINAL.pdf.

5 'IDP Convention–Now the Hard Work Begins', 26 October 2010. Available online at: http://allafrica.com/stories/200910261530.html.

the high turnout often observed for the regular bi-annual sessions of the African Union Summit, one may also wonder if the lack of a robust attendance by heads of state and government reveals certain ambivalence towards the Convention. Though a functioning consensus was ultimately achieved to ensure the Convention's adoption at the 2009 Summit, there was no guarantee that the Convention would be overwhelmingly signed and ratified. The perception that the Convention is only relevant to states affected by internal displacement might have also contributed to states' initial lukewarm response to the Convention.

That far fewer than expected number of states ratified the Convention understandably generated a certain level of frustration.[6] For some, this outcome was 'insufficient'.[7] For the ACHPR Special Rapporteur, this state of affair follows a 'rather unsatisfactory record of ratification and implementation of obligations under such instruments by African States'.[8] With the intention to encourage the ratification of the Convention and set an example, Uganda, the host of the 2009 Special Summit, became the first country to ratify the Convention on 29 January 2010. Its instrument of ratification was deposited on 4 March 2010. Sierra Leone followed suit by adopting the Convention on 8 October 2010. This was followed by the ratification of the Convention by the Central African Republic, Chad, Gabon, Gambia, Togo and Zambia which deposited their instruments of ratification at the AU Commission in 2011. Out of the 11 member states of the International Conference of the Great Lakes region (ICGLR), eight have already signed the Convention,[9] signalling that sub-regional legal developments might have also encouraged member states to ratify continent-level legal instruments. It must be noted that while several of the ICLGR states have signed the Convention, some key ICGLR states such as Sudan have not done so. As of July 2016, a significant number of the 25 states that have ratified the Convention are members of the ECOWAS.

The African Union is currently pursuing different strategies to speed up the ratification of the instrument.[10] The Convention is relevant to all states. Even countries which do not face complex emergencies may still experience precarious situations of displacement requiring legislative and institutional responses.[11] As duly highlighted by some commentators:[12]

6 African Countries' Reluctance to Ratify Kampala Declaration Questioned, *Afrik-News*, 29 June 2010, available online at: www.afrik-news.com/article17882.html. See also 'First Anniversary of the Kampala Convention: IDMC Calls for Ratification', Internal Displacement Monitoring Centre, 22 October 2010.

7 Michel Gabaudan and Kate Halff, 'African Leaders Must Follow Through on Kampala Convention', *The Huffington Post*, 27 October 2010.

8 Press Release by ACHPR Special Rapporteur. Available at: www.achpr.org/english/Press%20Release/KAMPALA%20CONVENTION_IDPs.pdf.

9 Kenya and Sudan have not yet signed the AU Convention.

10 Draft Plan of Action, 9.

11 Note 2 above, 9.

12 Ibid., note 7.

The Kampala Convention is not only about conflict and wars. It addresses displacement resulting from a wide range of causes, including natural and man-made disasters and development projects, as well as conflict, generalised violence and human rights violations. As such, it is of relevance to all 53 AU member states, whether or not they currently have any displaced populations, and whether or not they are or recently have been affected by war. All of them should, for example, be prepared for displacement caused by natural disasters, and they should take the necessary steps to minimise the impact of such displacement.

Legal and institutional reform

The Kampala Convention underscores the concept of national responsibility as a central framework. It provides that national authorities 'bear the primary duty and responsibility for providing protection and humanitarian assistance to internally displaced persons within their territory or jurisdiction without discrimination of any kind' (Art 5(1)). The responsibility of states to protect, respect and fulfil the rights of IDPs requires that all national authorities including the legislature, the judiciary and the executive take concrete steps to implement the Convention. These measures should be comprehensive in order to cover prevention of displacement, provide protection and assistance during displacement and seek durable solutions. At the minimum, authorities should develop domestic legislations, establish or designate an institutional focal point to coordinate activities on behalf of IDPs, and provide the necessary resources to deliver protection and assistance.[13]

The obligation of states to legislate, as provided for in Article 3, is premised on the assumption that the implementation of at least some of the Convention's provision requires domestication measures. Article 12, paragraph 2 requires states to 'establish an effective legal framework to provide just and fair compensations and other forms of reparations'. According to Article 4, paragraph 6 'state parties shall declare as offences punishable by law acts of arbitrary displacement that amount to genocide, war crimes or crimes against humanity'.

The objective of domestic legislative reform is not to grant legal status to IDPs. It is to facilitate a process aimed at meeting the specific needs of IDPs, taking into account their vulnerabilities. This is important to all states regardless of whether they are affected by regular incidents of internal displacement

13 The Framework for National Responsibility developed in 2005 by the Brookings-Bern Project on Internal Displacement identifies 12 steps for governments to take towards fulfilling national responsibility for internal displacement. These include: national legal framework, designation of a focal point, prevention, national awareness, data collection, training, national plan of action, role of national human rights institution, durable solution, participation of IDPs in decision making, allocation of adequate resource, and cooperation with international organizations. See *Addressing Internal Displacement: A Framework for National Responsibility* (Brookings Institution-University of Bern, 2005).

or not. Regional efforts including the adoption of the AU Convention and the Great Lakes Pact are expected to create momentum for legislative and policy reforms. Regarding Kenya, for instance, the former RSG notes:[14]

> The efforts of the Government of Kenya are in line with a growing trend that has been strongly reinforced by the Great Lakes Protocol, which requires Member States to incorporate the Guiding Principles into domestic legislation. With the adoption of the African Union Convention for the Protection and Assistance of Internally Displaced Persons in Africa (Kampala Convention), the demand for the elaboration of national policies and legislation relating to internal displacement is expected to increase. The Representative strongly supports these national initiatives and encourages the international community, in particular actors directly involved in legal issues pertaining to internal displacement, to support national authorities in these endeavors.

Multiple sources of guidance exist that may assist states on how to undertake necessary legislative reform. At the national level, states should draw on relevant domestic legislations and instruments. Experiences from other countries particularly those which share similar challenges of internal displacement and legal traditions may be quite useful. Legal and policy instruments at the regional and sub-regional levels need to be consulted. At the international levels, the Guiding Principles, their Annotations and the Manual for Law and Policy Makers are essential reference documents. Other resources include those that have been prepared under the guidance of the RSG including the Framework on Durable Solutions and Operational Guidelines on Human Rights and Natural Disasters. There are also specific manuals and studies by United Nations organisations and humanitarian institutions such as UNHCR and ICRC. In addition documents and studies prepared by CSOs such as IDMC and Brookings Bern Projects are quite important. Useful policy guidelines and normative standards being developed in the context of prevention of natural disaster such as the 2005 Hyogo Framework for Action and IFRC's guidelines for regulation of disaster relief laws may also be referred to.[15] With respect to the latter, it was noted that the development of the Guidelines for the Domestic Facilitation and Regulation of International Disaster and Relief and Initial Recovery Assistance would contribute 'to national legal preparedness by providing guidance to States interested in

14 Report of the Representative of the Secretary General on the Human Rights of Internally Displaced Persons, A/65/282, 11 August 2010, para. 2.

15 Hyogo Framework for Action 2005–2015: Building the Resilience of Nations and Communities to Disasters, Final report of the World Conference on Disaster Reduction, A/CONF.206/6 (2005). See also Introduction to the Guidelines for the Domestic Facilitation and Regulation of International Disaster Relief and Initial Recovery (Geneva: IFRC, 2008). Available online at: www.ifrc.org/PageFiles/41203/introduction-guidelines-en.pdf.

improving their domestic legal, policy and institutional frameworks concerning international disaster relief and initial recovery assistance'.[16]

Reviewing and amending existing legislations

IDPs are nationals or habitual residents of the state in which they are displaced. As such a range of national legislations thus have direct or indirect implications in shaping the domestic response to internal displacement. Constitutions and other key domestic legislations dealing with principles of equality, non-discrimination, socio-economic rights, freedom of movement, and the right to a family are quite important. Some domestic laws such as electoral laws may directly or indirectly discriminate against IDPs or create barriers to access essential social services.[17] It is recommended that states review the compatibility of these domestic legislations with provisions of the Convention and their adequacy with respect to issues such as the protection of vulnerable groups, compensation regime, responsibility of non-state actors, responsibility of government authority such as the police and the military. As has been stated in the context of the implementation of the Guiding Principles:[18]

> it is not sufficient simply to make general references to the Guiding Principles or even transcribe the Principles word-for-word in a national IDP law or policy; while valuable as a normative statement of commitment to the Principles, this does little to make them operational in a practical manner. Rather, what is required is to bring the range of relevant national legislation and policy in line with the international standards reflected in the Principles.

Constitutions have general application and as such may not directly address the specific needs and vulnerabilities of IDPs.[19] However, they are important tools for protecting IDPs.[20] They may provide key normative and institutional aspects of national protection for the human rights of persons in general. Constitutional provisions concerning freedom of movement, non-discrimina-

16 Guidelines for the Domestic Facilitation and Regulation of International Disaster Relief and Initial Recovery, 30IC/07/R4 annex, 1, para. 3.

17 Jeremy Grace and Jeff Fischer, 'Seeking Electoral Equality for IDP Voters', *Forced Migration Review: Special Issue* (2008): 26–27.

18 Note 4 above, 3.

19 Joe Oloka Onyango, 'Movement Related Rights in the Context of Internal Displacement', in *Incorporating the Guiding Principles on Internal Displacement into Domestic Law: Issues and Challenges*, ed. Walter Kälin *et al.* (Washington, DC: The American Society of International Law and Brookings Institution, 2010), 22.

20 The former RSG lists human rights directly relevant for the protection of IDPs as follows: (a) rights related to physical security and integrity (including protection of the right to life and violence against women); (b) fundamental rights related to basic necessities of life (e.g. the rights to food, potable water, adequate shelter, health services and sanitation); (c) rights related to other economic, social and cultural protection needs (for instance, the rights to

tion, equality, socio-economic rights, protection from gender-based violence are all key relevant norms and principles. Specific constitutional provisions or human rights norms relevant to the protection of marginalised or vulnerable groups such as women, children, the elderly, disabled persons and pastoralist groups are also key components of the national legal framework relevant to internal displacement. For instance, provisions on non-discrimination and equality may be used to determine the legality of any decision by local authorities to deny humanitarian assistance to those who may be associated with opposition parties, minorities and other groups.

Since constitutional provisions are often the hardest to change or amend; considerable attention should be made to their interpretation and actual implementation. In South Africa, a dynamic interpretative role by a constitutional court has been instrumental in promoting human rights.[21] The experience from Colombia also shows the impact judicial organs, particularly the highest judicial body, can make with respect to the response to internal displacement.[22] The Ethiopian Constitution not only declares that all international treaties the country ratifies are an integral part of the domestic law but also stipulates that constitutional provisions dealing with human rights ought to be interpreted based on key international human rights instruments to which the country is signatory (Article 13). During emergencies, state authorities often take measures which may restrict or suspend constitutionally guaranteed rights. Constitutional provisions regulating the state of emergency, therefore, are very important since people are often displaced during situations of emergencies. The presence of an institutional mechanism for monitoring how the suspension of civil liberty is regulated is also important.

Numerous aspects of the domestic criminal law are directly related to the protection and assistance of IDPs. Criminal law may provide for a criminalisation of arbitrary displacement. The Kampala Convention underscores that state parties shall 'ensure individual responsibility for acts of arbitrary displacement, in accordance with applicable domestic and international criminal law' (Art 3(1)g). Provisions declaring as offences punishable by law acts of genocide, war crimes and crimes against humanity are particularly relevant (Art 4(6)). It may also be directly relevant in providing for specific standards for the criminalisation of sexual and gender-based violence and harmful

work, receive restitution or compensation for lost property and to be provided with or have access to education); and (d) rights related to other civil and political protection needs (e.g. the rights to personal documentation, political participation, access to courts and freedom from discrimination). Protection of Internally Displaced Persons in Situations of Natural Disasters, The Report of the Representative of the Secretary General on the Human Rights of Internally Displaced Persons, A/HRC/10/13/Add.1, para. 29.

21 Johan De Waal, 'Constitutional Law', in *Introduction to South African Law*, ed. C. G. Van der Merwe and Du Plessis (The Netherlands: Kluwer International, 2004), 55–106.

22 See Rodolfo Rivadeneira, *Judicial Protection of Internally Displaced Persons: The Colombian Experience*, Brooking Bern Internal Displacement Project, November 2009.

traditional practices. The specific definition of torture under domestic legislation is quite important in preventing, mitigating and punishing one of the principal human rights breaches which leads to displacement. Criminal law can also address the situation of targeted attacks against human rights advocates and humanitarian workers and protect IDPs from abuse including by law enforcement organ.

Legislations regulating civil status can influence access by IDPs to documents which they have lost during their flight. Domestic laws should allow access to documentation and refrain from imposing undue restrictions such as return to areas of habitual residence to access documents. Laws regulating marital registration are particularly important in ensuring that women have equal access to get registration in their own names. They are also relevant in protecting women and children from the effects of traditional harmful practices which are identified by the Kampala Convention as one of the causes of internal displacement. Human rights framework and related legislations protect the rights of IDPs to organise and associate. States should also review their legislation on registration and regulation of NGOs and international humanitarian organisations.[23]

Electoral laws can play an important role with respect to guaranteeing of the exercise by IDPs of voting rights during displacement. Often IDPs cannot go back to their former place of residence to vote and yet existing legislations may require the fulfilment of certain requirements such as residence for a certain period in an area where an election may be held. The electoral legislative framework involves constitutional, legislative and administrative rules making it even more difficult to achieve the desired goal through an IDP specific legislation.[24] It is, however, recommended that states introduce new procedures to maintain existing registration, to transfer registration, or to waive requirements that would prevent IDPs from registering at the site of displacement.[25] Some laws also may not have the procedure of absentee registration in accordance to which IDPs may register in place of origin. In order to ensure that IDPs benefit from the fullest exercise of their right to vote, it is recommended national legislations allow IDPs to vote for the constituency of the place of origin or place of displacement.[26]

Many countries do not have specific legislations regulating the impacts of investment and development projects on the displacement of people.[27] These

23 David Fisher, 'The Right to Humanitarian Assistance', in *Incorporating the Guiding Principles on Internal Displacement into Domestic Law: Issues and Challenges*, ed. Walter Kälin *et al.* (Washington, DC: The American Society of International Law and Brookings Institution, 2010), 47–129.

24 Protecting Internally Displaced Persons: A Manual for Law and Policymakers (Brookings Bern Internal Displacement Project, 2008), 206.

25 Ibid., 207.

26 Ibid.

27 Chris de Wet, 'Improving Outcomes in Development Induced in Displacement and Resettlement Project', *Forced Migration Review* 12(2002): 7.

legislations are relevant not only with respect to the actions of the state but also that of private companies and organisations. Domestic legislations designed to facilitate access by potential investors to land have direct implications on the relocation of individuals. Building codes are important aspects of risk reduction strategies. Labour laws are key in ensuring that IDPs enjoy full access to livelihoods and are protected against discrimination while looking for employment opportunities. IDPs often suffer from lack of access to employment and an employment pension. Specific domestic legislations on land, housing, eviction and compensation are all important aspects of the domestic legal system on the protection and assistance of IDPs. This is particularly true with respect to internal displacement that may arise in the context of development projects. It is imperative to review if domestic legislations provide due process; protect women and children from unique vulnerabilities; ensure sufficient guarantees to communities with a special attachment to land, and provide for full and equitable compensations and remedies (Article 4(5)). The application of customary land tenure systems has consequences for dispute settlement, and for the protection of marginalised groups, and the role and participation of traditional authorities and resettlement policies. For instance in Burundi, it was found that the land identified by the government as being available in the government's scheme for reform is actually 'occupied' and used in accordance with customary land tenure system.[28] In traditional land tenure systems, the right to inheritance and usage rights are limited. It is observed that under statutory laws, property deeds are issued in the name of male heads of a household, limiting the access by women to land and property. In Cote d'Ivoire, a new land law requiring 'continuous and peaceful existence of customary rights' is said to be discriminatory to those who, despite their customary entitlement to a piece of land, could not prove 'continuous and peaceful use' due to their displacement from the area.[29]

Legislations relating to tax and visas are relevant for the movement of materials and personnel used for the provision of humanitarian assistance. It is important to evaluate if these legislations impose undue restrictions or limitations on the work of these organisations. Exceptions may be provided for the custom and related regulation for the movement of humanitarian goods and personnel. Laws and policies regulating disaster response are assuming great importance as countries increasingly grapple with the consequences of natural and man-made disasters. They involve a variety of legislative measures which relate to the disaster risk reduction, access and institutional mandate of local disaster preparedness and response. And yet very few countries have specific disaster-related legislations.[30] Some of the

28 See Jacquie Kigundu, *Why Land Tenure Matters for IDPs: Lessons from Sub-Saharan Africa* (Brooking-Bern Project on Internal Displacement, 2008).

29 See *Whose Land is This? Land Dispute and Forced Displacement in the Western Forest Area of Cote d'Ivoire*, Internal Displacement Monitoring Center, 2009.

30 *Law and Legal Issues in International Disaster Response* (Geneva: International Federation of Red Cross and Red Crescent Societies, 2007), 83.

issues regulated by these sets of rules include procedures on when international assistance and support can be requested by local authorities; facilitation of humanitarian assistance; establishment and allocation of special funds; safety and quality of humanitarian assistance; protection to victims; and compensation. Review of these laws may be undertaken based on emerging international standards including the Hyogo Framework.[31] Few African countries have specific national legislations on disasters.[32] In Uganda and Ethiopia, provisions have been incorporated in their respective constitutions to provide broad principles on the role of the state in preventing and regulating natural or man-made disasters.[33] Legislations defining the role and competence of members of the national defence force in civilian protection and assistance should also be examined. National legislations can provide for conditions under which forced evacuation may take place during disasters.[34] States can prescribe technical arrangements under which passage of humanitarian consignment and personnel may be allowed (Article 5(7)). It is important to consider if the relevant domestic legislations allow reparation or compensation to be provided when state institutions and authorities become negligent in providing the required assistance to those who are affected by natural or man-made disasters.

Current interest on climate change and its consequences for population movement has triggered a great deal of attention on how domestic environmental and climate-related legislations address concerns of human displacement. Legislations including on biodiversity, forestry, zoning and park protection are relevant in dealing with climate change and society's adaptation to its challenges. They play important roles in minimising the risk of human displacement generated by environmental factors. This also contributes to the prevention of conflicts stemming from competition among communities over the ever depleting natural resources. They enhance a state's capacity to implement and realise its obligation under the Convention with respect to internal displacement generated including by climate change (Article 5(4)). One must ask, for example, whether domestic environmental legislation requires prior environmental assessment to be undertaken for a project which may have certain environmental consequences prior to its entry into the implementation phase. An inquiry can also

31 See Hyogo Framework for Action 2005–2015: ISDR, See note 26 above. See also Protecting Persons Affected by Natural Disasters: IASC Operational Guidelines on Human Rights and Natural Disasters (Washington, DC: Brookings-Bern Project on Internal Displacement, 2006).

32 South Africa: Act No. 57, Disaster Management Act of 2002, Government Gazette No. 24252 (2003), Articles 24, 36, and 50; Algeria: Law No. 04–20 of December 25, 2004, concerning the prevention of major risks and the management of disasters in the framework of sustainable development.

33 See Arts 23 & 89(3) of the Constitution of the Federal Democratic Republic of Ethiopia and the Republic of Uganda respectively.

34 Art 4(4) f states: 'forced evacuations in cases of natural or human made disasters or other causes if the evacuations are not required by the safety and health of those affected'.

be made as to what extent domestic legal framework provides for compensation for individuals for environmental harm and damage. The review exercise should also look into how the competing protection needs of IDPs on the one hand and protection of the environment are being evaluated.

Enacting a specific legislation on internal displacement

Once a proper review of existing legislations has been undertaken, authorities are required to adopt and develop a specific legislation on internal displacement. Building on the national capacity to meet the challenges of internal displacement is a long process, and its legal and institutional dimension should form part and parcel of a meaningful strategy. As experience has often shown, an effective national response invariably requires a certain level of domestic legislative reform. For instance, in both the DRC and CAR, the former RSG recommended the prioritisation of legislative enactment within the national framework.[35] All countries benefit from a national legislation designed to implement provisions of the Convention. General domestic legislations, however, may not help address the specific protection and assistance needs of IDPs which are often neglected by such legislations.[36] It is understandable to expect countries that have had a long and unfortunate experience with slow onset natural disasters (Ethiopia) and conflicts (Somalia, Sudan, DRC, Sierra Leone, Liberia, Ethiopia, Eritrea, Burundi, Chad and CAR) to have specific national policies and legislations. As experiences in Kenya[37] and Cote d'Ivoire[38] clearly show, however, countries that have been once considered peaceful and thus immune from the eruption of conflicts may suddenly confront the realities of extreme crisis. Flooding in West Africa, particularly in Ghana and Benin has also shown that sudden natural disasters may cause considerable displacement in places that had not experienced a similar crisis in the past.[39]

35 Report of the Representative of the Secretary General on the Human Rights of Internally Displaced Persons, 3 August 2009, A/64/214, 47.

36 See Walter Kälin, *Internal Displacement and the Role of Parliamentarians in Times of Crisis*, 120th Meeting of Inter-Parliamentary Union, Addis Ababa, Ethiopia, 9 April 2009, available online at: www.brookings.edu/speeches/2009/0409_internal_displacement_kälin.aspx

37 See *Kenya: Speedy Reform Need to Deal with Past Injustices and Prevent Future Displacement* (Geneva: IDMC, 2010).

38 See *Cote d'Ivoire: Quest for Durable Solutions Continues as the Electoral Process Moves Forward* (IDMC, 2010).

39 In 2010, the number of persons displaced by a sudden onset disaster was estimated to be over 42 million people worldwide, See *Displacement Due to Natural Hazard-Induced Disasters: Global Estimates for 2009 and 2010* (Geneva: IDMC, 2011), 4. During the 10th Anniversary of the Guiding Principles, the Special Rapporteur on Refugees, Asylum Seekers, IDPs and Migrants noted:

> Displacement caused by natural disasters, the increasing incidence of flooding in recent times, as a result of changes in global weather patterns, has increasingly affected thousands of people in a number of African countries. The flooding in Togo, Ghana,

When sudden displacement occurs in an environment where the necessary legislative and institutional mechanisms are not put in place, provisions of humanitarian assistance and protections will encounter enormous obstacles. Domestic law making often takes considerable time. States may thus decide to adopt directives and regulations to address sudden and urgent incidents of displacement. But these measures should gradually be replaced by laws that are adopted by the highest state legislature and which may command respect from juridical institutions and other state organs.[40] A number of African countries have already adopted specific national legislations and policies.[41] Angola adopted its national legislation in 2000 which is the first national legislation developed in reference to the UN Guiding Principles on Internal Displacement. It was followed by Burundi (2001), Sierra Leone (2002), Liberia (2004), Uganda (2004) and Sudan (2009).[42] There have also been some legislative reform efforts in countries including Central African Republic, Chad, Nigeria, Cote d'Ivoire, Mozambique and Kenya.[43] From a review of these national legislative mechanisms, no single approach to domestic legal reform emerges. Neither does the Convention explicitly provide a typology of legal reform that member states should pursue. Experiences from countries that have adopted national legislations reveal that there are different approaches adopted by states in enacting national legislations.[44]

> Uganda, and Somalia during the last two years, caused the destruction of infrastructure, worth millions of dollars, and left several thousands of people homeless. Displacement caused by natural disasters, though not as traumatic as the conflict induced, can reverse gains of economic development, in areas which are in some cases marginalised communities, such as the case of Somalia and Northern Uganda which are conflict affected areas.

Statement by Bahame Tom Nyandunga, Commissioner, African Commission on Human and Peoples' Rights, 10 Years of Guiding Principles on Internal Displacement, Oslo Conference, 16–17 October 2009.

40 Note 24 above, 28.

41 Peter Neussl, 'Bridging the National and International Responses to IDPs', *Forced Migration Review* 20(2004): 42–44.

42 Similar national frameworks also exist in Bosnia and Herzegovina, Colombia, Georgia, Peru, Russia, and Turkey. For comparative information regarding national legislations on internal displacement, see the Brookings' Database on National and Regional Laws and Policies on Internal Displacement which is available at: www.brookings.edu/projects/idp/Laws-and-Policies/idp_policies_index.aspx.

43 'Kenya: Draft Policy on IDP offers new hope for IDPs', *IRIN*, 19 March 2010, available at www.irinnews.org/report.aspx?Reportid=88485. On the preparation of the draft legislative and national framework on internal displacement in CAR, see The Report of the Secretary General Representative on the Human Rights of Internally Displaced Persons, A/65/282, 11 August 2010, para. 19.

44 Making the Kampala Convention Work for IDPs: Guide for Civic Society on Supporting the Ratification and Implementation of the Convention for the Protection and Assistance of Internally Displaced Persons in Africa (Geneva, IDMC 2010), 12. See Jessica Wyndham, 'A Developing Trend: Laws and Policies on Internal Displacement', Brookings Institution, January 2007. Available online at http://reliefweb.int/rw/lib.nsf/ db900sid/JFRN-6Y2TC7/$file/brookings-idp-jan2007.pdf?openelement.

Endorsement of the Guiding Principles: Liberia

Liberia has struggled with the problem of internal displacement for over 17 years. The Transitional Government in 2004, through an official instrument signed by the Chairman of the Transitional Government, endorsed the UN Guiding Principles.[45] The instrument recognises the primary responsibility of government for the protection and assistance of IDPs; affirms several of the rights and entitlements of IDPs; recognises the international human rights and humanitarian law to which Liberia is a party; accepts the Guiding Principles as a source of guidance and framework for protection and assistance; and reiterates the determination of the government to 'foster a legal and institutional framework that can make use of the guidance provided by the Guiding Principles on Internal Displacement'.[46]

Selective approach: Burundi, Sierra Leone and Angola

IDP policies in Burundi,[47] Sierra Leone[48] and Angola[49] seek to address certain aspects of internal displacement such as return, resettlement or reintegration; specific rights of IDPs; or certain causes of displacement such as natural disasters. The case of Madagascar and Mozambique is also instructive. Owing to the repeated occurrence of natural disasters relating to cyclones in Madagascar and flooding in Mozambique, there has been an attempt to develop a more disaster-specific national response in these countries.[50]

Burundi had been mired in civil conflict which has generated the forced displacement of civilians for more than a decade. On 7 February 2001, the government signed the Framework Consultation Agreement with the UN humanitarian coordinator to facilitate the protection and assistance of IDPs based on the Guiding Principles.[51] The agreement was signed between the Minster of Human Rights of Burundi and the UN Humanitarian

45 The Guiding Principles on Internal Displacement: Instrument of Adoption, signed on 8 November 2004, available online at: www.brookings.edu/~/media/Files/Projects/IDP/Laws%20and%20Policies/Liberia/Liberia_GPadoption_2004.pdf.

46 Ibid.

47 National and Regional Laws and Policies on Internal Displacement: Burundi. Available at: www.brookings.edu/projects/idp/Laws-and-Policies/burundi.aspx.

48 Sierra Leone: Recovery Strategy for Newly Accessible Area, National Recovery Committee, adopted on May 2002. Available at: www.brookings.edu/~/media/Files/Projects/IDP/Laws%20and%20Policies/Sierra_Leone/SierraLeone_RecoveryStrategy_2002.pdf.

49 Norms on Resettlement of Internally Displaced Population (2001) attached to Council of Ministers Decree Number 1/01 (5 January 2001). Available online at: www.brookings.edu/~/media/Files/Projects/IDP/Laws%20and%20Policies/Angola/Angola_Norms2001.pdf.

50 Report of the Secretary General Representative on the Human Rights of Internally Displaced Persons, A/63/286, paras. 55–62.

51 See Tullio Santini, 'Addressing the Protection Gap: The Framework for Consultation on IDPs in Burundi', *Forced Migration Review* (2002): 43–46.

Coordinator and had the objective of promoting access, enhancing protection, and facilitating rapid assessment and response. The framework establishes a high-level Committee and a follow-up technical group. The Committee is composed of high-level government officials from relevant ministries and also representatives of the United Nations humanitarian system and NGOs.

The legislative framework in Angola covers both refugees and IDPs and addresses displacement generated by all causes including natural disasters. Its selective nature, however, stems from its focus on return and resettlement as a key aspect of the national response. Angola had been suffering from armed conflicts for decades until a ceasefire and a comprehensive peace agreement was signed between the government and UNITA in 2002.[52] At the peak of the armed conflict in Angola, over four million people were displaced from their homes. Angola's Ministry of Social Welfare, together with key international humanitarian organisations, prepared the Norms on Resettlement which was later enacted by the Council of Ministers.[53] The instrument promotes voluntary resettlement for both IDP and refugee returnees. It seeks to establish rules applicable to the resettlement of IDPs and refugees. It identifies provincial governments as responsible organs for the implementation of projects on resettlement and return of population. Through the role of the Humanitarian Coordination Group, NGOs and CSOs also participate in the projects.[54] It incorporates specific provisions concerning the identification of lands, security of relocation sites, sanitation, water, agricultural inputs for resettlement, rehabilitation on health posts, provision of food, social assistance and other concerns. Owing to the prevalence of landmines in many of the war-affected areas, the instrument provides specific standards with respect to mine clearance, awareness-raising initiatives, and security of the areas from the mines.[55] It involves traditional leaders in ensuring the participation of affected communities and individuals in the planning and implementation of the relocation process and refers to the role of international agencies, particularly UN organisations in assisting provincial governments.[56]

Based on specific recommendations from the RSG in 2001, the government issued another decree endorsing sets of specific operational procedures, further strengthening the implementation of the Norms.[57] Though most of

52 Luanda Memorandum of Understanding 2002 and Cease Fire Agreement between Angola and UNITA, 2002.

53 Ibid.

54 Art 3.

55 Art 4.

56 Arts 5, 6 & 7.

57 Standard Operational Procedures for the Enforcement of the 'Norms on the Resettlement of Displaced Populations', Council of Ministers Decree No. 79/02, 2 December 2002. Available online at www.brookings.edu/~/media/Files/Projects/IDP/Laws%20and%20Policies/Angola/Angola_SOPs_ResettlementNorms2002_Eng.pdf.

the Angolan IDPs have already returned home,[58] many of the displaced persons returned spontaneously with very little assistance and protection.[59] It was also cited that IDPs were often ordered by traditional leaders or members of the ruling party to return to their place of origin prior to any inspection of the areas by the displaced themselves.[60]

Comprehensive approach: Uganda

Best represented by the national IDP policy in Uganda, a comprehensive approach on internal displacement covers the salient elements of a national response to internal displacement involving key features, causes and phases of displacement.[61] Similar to the experience of the countries discussed above, Uganda has also been struggling with the consequences of protracted and vicious armed conflicts which left the displacement of almost close to a million people at the peak of the crisis. Since 2002, the government has been working with United Nations humanitarian institutions in developing the National Policy for Internally Displaced Persons.[62] Its framework is very comprehensive and covers all forms of displacement and its various phases. It provides for the protection of the rights of displaced persons, promotes resettlement and return and creates the *modus operandi* for the cooperation between the government and international organisations. The instrument establishes various policy and technical committees responsible for the implementation of the policy.

Domestic legislative and policy approaches discussed above should be examined in the light of the provisions of the Kampala Convention which provides sufficient flexibility for states to develop an approach as in addressing the unique situations of displacement prevailing in their context. While being specific to the most important and dominant forms of displacement, these national legislations should also be comprehensive enough. A mere endorsement of the Convention or the Guiding Principle is too simplistic and may not be sufficient to local authorities tasked with the responsibility of implementing the Convention. The national legislation should adopt a broad and comprehensive definition of IDPs which at the minimum complies with the definition as provided for under the Kampala Convention

58 UNHCR's 2010 country profile for Angola does not indicate the presence of IDPs population in the country. See Angola: 2010 Country Operation Profile. Available at: www.unhcr.org/cgi-bin/texis/vtx/page?page=4a03e30d6.

59 See Former IDPs Share the Common Challenge of Recovery and Reconstruction (Geneva: IDMC, 2007).

60 Ibid., 5.

61 Similar comprehensive national policy on internal displacement and a draft IDP Bill has recently been adopted in Kenya.

62 The National Policy for Internally Displaced Persons, Office of the Prime Minster, adopted in August 2004. Available at: www.brookings.edu/~/media/Files/Projects/IDP/Laws%20and%20Policies/Uganda/Uganda_IDPpolicy_2004.pdf.

and the Guiding Principles. The legislation should acknowledge and recognise the numerous rights and entitlements of displaced persons also identified in the Convention and the UN Guiding Principles. National instruments on IDPs must designate a national focal point and provide for the allocation of funds. It may also be useful to have specific provisions dealing with the protection of IDPs from retaliatory measures from the government concerned and its agents for seeking the protection of their rights. It should incorporate recognition of the rights of IDPs to receive international humanitarian assistance. The protection of vulnerable groups such as women, children, the elderly, minority groups and indigenous groups should also be incorporated as provided for under the provisions of the Convention. The specific needs of women to be protected from sexual and gender-based violence need to be taken into account.

In the exercise of drawing up national legislations and relevant policy frameworks, it is very important that an approach is adopted that involves a robust participation of IDPs themselves. In Nigeria, for instance, the process of developing a national framework for the protection of IDPs involved the participation of displaced communities and civic society organisations not only at the federal and national level but also at the local levels.[63] In terms of the content of the particular legislation, member states can draw important inputs not only from the provisions of the Convention but also from the UN Guiding Principles and the Annotations. The IASC Manual for Law and Policy Makers is also a useful reference tool. Member states may also be part of a regional grouping which have certain treatises or 'soft laws' as in the case of the International Conference on the Great Lakes Region. Based on these regional commitments and that of the UN Guiding Principles, some of the countries have already adopted legislations. These domestic legislations need to be designed with an eye on the specific challenges of displacement that characterise the particular country concerned.

National strategies and implementation plans

Beyond the adoption of new national legislations or the reviewing of existing laws, states should also develop strategies or action plans which will complement their domestic legislations and make them operational. The Kampala Convention provides that states shall 'adopt other measures as appropriate, including strategies and policies on internal displacement at national and local levels, taking into account the needs of host communities'. (Article 3(2)c). National policies, strategies, directives, manuals and procedures may be used to fill certain gaps or respond to specific emergencies. States may also tailor their policy to their unique circumstances or to the particular features or dominant forms of displacement. The Convention also

63 See note 4 above.

stipulates that states shall develop early warning systems, establish and implement disaster risk reduction strategies, emergency and disaster preparedness and management measures and, when necessary, provide immediate protection and assistance to internally displaced persons.

These national policies may either be specific to internal displacement or address other thematic concerns while incorporating key elements relevant to displacement. For instance, states may elaborate specific guidelines on temporary shelter and housing during evacuation and displacement. By the same token, a national policy on women or children may also address the particular needs of those affected by internal displacement. A number of key issues may be incorporated in a national strategy on internally displaced persons. These include budgeting and resource allocation, coordination of relevant national institutions, training and awareness creation, and identification of durable solutions.

National institutional framework

States that have ratified the Kampala Convention are obliged to give practical manifestation to their responsibility under the Convention, including by clearly designating a national coordination mechanism, and identifying institutions responsible for providing protection and assistance to IDPs. The Kampala Convention provides that states shall designate a coordinating body and assign responsibilities to appropriate organisations for protection and assistance including cooperation with international organisations or agencies, and civil society organisations.

The process of designation should take into account the existing institutional architecture within member states, and the respective roles and responsibilities of government offices. It is important to clarify the relationship between a dedicated national institution on internal displacement and the range of other institutions, both at the national and local levels, whose mandate and function directly or indirectly contribute to the implementation of the Convention. The institutional framework ought to clearly chart the relationship that exists between the national focal point and a range of other relevant national and local institutions.

A number of key elements may be drawn from the foregoing observations. First, states need to determine, based on the prevailing circumstances and existing institutional architecture, whether the establishment of a specific mechanism on internal displacement is warranted. Second, key responsibilities with respect to the provision of protection and assistance to IDPs may be assigned to different governmental organs and institutions while the role of the focal point focuses on coordinating the functions of these organs. While specifying the tasks and activities required from the coordination mechanism or from its constituent mechanisms, the Convention does not shed light on whether this should be made through parliamentary legislation, decrees or policy instruments. Neither has it been clarified at what political level the national institution should be represented. An effective national institutional arrangement creates linkages between the respective roles of the highest executive organ with specific technical committees and institutions. Third, the national consultation and deliberation on the establishment or designation of national focal points should also be conducted in a transparent and open process involving particularly those who are affected by internal displacement. The overall purpose of these institutional measures should focus on assisting states undertake an effective needs assessment at the national level, coordinate and provide humanitarian assistance to IDPs, address the protection needs of victims including through the protection of their human rights, and ensure durable solutions.

National coordination mechanism

State parties to the Kampala Convention shall determine whether its national experience with internal displacement warrants the establishment of a specialised domestic institutional mechanism or mechanisms to address dimensions of internal displacement. States need also determine whether the mandate of such a focal point should be comprehensive in nature or should rather focus on a specific aspect or aspects of internal displacement. Various states empower different government institutions to assume such responsibilities. Separate national coordination mechanisms or focal points may be set up to deal with displacement generated by armed conflicts and that generated by disasters. For example, Nigeria has established a separate national mechanism dealing with disaster preparedness and response. In Mozambique, the government, with support from donors has developed a national coordination mechanism responsible for addressing the challenges of displacement caused by natural disasters. The result of this exercise has been impressive and considered by the former RSG as a model to be emulated by others.[64]

The Kampala Convention also stipulates for the establishment of specialised mechanisms in order to address a number of key problems. For instance, Article 9(2) h provides that states shall take the 'necessary measures including the establishment of specialized mechanisms, to trace and reunify families separated during displacement and otherwise facilitate the re-establishment of family ties'. Moreover, Article 4(2) urges states to devise a national early warning system; and establish and implement disaster risk reduction strategies; emergency and disaster preparedness and management measures. Article 11(4) of the Kampala Convention also stipulates that states shall establish 'appropriate mechanisms providing for simplified procedures where necessary, for resolving disputes relating to the property of internally displaced persons'.

64 Report of the Representative of the Secretary General on the human rights of internally displaced persons, 9 February 2009, A/HRC/10/13, para. 63.

In light of the limited resources available to states and the need to ensure better coordination among the various domestic institutions that might be involved in national responses to internal displacement, an inter-sectoral coordination mechanism seems to be the most appropriate and cost-effective approach. Domestic legislative and policy instruments should, therefore, clearly determine both the composition and the tasks of the national coordination mechanism. It is important that representatives of IDPs, particularly vulnerable groups, are directly involved in the decision-making process. Angola's Norms on the Resettlement of Internally Displaced Populations provides that the Sub-Group on Displaced Persons and Refugees should include representatives of IDPs in the planning and management of resettlement programmes. The specific responsibilities and functions of a national coordination mechanism may vary from country to country depending on the prevailing specific challenges of internal displacement. Some of the key functions of national coordination mechanisms on internal displacement, however, may include: (a) deciding about the use of allocated budget and monitoring its implementation, (b) undertaking IDP profiling and needs assessment, (c) coordinating activities of different governmental institutions and local authorities, (d) running national awareness programmes on the rights and entitlements of IDPs, (e) coordinating activities with international organisations, CSOs and others, (f) developing national policies, manuals and tools, and ensuring that other national policies such as on education and health incorporate the specific needs of IDPs, (g) establishing or ensuring the establishment of a mechanism for evaluation of the compliance of assistance with international standards and norms, (h) designing specific programmes to enhance the capacity of key government institutions including the military and law enforcement organs through education, training and development of manuals, and (i) mobilising resources and technical assistance. While these activities principally focus on coordinating the roles and responsibilities of all the relevant institutions within the country, they may also facilitate the relationship between international institutions on the one hand and domestic actors on the other.

Undertaking a profiling and registration of IDPs is one of the most challenging tasks for a national focal point or designated local authorities. Guidelines on profiling of IDPs that have been developed at the international level may provide guidance and support. As experience shows, countries facing the problem of internal displacement often require the assistance of the international community to undertake this task. According to Article 5(5) of the Kampala Convention, when a state is unable to undertake the assessment of the situation of displacement, it shall facilitate the involvement of international actors. In recent years, there has been a growing call, particularly by donor countries, to develop common humanitarian needs assessment and action plans across agencies and countries, particularly those who are the recipients of such assistance who have often raised concerns that such an assessment needs to involve the participation and consultation of national authorities of concerned states. The engagement of national authorities may be coordinated by the national focal point.

Some countries elevate the political profile of the coordination mechanism by integrating it into the Officers of the President or the Prime Minster. Both in Uganda and Tanzania, the national coordination mechanism is located within the Office of the Prime Minster. While its function and responsibilities cascade down to the provincial and local level, the national focal point in Uganda is also supported by inter-ministerial and inter-agency sub-committees. In Angola, the national coordination group covers both refugees and IDPs. According to the Standard Operational Procedures for the Enforcement of the Norms on the Resettlement of Displaced Populations, the process of resettlement and return of IDPs is led by the following entities: (a) the National Commission for Social and Productive Reintegration of Demobilized Personnel and Displaced Populations; (b) The Provincial Commission, and (c) The *ad hoc* Group for Technical and Administrative Support. Both the provincial Commission and the *ad hoc* group report to the Commission. In Ethiopia, the National Authorities for Refugees and Returnees Affairs does not deal with internal displacement as such, and issues of natural disaster and associated challenges of displacement are covered by the Ministry of Agriculture and Rural Development. The federal office mandated with disaster prevention and response in Ethiopia is under the Ministry of Agriculture and Rural Development.

In countries such as Nigeria, Ethiopia and South Africa, local governments enjoy wide competence and powers. In situations like these, coordination activity between the federal and regional government should be considered carefully. It is also important that the national focal point works with ministries and departments dealing with children, women, people with disabilities and pastoralists with the view to mainstreaming displacement-related concerns in the respective mandate of each institution. Though the establishment of dedicated focal points on each protected category of displaced individual has occasionally been suggested, this may not be the most suitable choice in countries with resource and personnel constraints.

Parliamentary committees, sub-committees, informal groupings and other relevant non-parliamentary institutions

National or local parliaments may establish committees or sub-committees which specifically deal with internal displacement. These parliamentary committees or groups can play an instrumental role in legislative review. Moreover, they could also exercise a monitoring role by reviewing how the national focal point on IDP or various relevant government ministries or departments mainstream the responsibility of protecting and assisting IDPs within their respective mandate. They can also ensure that the national budget and its allocation to each government department reflects the prioritisation of IDP-related projects.[65] The working methods of these organs must involve the active participation of displaced persons themselves.

The national electoral body is often a catalyst for legislative and administrative measures which will facilitate the fullest exercise by IDPs of their right to vote. It has been recommended that these national electoral organs establish an IDP unit or focal point that will encourage legislative and administrative reforms.[66] Special commissions or land dispute settlement mechanisms may play an important role in handling communal disputes between returnees and local communities. For instance, the group of Human Rights Council's mandate holders which visited the DRC in 2009 recommended such mechanism for DRC.[67]

Courts and national human rights institutions

IDPs are nationals of the country in which they are displaced. They are, thus, direct beneficiaries of human rights and constitutional guarantees. Once the Convention has been domesticated, the role of courts in implementing its provisions becomes relevant. Even in situations where no binding international instruments exist, courts have proven to make significant contributions in domesticating the Guiding Principles.[68] Sometimes meeting the needs of IDPs may not necessarily require additional legislative reform. In this context, ensuring the application of existing legislations or human rights norms to displacement may become sufficient. This is where the responsibility of courts becomes very important. In African countries which follow the common law tradition, courts enjoy an even more pronounced role. IDPs' access to these courts and whether the latter can be effective institutional mechanisms for compensation and redress is, thus, crucial. This responsibility is key with respect to complaints brought by IDPs regarding evictions and property right protection, access to services, violation of civic and political rights, discrimination and breach of the right to equal treatment, and restriction of freedom of movement.

In common law African countries, the judiciary facilitates the domestic application of international norms including those relevant to internal displacement. The particular role of constitutional adjudication and decisions of the highest judicial organs are important. In Colombia, the Supreme Court provided principles guiding the measures to be taken by the government to address the discrepancy between the normative standards

65 Note 36 above.
66 Note 24 above, 209.
67 Report of the Representative of the Secretary General on the Human Rights of Internally Displaced Persons, A/64/214, para. 47.
68 See Rodolf Rivadeneira, *Judicial Protection of Internally Displaced Persons: The Colombian Experience* (Washington, DC: Brookings Bern Internal Displacement Project, 2009).

incorporated in the domestic law and the reality on the ground regarding internal displacement.[69]

National human rights institutions (NHRIs) will play a vital role in implementing the Convention.[70] They can promote and protect the rights of IDPs by undertaking tasks including developing or reviewing national legislations; handling individual complaints or facilitating access to legal remedies by IDPs; undertaking investigations; cooperating with the UN human rights mechanisms especially with the RSG, and promoting ratification of relevant legal instruments.[71] Their engagement both in reviewing national legislations and monitoring practices which result in internal displacement will particularly underline the human rights approach to national response to the problem of internal displacement. In Uganda, the National Human Rights Institution played a key role in the development of the national policy.[72] NHRIs may follow-up recommendations of human rights treaty bodies, the Human Rights Council and the regional human rights institutions on matters affecting IDPs. They are particularly relevant in monitoring those situations and practices which may lead to displacement of individuals and groups such as racial discrimination, harmful practiccs, discrimination and violations of human rights. They may handle individual complaints brought by IDPs themselves. The role of these institutions becomes more apparent as displacement lingers on and as the phase of emergency subsides. Following the crisis in the post 2007 election in Kenya, the National Human Rights Commission undertook a fact-finding mission regarding the problem of internal displacement and publicised its report.[73] National human rights mechanisms can establish fact-finding missions on major internal displacement situations or conduct visits to IDP camps. NHRIs can also play a critical role in creating awareness about the Convention through research and training and may also engage in advocacy work in promoting the ratification of the instrument by the concerned state. The independence of these mechanisms is an important element of the legitimacy of their specific initiative with respect to the protection and assistance of their rights and freedoms. This should also be relevant to institutions such as anti-corruption commissions or bodies which can play, among others, an important role in monitoring the distribution of humanitarian aid and assistance.

69 Ibid.

70 See, Report of the Workshop on the Role of African National Human Rights Institutions in Protecting the Human Rights of Internally Displaced Persons, Nairobi, Kenya, 25–26 October 2008, Office of the High Commissioner for Human Rights and the Brookings Institutions, available online at www.brookings.edu/~/media/Files/events/2008/1026_internal_displacement/0105_internal_displacement.pdf.

71 Ibid., 1.

72 Discussion with Professor Walter Kälin, 25 January 2011.

73 Kenyan National Human Rights Commission Progress Report on Investigating and Documenting Post-Election Violence, 27 March 2008. Available at www.knchr.org/dmdocuments/ProgressReport Draft_rev26MAR08%20_5_.pdf.

The military and law enforcement organs

The military and law enforcement organs are responsible for implementing several provisions of the Kampala Convention, particularly those related to the safety and security of humanitarian organisations. In certain situations, the presence of the police or even the military is required to ensure the protection of IDPs. At the same time, the actions of the state and its agents are too often the causes of internal displacement. This happens, for instance, when the military commits arbitrary displacement of civilians in violation of international humanitarian law or is otherwise involved in acts which result in human rights breaches. The same is true for other agents of the state such as the police or security services. During armed conflicts, the military is bound by relevant international humanitarian and human rights law to protect civilians and facilitate humanitarian access. The military should also ensure the safety and personal security of IDPs located in camps and settlement areas. If international humanitarian law and human rights law were fully respected, internal displacement and its various manifestations would not occur. But in reality, displaced persons trapped in conflicts face numerous challenges. For example, the military in CAR was criticised for failing to protect returnees and displaced persons from banditry and attacks by the Lord's Resistance Army. Under such circumstances, the government should meet its obligation including by ensuring accountability, enhancing the capacity of the armed forces and undertaking training. The military's manuals and instructions regulating displacement and guaranteeing access by returnees to their former places of residence need to be developed. These manuals may also serve as guidelines for national contingents which may participate in peace-keeping missions.

Particularly in situations of displacement generated by natural disasters, the military can play an indispensable role by deploying key assets in the areas of transportation of evacuated people and relief goods, rebuilding infrastructure and protecting the safety of victims including those who are displaced. International standards regulating the coordination between humanitarian actors and the military during natural disasters have been developed. National IDP policies such as the one developed in Uganda examine the relationship between the respective role of the military and the police. And yet several African countries do not have specific laws regulating the relationship between the military and civilian institutions.

The police assume protection responsibility in various contexts, including by investigating attacks and abuses of IDPs, and by helping to bring perpetrators to justice. In Somalia and Chad, it has been shown that often kidnapping of humanitarian officers has been perpetrated by gangs and those who encourage and participate in lawlessness.

The Kampala Convention and other relevant instruments could serve as essential elements of training provided to military and law enforcement institutions. Such specific training on IDP protection and assistance can be incorporated within training programmes that national authorities often conduct with their military and law enforcement officers. Specific manuals and procedures need to be developed at the national level which help these institutions respond effectively to the protection needs of vulnerable groups such as women and children. It is now common to see the establishment of departments or units within law enforcement institutions, which focus on sexual or gender-based offences. These institutions will definitely play an important role in addressing the concerns of women or children IDPs. Similar working procedures may also be developed with respect to the role of the military around IDP settlements and camps. Such manuals will help maintain the integrity and neutrality of the camps.

The role of traditional institutions

Among traditional societies, the role of traditional and customary institutions is profound. The role of these institutions becomes even more pronounced during emergencies where state institutions and the enforcement of formal laws face significant strain. National legislations and policy frameworks on internal displacement may, thus, consider the role of traditional, religious and other alternative dispute resolution mechanisms. These institutions play important roles in diffusing or preventing causes of displacement such as conflicts, serve as important interlocutors between affected communities, national authorities and international organisations, help address some specific concerns such as disputes between displaced persons and host communities, and can serve as effective focal points for addressing the specific needs of marginalised groups such as pastoralists and others with a specific relationship with land.

In Angola, traditional mechanisms were used by the government to involve IDPs in the planning and implementation of resettlement programmes. During the post-election violence and displacement in Kenya, the former RSG recommended the encouragement of a more robust role of community-based institutions in settling communal disputes and conflicts.[74] As is the case with the *Cacaca* courts in Rwanda, traditional institutions can also be important tools for dealing with the problem of impunity. As the experience from Angola shows, these institutions play key roles not only in helping the implementation of national policies and legislations but also in ensuring the protection of individual victims of displacement. As the role of women in traditional institutions is often minimal, traditional institutions may also face challenges guaranteeing the specific concerns of women and children.

The aforementioned problem calls for the inclusion, in relevant national legislations and policy frameworks, of sufficient safeguards ensuring the

74 Report of the Special Rapporteur on the human rights of internally displaced persons, Addendum: Mission to Kenya, 13 February 2012, A/HRC/19/54/Add.2, para. 64.

compatibility of the responsibility and role of traditional mechanisms with human rights standards. Articles 34, 35 and 78 of the Federal Constitution of Ethiopia recognise the role of customary and religious dispute settlement mechanisms in addressing family and property disputes. At the same time, Article 9 of the Constitution also guarantees the primacy of human rights and individual freedoms. Article 5, paragraph 1 of the new Kenyan Land Bill, adopted on 10 February 2012, also recognises customary land tenure systems to the extent that they are consistent with the provision of the Constitution. Such legal guarantees are crucial, as some traditional institutions reinforce harmful traditional practices which, as the Kampala Convention recognises, may even generate forced displacement.

Non-state actors

The Kampala Convention recognises the role of non-state actors such as armed groups, NGOs, *de facto* authorities and private companies in the protection and assistance of IDPs. Several provisions of the Convention are directly relevant and applicable to armed groups. In Chad, CAR, Sudan and Somalia, armed groups and insurgents are responsible for acts which result in the forced displacement of civilians, and for various forms of abuse perpetrated against civilians.

The Convention provides that states also assume responsibility to ensure that private companies and organisations are accountable for damages caused by their actions. Article 2(e) explicitly provides that states should 'provide for the respective obligations, responsibilities and roles of armed groups, non-state actors and other relevant factors, including civil society organizations, with respect to the prevention of internal displacement and protection of, and assistance to, internally displaced persons'. This means that states shall take legislative and other appropriate measures to punish forced displacement and arbitrary eviction caused by actions of non-state actors. It is also provided under Article 12(2) that states are also required to 'establish an effective legal framework to provide just and fair compensation and other forms of reparations, where appropriate, to internally displaced persons for damage incurred as a result of displacement, in accordance with international standards'.

The nature of NGOs and their contribution within the framework of a national response to internal displacement varies. Some of them may have broader human rights mandates while others focus on specific areas of expertise. These organisations are critical partners in the implementation of the national response during all phases of displacement. For instance, their participation in the preparation of needs assessments on a particular region or area may help to check if and whether the government is failing to take into account the needs of certain marginalised groups. In Kenya, an impressive array of NGOs and community organisations have been at the forefront of the elaboration of national policy on internal displacement with the view to implementing the Guiding Principles and the Great Lakes Protocol on Internal Displacement. In Somalia, local NGOs are important actors in the provision of humanitarian aid in areas where UN agencies and international non-governmental organisations do not enjoy access. The role and unique expertise of national Red Cross and Red Crescent societies have been quite important especially in the context of local response to natural disasters. The former RSG has found that while some governments allow NGOs to consult affected communities, often these organisations are not allowed to become a part of the national coordination mechanism, thus, having a considerably limited leeway to influence policies and their implementation at the national level. As experience shows, advocacy-oriented NGOs are particularly subjected to government restrictions and even expulsion.

Resource mobilisation and allocation

National policies and strategies need to identify how programmes and activities of national and local authorities in implementing the provisions of the Kampala Convention will be financed. Providing education, health, food, shelter and other social services requires considerable resources. Implementing projects aimed at achieving durable solutions demands even greater resources. Ensuring the allocation of sufficient resources is often the most difficult aspect of the national response to internal displacement, particularly in Africa where many states lack the necessary resources. Long after the adoption of a comprehensive national policy on internal displacement, the government in Uganda was slow in allocating funding for the implementation of the policy. In many situations, displacement is triggered by sudden events, leaving states with little time to raise funds. It is important, therefore, that states consider the establishment of emergency funds, or develop flexible procedures on the basis of which the required finance will be made available. For instance, Ethiopia has established a National Disaster Prevention and Preparedness Fund and Emergency Food Security Fund.

Within the framework of burden sharing and international cooperation, states are required to mobilise the necessary resources from international partners in situations where they face difficulties in finding the necessary resources from within. The government can only meet these requirements not only by cooperating with traditional humanitarian donors but also by forging new alliances with development actors such as the World Bank. In 2009, the World Bank launched a programme through which it has been assisting national and local authorities in finding durable solutions to the problem of internal displacement. National authorities should also explore new possibilities for partnership and resource mobilisation. The Cancun Climate agreement, for instance, has opened up new avenues for a global partnership for financing adaptation and mitigation measures.

The role of regional monitoring mechanisms

The primary responsibility of states in providing protection and assistance to IDPs is also reflected in how they cooperate with regional and international organisations, particularly in situations where they lack the capacity to effectively respond to situations of internal displacement. Too often states which experience some of the worst forms of internal displacement suffer from institutional fragility and resource constraints. Situations of internal displacement are often caused by conflicts with regional dimensions, thereby underlining the utility of regional organisations not only in meeting the protection and assistance needs of IDPs but also in addressing the root causes of displacement. In his report on internal displacement in Chad, for instance, the former RSG notes that internal displacement in the country is linked with the on-going armed conflict in Darfur.[75] In situations such as Chad's, the role of regional and sub-regional institutions in peace building and preventive diplomacy is crucial.

The Convention imposes obligations on member states to respect the competence and mandate of regional institutions particularly that of the African Union. Some of the implementation institutions such as the Conference of Parties are newly envisaged. Several provisions of the Convention, however, specifically mention the role of existing regional mechanisms, namely, the Executive Council, the African Commission on Human and Peoples' Rights, the African Court on Human and Peoples' Rights, and the Special Rapporteur on Refugees, Internally Displaced Persons and Migrants. As has been incorporated both in the Convention and the African Union Plan of Action, the role of these regional organisations involves the following key areas: (a) promoting the ratification of the Convention, (b) enhancing the capacity and resources of member states, (c) cooperating with relevant international organisations, (d) monitoring the policies and measures taken at the national level, and (e) engaging in mobilisation of resources. It must be stated that while international humanitarian organisations have developed mature and complex humanitarian assistance mechanisms over the years, similar capacity and tools, however, do not exist at the regional and sub-regional levels.

The Conference of Parties (COP)

The Conference of Parties is a forum intended to assist states to 'enhance their capacity for cooperation and mutual support'. It has a specific responsibility of monitoring and reviewing the implementation of provisions of the Convention. It is also responsible for the amendment of the Convention; a responsibility which it may undertake based on the advice of the Executive

75 See Report of the Representative of the Secretary General on the Human Rights of Internally Displaced Persons, A/HRC/13/21/Add.5.

Council. COP may also act as a dispute settlement mechanism to solve differences that may arise between state parties until such time as the matter is duly referred to and resolved by the African Court on Human Rights and Justice. Though the Convention does not specify the scope and frequency of COP meetings, the conference is expected to hold regular meetings.

An informal division of labour should exist between the COP and other regional processes, particularly the ministerial conferences on forced displacement and the regional human rights monitoring mechanisms. By building and implementing a procedure which allows it to review country compliance and thematic consideration, the COP can emerge as a key forum for sharing best practices and lessons learnt. The African Union has been effective in holding key ministerial conferences on forced displacement. Until such time that the Convention comes into force, these ministerial conferences may continue to serve as a key forum which facilitates policy deliberations, and reviews national policies and practices. The ministerial conference on forced displacement which preceded the 2009 special Kampala Summit had decided that similar meetings, which bring together ministers responsible for forced displacement matters across the continent, shall be held every two years with the view to reviewing the progress in the implementation of the Kampala Declaration. For instance, the ministerial conference on forced displacement held between 4 and 5 June 2010 was instrumental in the development and adoption of the African Plan of Action on forced displacement which seeks to implement the outcomes of the Kampala Summit. It endorsed and reiterated the decision made earlier on holding a ministerial conference every two years. As the Convention comes into force, these ministerial conferences and the COP may become redundant unless efforts are made to align and streamline these two processes.

Policy organs of the African Union

The role of the African Union in the prevention and protection of IDPs is comprehensively addressed in the Convention. The latter provides the organisation with general responsibilities and urges member states to respect the mandate of the African Union. It makes a direct reference to some of the African Union's key institutions, namely, the Assembly, the Executive Council, the African Commission on Human and Peoples' Rights, the African Court on Human Rights and Justice, and the African Commission (the secretariat). The Convention recognises the right of IDPs to have their concerns heard, and to enjoy full access to remedies provided by the African Commission on Human and Peoples' Rights and the African Court on Human and Peoples' Rights. Regarding the role of the Executive Council, the Convention states that the Council may advice the COP on proposals for amendments to the Convention. It is quite relevant that the implementation of the Convention is also examined in the light of other regional legal instruments, namely the AU Constitutive Act and the Protocol establishing the

Peace and Security of the African Union which sets forth relevant standards which grant key policy organs of the African Union powers and responsibilities relevant to the protection of IDPs.

The mandate of the AU touches upon a wider spectrum of protection and assistance activities ranging from authorising and undertaking regional interventions in certain extreme circumstances, to monitoring the implementation of the Convention, and to the coordination of humanitarian relief to IDPs. As is shown by the elaboration of the Convention itself, regional mechanisms can also play a critical role in developing relevant normative frameworks, and adapting international standards to regional contexts and situations. For instance, the African Union can authorise interventions based on the provisions of the Constitutive Act. The AU has not yet invoked Article 4 of the Consecutive Act which provides some of the Guiding Principles for AU's actions, including the right of the Union to intervene in response to grave situations such as war crimes, genocide and crimes against humanity. It also supports efforts initiated by member states in protecting and assisting IDPs, in particular, in: (a) strengthening support mechanisms and structures, (b) coordinating the mobilisation of resources, (c) collaborating with states, international organisations, humanitarian agencies and civic society organisations, (d) sharing information with the African Commission on Human and Peoples' Rights, and (e) cooperating with the Special Rapporteur on Refugees, Returnees, IDPs and Asylum Seekers.

Though Article 8 identifies the specific responsibilities of some key institutions such as the Assembly, the African Commission on Human and Peoples' Rights and the Special Rapporteur, it leaves out a number of other regional institutions and mechanisms; some of which are potential key players with respect to protecting and assisting victims of internal displacement. The roles and responsibilities of the Executive Council and the Peace and Security Council can be cited as an example. In accordance with the Constitutive Act and the Protocol on Peace and Security Council, these policy organs of the African Union, among others, have specific responsibilities to coordinate humanitarian relief and assistance programmes during emergencies.

As has been stated in the relevant AU instruments, the Assembly is responsible for providing direction and guidance regarding the management of conflicts and emergencies. It is the highest political organ of the African Union which has the responsibility to, among others, (a) authorise intervention in member states in accordance with Article 4 of the Constitutive Act, (b) adopt policy instruments and standards, (c) review and adopt reports of the African Commission on Human and Peoples' Rights and the African Court on Human and Peoples' Rights, and (d) deploy peace support missions to conflict areas. The Permanent Representatives Committee (PRC), particularly through its Sub-Committee on Refugees, Returnees and IDPs, as identified in the Constitutive Act and the Plan of Action, assumes a role of coordinating humanitarian issues. The Convention does not mention the role of the Permanent Representatives. As mentioned above, neither does it discuss the roles and responsibilities of the Peace and Security Council with respect to IDPs. The roles and responsibilities of these institutions, however, are particularly significant for the protection of civilians affected by armed conflicts. The PRC has established sub-committees on forced displacement with responsibility concerning humanitarian issues and has gradually become a key convener of member states, UN agencies and relevant civic society organisations on humanitarian issues. The Plan of Action recognises the role of additional stakeholders, namely the Economic, Social and Cultural Council, the Pan-African Parliament and the institutions created by the International Conference on the Great Lakes Region. The consequence of this responsibility with respect to the protection of civilians in general and that of IDPs in particular is important.

The increasing trend of considering humanitarian issues by AU policy organs has helped to clarify issues and identify potential challenges. Based on the decision of the Executive Council of the African Union, a Plan of Action has been developed which was later adopted by the ministerial conference on forced displacement held in June 2010. The objectives of the plan include: (a) implementing the vision of the AU in addressing the issues of forced displacement in Africa; (b) presenting an implementation and accountability mechanism; (c) promoting key components for information dissemination and advocacy; and (d) facilitating monitoring and follow-up. In the short term, the Action Plan sets out activities to be undertaken by member states, the different organs of the African Union, sub-regional institutions and other stakeholders in the promotion of a speedy ratification of the Convention. The long-term objectives will involve activities such as advocacy, capacity building, technical assistance, resource mobilisation, policy development, humanitarian assistance, and monitoring and reporting.

Under its peace-building and peace-keeping missions, the Peace and Security Council of the African Union also seeks to provide protection to civilians. In order to integrate and mainstream the protection of civilians during armed conflicts, the African Union has elaborated the Guidelines on Civilian Protection. Originally developed by a committee of military experts and having been scrutinised through a series of consultations involving member states, United Nations institutions, international organisations and civic society organisations, these Guidelines seek to ensure the mainstreaming of protection of civilians in African regional peace-keeping operations. The Action Plan makes reference to the Guidelines and considers them among the key standards that should be taken into account in the implementation of the Kampala Convention.

Another key policy area where the African Union has contributed relates to peace building and post-conflict reconstruction; a key area where regional and international institutions can facilitate and support durable solutions to the problems of displacement. Upon a decision by the Executive Council of the African Union, a policy on post-conflict reconstruction has been developed. This policy, developed through a wide consultation with member states and independent experts, was adopted at the 9th Session of the Executive Council in June 2006 in Gambia.[76] The policy contains the following elements, namely, security, humanitarian assistance, political governance and transition, socio-economic reconstruction and development, human rights, justice and reconciliation, and women and gender. This program aspires to be a regional complement to the works of the UN Peace Building Commission, and the roles and responsibilities of governments, regional and sub-regional organisations, international organisations and CSOs in order to coordinate support to countries that are emerging from conflicts with the view to assisting them adapt the policy into national laws, mobilise an African Volunteer Program and help build a roster of African expertise on post-conflict reconstruction and peace-making. It also seeks to conduct assessment missions and run specific programmes and projects on relevant areas. A Ministerial Committee has been established to monitor some of the AU activities and support the structures envisaged to implement the policy framework. So far the Committee has undertaken consultations and held a mission visit to Sudan. A follow-up technical meeting which will develop a roadmap to mobilise resources and support has also been considered.

Thanks to the partnership between the African Union and international humanitarian organisations, the Executive Council, the Peace and Security Council and the PRC are now increasingly examining reports on serious humanitarian concerns in the continent. These informed deliberations will help the further development of norms, ensure enhanced protection of civilians, and promote humanitarian space and access. But operationalising the African Union's broad mandate and competence is likely to face considerable challenges. The African Union has not so far made any intervention within the framework of Article 4 of the Constitutive Act. It is predicted that the implementation of this specific provision will be curtailed by lack of political will and resource constraint. It is equally difficult to proclaim that the AU and its institutions have become well-positioned to coordinate humanitarian assistance and relief during emergencies, as called for by the Constitutive Act. There is an overlap of competence particularly between the Executive Council and the PSC. There has also been fragmented policy platform at the African Union. The relationship between the ministerial conferences on forced displacement and policy organs of the AU, and particularly how the inputs of these special procedures will be incorporated in the deliberation of these policy organs has not been clarified. The most significant limitation to the authority of these key organs is their continuous difficulty in backing

76 See Decision on the AU Policy Framework on Post-Conflict Reconstruction and Development, DOC.EX.CL/274 (IX). Available at: http://africa-union.org/root/au/conferences/2007/july/PCRD/Decision%20om%post%20Post%20%Conflict.pdf, last visited on 20 June 2012.

their decision with the necessary resources and financing. The disproportionate number of humanitarian activities under the auspices of the African Union relies on outside support and assistance, rarely a sign of commitment and capacity of member states. A great portion of the funding required for the holding of the Special Summit in 2009 and additional follow-up meetings was financed through the support of AU partners.

The African Commission

Notwithstanding the existence of a formal coordinating mechanism on the protection and assistance of refugees and IDPs within the institutional framework of the former OAU, this mechanism had largely been ineffective mainly due to lack of funding and personnel. Partly owing to these challenges, no meaningful cooperation existed between the African Union secretariat and the ACHPR. Following the creation of the AU, however, several steps have been taken including the establishment of the portfolio of the commissioners, the reinvigoration of the composition and mandate of the Coordinating Committee on Assistance and Protection to Refugees, Returnees and Internally Displaced Persons in Africa (CCAR), and the strengthening of key departments within the Commission. In 2006, the latter also adopted its revised rules of procedure and identified key objectives, activities and benchmarks for implementation.[77]

The Kampala Convention provides that the African Union shall strengthen its institutional framework and capacity on internal displacement. The Plan of Action envisages the Commission as an 'overall coordinator and facilitator' of the implementation of regional activities on internal displacement. The Commission will also facilitate COP's meetings and activities.

Within the institutional architecture of the Commission, the chairperson plays an important role. The chairperson, for example, provides regular reports including on humanitarian issues to the AU's policy organs. These reports can serve as key tools in providing detailed and accurate humanitarian information which will then feed into policy debates in these mechanisms. Commissioners are also key players in coordinating the activities of the Commission on sectoral issues. In this capacity, the AU Commissioner for Political Affairs was at the forefront of not only providing the necessary secretariat role for the negotiation of the Kampala Convention but also in promoting the ratification of the Convention. The mandate and role of the Commissioner for Peace and Security is also crucial, as situations of internal displacement too often are triggered by armed conflicts and violence. Owing to potential overlaps between the two departments, coordination is often required particularly at the level of the Directorate for

77 See Revitalizing the AU Coordinating Committee on Assistance to Refugees, *The Reporter*, 25 November 2006.

Political Affairs, and the Directorate for Peace and Security which are under the supervision of the Commissioner for Political Affairs and the Commissioner for Peace and Security respectively.

The secretariat works closely with UN organisations, international humanitarian organisations and CSOs, some of which could also provide a much needed institutional support which could help the Commission to address some of its challenges. UNHCR had seconded officers to the Directorate for Political Affairs whose division on human and political affairs assumes an important role with respect to stirring humanitarian activities at the regional level. Since 2009, the capacity of the Humanitarian and Political Division has been boosted by the appointment of a new official and the assignment of additional staff. Despite these positive measures, however, the current level of staff and resources is far below what the division requires if it were to effectively implement its responsibilities.

Implementation challenges faced by the African regional human rights system

Principal regional human rights instruments, namely the African Charter on Human and Peoples' Rights, the Protocol to the African Charter on the Rights of Women in Africa and the African Charter on the Rights and Welfare of the Child are key human rights instruments supplementing the Kampala Convention. All these instruments are also clearly mentioned in the preamble of the Convention. The latter also provides key provisions outlining the role of African regional human rights institutions or mechanisms including the African Commission on Human and Peoples' Rights, and the African Court on Human and Peoples' Rights and ACHPR's Special Rapporteur. In addition, the African Committee of Experts on the Rights and Welfare of the Child and the African Peer Review Mechanism have also important roles to play.

The African Commission on Human and Peoples' Rights

The Commission has a number of tools at its disposal for the promotion and protection of the rights of IDPs. The Kampala Convention, however, specifically mentions the role the Commission in the examination of state reports. Under Article 14 of the Convention dealing with monitoring of the implementation of the provisions, the Convention only acknowledges the role of the Commission in examining states' reports. However, no mention has been made of the authority and competence of the Commission to examine individual or group complaints or its ability to conduct fact-finding missions. This vague provision may be cited as a ground to argue that the Convention did not intend to grant a competence to the Commission to consider communication relating to breaches of the provisions of the Kampala Convention.

Such an argument, however, does not stand a real test particularly when one looks at Article 20, paragraph 3, where the right of internally displaced persons to lodge a complaint with the African Commission on Human and Peoples' Rights or the African Court of Justice and Human Rights, or any other competent international body is explicitly recognised.

This reinforces Article 60 of the African Charter on Human and Peoples' Rights which states that 'the Commission shall draw inspiration from international law on human and peoples' rights, particularly from the provisions of various African instruments on human and peoples' rights'.

By lodging their formal complaints to the Commission, IDPs can seek remedies which they are denied by authorities. A body of jurisprudence has emerged from the Commission which could be used for the promotion of the rights of IDPs. In *SERAC and CESR v. Nigeria*, the Commission elaborated its important jurisprudence on the right to property and prohibition of eviction, by deciding that the right to housing may be read into the Charter's provisions on the right to health, family, and right to property.[78] In a recent landmark case inspired by the jurisprudence of the European Court of Human Rights and the Inter-American Court of Human Rights and which involved indigenous peoples in Kenya, the Commission held that the displacement of the Endorois peoples by the Kenyan government from their traditional land violated the Charter.[79] The most important outcome of this jurisprudence is reflected in the Commission's careful attempt to balance the implementation of the requirement of 'exhaustion of local remedies' on the one hand and the unique circumstances of displacement which make it extremely difficult for victims to take advantage of available remedies at the local level. In some of its most important decisions,[80] the Commission has underlined that complainants are not necessarily required to exhaust local remedies when the procedure of doing so in unduly long or where the remedies are unavailable or ineffective. The Commission's communication procedures suffer from a number of shortcomings, some of which are of particular relevance to the rights of IDPs. First, the Commission's findings

78 Communication No. 155/96, *The Social and Economic Rights Action Centre and the Centre for Economic and Social Rights v. Nigeria*, 15th Activity Report, para. 60.

79 *Centre for Minority Rights Development (Kenya) and Minority Rights Group International on Behalf of Endorois Welfare Council v. Kenya*, 276/2003, 27th Activity Report of the African Commission on Human and Peoples' Rights, 109–178.

80 Communication 87/93, *Constitutional Rights Project* (in respect of *Zamani Lekot & 6 others) v. Nigeria*, in 8th Annual Activity Report of the African Commission on Human and Peoples' Rights 1994–95, 18th Ordinary Session, 2–11 Oct. 1995, ACHPR/AHG/201/XXXI, Annex VI, 16, 18, para 6; Communication 71/92, *Recontre Africane poure la Defence des Droits de l'Homme (RADDHO) v. Zambia*, in 10th Annual Activity Report of the African Commission on Human and Peoples' Rights 1996–97, para. 12; and Communications 25/89, 47/90, 56–91, 100/93, *World Organization against Torture et al. v. Zaire*, in 9th Annual Activity Report of the African Commission on Human and Peoples' Rights 1995–96, 32nd Ordinary Session, 7–10 July 1996, AHG/207(XXXII), 2. 6, para. 37.

are often recommendations which ought to be considered by the political organs of the African Union before they are published. Importantly, the binding nature of these findings, often referred to as recommendations, has always been considered doubtful. Moreover, the Commission has so far failed to create a compensation regime based on which victims of breaches enjoy specific compensations.

The Commission has undertaken important fact-finding missions namely to Zimbabwe, Sudan and Mauritania. The Commission has also adopted a decision expressing its intention to undertake fact-finding missions into Somalia. The findings of these missions addressed key problems of internal displacement. These missions are often outcomes of the Commission's own initiative. Despite the concern over human rights and humanitarian violations in Darfur, attention to the findings of the mission was considerably low including by the institutions of the African Union themselves. For instance, there was no evidence which showed that the African Union Mission in Sudan (AMIS) took advantage of the report of the Commission. The decision of the Peace and Security Council in October 2010 endorsing the decision by the African Commission to undertake a fact-finding mission to Somalia is also remarkable in this context. Not only does this show an interest by a policy organ of the AU in the Commission's work, but it also underscores the Council's interest to strengthen and monitor such measures. This is contrary to how the Council dealt with the report of the fact-finding mission to Darfur in which case the delegation of Sudan chided the African Commission alleging that the latter has published its findings without taking into due account the government's reply.

As called for in the Kampala Convention, the Commission may use its power to examine states' report as a vehicle to monitor the implementation of the provisions of the Convention. This can be done if the Commission maintains its practices of broadly interpreting provisions of the Charter based on the current development of international human rights law and practices of other tribunals and regional human rights mechanisms. In its concluding observations, the Commission has often encouraged member states to enhance the implementation of national policies on IDPs and take specific measures with respect to the protection of IDPs. It is also true that despite concerns over the protection of the rights of IDPs in the country whose report is under consideration, the Commission, on a number of occasions, neglected to mention the issue in the examination of state reports. By way of example, one can mention the case of the Democratic Republic of Congo, where contrary to the determination by the Commission that massive displacement in the country makes it difficult for affected citizens to enjoy their rights under the Charter, the recommendation has kept silent on the matter.[81] It is, therefore, important for the Commission to clarify how it

81 See Concluding Observations and Recommendations on the Initial Report of the Democratic Republic of Congo (DRC), adopted at the 34th Ordinary Session of the African Commission on Human and Peoples' Rights, 6–20 November 2003.

intends to systematically integrate concerns over the implementation of the rights of IDPs in its concluding observations on initial and periodic reports of states under review.

The most significant legacy of the Commission for the protection and assistance of IDPs has been its decision to establish the mandate of the Special Rapporteur on Refugees, Migrants and Internally Displaced Persons in 2004. Since then the mandate has been a key focal point within the Commission on matters affecting IDPs. Though a direct responsibility for the Commission in the drafting of the Convention was never granted, its Special Rapporteur actively participated in the process and had contributed to the drafting process. As has been provided for both in the Convention and the Plan of Action, the Special Rapporteur will remain a key institutional link between the Commission and the Convention. The Plan of Action in particular suggests the revision and strengthening of the mandate. However, little detail has been incorporated regarding how this will actually be achieved.

The Commission faces several challenges in fulfilling its mandate on IDPs. Nothing stands between the Convention and its successful implementation by the Commission than the well-entrenched view which sidelines protection and assistance issues affecting IDPs as mere 'humanitarian' issue than a human rights agenda. Its relationship with UNHCR and the role and participation of NGOs can be used to enhance the capacity of the Commission. As has been shown in its fact-finding initiative on Somalia, the Commission's keen interest to undertake missions has been thwarted by governments' lack of willingness to accommodate such requests. In cases such as Darfur where the Commission has undertaken visits and made specific recommendations, its recommendations are not well respected and implemented.

The African Court on Human Rights and Justice

The African Court on Human Rights and Justice is a new institution established by the Protocol on the Statute of the African Court of Justice and Human Rights that merged the African Court on Human and Peoples' Rights and the African Court of Justice. The Convention's provision regarding the powers and authority of the Court anticipates the entry into force of the Protocol. However, only three states have so far ratified this new Protocol. The Kampala Convention does not expressly provide for the Court to assume responsibility for monitoring the compliance of member states with the Convention. Article 22, however, stipulates that when state parties fail to settle their disputes or differences over the interpretation or application of this Convention, either of the parties may refer the matter to the Court. That the Convention grants the Court the competence to settle interstate disputes over the interpretation and application of the Kampala Convention is simply a restatement of Article 19 of the Protocol on the African Court of Justice which grants broad responsibility of settling interstate disputes over treaty interpretation to the Court.

The potential role of the Court in overseeing the implementation and interpretation of the Convention is evident from its authority to determine contentious cases and provide legal advice and opinion based on a request by one of the executive organs of the Union or any other organisation recognised by the African Union. The Court's authority is articulated in a universalist term, meaning that it is empowered to consider breaches of any human rights instrument which the state concerned has ratified. Its role as a source of remedy to victims of internal displacement has also been indirectly recognised under Article 20(3) of the Kampala Convention where the right of IDPs to lodge complaints in regional and international organs including the African Court on Human Rights and Justice has been clearly stated.

The Court can only consider and determine individual cases where the matter involves states which made specific declarations and have accepted its jurisdiction over individual communication. To date only two states have made such a declaration, signalling the limited relevance of this procedure at least in the short term for individual victims including IDPs. Though a closer relationship between the Court and the Commission is envisaged in the Protocol, the Commission has shown far too little enthusiasm towards the Court as reflected in the limited referral of communications by the Commission to the Court. This is partly owing to the latter's fear of being overshadowed by a stronger court.

The first case was filed before the Court six years after the Court had been established. The Court, citing jurisdictional grounds, dismissed the case brought by a national of Chad against Senegal for initiating to prosecute Mr Hissene Habre, former President of Chad. In another high-profile case[82] referred to the Court by the African Commission on Human and Peoples' Rights involving 'serious and massive violations of human rights' in Libya, the Court determined that excessive use of force, unlawful arrest and detention amount to serious violations of the African Charter, and hence ordered the Libyan government to refrain from any action that would result in loss of life or violation of physical integrity of persons.

The Court also requested the government to report on measures it has taken to implement the decision within 15 days. Though the government failed to implement the decision, the Court's ruling showed the tools available within the regional human rights system to address pressing and challenging human rights situations which also involve massive forced displacement.

The African Committee of Experts on the Rights and Welfare of the Child

The African Committee of Experts on the Rights of the Child monitors the

82 Application No 004/2011–African Commission on Human and Peoples' Rights v. Great Socialist Peoples Libyan Arab Jamahiriya.

implementation of the African Charter on the Rights and Welfare of the Child (the African Charter) which, as described in greater detail in previous chapters, incorporates provisions dealing with displaced children including the responsibility of states to facilitate the protection and assistance of IDPs and the specific protection of those who are separated from their families as a result of displacement. Whereas both the Kampala Convention and the African Charter incorporate provisions relevant to the protection of the rights of displaced children, the Kampala Convention further complements the Charter by providing specific provisions covering issues such as right to education, access to documentation, protection against military recruitment, sexual violence, trafficking and abduction, and the protection of abandoned children and minors. As has been witnessed in conflict areas such as the DRC, Sudan and Somalia, displaced children are subjected to abuses such as forced military recruitment, lack of social services, forced labour and sexual violence.

The Committee adopted its first ever decision in *Nubian Minors v. Kenya* in March 2011. In this landmark decision which concerns children of Nubian descent in Kenya, it found the government of Kenya in violation of a number of key provisions of the Charter, including on the rights to birth registration, nationality and protection of statelessness.[83] The Committee recommended to the Kenyan government to take measures to ensure that children of Nubian descent in Kenya enjoy access to birth registration and nationality. It also requested the Kenyan government to take legislative, administrative and other measures to ensure the fulfilment of the right to the highest attainable standard of health and of the right to education, in consultation with the affected beneficiaries.

The Committee has recently made an admissibility decision on communication on violation of the rights of children in northern Uganda to consider a communication concerning conditions of children in northern Uganda.[84]

Similar to the African Commission, the Committee also examines state reports on the implementation of the African Charter, and also enjoys the competence to consider individual communications. Moreover, it also has the mandate to undertake investigations. Reports by states are expected to cover not only the progress achieved in the implementation of the African Charter but also the identification of the challenges faced by the state under review. As indicated in the Guidelines for the Initial Reports of the State Parties, the Committee requires, among others, specific information on

83 Decision on the Communication Submitted by the Institute for Human Rights and Development in Africa and the Open Society Initiative (On Behalf of the Children of Nubian Descent in Kenya) against the Government of Kenya, Communication: No. Com/002/2009, 22 March 2011. Available online at: www.ihrda.org/wp-content/uploads/2011/09/002-09-Nubian -children-v/kenya-Eng-pdf.

84 Report of the 18th session of the African Committee of Experts on the Rights and Welfare of the Child, para. 61.

measures states have undertaken to address situations affecting children such as separation from family including as a result of internal displacement, special protection for children under emergency and children affected by exploitation and abuse. While examining reports submitted by states experiencing armed conflicts, the Committee provides recommendations requesting specific information on the situation of children affected by armed conflicts. It has also appointed one of its members as a Rapporteur to follow on situations of children including refugees and IDPs who are affected by armed conflicts and natural disaster. The Committee has also held several workshops including on the protection of children during armed conflicts.

The effectiveness of the Committee's works has been undermined by several factors including the lack of visibility, absence of a well-functioning secretariat, low level of state reporting, lack of capacity and expertise by members of the Committee, and shortage of funding. Whereas the mandate given to the Committee under the Charter is more expansive than what is provided for to the Committee on the Right of the Child, some of the specific elements of its competence such as investigative mandate have been weakened by lack of resources. The Charter's somewhat limited reference to the role of non-state actors has also been considered as a shortcoming.

Strengthening the role of ACHPR Special Rapporteur

Since its establishment by the Commission in 2004 and the subsequent renewal of the mandate in 2007, the Special Rapporteur has played a significant role in the promotion and implementation of the rights of IDPs. The Rapporteur is mandated to seek, receive, examine and act upon information concerning the rights of refugees, asylum seekers and IDPs, undertake fact-finding missions to displacement situations, engage in dialogue with states and others relevant actors, develop strategies to better protect the rights of these groups, and raise awareness on relevant legal standards. The Special Rapporteur undertook missions in a number of countries and also participated in joint fact-finding missions together with other regional special procedures and mechanisms. That a number of important, *albeit* related, thematic topics have been covered under the terms of reference of the mandate meant that the mandate-holder had to share the limited resources at his disposal to concerns affecting each community. This is indeed a broad and challenging mandate.

The Plan of Action suggests a review and strengthening of the mandate of the ACHPR Special Rapporteur. Not much detail has been provided in the Plan of Action for the implementation of the Kampala Convention. Several ideas, however, can be considered. One option is to transfer the responsibility from a single individual to a body of experts or a working group. The Commission currently has five workings groups which include those dealing with the Commission's working methods, the rights of indigenous peoples, and socio-economic rights. This arrangement expands the opportunity to develop the support base for the mandate-holder and enhances the participations of key stakeholders, particularly humanitarian organisations and NGOs in the activities of the Commission. Additional efforts can also be made to enhance, within the framework of existing MOU between the African Commission and UNHCR, the cooperation between the ACHPR Special Rapporteur and the UNHCR. There had been a positive and collaborative working relationship between the ACHPR's Special Rapporteur and the former RSG; a relationship which had been strengthened through the RSG's participation in some of the sessions of the ACHPR and his close involvement in the elaboration of the Kampala Convention. There was also a plan to undertake a joint mission to Sudan. In light of current interest to strengthen the relationship between UN special procedure and regional mechanisms, considerable efforts should be undertaken to deepen the relationship through joint study, promotional work and even missions.

The African Peer Review Mechanisms

The African Peer Review Mechanism (APRM) has been identified both by the Kampala Convention and the Action Plan as one of the key mechanism of monitoring the implementation of the Convention.[85] The APRM is a review process under the New Partnership for African Development which allows member states to engage in a constructive self-assessment process and improve performance over a wide spectrum of standards and norms incorporated in the Declaration on Democracy, Political, Economic and Corporate Governance approved by the AU Summit in July 2002.[86] The review involves a number of key phases: (a) the development of self-assessment report and a Plan of Action for the country under review; (b) submission of the report and Plan of Action to the APRM secretariat; (c) examining the report through a country assessment team; and (d) a response from the country concerned which will then be submitted to the APRM forum.[87] The initial review is expected to be undertaken within 18 months following the acceptance of the review process by the state concerned. After the initial reporting, the periodic report will be held once in each 18 months. These reports are submitted directly to the small APRM secretariat based in Pretoria, South Africa.

Assessment of the legislative, policy and institutional reform undertaken by states within the framework of the APRM will have repercussions on efforts

85 See Art 14(4) of the Kampala Convention. Also note 16 above, para. 20.

86 Declaration on Democracy, Political, Economic and Corporate Governance, AHG/235(XXXVIII) Annex I, adopted during the 38th Ordinary Session of the Organisation of African Unity, 8 July 2002.

87 See the African Peer Review Mechanism: Organisation and Processes, NEPAD/HSGIC/03-2003/APRM Guidance, also available at: www.uneca.org/aprm/documents/book4.pdf.

by member states in the prevention of displacement, and the protection and assistance of those who are affected by it. The review under the sector on political governance, for instance, can be used to address the specific needs of IDPs. In some instances, a questionnaire addressed to the state under review requests information regarding the relationship between conflict and internal displacement.[88] Some of the Panel's final reports also include specific information and policy recommendations on displacement-related issues. This, for instance, has been true to the report of Uganda where a review of the status of IDPs in the country is incorporated. It has been stated that:

> The problem of IDPs needs a specific policy intervention. Displaced people face distinctive challenges in conditions of armed conflict. They often live in poor shelters, lack safe water, clothing, and domestic utensils and are exposed to poor environmental conditions. Many of the children have dropped out of school due to lack of educational necessities, displacement and limited school facilities. Orphans are the worst affected in these situations. To compound these problems, food production in and around the camps has been negatively affected by the lack of access to the fields. Among the displaced persons, women and girls are the most abused. In their written submission to the Country Review Mission (CRM), the National Women Councils (NAWOCO) of Uganda argued that many female Internally Displaced Persons (IDPs) fair worse than refugees, lacking basics such as sanitary towels, clean water, proper shelter, proper nutrition, all which may lead to reproductive health complications. Moreover, female IDPs also have to contend with violation of their rights such as rape from fellow IDPs, rebels and government forces.[89]

Under APRM, IDPs have been categorised as a vulnerable group. Country APRM reports recommend a number of policy actions including the capacity and role of mandated institutions in the designing and provision of tailor-made delivery services and importantly in the mainstreaming of the rights of vulnerable groups in peace-building initiatives and development programmes.[90] This has also been the case with respect to the review of Kenya whose APRM progress report states that the government has taken several measures to implement its commitments, namely, the enactment of the Refugee Act 2006, the resettlement of 106,651 IDPs following the post-election violence and the allocation of funds for resettlement of vulnerable groups such as landless individuals.

Not all APRM national reports include information on the examination of

88 Expert Questionnaire: Tanzania APRM, available online at www.aprmtanzania.org/sdocs/APRM%20EXPERT%20PANEL%20QUESTIONNAIRE.pdf.

89 APRM country Review Report No. 7, Republic of Uganda, May 2008. Available at: www.aprmtanzania.org/docs/Uganda%20CRR.pdf, para. 44.

90 Ibid., para. 429.

internal displacement. For example, despite a significant presence of IDPs in Algeria,[91] the country's APRM report provides no information of significance or recommendation to address their flight. Since the actual commencement of the APRM review in 2003, a number of countries have been reviewed including those that are affected by impacts of displacement. To its credit, the system of review is rigorous and technically detailed. But this also meant that it will take several years before all acceding states pass through the review process.[92] More than seven years after its establishment, there is an enormous gap in the relationship between the APRM secretariat based in South Africa and the structures and process of the African Union. The APRM process also provides a broad view of measures taken by the state which, though directly and indirectly relevant to the protection of displaced persons, may not have been examined in a single report. In order to address existing challenges and to integrate the APRM within the African Union, the Summit of the African Union in 2008 adopted a decision affirming the status of the structures of the APRM as an integral part of the African Union and requesting the same to negotiate and conclude a host agreement.[93]

Sub-regional mechanisms

The Plan of Action recognises the particular role of sub-regional institutions in the protection and assistance of IDPs.[94] ECOWAS in West Africa, SADC in Southern Africa, ICGLR in the Great Lakes region and IGAD in the East and the Horn of Africa have become key building blocks for the African Union's initiated programmes regarding forced displacement, peace building, conflict resolutions, human rights and peace-keeping. In the past, these institutions have robustly supported the Guiding Principles and can now undertake a number of key activities on behalf of IDPs. These activities include: (a) the appointment of focal points within their respective institutional frameworks; (b) the disseminations of standards including the Kampala Convention; (c) the development and promotion of a model law; (d) conducting training of law makers and policy makers; and (e) the integration of internal displacement in their programmes and activities.[95]

91 See Algeria: National Reconciliation fails to address needs of IDPs, Internal Displacement Monitoring Centre, 29 September 2009. Available at: www.unhcr.org/refworld/country,,IDMC,,DZA,,4ac310332,0.html.

92 Steven Gruzd, Africa's Evolving Governance Structure: Reflection on the African Peer Review Mechanism, Centre for Policy Studies, Policy Brief 54, January 2009, p.9.

93 Decision on the Africa Peer Review Mechanism, Decision 198 (XII), para. 16, adopted during the 11th Ordinary Session of the Assembly of the African Union, 30 June–1 July 2008, Sharm El-Sheikh, Egypt, p 16.

94 Plan of Action, para. 35.

95 See Roberta Cohen, The Role of Regional Organisations: ECOWAS, ECOWAS/IOM Workshop on International Migration in West Africa, 1 December 2010. Available online at: www.brookings.edu/speeches/2002/0930humanrights_cohen.aspx.

ECOWAS organised a major ministerial conference in July 2011 where member states made commitments to take several measures including the promotion of ratification by states, development of national policies on internal displacement, the incorporation of the Kampala Convention into ECOWAS's community law and the establishment of a regional task force to coordinate the implementation of the Convention.[96] IGAD also held a number of high-level meetings on internal displacement in which commitments were made to ensure the protection of IDPs including by establishing mechanisms within the sub-regional system that will ensure the integration of internal displacement in the activities of the organisation.[97] Currently, a dedicated unit has been established. The organisation has been very instrumental in the signing of peace agreements both in Sudan and Somalia which led to the deployment of a UN–African Union hybrid force in Sudan and the African Union Mission in Somalia (AMISOM) in Somalia respectively. IGAD's Early Warning and Conflict Resolution Mechanism (CEWARN) has also helped in the development of tools that will facilitate the sharing of information including on conflict-generated forced displacement.[98] Other sub-regional mechanisms are also developing early warning systems which seek to enhance the capacity and resources at the national and sub-regional levels to respond to the threat of conflicts and natural disaster.[99] Both ECOWAS and EAC have specialised courts with the potential for promoting and protecting the rights of IDPs.

International organisations have increasingly recognised the importance of working with sub-regional mechanisms in the promotion and protection of the human rights of IDPs. A MOU signed between UNHCR and ECOWAS to cooperate in a wide range of fields including on internal displacement can be mentioned.[100] A similar bilateral arrangement exists between UNHCR and SADC.[101]

96 ECOWAS Members Renew Commitment to Implement African Convention on IDPs, No. 117/2011, 9 July 2011. Available at: http://news.ecowas.int/presseshow.php?=117&lang=en&annee=2011.

97 Nairobi Declaration of the Ministerial Conference on Refugees, Returnees and Internally Displaced Persons in the IGAD Region, adopted on 21 February 2006.

98 See CEWARN Strategy: 2007–2011, CEWARN Unit, Addis Ababa, Ethiopia, located at: eastafrica.usaid.gov/(S(pmx5eu3ieiwr1n45ewgkaqqq))/.../1023.

99 See Strategic Indicative Plan for the Organ on Politics, Defence and Security Cooperation (Gaborone: SADC, 2004), pp. 17 and 19.

100 Memorandum of Understanding between UNHCR and ECOWAS, New York, 19 November 2001, available online at: www.adh-geneve.ch/RULAC/pdf_state/UNHCR-ECOWAS.pdf.

101 For information on the relationship between UNHCR and SADC, see UNHCR's website at: www.unhcrrlo.org/Regional_Partners/SADCC.html.

The role of international organisations

National and regional efforts in protecting and assisting IDPs in Africa face numerous challenges. These challenges mainly relate to lack of capacity, resources and expertise. Under such circumstances, the Special Rapporteur on the Human Rights of IDPs and other institutions such as the United Nations agencies and international humanitarian organisations can complement national and regional initiatives. Cooperation between organs of the African Union on the one hand and international organisations on the other including in areas of peace and security, protection of civilians during armed conflicts, disaster prevention, preparedness and response, human rights and humanitarian issues have consequences for the implementation of the Kampala Convention. African Union's close cooperation particularly with the former RSG, UNHCR and ICRC has been a catalyst in the development and refinement of national and regional measures. As has been examined previously, the elaboration of the Convention itself has been an important outcome of such close collaboration. Given the considerable resources and expertise available at the international level, the active involvement of international institutions in assisting national and regional developments should assume an important dimension of implementing the Convention. That the role and responsibility of some of these institutions have been explicitly mentioned in the Convention itself and that states are required to cooperate with and facilitate their access to displaced communities should be used as a basis of deepening the required relationship and cooperation.

The international human rights system

The Human Rights Council, treaty bodies and other oversight mechanisms can support and assist the implementation of the Kampala Convention. The reform of the Human Rights Council has introduced new mechanisms such as Universal Periodic Review that provide opportunities for stakeholders to provide recommendations to member states in improving the human rights of IDPs. Several UPR recommendations submitted to member states make reference to protection of IDPs within the country concerned and suggest ways of improving their plight. Among 15 countries with the problem of internal displacement that were reviewed during 2009, ten of them received specific recommendations.[102] As a follow-up to their commitments, states may incorporate such recommendations in their national human rights action plans. Moreover, organisations such as UNHCR are using the UPR to provide inputs regarding protection issues of refugees, stateless persons and IDPs during the adoption of the report

102 *Internal Displacement: Global Overview of Trends and Developments in 2009* (Geneva, Internal Displacement Monitoring Center, 2010), 10.

of the UPR Working Group.[103] Treaty bodies also now raise questions and incorporate recommendations on the protection of IDPs during the examination of national implementation of reports.

The Special Rapporteur functions as a global focal point of international efforts on behalf of IDPs. It has been the central institutional focal point for advocating the rights of IDPs. In addition to the mandate of the Special Rapporteur on the Human Rights of IDPs, the UN Human Rights Council has also established country mandates whose role in addressing the concerns of IDPs is quite important. Such country-specific mandates exist in key displacement-generating countries in Africa, namely, Sudan,[104] Burundi[105] and Somalia.[106] The promotional visits and reports of these mechanisms are important tools for highlighting IDPs' plight and for taking specific actions in order to address these challenges.

The Special Rapporteur on the Human Rights of Internally Displaced Persons

The Special Rapporteur on the Human Rights of Internally Displaced Persons (the Special Rapporteur) has been a key global focal point for the promotion and protection of the human rights of IDPs with a specific mandate of advocating for the rights of IDPs, mainstreaming the human rights of IDPs in the UN system and strengthening the responses to internal displacement at all levels.[107] Since the reinvigoration of the mandate in 2004, the Special Rapporteur has visited a number of countries in Africa, namely the CAR,[108]

103 See Submission by the High Commissioner for Refugees for the High Commissioner for Human Rights' Compilation Report – Universal Periodic Review: The Islamic Republic of Mauritania, Human Rights Liaison Unit, Division of International Protection (UNHCR), April 2010. Available online at: www.unhcr.org/refworld/pdfid/4bcd75222.pdf. See also Submission by the High Commissioner for Refugees for the High Commissioner for Human Rights' Compilation Report – Universal Periodic Review: Submission by the High Commissioner for Refugees for the High Commissioner for Human Rights' Compilation Report – Universal Periodic Review: Sudan, Human Rights Liaison Unit, Division of International Protection (UNHCR), 10 November 2010.

104 Situation of Human Rights in the Sudan, Human Rights Council Decision 14/117, adopted 7 October 2010, para. 10

105 Advisory Services and Technical Assistance for Burundi, Human Rights Council Resolution 9/19, adopted 24 September 2008, para. 8.

106 Assistance to Somalia in the Field of Human Rights, Human Rights Council Resolution 12/26, adopted on 2 October 2009, para. 10.

107 The Mandate of the Special Rapporteur on the Human Rights of Internally Displaced Persons, Human Rights Council, A/HRC/Res/14/6, para. 12, adopted on 17 June 2010.

108 See The Report of the Secretary General on the Human Rights of Internally Displaced Persons: Mission to the Central African Republic (French), A/HRC/8/6/Add.1, and 17 March 2008.

Chad,[109] the DRC,[110] Cote d'Ivoire,[111] Kenya,[112] Somalia[113] and Sudan.[114] These efforts are key components of the mandate of the Special Rapporteur which, according to the relevant resolution of the Council, should be pursued 'through continuous dialogue with Governments and intergovernmental and non-governmental organizations concerned, his [...] efforts to promote the protection of human rights of internally displaced persons'.[115]

The Special Rapporteur has supported countries such as Kenya, Sudan and Uganda and develops policies and domestic legislations on internal displacement.[116] He has also undertaken follow-up visits to countries such as Uganda.[117] The mandate-holder has also communicated with numerous African governments including Nigeria, Mozambique, DRC, Kenya, Sudan, Somalia, CAR, Chad, Cote d'Ivoire and Madagascar on a range of issues. Through some of these communications, the Special Rapporteur played a monitoring role by bringing to the attention of governments allegations of breaches of human rights of IDPs and has provided relevant recommendations.[118]

The Special Rapporteur has also been a catalyst for policy and legal developments at the regional and sub-regional levels. As has been mentioned in Chapter 3, the former SRG had been instrumental in the development of the Kampala Convention itself. The Manual for Law and Policy Makers and the normative instruments developed through the IASC have been widely used. Various policy makers from the region have also benefited from the San Remo course on the law of internal displacement whose development he has inspired.[119] There is evidence that the adoption of the Convention has already

109 See Report of the Secretary General on the Human Rights of Internally Displaced Persons: Mission to Chad, A/HRC/13/21/Add.5, and 22 December 2009.

110 See Combined Report of Seven Thematic Special Procedures on Technical Assistance to the Government of the Democratic Republic of the Congo and Urgent Examination of the Situation in the East of the Country, A/HRC/10/59, and 5 March 2009.

111 The Report of the Secretary General on the Human Rights of Internally Displaced Persons: Mission to Cote d'Ivoire, A/HRC/4/38/Add.2, and 18 October 2008.

112 Report of the Special Rapporteur on the Human Rights of Internally Displaced Persons: Mission to Kenya, Chaloka Beyani, A/HRC/19/54/Add.2, 6 February 2012.

113 Report of the Secretary General Representative on the human rights of internally displaced persons on Somalia, A/HRC/13/21/Add.2, 21 January 2010.

114 See Report of the Secretary General on the Human Rights of Internally Displaced Persons: Mission to Sudan, E/CN.4./2006/71/Add.6, 13 February 2006.

115 See Mandate of the Representative of the Secretary General on the Human Rights of Internally Displaced Persons, HRC Resolution 6/3, para. 7, 13 December 2007.

116 Report of the Secretary General Representative on the human rights of internally displaced persons on Somalia, para. 15.

117 Report of the Representative of the Secretary General on the Human Rights of Internally Displaced Persons, A/64/214, 3 August 2009, paras. 70–73.

118 Report of the Secretary General Representative on the Human Rights of Internally Displaced Persons on Somalia, A/HRC/10/13, 9 February 2009, para. 73.

119 The 7th Annual Course on Law of Internal Displacement took place between 7 and 12 June 2012, information on the web available at: www.iihl.org/Default.aspx?pageid=page10831.

started having an impact on the way countries perceive the mandate. Not only that, a number of African countries have now become co-sponsors of the resolution concerning the mandate of the Special Rapporteur and for the first time, Uganda became a co-lead sponsor of the resolution together with Austria.[120]

International humanitarian organisations

International humanitarian organisations can contribute immensely to the implementation of the Kampala Convention. Several provisions of the Convention call upon states to respect the mandate of international humanitarian organisations. As problems of internal displacement in several of the countries in the Horn of Africa and the Great Lakes region clearly show, the most serious situations of internal displacement occur in countries with weak state institutions, making the role of international humanitarian organisations even more important. That no single institution was mandated to coordinate the issue on internal displacement at the international level meant that often governments do not have a clear direction on how and with whom they should collaborate during emergencies. Since 2005, however, the humanitarian reform and the introduction of the cluster approach have helped to clarify the institutional division of labour.[121] The 'cluster approach' seeks to clarify the division of labour that should exist between UN agencies and non-governmental agencies by assigning lead agencies in humanitarian response in the area of agriculture, camp coordination and camp management, early recovery, education, emergency shelter; emergency telecommunications, health, logistics, nutrition, protection, and water, sanitation and hygiene.[122] For example, the field protection cluster is currently implemented in over 29 countries.[123]

United Nations organisations and international humanitarian institutions play a critical role in strengthening the capacity of the African Union. Beyond normative development, international organisations such as UNHCR, ICRC and IOM are working with the African Union in several areas. The United Nations and the African Union have agreed on a ten-year joint cooperation framework. This is reflected in the document titled Enhancing UN-AU Cooperation: Framework for the Ten Year Capacity-

120 In addition to Uganda, Ethiopia and Cote d'Ivoire were also among the co-sponsors of the Resolution. See Mandate of the Special Rapporteur on the Human Rights of Internally Displaced Persons, A/HRC/14/L.18, and 14 June 2010.

121 See Guidance Note on Using Cluster Approach to Strengthen Humanitarian Response Inter-Agency Standing Committee, 26 November 2006. Available online at: ochaonline.un.org/OchaLink Click.aspx?link=ocha&docid=34187.

122 Information on the cluster approach available online at: www.humanitarianreform.org/humanitarian reform/Default.aspx?tabid=70.

123 See The Digest: The Newsletter of the Global Protection Cluster, August 2011. Available online at: www.unhcr.org/refworld/docid/4e5603202.html.

Building Programme for the African Union.[124] In August 2010, the African Union signed a Memorandum of Understanding with OCHA.[125] The MOU focuses on three key areas of cooperation. These include (a) early warning, disaster preparedness and response, (b) coordination, and (c) civilian protection during natural disaster and conflicts. OCHA had earlier opened a liaison office in Addis Ababa, Ethiopia to work with the African Union in policy development and protection of civilians, emergency response coordination, advocacy and information management, and resource mobilisation.[126] The MOU facilitates the holding of briefings, training and deliberations involving member states, UN agencies and other organisations. It also seeks to provide an opportunity to enhance institutional cooperation and capacity building in areas including early warning, emergency response coordination, policy development, advocacy and information management, and resource mobilisation. In addition to achieving these, a two-year Action Plan has also been signed between the parties. The cooperation between OCHA and the African Union also focuses the AUC's humanitarian coordination mechanisms, mainly the Coordination Committee on Assistance to IDPs, Returnees and Refugees. Access to OCHA's wealth of information will also be critical in the role of the Commission to report to the policy organs of the African Union.[127] Outside the UN system, ICRC cooperates with the African Union and sub-regional organisations on a range of issues relevant to the protection of human rights of IDPs, particularly in the context of armed conflicts. It has fielded a liaison office to the African Union based in Addis Ababa and has also signed a Memorandum of Understanding with the latter.

It is not uncommon for the relationship between governments and international humanitarian organisations to experience some setbacks and challenges. These include issues of needs assessment, consent, the passage of humanitarian consignment and personnel and safety and security. States are generally obligated to allow 'rapid and unimpeded passage of all relief consignments, equipment and personnel to internally displaced persons'.[128] These frictions may become even more prevalent as the call for a more integrated and joint humanitarian assessment by agencies across the UN is sought.[129] Governments often complain about a lack of effective participation

124 Declaration: Enhancing UN-AU Cooperation: Framework for the Ten Year Capacity Building Program for the African Union, Annex, A/61/630, and 12 December 2006.

125 African Union Commission and OCHA finalise MOU, 26 August 2010. Available: www.reliefweb.int/rw/rwb.nsf/db900SID/VVOS-88PP28?OpenDocument.

126 Office for the Coordination of Humanitarian Affairs, African Union Liaison Office: Fast Facts, http://ochaonline.un.org/ocha2010/african-union.html.

127 Annual Report, Office for the Coordination of Humanitarian Affairs (Geneva, Switzerland: United Nations, 2009), 91.

128 Art 5(7).

129 See Strengthening of Coordination of Emergency Humanitarian Assistance of the United Nations, 2010(1) ECOSOC, 15 July 2010, para. 24.

in the coordination of the provision of humanitarian assistance.[130] Ideally, such assessments should be based on consultations with concerned national authorities and institutions. But states often express at different forums about the lack of transparency and involvement of states in the preparation of need assessments. Dependence on international assistance and aid encourages a situation whereby international organisations simply take over humanitarian assistance programmes, leaving few opportunities for local actors thereby undermining local ownership. In Uganda, for two decades international organisations were the main players in humanitarian assistance to such an extent that when peace returned, local capacity was significantly diminished.[131]

The Kampala Convention requires that states request international assistance when existing local resources are insufficient.[132] Specifically, states are obligated to allow rapid and unimpeded access to and assistance to IDPs. Ethiopia's expulsion of ICRC from the Ogaden region has been severely criticised.[133] There was equally severe criticism of the government of Sudan when it expelled over 13 international non-governmental organisations from Darfur.[134] The government of Eritrea has put in place administrative measures which significantly restrict the role of international actors.[135] With respect to the role of armed groups to allow international humanitarian operation, the Kampala Convention specifically stipulates that armed groups assume the obligation not to impede humanitarian assistance and passage of all humanitarian consignment, personnel and equipment.[136] Access to IDPs remains a concern to these organisations. Intimidation and direct attacks by armed groups has restricted access to IDPs in Somalia. In places such as Somalia, Chad, DRC and Sudan, international organisations are forced to deliver aid and assistance working not only through governments but also private security firms and armed groups. These bring two important challenges. The first one concerns the principle of neutrality which is at the heart of humanitarian operations. Article 6(3) of the Kampala Convention provides that international organisations should undertake their operation with neutrality, and should respect the human rights of IDPs. The second problem concerns the

130 See International Disaster Response Law Project: Report on Findings from South Asia, Southern Africa and Central America, Mar. 2003, at 17. Available online at: www.ifrc.org/Global/Publications/IDRL/country%20studies/IDRL_Fieldstudies_results0303.pdf.

131 *Internal Displacement: Global Overview of Trends and Developments in 2009* (Geneva, Switzerland, IDMC, 2010), 25.

132 Art 5(6).

133 ICRC, 'Ethiopia: ICRC deplores expulsion from Somalia regional state', Press Statement, 26 July 2007, available at www.icrc.org/eng/resources/documents/news-release/ethiopia-news-260707.htm.

134 'UN Expert Says World is Neglecting Major Internal Displacement Crises', Office of the High Commissioner for Human Rights, 13 March 2009, available online at www.unhchr.ch/huricane/huricane.nsf/0/30D38D2A6F00BB41C1257578004BBBF7?opendocument.

135 Note above 4.

136 Art 5(7)g.

potential tension between the legitimacy international organisations may give to local actors by working with those involved in human rights law violations and the responsibility of the international community to address impunity and ensure accountability. In Somalia, for instance, due to a lack of security and direct attacks, international organisations have adopted what is often considered as a system of remote management where the humanitarian operation is directed from Nairobi with the actual operation often being run by nationals. The former RSG noted that:[137]

> In the most difficult security environments, international humanitarian actors are increasingly forced to move to a form of remote management from outside the crisis area. This type of remote assistance places greater responsibility on national staff and local implementing partners and puts them at greater risk. While this approach may work for short periods, it presents concerns in the long-term with regard to quality, effectiveness and accountability issues.

The United Nations system and international humanitarian organisations are important in assisting states in achieving durable solutions to the problem of internal displacement. In countries such as Uganda, despite a return of a massive number of people, returnees still face enduring challenges. The UN Peace Building Commission is assisting countries such as Burundi, CAR, Sierra Leone and Guinea Bissau.[138] Based on the strategic framework for peace building, the Commission has identified a number of measures states can take. These include legislative reforms, institution building and strengthening and socio-economic integration of ex-combatants and IDPs.[139] The strategic framework identifies the commitments of government, civic society and that of the Commission with respect to restoring peace, strengthening national mechanisms on human rights, promoting training and capacity building. For instance, the strategic framework for CAR commits the government to take steps in implementing the Great Lakes Protocol on the Protection and Assistance of IDPs.[140] The financial assistance of the Commission to CAR was intended to fund, among others, a joint programme run by a number of UN organs to assist a sustainable return of IDPs.[141]

137 The Report of the Secretary General Representative on the Human Rights of Internally Displaced Persons, A/65/282, para. 66.

138 For documentation on country-specific works by the Peacebuilding Commission, see: www.un.org/peace/peacebuilding/pbc-countrymtgs.shtml.

139 See Report of the Peacebuilding Commission on its third session, A/64/341-S/2009/444, 8 September 2009.

140 See Strategic Framework for Peacebuilding in the Central African Republic 2009–2011, PBC/3/CAF/7, 14.

141 Central African Republic Receives New UN Peacebuilding Funds, United Nations News Service, 4 April 2010, located at www.reliefweb.int/rw/rwb.nsf/db900sid/EGUA-82CMHG?OpenDocument.

International criminal tribunals and arbitral institutions

The Kampala Convention provides for the responsibility of states to ensure the accountability of members of defence forces for the arbitrary displacement of civilians.[142] While a country's criminal law should facilitate the task of authorities to fulfil this important obligation, it is, however, often observed that countries lack the willingness and the capacity to bring to justice individuals responsible for acts of arbitrary displacement. In these situations, the role of mechanisms of transitional justice including international tribunals, inquiry bodies, fact-finding missions and arbitral bodies will be useful. As has happened in numerous situations, states may decide to incorporate the role of these bodies in peace agreements.[143] In other situations, accountability mechanisms may become critical elements of measures taken by the relevant international bodies such as the Security Council. This was the case when the United Nations Security Council decided to refer the situation in Sudan to the International Criminal Court.[144]

In other instances, states may show a willingness to avail themselves of available international instruments to address impunity. Both the Independent Expert on the Human Rights Situations in Somalia and the former RSG had suggested the establishment of an independent international inquiry into the human rights and humanitarian law breaches in Somalia.[145] Among others, this inquiry was considered to be useful in the egregious humanitarian violations and abuses that continue to take place against civilians. Several inquiries and fact-finding missions have investigated human rights development in the Darfur. The role of *ad hoc* and permanent international criminal tribunals such as the International Criminal Tribunal for Former Rwanda and the International Criminal Court is important in this respect.

Several African states are signatories to the Rome Statute establishing the ICC, which incorporate provisions designating deportation and forced transfer of population as crimes against humanity and war crimes.[146] Currently, there are cases from Central Africa Republic, Cote d'Ivoire, Kenya, Sudan, Uganda, DRC, Liberia and Libya being considered by the ICC. Exercising its mandate under Chapter VII, the Security Council referred the situation in Sudan to the ICC. In the cases of Uganda and DRC, governments them-

142 See Art 7 (4) & (5).

143 See, for example, Agreement between the Government of the Federal Democratic Republic of Ethiopia and the Government of the State of Eritrea, signed on 12 December 2000. Available online at: www.pca-cpa.org/showfile.asp?fil_id=138.

144 S/RES/1593(2005).

145 See Report of the Representative of the Secretary General in the Human Rights of Internally Displaced Persons: Mission to Somalia, A/HRC/13/21/Add.2, para. 60. See also Report of the Independent Expert on the Human Rights Situation in Somalia, A/HRC/10/85. 24 February 2009, para. 75.

146 Arts 7(1) (d) and 8(2) (a)(vii) and (b) (viii)).

selves self-referred the matter to the ICC. The situation in Kenya involves a *proprio motu* mandate of the prosecutor. Many including the former RSG had recommended that Kenya adopt a transitional justice mechanism to address abuses and breaches committed during the post-election displacement.[147] Though these cases are at different stages at the ICC, they show the potential of the ICC in addressing the challenges of impunity. Through the Ugandan self-referral, it is hoped that the Lord's Resistance Army will be brought to account for the vicious crimes and breaches it continues to commit. The warrant of arrest brought against LRA's leadership including Joseph Kony covers orders to target and kill civilians including those in IDP camps, enslavement of civilians in IDP camps, cruel treatment, pillaging IDP camps, murders, enlisting of children and inhuman acts.[148] The Prosecutor's action against six senior officials of Kenya also includes charges of 'forcible transfer of population'.[149]

Beyond the measures of accountability, these international mechanisms are important and key instruments of ensuring the right of IDPs to have access to appropriate remedies. The Eritrea Ethiopia Claims Commission was established as a component of the Peace Agreement signed between Ethiopia and Eritrea to settle their 1998–2000 war.[150] Its mandate was to determine the responsibility of each party to the conflict to wrongs and injuries caused to nationals of the other and determine compensations. It adopted several landmark decisions, ordering Eritrea and Ethiopia to ensure that civilian victims of internal displacement and deportation are duly compensated.[151] While this decision has never been fully implemented, it brings home the crucial role of tribunals and arbitration bodies in the provision of compensations to IDPs.

Peace-keeping missions and the implementation of the Convention

The relevance of the mandate of peace-keeping missions to the implementation of the Kampala Convention stems from a number of considerations.

147 The Report of the Secretary General Representative of the Human Rights of Internally Displaced Persons, A/HRC/10/13, 9 February 2009, para. 60.

148 The Prosecutor v. Joseph Kony, Vincent Otti, Okoth Odiambo and Dominc Ongwen, Pre-Trial Chamber II, Warrant of Arrest, ICC-02/04-01/05-53, 27 September 2005, pp.17–28, available online at www.icc-cpi.int/iccdocs/doc/doc97185.PDF (accessed on 13 September 2011).

149 Prosecutor's Application Pursuant to Article 58 as to William Samuel Ruto, Henry Kiprono Kosgey and Joshua Arop Sang, ICC-01/09-30RED, 15 December 2010, p. 11, available online at ICC-01/09-30RED (accessed on 13 September 2012).

150 See Allehone Abebe, 'Displacement of Civilians during Armed Conflict in the Light of the Case Law of the Eritrea-Ethiopia Claims Commission', *Leiden Journal of International Law* 22(2009): 823–851.

151 Ibid.

First, as has been noted on numerous occasions, the Convention reinforces the obligation of states to respect the mandate and authority of both the UN and the AU.[152] Second, the Convention furthermore involves numerous provisions which are directly relevant to the protection of IDPs particularly those who are trapped in armed conflicts. The Plan of Action further underlines the protection of IDPs during armed conflicts, the prevention of recruitment of children by armed groups and the prevention of sexual violence against women.[153] Acknowledging the specific role of peace-keeping missions in undertaking the aforementioned tasks, the Plan of Action, among others, supports the elaboration and operationalisation of African Union guidelines on the protection of civilians.[154] This is in line with the trend according to which, as identified by the seminal Brahimi report, 'peacekeepers may not only be operationally justified in using force (to protect civilians) but morally compelled to do so'.[155]

Translating national responsibility for the protection of displaced persons into reality particularly in the context of conflicts has always been a challenging task. States carry the responsibility to respond to the protection and assistance needs of IDPs at all times including in situations of armed conflicts. National responses examined in this chapter often concern countries that are experiencing or are emerging from decades of conflicts. It is precisely during these situations that states encounter enormous difficulty in responding to the problem of internal displacement and lack the capacity and willingness to implement norms and standards incorporated in the Kampala Convention. This had been true in situations of displacement crisis affecting counties such as Angola, Burundi, Liberia and Sierra Leone. Countries with current challenges of internal displacement such as Sudan, Somalia and DRC have also faced similar problems. There are situations where countries face a heightened level of conflict in a context where the authority and capacity of the state is severely weakened. In situations such as these, peacekeepers may be called upon to ensure stability and protect civilians.

At a strategic level, peacekeepers can support the implementation of peace agreements, facilitate confidence building and support initiatives on transitional justice, all areas incorporated in the Convention. At the tactical level, however, peace-keeping missions through their rules of engagement and standards of operations may undertake specific protection tasks and activities. Their role includes monitoring of ceasefire and peace agreements, disarmament and demining of areas, return and integration of displaced persons, protection of civilians and humanitarian personnel, establishing and

152 Arts 5(3) & 8.

153 Plan of Action, 14.

154 Ibid., 13.

155 Report of the Panel on United Nations Peace Operations, UN doc. A/55/305-S/2000/809, 2000, 21 August 2000, para. 50, available at: doc/UNDOC/GEN/G09/107/46/PDF/G0910746.pdf?OpenElement.

protecting humanitarian corridors, protecting vulnerable and marginalised groups such as women, children and persons with special needs, preventing displacement by developing contingency plans, and providing protection to areas under risk of attacks. In addition, peace-keeping missions enhance the capacity of national authorities to reform laws and policies, undertake training and capacity building for local police and military and help create conditions that facilitate reconstruction and recovery.

Civilian protection by peace-keeping missions in Africa

The United Nations had deployed peace-keeping missions in Africa in Sudan, DRC, Liberia, Rwanda, Burundi and Somalia and has currently seven peacekeeping operations in the continent.[156] The role of traditional peace-keeping missions in civilian protection has been minimal and in the early years of development of international coordination mechanism for the protection of IDPs rarely examined the role and responsibility of peacekeepers in any meaningful manner. The lack of response by the UNAMIR to the genocide in Rwanda showed the failure of UN peace-keeping missions in providing security to civilians.[157] Now the UN peace-keeping framework considers the issue of civilian protection by its peace-keeping missions and often sees attacks on civilians and humanitarian assistance as a breach of international peace and security. While adopting resolutions on peace-keeping missions, the Security Council now provides provisions on civilian protection in general and protection and assistance of IDPs in particular.[158] It has gradually developed a comprehensive framework for the protection agenda through its resolutions on children, women and armed conflicts.[159] Moreover, there is now a standing rule of engagement for peace operations that authorises the use of force to defend civilians in need of protection.[160] The revival of the UNSC's Working Group on Peacekeeping Missions and its informal group on civilian protection refocused the role of the organisation on the protection of civilians. While establishing UN peace-keeping missions, the Security Council has also increasingly incorporated provisions in its

156 These operations are located in the Sudan, South Sudan, the Democratic Republic of the Congo, Cote d'Ivoire, Darfur, Liberia and Western Sahara. Information available at: www.un.org/en/peacekeeping/operations/current.shtml.

157 See Comprehensive Report on Lesson Learnt from UNAMIR, United Nations, New York, Department of Peacekeeping Operations, 1996, available online at: http://reliefweb.int/node/33811.

158 Report of the Secretary General on the protection of civilians in armed conflict, Security Council, 1 November 2010, S/2010/579.

159 Kamel Morjane, 'The protection of Refugees and Displaced Persons', *Human Rights Protection in the Field*, ed. Bertrand Ramcharan (Leiden: Martinus Njihoff Publishers, 2006), 83.

160 Daniel Blocq 'The Fog of UN Peacekeeping: Ethical Issues Regarding the Use of Force to Protect Civilians in UN Operations', *Journal of Military Ethics* 5(2006): 201–213.

resolutions providing a mandate to civilian protection.[161] With the view to implementing the relevant resolutions of the Council on the protection of women including during armed conflicts, the Secretary General has appointed the first representative of the Secretary General on the protection of women from sexual violence and has made UN expertise available to assist states and their institutions to take protective measures including through the adoption of the necessary legal frameworks.[162]

The joint United Nations–African Union Peacekeeping Mission in Darfur represents the highest level of collaboration between the United Nations and the African Union peace-keeping mission. The AU has not yet undertaken any intervention invoking the provision of the Constitutive Act to address situations of genocide, war crimes and crimes against humanity; neither has it been asked by one or group of its member states to undertake such intervention to restore peace and order in one of the member states.[163] Its involvements in countries such as Somalia, Darfur, Comoros, and Burundi had explicit security and peace dimensions. The regional and sub-regional peace and security institutions and their involvement in preventive diplomacy have a direct link with the implementation of the provisions of the Kampala Convention in the prevention of internal displacement. They can facilitate the signing and adoption of peace agreements which incorporate specific language on the protection of IDPs. Moreover, the African Union has also come a long way in implementing the fullest realisation of the establishment of the African Union standby brigade and its sub-regional blocs. The protection of civilians has also been incorporated in the African Union Policy Framework on Standby Brigades. Upon a request by the Assembly, the African Union has also been developing a Framework for Action and Guidelines on the Protection of Civilians in Peacekeeping Operations.[164]

The AU had deployed missions in Burundi (2003–2004), Comoros and Sudan (2004–2007), and is currently involved in Somalia through the AMISOM. Its regional peace-keeping missions are deployed often in difficult

161 See Aide Memoire for the Consideration of Issues Pertaining to the Protection of Civilians during Armed Conflict, S/PRST/2009/1, available at: www.unic.or.jp/security_co/pdf/prst_2009_1.pdf.

162 See S/RES/1888 (2009).

163 In its 279th Session held in Addis Ababa on 18 May 2011, the African Union Peace and Security Council, while noting the efforts made by the AU Commission to develop such instruments, encouraged the Commission to mainstream the Draft Guidelines into the peace and security architecture of the African Union, including the development of Guidance Note on protection mandates and a framework for developing specific protection strategies. See Press Statement: PSC/PR/BR.(CCLXXIX), available at: www.au.int/en/sites/default/files/279%20PSC%20Statement%20Eng.pdf.

164 Progress Report on the Status of the Operationalization of the African Standby Force, 4th Ordinary Meeting of Specialized Technical Committee on Defense, Safety and Security Preparatory Meeting of Experts and 6th Meeting of the African Defense Staff and Heads of Security Services, 3–7 December 2010. Available at http//www.acoc-africa.org/docs/Dec2010ProgRepASF.pdf.

political environments, do not include explicit provisions in their mandate on civilian protection and suffer from resource constraints. Regional peace-keeping missions such as ECOMOG in Liberia in the past and AMISOM presently in Somalia not only have experienced significant hurdles in protecting civilians but had also been criticised for their direct participation in the violations of human rights and humanitarian law.[165] In order to address these concerns, the African Union has taken a number of steps including the development of the Guidelines on the Protection of Civilians in Peace Support Missions, and organised seminars and workshops which sought to raise awareness about the problem and the practical usefulness of such guidelines.[166] A number of key African Union institutions have already started making reference to these Guidelines. For instance, in its latest deliberation on the situation of Somalia, which also examined criticisms over human rights and humanitarian law breaches committed by AMISOM troops, the Peace and Security Council adopted a decision which 'encouraged the Commission to mainstream the draft AU Guidelines for the Protection of Civilians in Peace Support Missions ... into the activities of AMISOM'.[167] The utility of these Guidelines are widely recognised. But beyond their call for the protection of civilians from grave situations such as ethnic cleansing, genocide and war crimes, they provide little guidance on how to actually achieve full civilian protection, 'leaving it to those planning and implementing such operations to develop the conceptual approaches required to turn ambition into reality'.[168]

United Nations Organisations Stabilisation Mission in the Democratic Republic of Congo

The Democratic Republic of Congo has been a theatre of a series of vicious armed conflicts with both internal and international dimensions and involving government forces, militias and militaries of neighbouring countries. This conflict has created an environment of impunity and severe civilian

165 See *Harsh War, Harsh Peace: Abuses by Al Shabab, the Transitional Federal Government and AMISOM in Somalia* (New York: Human Rights Watch, 2000).

166 See African Union and Australian Government Holds International Symposium on the Protection of Civilians During Conflict Zones, Press Release No. 26, 2010. Available online at: www.africa-union.org/root/ar/index/PR-%20SYMPOSIUM%20ON%20PROTECTION%20OF%20CIVILIANS%20IN%20CLONFLICT%20ZONES%2005.03.10.doc.

167 Communiqué of the 245th Meeting of the Peace and Security Council, PSC/MIN/1(CCXXXXV), 15 October 2010, para. 7.

168 William Durch and Alison Giffen, *Challenges of Strengthening the Protection of Civilians in Multidimensional Peace Operations*, Background Paper Prepared for the 3rd International Forum for the Challenges of Peace Operations, 27–29 April 2010, Queenbeyan, Australia, Hosted by the Asia Pacific Civil-Military Centre of Excellence, note 41, located at: www.challengesforum.org/cms/images/pdf/Challenges_2010_BackgroundPaper_12April2010.pdf.

suffering. Currently, there are around 1.9 million IDPs in the country which is a staggering 2.9 per cent of the total population, many of whom are located in the eastern part of the country.[169] During the peak of the crisis in 2003, there were over 3.4 million IDPs.[170] These civilians have endured and continue to face all forms of abuse and neglect by armed groups. Rape of innocent civilians by armed groups remains one of the most horrific aspects of the conflict. Participation of troops from neighbouring countries such as Rwanda creates a situation where arbitrary displacement was and is committed not only by government forces but also by armed groups such as the FARDC (Forces Armées de la République Démocratique du Congo) but also by CNDP (Congrès national pour la défense du people) and FDLR (Forces démocratiques de libération du Rwanda), but also by members of the Rwandese armed forces.

The Security Council, under Chapter VI, established the United Nations Mission in the DRC in 2000 with a mandated force size of 5,500. The mandate of the force was principally focused on overseeing the implementation of the Lusaka Agreement. After the deployment of forces, MONUC cooperated with the Congolese army in a number of missions which were criticised for their violation of humanitarian law. Fully aware of the shortcomings inherent in MONUC's mandate, the Security Council passed Resolution 1484, this time within the framework of its mandate under Chapter VII, to strengthen the terms of reference of the force. Until the deployment of a more robust force, it also authorised a multinational force named ARTEMIS under the leadership of France.[171] Though the mandate of the new multinational force was considerably robust, it was limited to a certain geographical area meaning that many IDPs were beyond the reach of the peacekeepers.[172] But ARTEMIS played an important role in facilitating the deployment of the newly reinforced MONUC.

The Security Council has underlined the need for protection of civilians by MONUC. The difficult negotiation with the government of DRC which wanted to get rid of MONUC resulted in the establishment of the United Nations Organisations Stabilisation Mission in the Democratic Republic of Congo (MONUSCO). Its resolution renewing the mandate of the force has reflected this sentiment where the Council underscored the responsibility of the Mission to 'support the government's efforts, along with international partners and neighbouring countries, to create an environment conducive to the voluntary, safe and dignified return of internally displaced persons and refugees, or voluntary local integration or resettlement'.[173] The mandate

169 Note 4 above, 36.
170 Ibid.
171 S/RES/1484 (2002), para. 1.
172 William G. O'Neill, A New Challenge for Peacekeepers: The Internally Displaced, The Brooking-SAIS Project on Internal Displacement (Washington, DC: Brooking Bern Project on Internal Displacement, 2004), 36.
173 See S/RES/1925(2010). See also S/RES/1906(2009).

included the use of force to ensure the protection of civilians, including humanitarian personnel, under imminent threat of physical violence, and contribute to the improvement of the security conditions in which humanitarian assistance is provided, and assist in the voluntary return of refugees and IDPs. This development has helped the mission to clarify, through the adoption of the appropriate policy, how it will cooperate with the national defence forces. Among others, the new conditionality policy for cooperation prohibited the participation in joint operations of known violators of humanitarian law.[174] Within the framework of the cluster approach, MONUSCO troops will be deployed in areas where communities feel threatened by displacement.[175]

MONUC faced several problems right from the beginning. Its force size was particularly inadequate for a country as large as the DRC. Its actual deployment was also thinly spread in a large area which is not connected to the barest of infrastructure networks. The UN now deploys joint protection teams, composed of various UN divisions, with the mandate to work with government troops, armed groups, local communities and other stakeholders in order to mediate disputes, provide protection advice and separate children from armed groups. Regular meetings between MONUSCO military and civilian officers and UN agency participants of the cluster approach have also been increasingly taken with the view to coordinate protection activities.

African Union Mission in Somalia (AMISOM)

The African Union Peace and Security Council established AMISOM on 6 December 2006. The Council authorised the force during its 19th meeting held on 19 January 2007.[176] The mandate of the mission included the facilitation of humanitarian assistance and the repatriation of refugees and IDPs. Originally it was considered as a transitional measure where the United Nations will authorise a UN peace-keeping mission at the expiration of AMISOM's mandate in six months. By its Resolution 1744, the United Nations Security Council partially lifted its earlier arms embargo and authorised the deployment of Somalia in 2007.[177] Since then, the Council has consistently renewed the mandate of the mission.[178]

174 *Always on the Run: The Vicious Cycle of Displacement in Eastern Congo* (New York, Human Rights Watch, 2010), p. 17.

175 Report of the Representative of the Secretary-General on the Human Rights of Internally Displaced Persons: Mission to the Democratic Republic of Congo, A/HRC/8/6/Add.3, para. 35.

176 See Communiqué of the 69th Meeting of the African Union Peace and Security Council, PSC/PR/Comm/(LXIX).

177 Security Council Resolutions 1744 and 1772 (2007).

178 Security Council Resolution 1744 (2007), Security Council Resolution 1766 (2007), Security Council Resolution 1772 (2007), Security Council Resolution 1801 (2008), Security Council Resolution 1811 (2008), Security Council Resolution 1831 (2008), Security Council Resolution 1863 (2009), Security Council Resolution 1910 (2010), and Security Council Resolution 2010 (2011).

The objective of AMISOM's deployment is to provide a secure environment for the TFG to implement its responsibility in maintaining order and security under the Djibouti agreement.[179] The capacity of the TFG to respond to the massive displacement challenge has been extremely limited. There has not been any entity dealing with the concerns of IDPs.[180] Though its National Refugee Commission assumed responsibility to provide assistance and protection to IDPs, it has never mounted effective projects and policy. Increasingly TFG forces and AMISOM troops have expanded their control in key areas in Mogadishu. Troops from neighbouring Ethiopia and Kenya have also intervened in the country providing support for TFG in other parts of the country. Recently, the Kenyan government has made a decision to integrate its troops into AMISOM command. Though they are known to operate in the country, Ethiopian troops remained outside of AMISOM's command structure.

AMISOM's potential in providing protection and assistance to IDPs should be considered from the perspective of both its mandate in civilian protection and the practical challenge it faces such as personnel, equipment and finance. Since recently resolutions of the SC on Somalia are increasingly making reference to human rights and humanitarian situations on the ground and have instituted a sanction regime on those individuals and entities which are involved including in obstructing humanitarian assistance. With respect to the AUPSC, the growing criticism of the role and participation of AMISOM in human rights and humanitarian violations has generated some interest within members of the Council to consider human rights and decide to support the request by the African Commission on Human and Peoples' Rights to undertake a fact-finding mission in Somalia.

AMISOM faced considerable problems as it lacks troops, resources and equipment. Though by October 2010, the AUPSC passed a decision calling for an increase of the troops to 20,000, the United Nations Security Council remains cautious about authorisation of such a force. It is also unable to stabilise a large portion of the country's territory which is controlled by the insurgent groups. It became a target of insurgents who used rocket-propelled grenades, mines and suicide attackers. It remained unable to contain the ever increasing displacement of civilians which remains extremely high. Al Shabaab has prohibited, restricted and even expelled humanitarian organisations insisting on the signing of Memorandum of Understanding and payment of lofty fees from humanitarian organisations. There has been an allegation that humanitarian assistance has been channelled to armed

179 Agreement between the Transitional Federal Government of Somalia (Security Council Resolution 1766 (2007), FG) and the Alliance for the Re-Liberation of Somalia (ARS), Djibouti, 9 June 2008, para. 3.

180 Hassan Noor, 'Emergency within an Emergency: Somali IDPs', *Forced Migration Review* 28(2007): 30.

groups.[181] Attacks and unreasonable demands had forced WFP to suspend its operation in the south part of Somalia, affecting a population of over a million people in January 2010. There have also been allegations that the troops themselves have been involved in direct shelling against civilian populations thereby becoming a direct cause of displacement themselves.[182] As the UN office was operating from Kenya, it was indeed very difficult for OHCHR to monitor developments on the ground. With respect to immunities and privileges, it is provided in the Status of Agreement signed between AMISOM and the TFG that AMISOM and its members enjoy benefits and privileges as provided for under the African Convention on Diplomatic Privileges and Immunities.[183]

Coordination and consultative meetings were held between AMISOM and UN humanitarian organisations to exchange information and coordinate actions in order to address the needs of vulnerable groups particularly women, children and displaced persons.[184] Despite the need for protection and humanitarian assistance, the participation and presence of international humanitarian organisations in South and Central Somalia has been very restricted. The role of AMISOM in assisting humanitarian access by international organisations is considerably limited. As AMISOM is not seen as an independent and neutral force by insurant groups, any association between the force and international organisation will be perceived as political. In September 2011, the Security Council encouraged the UN to work with the African Union to establish and develop AMISOM's Guard Force with the view to 'provide security, escort and protection services to personnel from the international community'.[185] Despite some recent gains, the force also control a very limited area within Mogadishu, and most of the civilians who require international assistance and support are outside its reach.

The Joint United Nations–African Union Mission in Darfur (UNAMID)

The United Nations–African Union Mission in Darfur was established by Security Council Resolution 1769 (July 2007) under Chapter VII to replace the AMIS that was deployed in 2004. Between 2004 and 2008, AMIS had faced multiple challenges to provide the necessary protection to civilians.

181 Press Conference by UN Resident and Humanitarian Coordinator for Somalia, 21 July 2010, located at www.un.org/News/briefings/docs/2010/100721_Bowden.doc.htm (accessed on 13 September 2010).

182 See *Harsh War, Harsh Peace: Abuses by Al Shabaab, the Transitional Federal Government and AMISOM in Somalia* (New York, Human Rights Watch, 2005).

183 Status of Mission (SOMA) Agreement between the Transitional Federal Agreement and the African Union, 6 March 2007, Art III. Available at: www.amisom-au.org/uploads/Status%20of% 20Mission%20Agreement%s20on%20AMISOM.pdf.

184 Report of the Chairperson on Situation in Somalia, PSC/PR/2(CCXIV), para. 34.

185 S/RES/2010(2011), para. 5.

First, AMIS's mandate justified the use of force only 'under imminent threat and in the immediate vicinity and within its resources and capability'.[186] Not only was this mandate vaguely interpreted, it was also claimed that its Rules of Engagement and Standard Operating Procedures were unclear.[187] Lack of personnel and other resources meant that AMIS troops did not have the inputs necessary to play any meaningful role in civilian protection. Resolution 1769 authorises UNAMID to take the necessary action in the areas of deployment of its forces: (a) protect its personnel, facilities, installations and equipment, and to ensure the security and freedom of movement of its own personnel and humanitarian workers, (b) support early and effective implementation of the Darfur Peace Agreement, (c) prevent the disruption of its implementation and armed attacks, and (d) protect civilians, without prejudice to the responsibility of the government of Sudan. The specific tasks to be performed by the peace-keeping mission include facilitating humanitarian access and provision, protecting civilians, creating a secure environment for a sustainable return of IDPs and refugees, and assisting the monitoring and strengthening of national institutions such as NHRIs, judiciary organs and prison administrations.[188]

UNAMID has been mandated to 'contribute to the protection of civilian populations under imminent threat of physical violence and prevent attacks against civilians' including by deterring violence and deploying police force in areas where IDPs have settled.[189] The force is also mandated to facilitate the provision of humanitarian assistance and facilitate durable solution through the sustainable and durable return of refugees and displaced persons including by deploying a civilian police force in areas where IDPs population has been concentrated. UNAMID has faced challenges in fulfilling its protection mandates. Resolution 1769 also places responsibility on the government of Sudan and other parties to the conflict. The government and armed groups are obliged to cooperate with humanitarian organisations, cease attack against civilians including aerial bombardment, ensure special protection to women and girls from sexual and gender-based attacks, and address impunity including through cooperation with the International Criminal Court.

Conclusion

The elaboration of the Kampala Convention is a significant achievement. Ensuring its implementation through a robust complementary role of national, regional and international institutions is an urgent and critical task.

186 *Darfur 2007: Chaos by Design: Peacekeeping Challenges for AMIS and UNAMID* (New York: Human Rights Watch, 2000), 49.
187 Ibid., 62.
188 Report of the Secretary General and the Chairperson of the Commission of the African Union on the Hybrid Operation in Darfur, S/2007/307/Rev. 1, para. 55.
189 Ibid.

The first important step to be taken by states is to ratify the instrument. They should then adopt the necessary legislative review and designate a coordination mechanism with the view to facilitating the implementation of the Convention. In taking these measures, national authorities should cooperate with the African Union, other regional and sub-regional organisations and with international institutions and mechanisms. Undertaking a successful implementation of the Convention, however, encounters several challenges which states and their regional and international partners should effectively tackle if the objectives of the Convention are to be realised.

The process of ratification of the Convention has been slow. In more than two years since the adoption of the Kampala Convention, the instrument has not yet come into force. The problem of ratification has been a common challenge to African human rights instruments whose entry into force has been significantly slowed or hampered by, among others, sluggish ratification. This, however, should not be inevitable. First, during the drafting of the Convention, several controversial issues such as displacement generated by lack of development, intervention by the African Union, the concept of responsibility to protect, and the establishment of the African Union High Commissioner for Human Rights were taken out of the draft principally to make the text acceptable to states. Second, the content of the Convention is similar to much of the provisions of the UN Guiding Principles which in turn reflect international human rights and humanitarian laws. Third, around 11 members states, four states less than the number of instruments of ratification required to trigger the entry into force of the Convention, have already ratified the ICGLR. Fourth, while a number of African states namely Angola, Burundi, Sudan, Liberia, Sierra Leone and Uganda have already adopted national laws and policies on internal displacement, several others are in the process of doing so. Ratification of these instruments will significantly support and reinforce measures that have already been undertaken.

A number of factors might have underpinned the problem encountered so far with respect to ratification. Some countries may still be resistant towards some of the contents of the Convention. As has already been mentioned, several controversial provisions of the draft Convention were excluded during the drafting process and the text was finally adopted by consensus. It also does not explain why states which have become parties to the Great Lakes Protocol have not yet ratified the Convention. Even if states do not have a specific policy position concerning the content of the Convention, national policy makers in countries where complex emergencies do not often occur may not consider the ratification of the Convention as a national priority.

The African Union has adopted an Action Plan which, while setting out several activities aimed at promoting the ratification of the Convention, also provides a roadmap for specific measures at the national and regional level. The African states have already expressed their commitments to several international and regional legal instruments which have direct and indirect ramifications to protecting and assisting IDPs. Several governments, subregional organisations and African Union institutions have also expressed their endorsement of the Guiding Principles. There is a conviction that based on these instruments and the Guiding Principles, a framework for implementation can be developed even while the Convention awaits ratification.

IDPs are either nationals or residents of the state within whose boundary they are displaced. As such, they are entitled to all protection and assistance of nationals and residents are beneficiaries from under the country's domestic laws. In order to fully realise the objectives of the Convention, a certain level of legislative reforms is required. The Convention is not too prescriptive as to the scope and depth of the legislative reform required. Nevertheless, it is provided that the reform should incorporate both a review and amendment of existing legislations and consideration of the enactment of a new domestic law. While this is no small task, particularly for countries with severe constraints on expertise and resources, they can rely both on the provisions of the Convention and several other instruments, standards and manuals developed both at the regional and international levels. Starting with the national Constitution and some general human rights related legislations, several legislations touching on areas of criminal justice, land tenure, protection of vulnerable groups, environment, disaster, education, elections, employment, investment, tax and customs should be considered during the national review exercise. Even when amendments of these legislations are found unnecessary or extremely difficult, the process will facilitate the Convention's implementation. By undertaking an assessment of its own experience with internal displacement, the state needs to determine whether it should enact a specific national legislation on internal displacement or not. There is broad support for the adoption of displacement-specific legislation even in countries that do not often experience national emergencies and those located in a fragile environment. The scope and nature of the Convention, however, should be decided by the state taking full account of its national experience and identified gaps in its legislations.

The Kampala Convention requires states to take concrete steps in ensuring legislative reform and designate national mechanisms with the responsibility of ensuring the implementation of the Convention at the national level. All states including those which do not experience complex emergencies need a coherent national policy and legislation dealing with internal displacement. A number of African countries namely Angola, Burundi, Liberia, Sierra Leone, Sudan and Uganda each have a specific national framework on internal displacement. The review of these domestic codifications reveals some broad trends. The first approach is represented by the Liberian model where a rather brief legal instrument is adopted to declare the state's recognition of the Guiding Principles and its readiness to implement the latter through additional legislative and administrative measures. A number of countries namely Angola, Burundi and Sierra Leone chose a more detailed national legislative which essentially focused on a set of priority areas such as the question of return or a durable solution. The third approach is pursued by Uganda which, through the adoption of a much broader framework on internal displacement, seeks to address some of the salient elements of internal displacement. In the majority of cases, displacement policies and laws tend to focus on addressing the protection and assistance needs of those displaced by armed conflicts. This has been principally due to the fact that most of these countries have been disproportionately affected by armed conflicts. It should, however, be stated that the national policy framework in Angola and Uganda deals with internal displacement generated both by armed conflict and disasters.

Within the framework of the Guiding Principles, countries opted for different approaches to tackle legal problems associated with internal displacement. Within this flexible arrangement, however, states need to ensure that their domestic legislations fulfil certain requirements. A comprehensive approach which adopts the broad definition of IDPs as recognised in the Convention and the UN Guiding Principles should be pursued. The domestic law should also be in a position to identify responsibilities for coordination and provide guidance on a framework for a division of labour. In light of the unique and specific experience of vulnerable groups including women and children, it is imperative to ensure that the domestic law makes reference to these groups and that specific guidance is provided on how the monitoring of the legislation will also take into account specific laws on children and women that might have been adopted. It is also important that the national legislation recognises that IDPs are not only victims who require humanitarian assistance but are also holders of rights and entitlements such as freedom of movement, the right to property and socio-economic rights. A provision dealing with how IDPs who suffered injury or harm will benefit from compensation should also be incorporated into the national legislation.

That quite a considerable number of situations of internal displacement have been triggered by armed conflicts in Africa makes regional institutions on peace-making and conflict resolution important players in the prevention of internal displacement. The Convention also duly recognises the role of regional institutions in the protection and assistance of IDPs; a strategy that complements some of the regional legal instruments which grant the Council of Ministers and the AU Peace and Security Council the responsibility of coordinating humanitarian and relief assistance. While the primary responsibility lies with states to implement and promote the human rights of IDPs, regional and sub-regional institutions also play an important role in monitoring the implementation of the provisions of the Convention. Different categories of regional and sub-regional institutions are important in this respect. The first ones are those identified under the Convention itself as having specific responsibilities. These include the COP, the African Commission on Human and Peoples' Rights, and the Special Rapporteur on Refugees, Asylum Seekers and Internally Displaced Persons. The second category of mechanisms includes those that, though not specifically mentioned in the Convention, nonetheless play a rather critical role. These include the African Peace and Security Council, the Committee of Permanent Representatives, African Committee on the Rights and Welfare of the Child, the APRM to mention just a few. The third layer of organisations is sub-regional blocs and the various mechanisms they have built with respect to issues concerning internal displacement.

Greater collaboration and cooperation is required between national and regional mechanisms. The relationship between the Special Rapporteur and the Commission of the African Union has been largely *ad hoc*. Despite the recent decision to integrate NEPAD and the APRM structures within the African Union, these institutions are largely unknown. The same applies to the Committee of Experts on the Rights and Welfare of the Child, the efficacy of whose mandate has been weakened by a number of shortcomings. For these institutions to play a more coherent and effective role, the following issues ought to be addressed: (a) the relationship between the African Commission and the African Court ought to be well-coordinated and planned; (b) the role of the Special Rapporteur in the formulation of policy instruments and provision of inputs to the regional effort in the protection and promotion of human rights of IDPs need to be considered very closely; (c) the ACHPR should further consolidate and clarify its jurisprudence specially by focusing on certain specific aspects affecting IDPs. Human rights reporting both under the African Charter on Human and Peoples' Rights and the APRM will only be effective to the extent to which these institutions are ready to integrate the protection and assistance of IDPs within their mandate and operation; and also the willingness of state parties to include in their national reports information on measures taken at the national level to implement commitments. Much more is needed in terms of harmonising reporting under these mechanisms. The current practice of fragmented reporting, as shown by poor reporting performance by member states, has not been effective.

The future role of the COP as a forum for cooperation and assistance among states is important. However, its role should be examined in light of the fact that already the African Union has held three ministerial meetings on forced displacement. These meetings have provided the space for policy development and guidance. Member states have agreed on holding such meetings once every two years. Some of the envisaged activities have also been outlined in the African Union Plan of Action. During the period when the Convention awaits ratification, the ministerial conference may act as a substitute for the COP. Once the Convention secures the minimum ratification of 15 member states and enters into force, it is incumbent upon member states to identify the relationship between the COP and ministerial conferences. A policy platform which transcends the technical requirements of ratifications is appealing, especially as the ratification of the instrument becomes slow. It will help policy makers from all countries to be involved in the process thereby gradually encouraging ratification. On the other hand, some of the tasks mandated to the COP evince legal obligations on the part of ratifying states. It is, therefore, possible to design a procedure whereby state parties to the Convention undertake COP meeting during one of the sessions of the ministerial conference.

As a regional legal instrument, the implementation of the Convention principally falls within the parameters of national and regional initiatives. However, international institutions, namely, humanitarian organisations and agencies, UN human rights mechanisms, tribunals and transitional justice mechanisms and peace-keeping missions have important protection and assistance roles thereby contributing to the fulfilment of the Convention's objectives. The international system has a far more developed system of resource mobilisation, expert reservoir and experience in organisation of humanitarian and relief action.

The reform of the UN Human Rights Council led to the creation of innovative mechanisms such as the Universal Periodic Review which are being used to proffer recommendations which seek to improve conditions of human rights of IDPs. During the evaluation of national implementation reports, treaty bodies have also been increasingly invoked in displacement-related recommendations. At the international level, however, the Special Rapporteur on the human rights of IDPs is a key focal point. Beyond his contribution to the development of normative standards including some specific instruments addressing carefully identified areas, he has undertaken several missions to a number of African countries where he has made a concerted impact on shaping the local response to challenges of internal displacement. The Special Rapporteur has provided specific inputs to the development of the Convention itself and is well-positioned to play a key role in the future implementation of the Convention. The mandate-holder has also worked with a number of thematic and country-specific procedures. Through the role of country-specific mandate holders in Burundi, Somalia and Sudan, concerns on protections and assistance gaps have been raised and examined. The adoption of the Convention has already influenced the behaviour of states towards the mandate-holder. Not only are an increasing number of states co-sponsoring the resolution relating to the mandate of the Special Rapporteur, but Uganda has co-led the negotiation process over the recently adopted resolution of the Human Rights Council.

The role of a number of key UN agencies and humanitarian organisations has been instrumental for the successful elaboration of the Convention. Now both at the national and regional level, these institutions are critical partners in the implementation of national policies and legislations. This is particularly so given that most situations of internal displacement occur in national contexts where the resources and institutional capacities of states and regional actors are considerably limited. The cluster approach has been implemented where the specific role and contribution of each international organisation is clarified. New institutions such as the Peace Building Commission are assisting countries such as Burundi, CAR and Guinea Bissau to secure durable solutions through legislative reform, institutional capacity building and post-conflict development and reconstruction. But it is in the provision of material assistance to displacement-affected communities that the role of international organisations is particularly felt. International organisations, however, face quite a number of limitations. In some situations, continued and excessive reliance on international assistance means that considerably little attention is being given to the strengthening of local capacity. Several governments such as Algeria, Eritrea and Sudan restrict the role of international actors. Moreover in places such as Somalia, the DRC, Chad and Southern Sudan, lack of security makes it difficult for international organisations to play their role.

International and regional peace-keeping missions are increasingly playing a role in the protection of civilians including those who are uprooted from their homes and residences. The deployment and operationalisation of peace-keeping missions in Sudan, DRC and Somalia reveal the challenges of protecting IDPs trapped in conflicts. Both in Sudan and DRC, the international peace-keeping missions are not provided with the manpower and resources to provide the fullest protection required for civilians. In Somalia, the African Union peace-keeping mission, AMISOM, is being criticised for direct involvement in generating civilian displacement, and human rights and humanitarian violations.

7 Conclusions

The Kampala Convention is a pioneering regional legal instrument that provides a comprehensive and binding legal framework for the protection and assistance of IDPs in Africa. The importance of its adoption was widely recognised by international and regional bodies and organisations, namely, the General Assembly, the Human Rights Council, the Executive Committee of UNHCR and the former RSG. The African Commission on Human and Peoples' Rights endorsed the Convention, and the Special Rapporteur of the Commission recognised it as one of the most important legal instruments in the continent. Africa can truly take pride in being the region to have adopted the first binding legal instrument on internal displacement. This book has examined the background, evolution and the future implementation challenges facing this pioneering legal instrument. It underscored the need to examine the Convention within the institutional and normative developments both at the regional and the international levels.

Undertaking an in-depth study on a regional treaty in Africa is not an easy task, not least due to the fact that many of the regional legal instruments are not accompanied with detailed *travaux preparatoire*. Studying the background of the AU Convention is not an exception. This book has sought to fill this lacuna by incorporating information collected including two study visits by the author to the headquarters of the African Union where all the expert meetings during the negotiation of the Convention were held. A number of key participants in the process including member states, representatives of international organisations, officials of the African Union, representatives of civic society organisations and experts were interviewed. Chapter 4 of the research on the background of the drafting process relied on information gleaned from the reports of the meetings and that provided by these informants. Different versions of the Convention appeared at various stages of the negotiation process, providing a useful insight into how the provisions of the Convention evolved.

The adoption of the Convention is a culmination of an important regional approach to address the challenges of internal displacement. That the text has been adopted by a Special Summit of the African Union, the first time a regional legal instrument has been considered at the highest political level, is also revealing of the political importance attached to the initiative. The drafting of the Convention is yet another proof of regional organisations' relevance not only in transforming international norms to local contexts but also in filling gaps with respect to which international consensus was difficult to consolidate. While the text is truly an African initiative, it involved an exemplary collaboration between the African Union on the one hand and its international partners which included a wider range of actors such as the former RSG, ACHPR Special Rapporteur, UN agencies, international organisations and CSOs. By encouraging a solid partnership with these international partners, the codification process also provided an exemplary relationship between regional mechanisms and international organisations in standard setting. This collaboration not only injected the financial and logistical support to the initiatives but also provided the much needed expertise that guaranteed that provisions of the Convention are consistent with relevant international standards and norms.

Framework and evolution of the African regional system

There is a need to consider the Kampala Convention within the broader regional system of the African Union which covers issues such as human rights, conflict resolution, post-conflict reconstruction, recovery and development. The elaboration of the Kampala Convention was rationalised on the basis of a number of key factors related to the presumed protection gaps and the role these mechanisms will play in addressing these gaps. Both the Annotated Outline and the preamble of the Convention recognise that there has been a clear 'legal vacuum' with respect to protecting and assisting IDPs which needed to be filled. It was thought that a regional Convention can easily circumvent tricky, challenging and often protracted negotiations that a proposal on a global treaty on internal displacement would normally trigger. It was also argued that regional instruments are well-positioned to address protection and assistance challenges unique or particular to the region. This has been further strengthened by a trend in an increasing and emphatic involvement of regional organisations, including in the development of regional norms. While this may present a risk of fragmentation of international norms and standards, it has shown that the Kampala Convention has significantly helped the process of 'regionalising' the widely accepted UN Guiding Principles on Internal Displacement. The adoption of the Kampala Convention is, therefore, a natural progression from years of experience with international efforts to clarify the normative basis for the protection and assistance of IDPs and the reinforcing and streamlining of institutional mechanisms at the global level. It is also a validation of the increasingly wide acceptance of the Guiding Principles by states, international organisations and regional actors.

Proposals which sought to provide protection to IDPs through a revision of the African Charter on Human and Peoples' Rights and the 1969 OAU

Refugee Convention were rejected. For instance, the joint consultation held between UNHCR and the ACHPR in 2003 recommended the elaboration of an additional Protocol to the 1969 Convention which would have focused on the protection of IDPs.

Placing the protection and assistance of IDPs in the human rights framework faces challenges. Despite its status as one of the most significant pillars of the African regional legal instruments, the 1969 OAU Refugee Convention had not been fully integrated into the regional human rights system. The African Commission had not developed an extensive jurisprudence on the protection of refugees and IDPs. In recent times, however, the ACHPR has taken certain steps including adopting decisions on key communications with implications for the protection of victims of forced displacement and undertaking fact-finding missions which may provide a realistic chance that it may well play an active role in the implementation of the Convention once the latter comes into force. The establishment and operationalisation of the mandate of the ACHPR's Special Rapporteur assisted this trend.

The 1969 OAU Refugees Convention has been predominantly considered as a unique regional instrument to address the attributes of refugee problems in Africa and meet their protection and assistance needs. The Convention has been cited in order to show the possibility and usefulness of regional approaches in addressing complex issues. But even this regional instrument did not articulate the problem of forced displacement in a comprehensive manner. Much like developments at the international level, however, regional refugee protection mechanisms, particularly the Commission of Fifteen, the ministerial conferences and key consultative meetings between the OAU and UNHCR led to an increasing acknowledgement of multifaceted problems faced by broad categories of displaced persons which also included returnees and IDPs.

Some key regional developments made important contributions to the emergence and evolution of the Kampala Convention. As is represented by the 1969 OAU Refugee Convention, the African region has a long tradition of regional approaches in addressing the problem of displacement in the continent. A series of ministerial conferences took place with a view to not only discussing some of the challenges of implementing the Refugee Convention, but also to identifying ways and means of tackling contemporary challenges including those affecting groups such as returnees and IDPs. There were also a few regional legal instruments preceding the Kampala Convention, which provided explicit recognition to IDPs. The African Charter on the Rights and Welfare of the Child and the Protocol on the Rights of Women in Africa are the first binding regional instruments providing for the protection and assistance of internally displaced children and women respectively. It is also important to note that the African Commission on Human and Peoples' Rights adopted key decisions with important implications for the promotion of the human rights of IDPs. Since 2004, the

Commission has also used its Special Rapporteur to advance the cause of displaced persons. The transformation of the OAU into the African Union and the adoption of several instruments including the Constitutive Act have been important developments. Unlike the case of the Charter of the former OAU, the Constitutive Act of the African Union elevates the position of human rights. It provides for groundbreaking norms such as regional intervention in situations of grave breaches of international human rights and international humanitarian law including genocide, crimes against humanity and war crimes. The Constitutive Act and other regional instruments such as the Protocol on the establishment of the African Union Peace and Security Council provide for specific norms with far-reaching implications for the protection of IDPs.

The Kampala Convention has been elaborated as a standalone regional instrument. But it took into account these regional instruments. Sub-regional treaties particularly the Great Lakes Protocols relating to internal displacement were particularly important and served as useful sources. The preamble of the Convention explicitly mentions many of these regional instruments. The influence of these treaties is notable in those provisions of the Convention dealing with institutional issues such as the role of the African Union, the African Court on Human and Peoples' Rights, the African Commission on Human and Peoples' Rights and the African Peer Review Mechanism. The concept of regional intervention in the context of genocide, war crimes and crimes against humanity has its roots in the Constitutive Act. There are a number of concepts drawn from the refugee law especially from the OAU Convention. The protection of IDPs from forced return to areas where their safety and security is no more guaranteed has its roots in refugee law. The preamble's focus on the African traditional generosity in hosting refugees seems to be transplanted from the refugee instrument. The Convention also reinforces some regional soft laws such as the Addis Ababa Document on Refugees and Forced Displacement of Populations in Africa. The innovative provisions of the Constitutive Act on regional interventions during grave and serious violations inspired the inclusion of similar provisions in the Convention which outlines the responsibilities of the African Union in certain situations of serious and grave situations.

The international context and source of the Convention

The success of the elaboration of the AU Convention should be seen within the normative and institutional developments which have helped shape the discourse and response to the protection and assistance needs of IDPs at the international level. The Guiding Principles represent the climax of the international effort in providing sufficient protection and assistance to IDPs. The Convention is cast as an attempt to give a binding expression to this important normative framework, making it suitable for the African context. The protection of IDPs has definitely been influenced by changes in international law relating to the articulation of sovereignty, civilian protection, state responsibility and the rights of individuals. But the search for developing an appropriate model of protecting IDPs has also contributed significantly to the development of international law itself. This has been particularly facilitated by the establishment of the mandate of the former RSG by the former UN Commission on Human Rights and the mandate's continued renewal by the new Human Rights Council. The approach used by the mandate holder examined the potential and limitation of existing international law, mainly international human rights law and international humanitarian law in the protection of IDPs. Despite states' continued invocation of the doctrines of non-intervention, state sovereignty and non-interference, the aforementioned exercise showed to what extent international law can be used to provide protection and assistance to erstwhile neglected individuals and groups. The various reports of the former RSG have also identified gaps and 'grey areas' which necessitate the systematic and comprehensive elaboration of norms regulating internal displacement.

The preamble of the Kampala Convention recognises the role of the Guiding Principles as a source of normative development on internal displacement. The Convention draws on fields of international law such as international human rights law, international humanitarian law and refugee law. It is notable that current developments particularly in the field of international criminal law and climate change have also been taken into account. Moreover, the Convention also relied on the Annotation prepared by the former SRG. Though not as explicit and robust as the endorsement given to the Annotation by the Great Lakes Protocol, the drafting background has shown that the drafters and negotiators often cited the Annotations. The contribution of the Consultative Group, constituting the former RSG, ICRC and UNHCR, helped ensure compatibility of the text with the Guiding Principles and other norms.

The success of the elaboration of the Convention partly stems from the strong support given by the international community, particularly by relevant UN agencies, international organisations, civic organisations and the former SRG. These actors had already built a strong relationship with the African Union. This cooperation and collaborative relationship is aimed at supporting the latter's initiative to develop a robust regional mechanism which will effectively deal with conflicts, human rights violations and forced displacement. For some of these organisations, the development of a regional instrument that recognises and endorses their role in providing assistance and protection to IDPs is a welcome development. This is particularly so in the light of the fact that many states had been vociferously 'objecting' to the exercise of a mandate by these organisations with respect to categories of persons who have not been recognised under international law or with respect to an issue often recognised as falling within the internal affairs of the state. Supporting an effective legal and institutional regime on internal displacement also reduces the risk of external outflows of persons. Preventing or reducing such a risk has traditionally been supported by Western governments and donors.

The background and drafting history of the Convention

As was noted already, the Convention should be seen as an outcome of a broad regional approach by the African Union, which aims at addressing protection gaps not only *vis-a-vis* IDPs but also with respect to refugees and returnees. The series of ministerial meetings and the Kampala Summit organised by the African Union adopted such an inclusive agenda. In addition to developing a binding regional instrument regulating internal displacement, 'soft laws' have been adopted charting some of the key activities to be undertaken with respect to the protection of refugees and returnees. Ever since the first decision of the AU's Executive Council was passed in 2004 requesting the AU Commission to elaborate a legal framework for protecting and assisting IDPs, several measures have been undertaken to develop the Convention. The African Union secured the expertise of Dr Chaloka Beyani, a prominent African international lawyer from the London School of Economics, to prepare the first draft of the text. He prepared the Annotated Outline which was then commented upon by a group of independent legal experts which involved the former SRG, representatives of organisations such as UNHCR, IOM and the ICRC, and a member of civic society organisations such as African Humanitarian Action. Beyond the responsibility of preparing the first draft text of the Convention, the drafter played a critical role during the entire negotiation process, often serving as a resource person and a shadow rapporteur.

In 2007 and 2008, a series of meetings of member states were held to negotiate the Convention. The African Union Commission organised and provided secretariat services to these meetings. The participation of the PRC sub-committee on Refugees, Returnees and Displaced Persons and ACHPR Special Rapporteur has been quite important. The first meeting of legal experts was held from 15 to 17 December 2007. This was followed by the second expert meeting held from 1 to 6 June 2008. The third meeting of legal experts was held on 9 November 2009. Though faced with some 'logistical' problems such as lack of sufficient time and translation inconsistencies between the various versions of the text of the Convention, these meetings were generally successful. The African Union's Department for Political and Humanitarian Affairs served as the secretariat of the meeting. The Office of the Legal Counsel was also closely involved in the process. At these meetings, a number of issues were found particularly challenging and controversial. These included the role and responsibility of armed groups, displacement caused by lack of development, the proposed establishment of a regional office for the protection of and assistance to IDPs, and the role of external intervention to prevent arbitrary displacement.

The third ministerial meeting on refugees, returnees and displaced persons adopted the final text which was then forwarded for adoption to the Special Summit of the African Union held in Kampala, Uganda in October 2009. As a country which has experienced severe forms of forced displacement throughout its history, Uganda was undoubtedly a fitting venue for hosting the special Summit which adopted the text of the Convention, 17 African states becoming signatories to the Convention at the conclusion of the historical event. In addition to the Convention, the Assembly also adopted the Kampala Declaration. While awaiting the entry into force of the Convention, it was felt that the Declaration will provide the necessary guidance to the African Union and its member states in their efforts to ensure protection and assistance to IDPs. The desirability of the Declaration was also occasioned by the need to consider the issues relating to refugees and returnees which are not covered by the Convention.

Earlier drafts of the Convention lay bare the intention of the drafters to expand the scope of the Convention by extending its reach far beyond what has been provided for under the UN Guiding Principles. The definition of internally displaced persons was intended to include those displaced as a result of lack of development. Its provisions dealing with the role and responsibility of the African Union also toyed with the idea of providing authority to the African Union to intervene in member states in order to prevent arbitrary displacement and ensure the protection and assistance of IDPs. A much earlier version of the draft Convention had also incorporated a provision establishing an African Union Office which would have had the responsibility of ensuring the implementation of the Convention. The draft Convention's reference to reparations also triggered the relevance and applicability of such forms of relief to individuals who have become internally displaced. Most of these proposals did not make it to the final version of the text.

Key relevant international organisations actively encouraged the African Union to consider the development of a regional instrument on internal displacement. Once the African Union initiated the process, they were intimately involved in the elaboration of the Kampala Convention. They have also been involved in funding the series of meetings held prior to the adoption of the Convention. If the development of the Guiding Principles was innovative in that it happened outside the framework of an intergovernmental negotiation, the drafting of the Convention involved a very active participation and input from the RSG, the ACHPR Special Rapporteur, UN agencies and to a limited extent CSOs. It is indicative not only of the growing role of these actors in international law making but also reveals the changing views of states with respect to the mandates and role of particularly United Nations agencies with respect to IDPs. It should be noted that there has been a long tradition of cooperation between the OAU/AU and institutions such as UNHCR and ICRC. As far back as 1998, the Council of Ministers of the OAU adopted a decision that recognised and acknowledged the role of ICRC in situations of internal displacement. A similar relationship also existed between the UNHCR and the continental organisation. In light of the lack of the necessary knowledge and awareness about internal displacement and some of the protection issues it raises, particularly among those who were directly involved in the negotiations, the involvement and role of these international organisations has therefore been very useful.

Objectives of the Convention

The Kampala Convention has, as its principal objective, the provision of a binding legal framework for protecting and assisting IDPs. It does so by transforming the Guiding Principles into a binding set of norms. It is rather clear from the text of the Convention that several new developments from fields of international humanitarian law and human rights law have left their marks on the Convention. The active participation of the former RSG had been instrumental in ensuring compliance with the existing international legal framework, particularly the Guiding Principles, as was the involvement of ICRC in ensuring that the provisions of the Convention comply with international humanitarian law.

There are some key similarities and differences between the Convention and the Guiding Principles. The Convention and the Guiding Principles both adopt quite a similar definition to internally displaced persons. Both instruments also examine the problem of internal displacement through the perspective of the three important phases of displacement. Both instruments also seek to reinforce relevant international human rights law and international humanitarian law. A closer examination and comparison of the two texts, however, reveals important and key differences. The Convention represents a binding instrument. Rather than focus on the enumeration of the rights of IDPs, the Convention also adopts a framework of state responsibility where the obligation of states during each phase of the displacement is clearly laid out. There are far more detailed provisions on the application of international humanitarian law and issues of protection of IDPs during situations of conflicts. The Convention's provisions on the role and responsibility of non-state actors such as armed groups, businesses and companies are also clearly laid out. Taking into account contemporary developments which have become increasingly prominent in recent years, the Convention also has a number of important provisions dealing with issues of protection during natural disasters and climate change. It urges states to undertake effective measures to implement early warning systems and risk reduction strategies. Compared to the Guiding Principles, there is also a strong framework for accountability for breaches of the Convention where states are urged to ensure that violations of these norms are appropriately addressed through judicial processes. Starting from the development of the Annotated Outline and the preparation of the first draft, the exercise had a much broader agenda than the mere transformation of the Guiding Principles into binding laws. For instance, there was a desire to include situations of displacement triggered by not only development projects but also poverty and lack of development.

From the perspective of the institutional framework, the Convention not only reinforces the role of existing mechanisms such as the ACHPR, the African Court of Human and Peoples' Rights and the APRM but also creates the Conference of Parties which has been given the mandate to monitor and oversee the implementation of the Convention.

Scope and elements of the Convention

The Kampala Convention incorporates 23 articles, arranged around key issues involved in the three phases of displacement. It adopts a comprehensive approach on internal displacement. Its definition of IDPs is both comprehensive and consistent with the Guiding Principles. It underscores the principles that the definition of IDPs should not result in any separate legal status. In addition to those who are displaced, the Convention also provides for the protection of host communities. Its provisions on the problem of internal displacement in the context of climate change are relevant to addressing protection issues emanating from the nexus between displacement and climate change. The Convention innovatively incorporates provisions which require states to implement disaster risk reduction strategies, develop early warning systems, prevent and mitigate the degradation of the environment in areas where IDPs are located, protect vulnerable communities, promote environmental assessment prior to the implementation of development projects and guarantee durable and sustainable solutions to internal displacement situations including those induced by natural disasters and environmental concerns. Its provisions reinforce both regional and international instruments relevant to the protection and assistance of IDPs. By adopting a framework of state responsibility, it lays out the responsibility of states in preventing arbitrary displacement, protecting and assisting IDPs during displacement, and facilitating durable solutions. It provides a comprehensive definition of situations which constitute arbitrary displacement. Accordingly, the following non-exhaustive lists of situations are categorised as arbitrary displacements: displacement based on racial discrimination or similar practices; displacement of civilians during armed conflicts not justified on the basis of civilian protection or military necessity; intentional violations as a component of violations of human rights law and international humanitarian law; displacement as a result of harmful traditional practices; and forced evacuations during disasters which are not justified by safety and health reasons.

Within the framework of the responsibility of states, the Convention reconceptualises the doctrine of state sovereignty and non-intervention in the internal affairs of states. The legal recognition that internal displacement is a phenomenon with respect to which a regional and international response might be warranted has itself been a remarkable reformulation of previous positions. This is not, however, to suggest that the Convention redraws the fundamental relationship between African states and the long cherished doctrines of sovereignty and non-interference. But the Convention introduces key provisions which will shape the policy of African governments towards the rights of IDPs, and their relationship with other actors which may want to provide assistance to affected communities when the state concerned is unable or unwilling to provide the required assistance and protection. Taking its cue from the African Union's Constitutive Act, the Convention, for example, provides for the authority of the AU and the right of member states to request regional intervention during grave situations such as genocide, crimes against humanity and war crimes. Proposals to include concepts such as the responsibility to protect and humanitarian intervention were put aside as drafters and negotiators alike felt that the inclusion of doctrines and concepts on which general consensus is lacking makes it hard for states to finally accept and ratify the Convention.

While endorsing the framework of state responsibility as an overarching doctrine, the Convention also incorporates provisions underlining the human rights of IDPs including protection against discrimination, freedom of movement and the right to choose one's residence. It recognises 'the inherent rights of internally displaced persons' and affirms the responsibility of states to 'respect, protect and fulfil the human rights' of IDPs. It calls on governments to provide special measures to protect and assist those with special needs, including children, female heads of households, the elderly, people living with HIV/AIDS, expectant mothers and disabled persons. Responding to the concern that the regime on internal displacement may undermine the institution of asylum, the Convention declares that its provisions may not prejudge the rights of individuals to seek asylum. The right of persons to seek safety in any part of the country has also been provided for. In terms of monitoring and overseeing the implementation of the rights of IDPs, the Convention does not prejudice the right of IDPs to bring their complaint under regional human rights mechanisms including the African Commission on Human and Peoples' Rights and the African Court on Human and Peoples' Rights. It also provides for a specific role of ACHPR's reporting mechanism, the APRM and the Special Rapporteur on Refugees, Asylum Seekers, Migrant Workers and Displaced Persons in guaranteeing states' compliance with the Convention's provisions.

The Convention incorporates provisions on the role and responsibilities of non-state actors including armed groups, private military and security companies and multinational companies. Its provisions on armed groups was one of the most contested provisions which led to the reopening of the text during the African Union Summit in October 2009 in Kampala, well after a meeting of minsters responsible for forced displacement had adopted the text of the draft Convention. The fear that detailed provisions on the role and responsibility of armed groups may elevate their legal status underpins such anxiety.

This has resulted in the inclusion of a provision as the Convention which declares that the Convention should not be interpreted as giving or legitimising the status of armed groups. Furthermore it is stated that the application of the Convention should not be prejudicial to the criminal responsibility of armed group members. The Convention's provisions on private businesses and multinational companies, particularly those which are involved in the exploration of economic and natural resources, obligates states to ensure their accountability for the displacement of populations on account of their actions. The Convention calls for these entities to undertake environmental assessment studies prior to the implementation of their projects.

From the perspective of the institutional framework within which the monitoring of the implementation of the Convention will be undertaken, the Convention establishes a Conference of Parties whose meeting will be held on a regular basis. During the drafting process, there was a suggestion that the meeting of the Conference of Parties should take place once every two years. This was further changed into a provision which stipulates that the COP's meeting shall take place on a regular basis. By eschewing the proposal to establish a permanent office on internal displacement, states created a mechanism which for all intents and purposes resembles the ministerial meetings on forced displacement which had been held, if not on a regular basis, on a number of occasions. In addition to the COP, the Convention also envisages the role of ACHPR, African Court of Human and Peoples' Rights, the Special Rapporteur on Refugees, Asylum Seekers and IDPs and the African Peer Review Mechanisms as institutional mechanisms on oversight and implementation. The role and responsibilities of regional and international organisations is another set of important provisions. It incorporates a detailed provision on the role of the African Union as a coordination mechanism for regional efforts and measures being taken on behalf of IDPs. The Convention also provides for the role of international organisations and CSOs.

Significance of the Convention

The central objective of the entire initiative of drafting a regional Convention on internal displacement has been to fill the existing 'legal vacuum' in the protection of and assistance to IDPs. By becoming the first binding regional legal instrument on the protection of IDPs, the Convention makes an important contribution in filling such legal vacuum. Its emphasis on the framework of state responsibility as an overarching normative premise refocuses the shift away from the traditional preoccupation of African states with sovereignty and non-intervention. The reference to the Constitutive Act's provision on regional intervention will also cast sovereignty as incorporating a responsibility to protect one's citizens. By providing detailed provisions on the responsibility of states in all phases of displacement, the Convention also supplements the Guiding Principles whose provisions outline the needs and entitlements of IDPs.

The Convention's provisions on issues of protection and assistance of displaced persons in the context of natural disasters and climate change make the Convention relevant in addressing current and topical challenges. Indeed, the reference to early warning systems, risk reduction strategies and environmental rehabilitation programmes are quite innovative. With reference to international humanitarian law, its key provisions such as those dealing with the responsibility of armed groups and private military entities advance international humanitarian law.

Despite the regional scope of the Convention, a number of its provisions have international scope. The Convention reinforces the role of international organisations in the area of protecting and assisting IDPs. The significance of this should be examined in light of states' past criticisms of the involvement of these organisations in what has been considered an issue falling within the domestic sphere. Several provisions of the Convention expressly mention the role of international organisations. The preamble of the Convention recognises the role being played by the UN Inter-Agency Standing Committee and the specific mandates and roles of institutions such as the UNHCR and ICRC.

Implementation and its challenges

As of January 2016, 24 states have ratified the Kampala Convention while 40 states have become signatories. Ratifying states are expected to adopt national legislations, policies and strategies to domesticate and implement the Convention. Establishment or designation of a national institutional mechanism is also required under the Convention with the responsibility of coordinating response at the national level. These measures include mobilisation of resources, establishment and strengthening of early warning systems and risk reduction strategies. States are also urged to establish a national registry on IDPs and issue documentation to IDPs. It is also provided that an assessment of the condition of displacement in the country should be undertaken with the view to determine the prevalence of the problem. During the drafting process, questions were raised whether African countries indeed posses the required capacity to undertake all these monumental tasks. The Convention's provision on international cooperation and assistance may be used to address some of these shortcomings.

The Convention includes strong provisions on the prevention of arbitrary displacement and the protection of IDPs from arbitrary displacement. This makes the role of human rights institutions and a human rights framework considerably relevant. As has been noted also, the Convention provides for a strong endorsement of the framework of non-discrimination and equality. Human rights institutions such as the African Court on Human and Peoples' Rights, the African Commission on Human and Peoples' Rights, the African Peer Review Mechanism, the Special Rapporteur on Refugees, Asylum Seekers, Migrant Workers and IDPs all have important roles to play in monitoring the implementation of the Convention. Human rights institutions exhibit some obvious advantage. First, a number of key regional instruments such as the African Charter on the Rights and Welfare of the Child and the African Protocol on the Rights of Women in Africa incorporate norms and rules on the protection of displaced children and women respectively. Mainly through the work of the Special Rapporteur, the ACHPR has also since 2004 closely considered issues affecting IDPs. Its communication procedures have also increasingly pushed the development of the regional human rights jurisprudence towards addressing the specific human rights challenges of IDPs. The Convention also provides that states should also present information on the protection of IDPs in their report and assessment exercise under the APRM. As the experience of countries reviewed under this process clearly show, the APRM can be used as a vehicle for addressing the protection and assistance needs of IDPs.

A considerable amount of investment is required both at the national and regional levels if the implementation of the Convention is to be fully realised. This is particularly true as governments are required to establish and strengthen national mechanisms, set up an information mechanism on IDPs, design and implement early warning systems and risk reduction studies, provide sufficient humanitarian assistance during their displacement and ensure that conditions are met that facilitate durable solutions. Very few countries in Africa will have the resources required to fully realise these commitments on their own. The relevant provision of the Convention on international cooperation should therefore urgently be implemented. There are practical tools that can be pursued. For instance, the Kampala Declaration requires that states take the initiative to ensure that a certain portion of development assistance is dedicated to the protection of IDPs. While such welcome measures underscore the linkage between response to IDPs and development, it is also critical that the specific modality of how this will be rationalised should be worked out.

Bibliography

Reports

Activity Report of the Special Rapportuer on Refugees, Asylum Seekers, Migrants and IDPs in Africa (41st). The text of this report can be located at ACHPR's website at www.achpr.com

Analytical report of the Secretary General on internally displaced persons, E/CN.4/1992/23(1992)

Annual Report, Office for the Coordination of Humanitarian Affairs. Geneva, Switzerland: United Nations, 2009

APRM country review report No. 7, Republic of Uganda, May 2008

Compilation and Analysis of Legal Norms, Part II: Legal Aspects Relating to the Human Rights to be Protected against Arbitrary Displacement, Report of the Representative of the Secretary General on Internally Displaced Persons to the UN Commission on Human Rights, UN Doc. E/CN.4/1998/Add.1(1998)

Comprehensive Report on Lesson Learnt from UNAMIR, United Nations, New York, Department of Peacekeeping Operations, 1996

Conclusions and Recommendations of the Consultative Meeting between the African Commission on Human and Peoples' Rights and the United Nations High Commissioner for Refugees, Addis Ababa, 20 and 21 March 2003

Conference on internal displacement in the IGAD sub-region. Report of the experts meeting, Khartoum, Sudan, 30 August–2 September 2003, Brookings Institution and SAIS Project on Internal Displacement

International Commission on Intervention and State Sovereignty: Responsibility to Protect (2001)

National Emergency Management Agency (NEMA), *Nigeria: Promoting Disaster Risk Reduction in Post Disaster Recovery and Reconstruction Efforts*, (PowerPoint Presentation to the ISDR ECOSOC Side Event, 19 July 2006)

OAU Experts and Ministerial Meetings on Refugees, Returnees and Internally Displaced Persons in Africa, 10–14 December 1998, Khartoum, Sudan. UNHCR Report

Office of the High Commissioner for Human Rights and the Brookings Institutions, *Report of the Workshop on the Role of African National Human Rights Institutions in Protecting the Human Rights of Internally Displaced Persons,* Nairobi, Kenya, 25-26 October 2008

Parsett, Piero Calivi. International Disaster Response Law Project: Report on Findings from South Asia, Southern Africa and Central America, March 2003

Preliminary Report on the protection of persons during disasters, Mr Eduardo Valencia-Ospina, Special Rapportueur, International Law Commission, 60th Session, A/CN.4/598

Recommendations from the Arusha Conference on the Africa Refugee Problem, (Uppsala: Scandinavian Institute of African Studies, 1981)

Regional Conference on Internal Displacement in West Africa (Report), Abuja, Nigeria, 26–28 April 2006, Brookings-Bern Project on Internal Displacement

Report of the Chairperson on Situation in Somalia, PSC/PR/2(CCXIV)

Report of the African Commission's Working Group of Experts, submitted in accordance with the Resolution on the Rights of Indigenous Populations/ Communities in Africa, adopted by the African Commission on Human and Peoples' Rights at its 28th Ordinary Session (2003)

Report of the Representative of the Secretary General, Mr Francis M. Deng, submitted pursuant to Commission on Human Rights resolution 1995/57, Compilations and analysis of legal norms, E/CN.4/1996/52/Add.2, 1995

Report of the Representative of the Secretary General, Mr. Francis M. Deng, submitted pursuant to Commission on Human Rights resolution 1997/39, Compilations and analysis of legal norms, Part II, E/CN.4/1998/53/Add.1, 1998

Report of the Representative of the Secretary-General on the human rights of internally displaced persons, A/HRC/10/13/Add.3

Report of the Group of Governmental Experts on International Co-operation to Avert New Flows of Refugees. New York: United Nations, UN Document A/41/324

Report of the Representative of the Secretary General on the Human Rights of Internally Displaced Persons, 3 August 2009, A/64/214

Report of the Secretary General Representative on the Human Rights of Internally Displaced Persons, A/63/286

Report of the Secretary General Representative on the Human Rights of Internally Displaced Persons, A/65/282, 11 August 2010

Report of the Secretary General Representative on the Human Rights of Internally Displaced Persons in Somalia, A/HRC/13/21/Add.2

Report of the Secretary General on the protection of civilians in armed conflict, Security Council, 1 November 2010, S/2010/579

Report of the African Commission on Human and Peoples' Rights' Fact-Finding Mission to the Republic of Sudan in the Darfur Region, EX. CL/364(XI), Annex III

Report of the African Commission's Working Group of Experts on Indigenous Populations/Communities, adopted at the 34th Ordinary Session in November 2003, the 17th Annual Activity Report of the African Commission later noted and authorized for publication by the 4th Ordinary Session of the AHSG of the AU held in January 2005 in Abuja, Nigeria (Assembly/AU/Dec.56 (IV))

Report of the Ministerial Conference on Refugees, Returnees and Displaced Persons in Africa, 1–2 June 2006 Ouagadougou, Burkina Faso, at 7. AU/MIN/HARDP/Rpt.

Report of the African Commission on Human and Peoples' Rights, 1994–95, ACHPR/APT/8th, Annex VII; Resolution on Liberia, Eight Annual Activity Report of the African Commission on Human and Peoples' Rights, 1994–95, ACHPR/APT/8th, Annex VII

Report of the Meeting of the Drafting Committee of the African Union member States Legal Experts on the Draft AU Convention for the Protection and Assistance of Internally Displaced Persons in Africa, Addis Ababa, Ethiopia, 25–29 July 2008

Report on the Extraordinary Session of the Executive Council on Refugees, Returnees and Internally Displaced Persons held in Kampala, Uganda, 19–20 October 2009, Ext. EX.CL/PA/Rpt.(1)

Report of the Panel on United Nations Peace Operation, UN doc. A/55/305-S/2000/809, 2000

Report of the Special Rapporteur on Refugees, Asylum Seekers, Migrant Workers and Internally Displaced Persons for the period November 2008–May 2009

Report on the Third Meeting of Legal Experts of the African Union on the Draft AU Convention for the Protection and Assistance of Internally Displaced Persons in Africa, Addis Ababa, Ethiopia, November 2008

43rd Report of Activities by the Commissioner Bahame Tom Nyandunga, Special Rapporteur for Refugees, Asylum Seekers, Migrants and IDPs for November 2007 to May 2008

Report of the Peace building Commission on its third session, A/64/341-S/2009/444, 8 September 2009

Second Meeting of Legal Experts of member states of the AU on the Draft AU Convention for the Protection and Assistance of Internally Displaced Persons in Africa, Addis Ababa, Ethiopia, 2–6 June 2008

Special Procedures and Regional Human Rights Mechanisms: Areas for Strengthening Cooperation, Item IV(d), 15th Annual Meetings of the Special Procedures Mandate Holders, available www2.ohchr.org/english/bodies/chr/special/annual_meetings/docs/SP_regional_human_rights_systems_en.pdf, accessed on 10 September 2010

The Status and Treatment of Refugees. The Asian African Legal Consultative Organization, 2009

Summary record of the 39th meeting of the Sub-Commission, E/CN.4/1996/SR.39(1996)

UN High Commissioner for Refugees, Recommendations of the OAU/UNHCR symposium on refugees and forced population displacements in Africa, 21 September 1994, EC/1994/SCP/CRP.7/Add.1

Legal instruments (treaties, resolutions, decisions etc.)

Act No. 57, Disaster Management Act of 2002, Government Gazette No. 24252 (South Africa, 2003)

The Addis Ababa Document on Refugees and Forced Population Displacements in Africa. Adopted by the OAU/UNHCR Symposium on Refugees and Forced Population Displacements in Africa, 8–10 September 1994

African Charter on Human and Peoples' Rights, adopted 27 June 1981, OAU Doc. CAB/LEG/67/3 rev. 5, 21 I.L.M. 58 (1982), entered into force 21 Oct. 1986

African Charter on the Rights and Welfare of the Child, OAU Doc. CAB/LEG/24.9/49 (1990), entered into force 29 Nov. 1999

African Commission on Human and Peoples' Rights Resolutions: Resolution 68/2004; Resolution 74/200; Resolution 93/2005; Resolution 102/2006;

Resolution on the Renewal of the Mandate of the Special Rapporteur on Refugees, Internally Displaced Persons and Migrants in Africa, ACHPR/Res.116(XXXXII), 2007; Resolution on the Mandate and Composition of the Working Group on working methods of the Commission, the African Commission on Human and Peoples' Rights (the African Commission) meeting at its 42nd Ordinary Session held from 15–28 November 2007, Brazzaville, the Republic of Congo; Resolution on the Composition and Renewal of the Mandate of the Working Group on Indigenous Populations/Communities in Africa, ACHPR/Res.123 (XXXXII) 07; Resolution on the Appointment of the Chairperson and Members of the Working Group on Economic, Social and Cultural Rights in Africa, ACHPR/Res.124 (XXXXII) 07

The African Regional Strategy for Disaster Risk Reduction and Plan of Action 2006–2010 and Plan of Action, EX.CL/Dec.250 (VIII)

The African Union Convention for the Protection and Assistance of Internally Displaced Persons in Africa, adopted by the Special Meeting of the Heads of State and Government held on 23 October 2009

Agreement between the Government of the Federal Democratic Republic of Ethiopia and the Government of the State of Eritrea, 12 December 2000

Agreement between the Transitional Federal Government of Somalia (TFG) and the Alliance for the Re-Liberation of Somalia (ARS), Djibouti, 9 June 2008

Charter of the Organisation of African Unity, adopted in Addis Ababa, Ethiopia in May 1963 and entered into force in September 1963

Commission for Human Rights: ACHPR/Res.68 (XXXV) 04, ACHPR/Res.74 (XXXVII) 05 and ACHPR/Res.93 (XXXVIII) 05, and ACHPR/Res.102(XXXX) 06; CHR Res. 1992/73; E/CN.4/RES/1998/50; CHR Dec. 2004/118; Resolution on Situation in Rwanda, Seventh Annual Activity Report of the African Commission on Human and Peoples' Rights, 1993–94, ACHPR/APT/7th, Annex II; Resolution on Burundi, Ninth Annual Activity Report of the African Commission on Human and Peoples' Rights, 1995–96, ACHPR/APT/9th, Annex VII; Resolution on Sudan, Eeight Annual Activity; ACHPR/Res.116 (XXXXII) 07: Resolution on the Renewal of the Mandate of the Special Rapporteur on Refugees, Asylum Seekers, Internally Displaced Persons and Migrants in Africa; Resolution on the Mandate of the Special Rapportuer on Refugees, Asylum Seekers and Internally Displaced Persons in Africa, 23 November–7 December 2004, ACHPR/Res. 72/(XXXVI)04

Communiqué of the 245th Meeting of the Peace and Security Council, PSC/MIN/1(CCXXXXV), 15 October 2010

The Constitutive Act of the African Union, 2000, OUA Doc. CAB/LEG/23.15, entered into force 26 May 2001

Constitutions: The Constitution of the Federal Democratic Republic of Ethiopia; The Constitution of the Republic of Uganda

Convention Governing the Specific Aspects of Refugee Problems in Africa, 1001 U.N.T.S. 45, entered into forced 20 June 1970

Convention on the Elimination of All Forms of Discrimination against Women, G.A. res. 34 U.N. GAOR Supp. (No.46) at 193, U.N.Doc.A/34/46

Convention on the Prevention and Punishment of the Crime of Genocide Adopted by Resolution 260 (III) A of the UN General Assembly on 9 December 1948, entered into force 12 January 1951

Convention on Prohibitions or Restrictions on the Use of Certain Conventional

Weapons which may be deemed to be Excessively Injurious or to Have Indiscriminate Effects and Protocols, 10 October 1980 v. 1342 U.N.T.S

Convention on the Prohibition of the Development, Production and Stockpiling of Bacteriological (Biological) and Toxin Weapons and on their Destruction. Opened for Signature at London, Moscow and Washington, 10 April 1972

Convention on the Prohibition of the Development, Production, Stockpiling and Use of Chemical Weapons and Their Destruction, Doc.CD/CW/WP.400/Rev

The Convention on the Prohibition of the Use, Stockpiling, Production and Transfer of Anti-Personnel Mines and on Their Destruction (1997) 36 ILM 1507

Dar es Salaam Declaration on Peace, Security, Development in the Great Lakes Region, International Conference on Peace, Security and Development in the Great Lakes Region, First Summit of Heads of state and Government, Dar es Salaam, 19–20 November 2004. Available at www.icglr.org/key-documents/declarationspacts/Dar%20Es%20Salaam%20Declaration%20on%20Peace%20Security%20Democracy%20and%20Development.pdf

Decision of the Assembly (OAU/AU): Decisions Assembly/AU/Dec. 45(III) adopted during the 3rd Assembly Summit in Addis Ababa, Ethiopia held between 6–8 July 2004. See also Decision Assembly/AU/Dec. 83(V) adopted during the 5th Assembly Summit in Sirte, Libya held between 4–5 July 2005; Decision on the Draft Protocol to the African Charter on Human and Peoples' Rights Relating to the Rights of Women (Assembly/AU/Dec.19(II); Decision on the Draft Protocol of the Court of Justice of the African Union (Assembly/AU/Dec.25(II)); and Decision on the Draft Convention on the Prevention and Combating of Corruption (Assembly/AU/Dec.27(II)); Decision on the Holding of a Special Session on a consideration and resolution of conflicts in Africa, Assembly/AU/Dec.266(XIII); Assembly of the African Union, 11th Ordinary Session, 30 June–1 July 2008, Sharm El-Sheikh, Egypt, Decision 198 (XII)

Decision of the Executive Council of the African Union on the ministerial conference on Refugees, Returnees and Internally Displaced Persons Doc. EX.CL/254 (IX)

Decision of the Executive Council of the African Union on the ministerial conference on Refugees, Returnees and Internally Displaced Persons Doc. EX.CL/259 (IX)

Decision of the Executive Council of the African Union on the Situation of Refugees, Returnees and Displaced Persons, EX.CL/Dec.127 (V)

Declaration of heads of state and government of the Assembly on the establishment within the OAU of a Mechanism for Conflict Prevention, Management and Resolution, AHG/DEC L.3(XXIX)

Declaration: Enhancing UN–AU Cooperation: Framework for the Ten Year Capacity Building Program for the African Union, Annex, A/61/630, 12 December 2006

Declaration of Minimum Humanitarian Standards, Turku/Abo, 2 December 1990

Draft AU Convention for the Protection and Assistance of Internally Displaced Persons (August 2007)

Draft Declaration on the Rights and Duties of States. Adopted by the General Assembly resolution 375 (IV) of 6 December 1949

ECOSOCC Res. 1990/78 of July 1990

Executive Council OAU/AU: Decision of the 3rd Ordinary Session of the Executive Council of the African Union, EX/CL/Dec.33(III); EX.CL/Dec.284 (IX); OAU Decisions, CM/Dec.388(LXVII) adopted during the 67th Ordinary Session of the Council of Ministers, Addis Ababa, 23–27 February 1998; Decision on the situation of refugees, returnees and internally displaced persons in Africa, DOC.

EX.CL/372(XII); EX.CL/Dec.381; Resolution on the Situation of Refugees in Africa, CM/Res. 1117 (XLVI); Executive Council, Decision on the Situation of Refugees, Returnees and Displaced Persons, Doc. EX.CL/254(IX); EX.CL/Dec.529 (XVI); Ex.CL/Dec.228 (VII)

General Assembly Resolutions 2625 (XXV) of 24 October 1970; GA Res. 63/1970; GA Res. 2956 (XXVII) Resolution (1972); GA Res. 32/127 (1977); GA Res. 43/116(1988); 46/182, 19 Dec. 1991; Resolution/47/105(1992); Resolution 48/135, 20 Dec. 1993; GA Res. 48/42 (1993); A/RES/48/116(1994); A/RES/49/169(1995); GA Res. 49/57(1995); A/RES/150/152 (1996); A/RES/51/75(1997); A/RES/53/125 (1999); GA Res. 54/167 9 (17 December 1999); A/RES/54/146(2000); A/RES/55/74 (2001); A/RES/57/150 (2002);. A/RES/57/187(2003); A/RES/58/151(2004); A/RES/59/170(2005); GA Res. 60/1(2005).; A/RES/60/129 (2006); A/RES/61/137(2007); and A/RES/62/124(2008); GA RES/62/125 (24 January 2008)

Geneva Convention (I) for the Amelioration of the Condition of the Wounded and Sick in Armed Forces in the Field. Geneva, 12 August 1949

Geneva Convention (II) for the Amelioration of the Condition of Wounded, Sick and Shipwrecked Members of Armed Forces at Sea. Geneva, 12 August 1949

Geneva Convention (III) relative to the Treatment of Prisoners of War. Geneva, 12 August 1949

Geneva Convention (IV) relative to the Protection of Civilian Persons in Time of War. Geneva, 12 August 1949

Grand Bay Declaration and Plan of Action, adopted at the OAU First Ministerial Conference on Human Rights in Africa, 16 April 1999

Guidelines for Initial Reports of State Parties, CMTTE/ACRWC/2II

Guidelines for the Domestic Facilitation and Regulation of International Disaster Relief and Initial Recovery Assistance, adopted by the Thirtieth International Conference of the Red Cross and Red Crescent in 2007, available at http://icrc.org/web/eng/siteengO.nsf/htmlall/p1108/$File/ICRC_002_1108.pdf!Open

Guidelines on the Use of Foreign Military and Civil Defence Assets in Disaster Relief. UN Office for the Coordination of Humanitarian Affairs, OCHA, 2007

Guiding Principles on Internal Displacement, 22 July 1998, E/CN.4/1998/53/Add.2

Hague Convention IV (18 October 1907) Convention Respecting the Laws and Customs of War on Land, entry into force, 26 January 1910

Human Rights Council: Resolution 9/9, 24 September 2008; Resolutions 6/20(2007); Human Rights Council Decision 14/117, Human Rights Council Resolution 9/19; Human Rights Council Resolution 12/26; A/HRC/6/19/, 28 November 2007. A/HRC/Res?14/6 Resolution 7/20 ; Resolution S-8/1 HRC Resolution 6/32; A/HRC/10/13

Hyogo Framework for Action 2005–2015: Building the Resilience of Nations and Communities to Disasters, in Final report of the World Conference on Disaster Reduction, A/CONF.206/6 (2005)

International Covenant on Civil and Political Rights, adopted and opened for signature, ratification and accession by General Assembly resolution 2200A (XXI) of 16 December 1966, entry into force 23 March 1976

International Covenant on Economic, Social and Cultural Rights, adopted and opened for signature, ratification and accession by General Assembly resolution 2200A (XXI) of 16 December 1966, entry into force, 3 January 1976

Intersession Activities by Commissioner during the 41st Session of the African Commission on Human and Peoples' Rights, 16–30 May 2007, Accra, Ghana

Kampala Declaration on Refugees, Returnees and Internally Displaced Persons in Africa, 23 October 2009, Ext/Assembly/AU/PA/Draft/Decl.(I) Rev.1, available at: www.unhcr.org/refworld/docid/4af0623d2.html [accessed 1 May 2010]

Khartoum Declaration of the OAU Ministerial Meeting on Refugees, Returnees, Internally Displaced Persons in Africa, 13–14 December 1998

Kigali Declaration, Adopted at the Ministerial Conference on Human Rights in Africa, 8 May 2003

Law No. 04–20 of 25 December 2004, concerning the prevention of major risks and the management of disasters in the framework of sustainable development (Algeria)

In the Matter of Michelot Yogogobaye versus the Republic of Senegal: Judgment, Application No 001/2008, text available at www1.umn.edu/humanrts/africa/comcases/1-2008.pdf, accessed on 12 September 2010

Memorandum of Understanding between the SGR and ERC, Document HR/4584, REF/1172, 18 April 2002

Memorandum of Understanding between UNHCR and ECOWAS, New York, 19 November 2001

Minimum Humanitarian Standards (26 August 1994) Sub-Commission Res. 1994/26

Nairobi Declaration of the Ministerial Conference on Refugees, Returnees and Internally Displaced Persons in the IGAD region, 21 February 2006

Norms on Resettlement of Internally Displaced Population (2001) attached to Council of Ministers Decree Number 1/01 (5 January 2001) (Angola)

Oslo Declaration and Plan of Action on the plight of refugees, returnees and displaced persons in Southern Africa, SARRED Doc. 88/5 (24 August 1988)

Ouagadougou Declaration of the Ministerial conference on Refugees, Returnees and Internally Displaced Persons, Ouagadougou, Burkina Faso from 29 May to 2 June, 2006

Outcome of the brainstorming session between organs of the African Union with a human rights mandate, held in Ouagadougou, Burkina Faso, from 28 to 30 September 2008, www.achpr.org, accessed on 13 April 2010

Pan-African Parliament Resolutions: Resolution on Conflict Resolution, PAP. Res. 002/04; Resolution on the Dispatch of the Pan-African Parliament Peace Mission to the Democratic Republic of Congo, PAP-Res. 007/05, adopted on 11 April 2005.; Resolution on the Dispatch of the Pan-African Parliament Peace Mission to Cote D'Ivoire, PAP-Res. 06/05 (Adopted 11 April 2005)

Pan-African Parliament: One Africa–One Voice: Pan-African Parliament Strategic Plan 2006–2010, November 2005

Principles and Rules for Red Cross and Red Crescent Disaster Relief, adopted by the Twenty-first International Conference of the Red Cross (Istanbul, 1969), reprinted in *International Review of the Red Cross*, No. 310 (February 1996), annex IV

Protocol to the African Charter on Human and Peoples' Rights on the Rights of Women in Africa, adopted by the 2nd Ordinary Session of the Assembly of the Union, Maputo, CAB/LEG/66.6 (Sept. 13, 2000), entered into force 25 November 2005

Protocol on the Protection and Assistance to Internally Displaced Persons
The Protocol on the statute of the African Court of Justice and Human Rights, 1 July 2008
Protocol Additional to the Geneva Conventions of 12 August 1949, and relating to the Protection of Victims of International Armed Conflicts (Protocol I), 8 June 1977
Protocol Additional to the Geneva Conventions of 12 August 1949, and relating to the Protection of Victims of Non-International Armed Conflicts (Protocol II), 8 June 1977
Protocol Relating to the Status of Refugees, 31 January 1967, United Nations, Treaty Series, vol. 606
Resolution of the Council of Ministers on the issues of Refugees (OAU/AU): CM/Res. 1117 (XLVI) 1987; CM/Res. 1084 (XLV; CM/939 (XL); Resolution CM/Res. 1022 (XLIII)
Resolution on the Division of Africa into five regions, CM.Res 464.(XXVI)
Resolution on Cooperation between the African Commission on Human and Peoples' Rights and the African Committee of Experts on the Rights and Welfare of the Child in Africa, The Organisation of African Unity institutional mechanism, ACHPR/Res144 (XXXXV) 09
Resolution on the Mandate of the Special Rapporteur on the refugees, asylum seekers, migrants and internally displaced persons in Africa, adopted at the 36th Ordinary Session of the African Commission on Human and Peoples' Rights in Dakar, Senegal, 4 December 2004
Rules of Procedure of the Assembly of the African Union, 1st Ordinary Session, 9–10 July 2002, Durban, South Africa
Rules of Procedure of the Permanent Representatives' Committee, adopted during the 1st Ordinary Session of the Assembly of the African Union, 9–10 July 2002, Durban, South Africa
Security Council Resolutions: SC Res. 1674(Apr. 28, 2006); SC/RES/1625 (2005; SC Res. 1286(2000); SC Res. 688, U.N. SCOR, 46th Sess., U.N. Doc. S/Res/688(1999); S.C. Res. 787, U.N. SCOR, 47th Sess., at 2–3, U.N. Doc. S/RES/700(1992); S.C. Res. 770, U.N. SCOR, 47th Sess (1992); S.C. Res. 820, U.N. SCOR, 48th Sess., at 4–5, U.N. Doc. S/RES(1993); S.C. Res. 819, U.N. SCOR, 48th Sess., at 2, U.N. Doc. S/RES(1993); S.C. Res. 836, U.N. SCOR, 48th Sess., at 4, U.N. Doc. S/RES 836(1992; S.C. Res. 929, U.N. SCOR, 49th Sess., at 3. U.N. Doc. S/Res/929(1994); SC/RES/251/84 ; Resolution 1593, 2005; S/RES/1484 (30 May 2002)
Standing Committee, Recommendation 1631(2003), Text adopted acting on behalf of the Assembly, on 25 November 2003
Statute of the International Criminal Court, UN Doc, A/CONF.183/9
Statute of the International Tribunal for War Crimes in former Yugoslavia (as adopted by the Security Council in resolution 841/1993)
The Statute of the International Criminal Tribunal for Rwanda, annexed Security Council Resolution 955, adopted 8 November 1994, United Nations document S/RES/955 (1994)
Statutes of the Commission of the African Union, ASS/AU/2(1), adopted at the 1st Ordinary Session of the African Union, 9–10 July 2002
Statutes of the Economic, Social, and Cultural Council of the African Union, adopted during the 3rd Ordinary Session of the African Union held in Addis Ababa, Ethiopia, 6–8 July 2004

The Statute of the African Union Commission on International Law, EX.CL/478(XIV)
Status of Mission (SOMA) Agreement between the Transitional Federal Agreement and the African Union, 6 March 2007
Uganda National Policy for Internally Displaced Persons, Office of the Prime Minister, Department of Disaster Preparedness and Refugees, August 2004
Universal Declaration of Human Rights adopted by General Assembly resolution 217 A (III) of 10 December 1948
United Nations Charter June 26, 1945, 59 Stat. 1031, T.S. 993, 3 Bevans 1153
United Nations Declaration on the Rights of Indigenous Peoples (A/RES/61/295)
UN Declaration on principles of international law concerning friendly relations and co-operation among states in accordance with the Charter of the United Nations, A/RES/25/2625, 24 October 1970
United Nations Principles on Housing and Property Restitution for Refugees and Displaced Persons (Pinheiro Principles)
Vienna Declaration and Programme of Action of the World Conference on Human Rights, held at Vienna, 14–25 June 1993, United Nations document A/CONF.157/23, Part I

Selected judicial decisions (ICJ, African Commission on Human and Peoples Rights etc.)

Advisory Opinion on the African Commission on Human and Peoples' Rights on the UN Declaration on the Rights of Indigenous Peoples, adopted during the 41st Session of the African Commission on Human and Peoples' Rights, May 2007
Barecelona Traction Light and Power Company, Ltd. (Belgium and Spain) (Second Phase), International Court of Justice, Judgment of 5 February 1970, 1970 ICJ Rep.3
Corfu Channel Case (United Kingdom v. Albania); Assessment of Compensation, 15 XII 49, International Court of Justice (ICJ), 15 December 1949
Communication 87/93, *Constitutional Rights Project* (in respect of *Zamani Lekot & 6 others v. Nigeria)*, in Eighth Annual Activity Report of the African Commission on Human and Peoples' Rights 1994–95, 18th Ordinary Session, 2–11 October 1995, ACHPR/AHG/201/XXXI, Annex VI, 16, 18
Communication 71/92, *Recontre Africane poure la Defence des Droits de l'Homme (RADDHO) v. Zambia*, in Tenth Annual Activity Report of the African Commission on Human and Peoples' Rights 1996–97
Communications 25/89, 47/90, 100/93, *World Organization Against Torture et al. v. Zaire*, in Ninth Annual Activity Report of the African Commission on Human and Peoples' Rights 1995–96, 32nd Ordinary Session, 7–10 July 1996
Communication No. 101/93, Civil Liberties Organization in respect of the *Nigeria Bar Association v. Nigeria*, 8th Annual Activity Report of the African Commission on Human and Peoples' Rights 1994–1995
Communication No. 60/91, *Constitutional Rights Project v. Nigeria*, Eighth Annual Activity Report of the African Commission on Human and Peoples' Rights 1994–1995
Communication No. 87/93, *Constitutional Rights Project v. Nigeria*, Eighth Annual Activity Report of the African Commission on Human and Peoples' Rights 1994–

1995
Communication 159/96, *Union Interafricaine des Droits de l'Homme, Fédération Internationale des Ligues des Droits de l'Homme, Rencontre Africaine des Droits de l'Homme, Organisation Nationale des Droits de l'Homme au Sénégal and Association Malienne des Droits de l'Homme v. Angola*, November 1997, 11th Annual Activity Report
Communication No. 155/96, *The Social and Economic Rights Action Center and the Center for Economic and Social Rights v. Nigeria*, 15th Activity Report
Communication No. 232/99 (2000), Iohn D. Ouko v. Kenya, 14th Annual Activity Report, 2000
Communications 54/91, 61/91, 98/93, 164/97, 196/97, & 210/98, Malawi African Association, Amnesty International, Ms Sarr Diop, Union Inter Africaine des Droits de l'Homme v. Mauritania (Merits) in 13th Annual Activity Report of the African Commission on Human and Peoples' Rights 1999–2000, ACHPR/AHG/222 (XXXVI) Add. 136, 158 (2000)
Communication 211/1998, *Legal Resources Foundation v. Zambia*, 14th Annual Activity Report, Annex V
Communication 276/2003 – Centre for Minority Rights Development (Kenya) and Minority Rights Group International on behalf of *Endorois Welfare Council v. Kenya*
Concluding Observation of the African Commission on the third periodic report of the Republic of Uganda, 45th Ordinary Session of the African Commission on Human and Peoples' Rights, Banjul, the Gambia, from 13–27 May 2009
Concluding Observation of the African Commission on Human and People's Rights on the Initial Report of Kenya, adopted at its 41st Ordinary Session held in Accra, Ghana from 16–30 May 2007
Concluding observation on the periodic report of the Republic of Sudan, presented to the 35th Ordinary Session of the African Commission on Human and Peoples' Rights held in Banjul, The Gambia, from 21 May to 4 June 2004
Case Concerning Military and Paramilitary Activities In and Against Nicaragua (Nicaragua v. United States of America); Merits, International Court of Justice (ICJ), 27 June 1986
Eritrea Ethiopia Claims Commission: Partial Award in Ethiopia's Central Front Claims, 43 ILM 1275(2004)
Final Communiqué of the 42nd Ordinary Session of the African Commission on Human and Peoples' Rights, Brazzaville, Republic of Congo, 15 to 28 November 2007
Michelot Yogogombaye vs. the Republic of Senegal, African Court on Human and Peoples' Rights application No. 001/2008
Prosecutor's Application Pursuant to Article 58 as to William Samuel Ruto, Henry Kiprono Kasseny and Josha Arop Sad, ICC-01/09-30RED
Prosecutor v. Blagojević et al., IT-02-60-T, Judgment, 17 January 2005
The Prosecutor v. Joseph Kony, Vincent Otti, Okoth Odiambo and Dominc Ongwen, Pre-Trial Chamber II, Warrant of Arrest, ICC-02/04-01/05-53
Prosecutor v. Krnojelac, IT-97–25, Trial Chamber Judgment of 15 March 2002
Prosecutor v. Radislav Krstić, Judgment of Trial Chamber I, IT-98-33, 2 August 2001

Articles, Books etc.

Abebe, Allehone. 'Legal and Institutional Dimension of Protecting and Assisting IDPs in Africa'. *Journal of Refugee Studies* 22(2009): 155–176

———. 'Shaming and Bargaining: African States and the Universal Periodic Review of the UN Human Rights Council'. *Human Rights Law Review* 1(2009): 1–35

———. 'Displacement of Civilians during Armed Conflict in the Light of the Case Law of the Eritrea-Ethiopia Claims Commission'. *Leiden Journal of International Law* 22(2009): 823–851

———. The African Union Convention on the Protection and Assistance of Internally Displaced Persons as an emerging regional legal regime for humanitarian assistance during natural disaster, paper presented during the 15th Humanitarian Conference, 18–19 February 2010, Webster University, Geneva

———. *Addressing Internal Displacement: Framework for National Responsibility.* Washington, DC: Brooking–Bern Project on Internal Displacement, 2005

———. 'The African Union Convention on Internal Displacement: Its Codification Background, its scope and Enforcement Challenges'. *Refugee Survey Quarterly* 29(2010)

Acquaviva, Guido. Forced Displacement and International Crimes, Legal and Protection Policy Research Series, UNHCR, June 2011

'Africa: IDP Convention–Now the Hard Work Begins'. *IRIN*, 26 October 2006

'African Countries' Reluctance to Ratify Kampala Declaration Questioned'. *Afrik-News*, 29 June 2010

African Union and Australian Government holds international symposium on the protection of civilians during conflict zones, Press Release No. 26, 2010

'African Ministers Have Adopted an Action Plan'. African Press Organization, 8 June 2010

'African IDP Convention Fills a Void in Humanitarian Law'. *IRIN*, 27 October 2009

African Humanitarian Action. *Partnership to Protect: CSOs and the AU: An advocacy toolkit for civilian protection.* Addis Ababa, 2008

African Union News. African Commission Newsletter, Issue 36, December 2008

———. Ministerial Meeting Prepares for Special Summit on Refugees, Returnees and Internally Displaced Persons, AU Newsletter, Issue 36, December 2008

Aiboni, Sam. *Protection of Refugees in Africa.* Uppsala: Svenska Institute for Internaionell Rott, 1978

Aide Memoire, The Third Conference of African Union Minsters in Charge of Forced Displaced Matters (4–5 June 2010)

Alborzi, Mohammad. *Evaluating the Effectiveness of International Refugee Law: Protection of Iraqi Refugees.* The Hague: Martinus Njihoff Publishers, 2006

Anker, Debora. 'Refugee Status and Violence against Women in the 'Domestic' Sphere: The Non-state actor Question'. *Georgetown Immigration Law Journal* 15(2001): 391–402

Annotated Outline of a Draft Legal Framework for the Protection and Assistance of Internally Displaced Persons in Africa, AU/EXP/HARDP/2(V-ii)

Ankumah, Evelyn. *The African Commission on Human and Peoples' Rights: The System in Practice 1986–2000.* Cambridge: Cambridge University Press, 2008

Aukot, Ekuru. 'Refugee Protection in Africa: A Developing Country's Dilemma Towards Effective Protection'. *East African Journal of Peace and Human Rights* 9(2003), 213–254

Badnsky, Daniel and Crook, John. 'Symposium: The ILC's Articles: Introduction and Overview'. *American Journal of International Law* 96(2002): 773–791

Bagshaw, Simon. *Developing a Normative Framework for the Protection of Internally Displaced Persons.* New York: Transnational Publishers, 2005

———. *Developing the Guiding Principles on Internal Displacement: The Role of a Global Public Policy Network.* Italy: European University Institute, 1999

———. 'Internally Displaced Persons at the Fifty-Fourth Session of the United Nations Commission on Human Rights, 16 March–24 April 1998'. *International Journal of Refugee Law* 10(1998): 548–556

Banda, Fareda. 'Protocol to the African Charter on the Rights of Women to Africa' in *The African Charter on Human and Peoples' Rights: The System in Practice 1986–2000* eds. Malcom Evans and Rachel Murray, 441–475. Cambridge: Cambridge University Press

Bayefsky, Anne and Fitzpatrick, Joan, eds. *Human Rights and Forces Displacement.* The Hague: Martinus Nijhoff Publishers, 2000

Benedek, Wolfgang. 'The African Charter and Commission on Human and Peoples' Rights: How to Make it More Effective'. *Netherlands Quarterly of Human Rights* 11(1991): 25–40

Bertrand, Pierre. 'An Operational Approach to International Refugee Protection'. *Cornell International Law Journal* 26(1994): 495–500

Beyani, Chaloka. 'Recent Developments: The Elaboration of a Legal Framework for the Protection of Internally Displaced Persons in Africa'. *Journal of African Law* 50(2006): 187–192

———. *International Displaced Persons under International Law.* Oxford: RSP Documentation Center, 1995

———. 'State Responsibility for the prevention and Resolution of Forced Population Displacement in International Law'. *International Journal of Refugee Law* (Special Edition, 1995): 131–137

Blocq, Daniel. 'The Fog of UN Peacekeeping: Ethical Issues Regarding the Use of Force to Protect Civilians in UN Operations'. *Journal of Military Ethics* 5(2006): 201–213

Bodnsky, Daniel and Crook, John. 'Symposium: The ILC's Articles: Introduction and Overview'. *American Journal of International Law* 96(2002)

Boyle, Alan. 'Some Reflection on the Relationship of Treaties and Soft Law'. *International and Comparative Law Quarterly* 48(1999): 901–913

Brandl, Ulrike. 'Soft Law as a Source of International and European Refugee Law' in *Who is a Refugee? A Comparative Case Law Study,* edited by Jean-Yves, Dirke Venheule, Klaus Hullmann and Carlos Galiano, 203–226. Hague, London, Boston: Kluwer Law International, 1997.

Briefing note: Mitigating Vulnerabilities of Women and Children in Armed Conflicts, PSC/PR/3(CCXXXIII), 30 March 2010

Brooking-Bern Project on Internal Displacement. *An African Solution to Internal Displacement: AU Leaders Agree to Landmark Convention,* 23 October 2009

Brownlie, Ian. 'Kosovo Crisis Inquiry: Memorandum on the International Law Aspects'. *The International and Comparative Law Quarterly* 49(2000): 878–905

———. *Principles of Public International Law,* 3rd edn., Oxford: Oxford University Press, 1976

Burton, Eve. 'Leasing Rights: A New International Instrument for Protecting Refugees and Compensating Host Communities'. *Colombia Human Rights Law Review* 19(1987): 307–332

Carsten, Stahn. 'Responsibility to Protect: Political Rhetoric or Emerging Legal Norm?' *American Journal of International Law* 101(2007): 99–120

Cassell, Doug. 'Enhancing Human Rights and Legal Protection' in *Invisible Refugees*, edited by James H. Williams, 13–19. Washington, DC: Chicago–Kent College of Law and Pax International, 2003

Cassese, Antonio. '*Ex iniuria ius oritur:* Are We Moving towards International Legitimation of Forcible Humanitarian Countermeasures in the World Community?' *European Journal of International Law* 10(2000): 23–30

Ceasare Romano and Elizabeth Burleson. 'The Cancun Climate Conference'. *ASIL Insight* 15(2011)

Central African Republic Receives New UN Peace Building Funds, United Nations News Service, 4 April 2010, located at www.reliefweb.int/rw/rwb.nsf/db900sid/EGUA-82CMHG?OpenDocument, accessed on 5 November 2010

Chenwi, Lilian. 'Breaking New Ground: The Need for a Protocol to the African Charter on the Abolition of Death Penalty in Africa'. *African Human Rights Law Journal* 5(2005): 89–104

Chesterman, Simon. *Just War or Just Peace: Humanitarian Intervention and International Law*. Oxford: Oxford University Press, 2001

Chukwumeriji, Okezie. 'Peer Review and the Promotion of Good Governance in Africa'. 32 *North Carolina Journals of International Law and Commercial Regulations* 49(2006–2007): 49–111

Cilliers, Jakkie and Sturman, Kathryn. 'The right of intervention: Enforcement challenges for the African Union'. *Africa Security Review* 11(2002): 3–11

Clarke, Tom and Crepeau Francois. 'Mainstreaming Refugee Rights: The 1951 Refugee Convention and International Human Rights Law'. *Netherlands Quarterly of Human Rights* 17(1999): 389–410

Cohen, Roberta. 'Strengthening Protection of IDPs: The UN's Role'. *Law and Ethics*, Winter/Spring 2006

———. 'The Forgotten Ones: A Survey of Recent Literature on Displaced Persons'. *Harvard International Review* (Winter/Spring 2000)

———. 'The Development of International Standards to Protect Internally Displaced Persons'. in *Human Rights and Forced Displacement*, edited by Anne Bayefsky and Joan Fitzpatrick, 76–89. The Hague: Martinus Nijhoff Publishers, 2000

———. *Protection and Assistance For Disaster IDPs: An Institutional Gap*. Washington, DC: Brookings Institution, 2008

———. *The Role of Regional Organisations*. Washington, DC: Brookings Institutions, 2000

———. The role of regional organisations: ECOWAS, ECOWAS/IOM Workshop on International Migration in West Africa, 1 December 2010

———. 'The Guiding Principles on Internal Displacement: An Innovation in International Standard Setting'. *Global Governance* 10(2004)

Cohen, Roberta and Deng, Francis. 'Normative Framework of Sovereignty' in *Sovereignty as Responsibility: Conflict Management in Africa*, edited by Francis Deng, Sadikiel Kimaro, Terrence Lyons, Donald Rothchild and I. William Zartman. Washington, DC: Brookings Institution 1996

Cohen, Roberta, Kälin, Walter and Mooney, Erin. *Guiding Principles on Internal Displacement and the Laws of the South Caucasus*. Washington, DC: American Society of International Law and the Brookings Institution Project on Internal, 2003

Cohen, Roberta and Deng, Francis. *Masses in Flight: The Global Crisis of Internal Displacement.* Washington, DC: Brookings Institution Press, 1998

Cohen, Roberta and Eueno, Jaques. *Improving Institutional Arrangements for* IDPs. Washington, DC: Brookings Institution-Refugee Policy Project on Internal Displacement, 1995

Crawford, James. *Human Rights and State Responsibility.* Thomas J Dodd Research Centre, University of Connecticut, 2007

Davis, Kristin. 'Emperor is Still Naked: Why the Protocol on the Rights of Women in Africa Leaves Women Exposed to More Discrimination'. *Vandebilt Journal of Transnational Law* 42(2009): 949–991

de Wet, Chris. 'Improving Outcomes in Development Induced in Displacement and Resettlement Project'. *Forced Migration Review* 12(2002): 6–10

De Waal, Johan. 'Constitutional Law' in *Introduction to South African Law*, eds. C. G. Van der Merwe and Du Plessis. The Netherlands: Kluwer International, 2004: 55–106

Deng, Francis. Comprehensive Study pursuant to Human Rights Commission resolution 1972/73, E/CN.4/1993/5

———. Report of the Representative of the Secretary General submitted pursuant to Commission resolution 1998/50, E/CN.4/1999/79/Add.2

———. Compilation and Analysis of Legal Norms (UN New York and Geneva, E/CN.4/1996/52/Add.2, 1998)

———. 'The Global Challenge of Internal Displacement'. *Washington University Journal of Law and Policy* 5(2001): 141–155

———. *Protecting the Dispossessed: A Challenge for the International Community.* Washington, DC: Brookings Institution, 1995

———. 'Frontiers of Sovereignty: A Framework of Protection, Assistance and Development for the Internally Displaced'. *Leiden Journal of International Law* 8(1995): 249–286

Deng, Francis. *et al. Sovereignty as Responsibility: Conflict Management in Africa.* Washington, DC: Brookings Institution Press, 1996

Doebbler, Curtis. *International Human Rights Law: Cases and Materials.* Washington, DC: CD Publishing, 2004

d'Orsi, Cristiano 'Sub-Saharan Africa: Is a New Special Regional Refugee Law Regime Emerging?' *Zeitschrift für ausländisches öffentliches Recht und Völkerrecht* 68(2008): 1057–1081

Dorr, Noel. 'The responsibility to Protect – an Emerging Norm?' *Irish Studies in International Affairs* 19(2008): 189–207

Draft Plan of Action for Implementation of the Outcome of the African Union Special Summit on Refugees, Returnees and Internally Displaced Persons in Africa (undated, a copy available with the author)

Draft Programme, Legal Experts meeting on the draft AU Convention for the Protection and Assistance of Internally Displaced Persons in Africa, Addis Ababa, Ethiopia, 9 November 2008

Draft Agenda, Extraordinary Session of the Executive Council, Kampala, Uganda, 19–20 October 2009

Draft Agenda, Meeting of the Assembly of the Heads of State and Government Kampala, Uganda, 22–23 October 2009

Dugard, John. 'The Organisation of African Unity: An Inquiry into the Plea of Self-Defence as a Justification for the Use of Force in Eradication of Colonialism'. *The*

International and Comparative Law Quarterly 16(1967): 157–90

Durch, William and Giffen, Alison. *Challenges of Strengthening the Protection of Civilians in Multidimensional Peace Operations,* Background paper prepared for the 3rd International Forum for the Challenges of Peace Operations, 27–29 April 2010, Queenbeyan, Australia. Hosted by the Asia Pacific Civil-Military Centre of Excellence, note 41, located at www.challengesforum.org/cms/images/pdf/Challenges_2010_BackgroundPaper_12April2010.pdf, accessed on 15 November 2010

Eckengard, Arvid. *The African Union Mission in Sudan (AMIS): Experiences and Lessons Learnt.* Stockholm: Sweden Defence Research Agency, 2009

Elias, Taslim. *Africa and the Development of International Law*, 2nd edn. Netherlands: Martinus Nijhoff, 1988

Evans, Malcolm and Murray, Rachel. *The African Charter on Human and Peoples' Rights: The System in Practice.* Cambridge: Cambridge University Press, 2004

Evolution and current situation of forced displacement in Africa, Background Paper, Expert Meeting, Special Summit on Refugees, Returnees and Displaced Persons in Africa, Addis Ababa, Ethiopia, 5–7 November 2008

Ewumbue-Monono, Churchill and von Flue, Carlo. 'Promotion of International Humanitarian Law through Cooperation between the ICRC and the African Union'. *International Review of the Red Cross* 85(2003): 749–773

Ferris, Elizabeth. 'Assessing the Impact of the Principles: An Unfinished Task'. *Forced Migration Review* (Special Edition, 2008): 10–11

Ferris, Elizabeth. *Comparative Perspectives on Laws and Polices Addressing Internal Displacement.* Washington, DC: Brookings Bern Institution, 2009

Fisher, David. 'The Right to Humanitarian Assistance' in *Incorporating the Guiding Principles on Internal Displacement into Domestic Law: Issues and Challenges,* edited by Walter Kälin, Rhodri William, Khalid Koser and Andrew Solomon, 47–129. Washington, DC: The American Society of International Law and Brookings Institution, 2010

Fitzpatrick, Joan. 'Human Rights and Forced Displacement: Converging Standards' in *Human Rights and Forced Displacement*, edited by A. Bayefsky and J. Fitzpatrick. 3–26. The Hague, Netherlands: Martinus Nijhoff Publishers, 2000

Foster, Michelle. *International Refugee Law and Socio-Economic Rights: Refuge from Deprivation.* Cambridge: Cambridge University Press, 2007

Franck, Tomas. 'Who killed Article 2(4) or Changing Norms Governing the Use of Force by States'. *American Journal of International Law* 64(1970): 809–37

Franco, Leonardo. 'An Examination of Safety Zones for Internally Displaced Persons as a Contribution toward Prevention and Solution of Refugee Problem' in *International Law Conference.* The Netherlands: Kluwer Law International, 1994

Freedman, Paul. 'International Intervention to Combat the Exposition of Refugees and Internally Displaced Persons'. *Georgetown Immigration Law Journal* 9(1995): 565–601

Funke, Norbert and Nsouli, Saleh. The New Partnership for Africa's Development (NEPAD): Opportunities and Challenges, IMF Working Papers 03/69, 2003

Gabaudan, Michel and Halff, Kate. 'African Leaders Must Follow Through on Kampala Convention'. *The Haffington Post,* 27 October 2010

Garvey, Jack. 'The New Asylum Seekers: Addressing their Origin' in *The New Asylum Seekers: Refugee Law in the 1980s*, edited by David Martin, 181–195. The Netherlands: Martinus Nijhoff Publishers, 1988

Geissler, Nils. 'The International Protection of Internally Displaced Persons'. *International Journal of Refugee Law* 11(1999): 451–478

Ghai, Yash. 'Human Rights Governance: The Asian Debate'. *Asia Pacific Journal of Human Rights and Law* (2000): 9–52

Gittleman, Richard. 'The African Charter and the Commission on Human and Peoples' Rights: A Legal, Analysis'. *Virginia Journal of International Law* 22(1981): 667–714

Goldman, Robert. 'Codification of International Rules on Internally Displaced Persons'. *International Review of the Red Cross* 324(1998): 463–466

Goodwin-Gill, Guy and McAdam, Jane. *The Refugee in International Law*, Third Edition. Oxford: Oxford University Press, 2007

Goodwin-Gill, Guy. 'The Limits of the Power of Expulsion in Public International Law'. *British Year Book of International Law* 47(1974–75): 56–122

———. 'State Responsibility and the "Good faith" Obligation in International Law'. in *Issues of State Responsibility before International Judicial Institutions*, edited by M. Fitzmaurice and D. Sarooshi, 75–104, Oxford: Hart Publishing, 2004

Gorlick, Brian. 'Human Rights and Refugees: Enhancing Protection through International Human Rights Law'. Working Paper, No. 1, *New Issues in Refugee Research*. New York: UNHCR, 2000

Grace, Jeremy and Fischer, Jeff. 'Seeking Electoral Equality for IDP Voters'. *Forced Migration Review* (2008): 26–27

Gray, Christine. *International Law and Use of Force*. Oxford: Oxford University, 2004

Greenwood, Christopher. 'International Law and the NATO Intervention in Kosovo'. *International and Comparative Law Quarterly* 49(2000): 926–934

Gururaja, Shrilakshemi. 'Gender Dimensions of Displacement'. *Forced Migration Review* 9(2000): 13–16

Guteres, Antonio. Current Trends in Forced Displacement and Humanitarian Action, 2010 Harrell-Bond Human Rights Lecture, Refugee Studies Centre, University of Oxford, 13 October 2010

Gruzd, Steven. Africa's Evolving Governance Structure: Reflection on the African Peer Review Mechanism, Centre for Policy Studies, Policy Brief 54, January 2009

Gye-Wado, Onje. 'A Comparative Analysis of the Institutional Framework for the Enforcement of Human Rights in Africa and Western Europe'. *American Journal of International Law* 2(1990): 187–200

Hatchard, John. 'Ratification of International and Regional Human Rights Instruments by African States'. *Journal of African Law* 36(1992): 186–192

Hathaway, James. 'Preconceiving Refugee Law as Human Rights Protection' in *Problems and Prospects of Refugee Law,* edited by Vera Gowlland and Klaus Samson. 9–30. Geneva: The Graduate Institute of International Studies, 1992

———. *Proceeding of the American Society of Public International Law*. Washington DC: Society of International Law, 1996

———. *The Rights of Refugees under International Law*. Cambridge: Cambridge University Press, 2005

Hathaway, James and Foster, Michelle. 'Internal Protection/Relocation/Flight Alternative as an Aspect of Refugee Status Determination' in *Refugee Protection in International Law: UNHCR's Global Consultations on International Protection*, edited by E. Feller, Volker Turk and Frances Nicholsen, 353–413. Cambridge: Cambridge University Press, 2003

Henkin, Louise. 'An Agenda for the Next Century: The Myth and Mantra of State Sovereignty'. *Virginia Journal of International Law* 35(1994): 115–120

Henckaerts, Jean-Marie. *Mass Expulsion in Modern International Law and Practice*. Dordrecht, Netherland: Martinus Nijhoff Publishers, 1995

Henckarts, Marie and Doswald-Beck, Louise. *Customary International Humanitarian Law, Volume I: Rules*. Cambridge: Cambridge University Press, 2005

Heyns, Christof. 'The African Regional Human Rights System: In Need of a Reform?' *The African Human Rights Law Journal* 2(2001): 155–175

Heyns, Christof and Kallender, Magnus. 'Africa in International Human Rights Text Books'. *African Journal of International and Comparative Law* 15(2007) 147–153

Human Rights Watch. *Harsh War, Harsh Peace: Abuses by Al Shabab, the Transitional Federal Government and AMISOM in Somalia*. New York: Human Rights Watch, 2000

———. *Darfur 2007: Chaos by Design: Peacekeeping Challenges for AMIS and UNAMID*. New York: Human Rights Watch, 2000

———. Always on the Run: The Vicious Cycle of Displacement in Eastern Congo. HRC: New York, 2010

ICRC, 'Internally Displaced Persons: The Mandate and Role of the International Committee of the Red Cross'. *International Review of the Red Cross* (2000): 838

'IDP Convention–Now the Hard Work begins', United Nations Office for the Coordination of Humanitarian Affairs – Integrated Regional Information Networks (IRIN), 26 October 2010

Information Note on African Union Special Summit of Heads of State and Government on Refugees, Returnees and Internally Displaced Persons. October 2009

Internal Displacement Monitoring Centre. *Global Overview of Trends and Developments in 2000*. Geneva: Internal Displacement Monitoring Center, 2001

———. *Former IDPs Share the Common Challenge of Recovery and Reconstruction*. Geneva: IDMC, 2007

———. *The Great Lakes Pact and the Rights of Displaced People: A Guide for Civil Society*. Geneva: IDMC, September 2008

———. *Internal Displacement: Global Overview of Trends and Developments in 2009*. Geneva: IDMC, 2010

———. *Whose Land is This? Land Dispute and Forced Displacement in the Western Forest Area of Cote d'Ivoire*, 2009

———. *Kenya: Speedy Reform Need to Deal with Past Injustices and Prevent Future Displacement*. Geneva: IDMC, 2010

———. *Cote d'Ivoire: Quest for Durable Solutions Continues as the Electoral Process Moves Forward*. Geneva: IDMC, 2010

———. *Making the Kampala Convention Work for IDPs: Guide for Civic Society on Supporting on the Ratification and Implementation of the Convention for the Protection and Assistance of Internally Displaced Persons in Africa*. Geneva: IDMC, 2010

———. *Eritrea: Uncertain Future for Thousands of Returning IDPs*. Geneva: IDMC, 2006

———. *Ethiopia: Human Rights Violations and Conflicts Continue to Cause Displacement*. Geneva: IDMC, 2009

———. *Displacement due to Natural Hazard-Induced Disasters: Global Estimates for 2009 and 2010*. Geneva: IDMC, 2011

International Federation of Red Cross and Red Crescent Societies. *Law and Legal Issues in International Disaster Response*. Geneva: Switzerland, 2007

Interview with Mr Micheal Kabai, South African Permanent Mission, 25 January 2005. File with the author

Interview with the head of delegation of Sudan, October 2009, Geneva, Switzerland

Interview with a counsellor at the Embassy of Congo, Addis Ababa, Ethiopia, 10 February 2009

Interview with an Ethiopian delegate who participated in the meeting, 11 January 2008

Interview with Ms Dolly Joiner, African Union Commissioner for Political Affairs, 27 January 2009

Jackson, Ivor. *The Refugee Concept in a Group Situations*. The Hague: The Netherlands, Kluwer Law International, 1999

Jalloh, Charles. 'International Decision: Michelot Yogogombaye v. Republic of Senegal. App. No. 001/2008'. *Journal of American International Law* 104(2010): 620–628

Jennings, Robert. 'Sovereignty and international law' in *State, Sovereignty and International Governance*, edited by G. Krejer. Oxford: Oxford University Press, 2002

Jennings, Robert and Watts, Arthur. *Oppenheim's International Law*, 9th edition, Vol. I. Harlow: Longman, 1992

Josee, Alvarez. *International Organizations as Treaty Makers*. Oxford Scholarship Monograph, 2006

Kaime, Toko. 'The Protection of Refugee Children under the African Human Rights System: Finding Durable Solution in International Law' in *Children Rights in Africa*, edited by Julia Sloth Nielsen, 183–199. Abingdon: Ashgate Publishing Limited, 2008

Kälin, Walter 'The Guiding Principles on Internal Displacement as International Minimum Standard and Protection Tool'. *Refugee Survey Quarterly* 24(2005): 27–36

———. *How Hard Is Soft Law? The Guiding Principle on Internal Displacement and the Need for A Normative Framework*. Washington, DC: Brookings Institute, 2001

———. *The Guiding Principles on Internal Displacement: Annotations*, 2nd Edition. Washington, DC: The American Society of International Law, 2008

———. Statement of the Representative of the UN Secretary-General for the Human Rights of Internally Displaced Persons, on the Occasion of the 40th Ordinary Session of the African Commission on Human and Peoples' Rights, 18 November 2006

———. 'Legal Protection of Internally Displaced Persons – Protection in International Human Rights Law' in Lavoyer, Jean-Philippe (ed.), Internationally displaced persons, report of the symposium Geneva 23–25 October 1995, International Committee of the Red Cross, 1996, pp. 15–26

———. 'The Great Lakes Protocol on Internally Displaced Persons: Response and Challenges', paper presented at International Law Project Symposium on International Law in Post Conflict Situations: The Great Lakes Process, 27 September 2007

———. Internal Displacement and the Role of Parliamentarians in Times of Crisis,

120th Meeting of Inter-Parliamentary Union, Addis Ababa, Ethiopia, 9 April 2009

———. 'The Future of the UN Guiding Principles on Internal Displacement'. *Forced Migration Review*. Special Edition, 2006

Kälin, Walter, Williams, Rhodri, Koser, Khalid and Solomon, Andrew (eds), *Incorporating the Guiding Principles on Internal Displacement into Domestic Law: Issues and Challenges*. Washington, DC: ASIL, 2010

Kassa, Getahun. 'Mechanisms of Constitutional Control: A Preliminary Observation of the Ethiopian System' in *Federalism and the Protection of Human Rights*, edited by Eva Brems and Chiristoher van de Berken, 86–107. Vienna: Lit Verlag Gmbh and Co. KG, 2008

'Kenya: Draft Policy on IDP Offers New Hope for IDPs', *IRIN*, 19 March 2010

Kibraeb, Gaim. Reflections on the African Refugee Problem: A Critical Analysis of Some Basic Assumptions. Research Report No 67, Uppsala, 1983

Kigundu, Jacquie. *Why Land Tenure Matters for IDPs: Lessons from Sub-Saharan Africa*. Brooking-Bern Project on Internal Displacement, 2008

Killander, Magnus and Adjolohoun, Horace. 'Introduction' in *International Law and Domestic Legal Litigation in Africa*, edited by Magnus Killander, 3–25. Pretoria: Pretoria University Law Press, 2010

Kindiki, Kithure. 'The Normative and Institutional Framework of the African Union Relating to the Protection of Human Rights and the Maintenance of Peace and Security: A Critical Appraisal'. *African Human Rights Law Journal* 3(2003): 97–118

Kneebone, Susan and Rawlings-Senaei, Felicity. *New Regionalism and Asylum Seekers: Challenges Ahead*. New York: Berghan Books, 2007

Kioko, Ben. 'The Right of Intervention under the African Union's Constitutive Act: From Non-interference to Non-intervention'. *International Review of the Red Cross* 85(2003): 807–825

Koskenniemi, Martti. 'The Police in the Temple. Order, Justice, and the UN: A Dialectical View'. *European Journal of International Law* 6(1995): 328–345

Kufour, Kofi. *Human Rights in Africa: Interpreting the Organisations of Africa Unity's Grand Bay Declaration and Plan of Action*, available online at www.uel.ac.uk/law/research/publications/index.htm. Accessed March 2010

Kuwali, Dan. 'The End of Humanitarian Intervention: Evaluation of the Union's Right of Intervention'. *African Journal of Conflict Resolution* 29(2009): 41–61

Lauterpacht, Hersch. 'The Grotian Tradition in International Law'. *British Yearbook of International Law* 46(1946): 1–53

Lavoyer, Jean-Philippe. 'Guiding Principles on Internal Displacement'. *International Review of the Red Cross* 324(1998): 467–480

Lee, Luke. 'Internally Displaced Persons and Refugees: Toward a Legal Synthesis?' *Journal of Refugee Studies* 9(1996): 27–42

———. 'The London Declaration of International Law Principles on Internally Displaced Persons'. *The American Journal of International Law* 95(2001): 454–459

———. 'The Case for an International Convention on Displaced People' in *Invisible Refugees*, edited by James H. Williams. Washington, DC: Chicago–Kent College of Law and Pax International, 2003

Letter from Dr Dawit Zewde, President of African Humanitarian Action to the AU Political Affairs Department, 15 January 2007

Levitt, Jeremy. 'Africa: As a Maker of International Law' in *Africa: Mapping New*

Boundaries in International Law, edited by Jeremy Levitt. Oxford, Portland OR: Hart Publishing, 2008

———. 'The Peace and Security Council of the African Union: The Known Unknowns'. *Transnational Law and Contemporary Problems* 13(2003): 109–137

Lillich, Richard. 'Current Developments: The Paris Minimum Standards of Human Rights Norms in a State of Emergency'. *American Journal of International Law* 49(1985): 1072–1081

Lloyd, Amanda. 'A Theoretical Analysis of the Reality of Children's Rights in Africa: An Introduction to the Rights and Welfare of the Child'. *African Human Rights Law Journal* 2(2002): 11–33

Lloyd, Amanda and Murray, Rachel, 'Institutions with the Responsibility for Human Rights Protection under the African Union'. *Journal of African Law* 48(2004): 165–186

Loescher, Gil. *The UNHCR and World Politics – A Perilous Path*. Oxford: Oxford University Press, 2001

Lyons, Donald Rothchild and Zartman, William. *Sovereignty as a Responsibility: Conflict Management in Africa*. Washington, DC: Brookings Institution, 1996

McAdam, Jane. *The Refugee Convention as a Rights Blueprint for Persons in Need of International Protection*. Geneva: UNHCR (New Issues in Refugee Research, No. 125: 2006

McNamerra, Dennis. 'Introduction'. *Refugee Survey Quarterly* 14(1995): 1–2

Maluwa, Tiyanjana. 'Reimagining African Unity: Some Preliminary Reflections on the Constitutive Act of the African Union (2002)'. *African Yearbook of International Law* 9(2001): 3–38

———. 'The Constitutive Act of the African Union and Institution-Building in Postcolonial Africa'. *Leiden Journal of International Law* 16(2003): 157–170

———. 'International Law-Making in the Organization of African Unity: An Overview'. *African Journal of International and Comparative Law* 12(2000): 201–205

Mashabane, Maite Nkoana. Statement as a Chairperson of the African Union (AU) Post-conflict Reconstruction and Development (PCRD) Committee, on the occasion of the AU PCRD Ministerial, Sudan, 26 October 2006

Mayanja, Macrine. 'The Guiding Principles and the Challenges of Forced Displacement in Africa: The Response of the African Union', The Conference on Ten Years of the UN Guiding Principles on Internal Displacement: Achievements and Future Challenges, Oslo, Norway, 16–17 October 2008

Menon, Nitya, Protocol on the Protection and Assistance to IDPs, December 2007, www.lse.ac.uk/collections/law/projects/greatlakes/Session%201%20 Documentation.pdf

Meron, Theodor. 'On the Inadequate Reach of Humanitarian and Human Rights Law and the Need for a New Instrument'. *American Journal of International Law* 77(1983): 589–606

———. 'State Responsibility for Violations of Human Rights'. *Proceedings of the American Society of International Law* (1989): 372–385

———. 'Internal Strife: Applicable Norms and a Proposed Instrument' in *Humanitarian Law of Armed Conflict: Challenges Ahead*, edited by Astrid Delissen and Gerard Tanja, 249–269. The Hague: T.M.C. Asser Institute, 1991

———. *The Humanisation of International Law*. The Netherlands: Martinus Nijhoff Publishers, 2006

Mahmud, Sakha. 'The State and Human Rights in the 1990s: Perspectives and Prospects'. *Human Rights Quarterly* 15(1993): 485–498

Mezmur, Benyam. 'Still an Infant or Now a Toddler? The Work of the Committee of Experts on the Rights and Welfare of the Child and its 8th Ordinary Session'. *African Human Rights Law Journal* 7(2007): 258–276

Moggah, Robert. 'A Tale of Two Solitudes: Comparing Conflict and Development-Induced Internal Displacement and Involuntary Resettlement'. *International Migration* 41(2003): 5–28

Mooney, Erin. 'Towards a Protection Regime for Internally Displaced Persons' in *Refugees and Forced Displacement*, edited by Newman Edward and Joanne van Selm, 159–181. Tokyo/New York/Paris: United Nations University Press, 2003

———. 'The Guiding Principles and Responsibility to Protect'. *Forced Migration Review* (Special Issue 2008): 11–13

———. 'Developing National Law, Policy and Strategies around the African Union Convention for the Protection and Assistance of Internally Displaced Persons in Africa'. African Union–Civil Society Organizations Pre-Summit on Internally Displaced Persons in Africa Kampala, Uganda, 13–15 October 2009

Morjane, Kamel. 'The Protection of Refugees and Displaced Persons' in *Human Rights Protection in the Field*, edited by Bertrand Ramcharan, 79–87. The Netherlands: Martinus Njihoff Publishers, 2006

Mumba, K.C. 'Prospects for the Regional Protection of Human Rights in Africa'. *Holdsworth Law Review* 12(1982): 101–120

Murithi, Tim. 'Towards a Symbiotic Partnership: The UN Peace Building Commission and the Evolving African Union/NEPAD Post-Conflict Reconstruction Framework' in *A Dialogue of the Deaf: Essays on Africa and the United Nations*, edited by Adekeye Adebajo and Helen Scanlon, 243–260. Johannesburg: Jacana, 2006

Murphy, Sean. *Humanitarian Intervention: The United Nations in an Evolving World Order*. Philadelphia: University of Philadelphia, 1996

Murray, Rachel. *Human Rights in Africa: From the OAU to the African Union*. Cambridge: Cambridge University Press, 2004

———. 'Refugees and Internally Displaced Persons and Human Rights: the African System'. *Refugee Survey Quarterly* 24(2005): 56–66

Mutua, Makau. 'The Banjul Charter and African Cultural Fingerprint: An Evaluation of the Language of Duties'. *Virginia Journal of International Law* 35(1995): 339–80

———. 'The African Human Rights System in a Comparative Perspective: The Need for Urgent Reformulation'. *Legal Forum* 5(1993): 31–35

———. 'Refugees and Internally Displaced Persons and Human Rights: The African System'. *Refugee Survey Quarterly* 24(2005): 56–66

———. 'The African Human Rights Court: A Two-Legged Stool'. *Human Rights Quarterly* 21(1999): 342–363

Naldi, Gino. *The Organization of African Unity: An Analysis of its Role*, Second Edition. London and New York: Mansell, 1999

———. 'Reparations in the Practice of the African Commission on Human and Peoples' Rights'. *Leiden Journal of International Law* 14(2001): 681–693

———. 'The African Union and the Regional Human Rights System' in *The African Charter on Human and Peoples Rights: The System in Practice 1986–2000* in Malcolm Evans and Rachel Murray, 2nd edn, 20–48. Cambridge: Cambridge

University Press, 2008

Neussl, Peter. 'Bridging the National and International Responses to IDPs'. *Forced Migration Review* 20(2004): 42–44

New treaty for internally displaced persons in Africa, News and Media, United Nations Office in Geneva, 22 October 2009

New African Union Convention Protects Internally Displaced Persons, October 26, 2009, Refugee International

The New Partnership for Africa's Development – The African Peer Review Mechanism, 8 July 2002, paragraphs 1–3, Organisation of African Unity

Nigeria: Promoting Disaster Risk Reduction in Post Disaster Recovery and Reconstruction Efforts, PowerPoint Presentation to the ISDR ECOSOC Side Event, National Emergency Management Agency (NEMA), July 19, 2006

Noor, Hassan. 'Emergency within an Emergency: Somali IDPs'. *Forced Migration Review* 28(2007): 29–32

Nmehielle, Vincent. *The African Human Rights System: Its Laws, Practices and Institutions*. The Netherlands: Njihoff Publishers, 2001

Nsibirwa, Martin. 'A Brief Analysis of the Draft Protocol to the African Charter on Human and Peoples' Rights on the Rights of Women'. *African Journal of Human Rights* 1(2001): 40–63

Nyaduga, Bahame. Statement during 10th Anniversary of the Guiding Principles on Internal Displacement: An African Perspective, Statement of Commissioner, African Commission on Human and Peoples' Rights, Oslo, October 16/17, 2008

———. 'The Challenges of Internal Displacement in Africa'. *Forced Migration Review* 21(2004): 58

Nyandunga, Bhame Tom. 'The African Union IDP Declaration, The Kampala Convention and Recommendation: The Challenges Faced and Strategies Needed to Ensure Speedy Signature, Ratification and Implementation,' page 8. Available at: www.unhcrrlo.org/Conference_Special_Events/Docs/AU%20IDP%20Convention_Advocate%20Bahame%20Tom%20Nyanduga.pdf.

———. 'Working Groups of the African Commission and their Role in the Development of the African Commission on Human and Peoples' Rights' in Malcolm and Murray, *African Charter on Human and Peoples' Rights*.

Nyinah, Mihael Kingsley. 'What may be borrowed: What is news? Debate'. *Forced Migration Review* (1999): 29–31

Odinkalu, Chidi. 'Back to the Future: The Imperative of Prioritising for the Protection of Human Rights in Africa'. *Journal of Africa Law* 47(2003): 1–37

———. 'The Individual Complaint Procedures of the African Union on Human and Peoples' Rights: A Preliminary Assessment'. *Transitional Law & Contemporary Problems* 8(1998)

Ogata, Sadago. 'Keynote Address' in *Problems and Prospects of Refugee Law*, edited by Vera Gowlland and Klaus Samson, xix–xiv. Geneva: The Graduate Institute of International Studies, 1992

Ojo, Olusola and Sesay, Amadu. 'The OAU and Human Rights: Prospects for the 1980s and Beyond'. *Human Rights Quarterly* 86(1986): 89–103

Okafor, Obiora Chindu. *The African Human Rights System, Activist Forces and International Institutions*. Cambridge: Cambridge University Press, 2007

Okoth-Obbo, George. 'Thirty Years On: A Legal Review of the 1969 OAU Refugee Convention Governing the Specific Aspects of Refugee Problems in Africa'. *Refugee Survey Quarterly* 20(2001): 79–138

Oloka-Onyango, Joe. 'The Plight of the Larger Half: Human Rights, Gender Violence and the Legal Status of Refugees and Internally Displaced Women in Africa'. *Denver Journal of International Law and Policy* 24(1996): 349–394

———. 'Forced Displacement and the Situation of Refugee and Internally Displaced Women in Africa'. *East African Journal of Peace and Human Rights* 5(1998): 1–31

———. 'Human Rights, the OAU Convention and the Refugee Crisis in Africa: Forty years after Geneva'. *International Journal of Refugee Law* 3(1991): 453–460

———. 'The Place and Role of the OAU Bureau for Refugees in the African Refugee Crisis'. *International Journal of Refugee Law* 6(1994): 34–52

———. 'Movement Related Rights in the Context of Internal Displacement', in *Incorporating the Guiding Principles on Internal Displacement into Domestic Law: Issues and Challenges,* edited by Walter Kälin, Rhodri William, Khalid Koser and Andrew Solomon, 9–47. Washington, DC: The American Society of International Law and Brookings Institution, 2010

O'Neill, William G. *A New Challenge for Peacekeepers: The Internally Displaced, The Brooking – SAIS Project on Internal Displacement.* Washington, DC: Brooking Bern Project on Internal Displacement, 2004

Oucho, John. 'Internal Displacement of Populations in the SADC Region: An Overview'. Paper presented at a seminar on internal displacement in the SADC region, 24–25 August 2005, Gaborone, Botswana, www2.warwick.ac.uk/fac/soc/afrobrain/oucho/publications. Accessed on 12 March 2010

Ouguergouz, Fatsah. 'The Bamako Convention on Hazardous Waste: A New Step in the Development of the African International Environmental Law'. *African Yearbook of International Law* 1(1993): 195–216

Packer, C. and Rukare, D. 'The New African Union and its Constitutive Act'. *American Journal of International Law* 96(2002): 365–379

Petrasek, David. 'New Standards for the Protection of Internally Displaced Persons: A Proposal for a Comprehensive Approach'. *Refugee Survey Quarterly* (Spring/Summer, 1995): 285–290

Phuong, Catherine. *The International Protection of Internally Displaced Persons.* Cambridge: Cambridge University Press, 2005

Plender, Richard. 'The Legal Basis of International Jurisdiction to Act with Regard to the Internally Displaced' in *The Problem of Refugees in the Light of Contemporary International Law Issues*, edited by Vera Gowaland-Debbas, 119–134. The Netherlands: Kluwer Law International, 1995

Ramcharan, Bertrand. 'State Responsibility for Violations of Human Rights'. in *Contemporary Problem of International Law: Essays in Honour of George Schawazenberger*, edited by Edith Browne, Bin Cheng and Georg Schwarzenberger, 246–261. London: Stevens and Son, 1988

———. 'Complementarity between Universal and Regional Human Rights Organizations: Perspective from the United Nations High Commissioner for Human Rights'. *Human Rights Law Journal* 21(2000): 324–326

———. 'The Travaux Preparatoires of the African Commission on Human Rights'. *Human Rights Law Journal* 13(1992): 307–314

Reisman, Michael. 'Sovereignty and Human Rights in Contemporary International Law'. *American Journal of International Law* 84(1990): 869–873

Review of the Multilateral Treaty-making Process, UN Legislative Series, No. 21,

ST/LEG/SER.B/21 UN sales No. E/F.83.V8 (1985)

Revitalizing the AU Coordinating Committee on Assistance to Refugees, *The Reporter*, 25 November 2006.

The Rights and Guarantees of Internally Displaced Children During Armed Conflict. Office of the Representative of the Secretary General for Children and Armed Conflict, Working Paper No. 2, 2010

Rivadeneira, Rodolfo. *Judicial Protection of Internally Displaced Persons: The Colombian Experience.* Brooking Bern Internal Displacement Project, November 2009

Rosenberg, Matthew. 'Refugee Law and Displacement Loophole'. *Hertfordshire Law Journal* 2(2004): 19–25

Ruddick, Elizabeth. 'Note: The Continuing Constraint of Sovereignty: International Law, International Protection, and the Internally Displaced'. *Boston University Law Review* 77(1997)

Sadruddin, Aga Khan. *The United Nations Study on Human Rights and Mass Exodus.* E/CN.4/1503, 1981

Santini, Tullio. 'Addressing the Protection Gap: The Framework for Consultation on IDPs in Burundi'. *Forced Migration Review* (2002): 43–46

Sarkin, Jermey. 'The Role of the United Nations, the African Union and Africa's Sub-Regional Organisations in Dealing with Africa's Human Rights Problems: Connecting Humanitarian Intervention and the Responsibility to Protect'. *Journal of African Law* 53(2009): 1–33

Sassoli, Marco. 'State Responsibility for Violations of International Law'. *International Review of the Red Cross* 84(2002): 401–434

Scillianos, Linos Alexander. 'The Classification of Obligations and the Multilateral Dimensions of the Relations of State Responsibility'. *European Journal of International Law* 13(2002): 1127–45

Senui, Mebrat. Brief Report on AU Consultative Meeting, 16 May 2007. Addis Ababa, African Humanitarian Action

Schafer, David. 'Towards a Modern Doctrine of Humanitarian Intervention'. *University of Toledo Law Review* 23(1992): 253–93

Schachter, Oscar. *International Law in Theory and Practice.* The Netherlands: Martius Nijhoff Publisher, 1991

Scheinin, Martin. 'Forced Displacement and the Covenant on Civil and Political Rights' in *Human Rights and Forced Displacement,* edited by Anne Bayefsky and Joan Fitzpatrick, 66–76. The Hague: Kluwer Law International, 2000

Schmidt, Patrick. 'The Process and Prospects for the UN Guiding Principles on Internal Displacement to become Customary International Law: A Preliminary Assessment'. *Georgetown Journal of International Law* 35(2003–2004): 483–503

Schroth, Peter. 'The African Union Convention on Preventing and Combating Corruption'. *Journal of Africa Law,* 49(2005): 24–38

Shacknove, Andrew. 'Who is a Refugee?' *Ethics* 95(1985): 274–284

Simma, Bruno. 'Self-contained Regimes'. *Netherlands Yearbook of International Law* 16(1985): 111–136

Simons, Marco. 'The Emergence of a Norm Against Arbitrary Forced Relocation'. *Colombian Human Rights Law Review* 95(2003)

Speech by Prime Minster of Uganda to the Extraordinary Session of the AU Executive Council, 19 October 2009

Stahn, Cartsen. 'Responsibility to Protect: Political Rhetoric or Emerging Legal

Norm?' *American Journal of International Law* 101(2007)

Statement by Ibrahim Gambari to the United Nations Security Council, 14 June 2010

Statement of Ms Julia D. Joiner, AU Commissioner for Political Affairs, UNHCR EXCOM Side Event, 7 October 2008

Statement of Ambassador Emile Ognimba, Director for Political Affairs, the African Union Commission, 60th Session of the Executive Committee of the High Commissioner's Program, 28 September–2 October 2009

Stavropoulou, Maria. 'The Right Not to Be Displaced'. *American University Journal on International Law and Policy* 9(1994)

———. 'Displacement and Human Rights: Reflections on UN Practice'. *Human Rights Quarterly* 20(1998): 515–554

Strategic Indicative Plan for the Organ on Politics, Defence and Security Cooperation. Gaborone: SADC, 2004

Strategic Plan 2009–2012, African Union Commission, EX.CL/501(XV)

Strategic Framework for Peacebulding in the Central African Republic 2009–2011, PBC/3/CAF/7

Sztucki, Jerzy. 'The Conclusions on the International Protection of Refugees Adopted by the Executive Committee of the UNHCR Programme'. *International Journal of Refugee Law* 1(1989): 285–318

Taylor, Paul. *International Organisations in the Modern World: The Regional and Global Progress*. New York: Pinter, 1993

Tigere, Patrick and Amukhobu, Rita. 'The African Union's Institutional Framework for Responding to Forced Displacement in Africa'. *Conflict Trends* 3(2005): 48–55

Tomuschat, Christian. 'State Responsibility and the Country of Origin' in *The Problem of Refugees in the Light of Contemporary International Law Issues*, edited by Vera Gowlland Debbas, 59–81. The Hague: Kluwer Law International, 1996

Umozurike, Uo. 'The Protection of Human Rights under the Banjul Charter on Human and Peoples' Rights'. *African Journal of International Law* 1(1986): 65

UNHCR's Role in Support of an Enhanced Humanitarian Response to Situations of Internal Displacement. Policy Framework and Implementation Strategy (June 2007), EC/58/SC/CRP.18

UNHCR, Revitalising the African Union Coordinating Mechanism on Assistance to Refugees, Returnees and Internally Displaced Persons, 17 November 2006, available online at www.unhcrrlo.org/AfricanNews/Press_Release/CCAR.pdf. Accessed on 13 March 2010

———. African Ministers Adopt Historic Draft IDP Convention, Geneva, 2008

Viljoen, Frans. 'Supra-national Human Rights Instruments for the Protection of Children in Africa: The Convention on the Rights of the Child and the African Charter on the Rights and Welfare of the Child'. *The Comparative and International Law Journal of Southern Africa* (1998): 99–210

———. 'The Realisation of Human Rights in Africa through Sub-regional Institutions'. *African Year Book of International Law* 7(1999): 185–214

'Violence in Mogadishu Swells Number of Displaced Somalis-UN survey', UN News Center, 1 October 2010

Wall, Johan De. 'Constitutional Law' in *Introduction to South African Law*, edited by C. G. Van der Merwe and J. E. Du Plessis, 55–106. The Netherlands: Kluwer International, 2004

Weiss, Edith. 'Invoking State Responsibility in the Twenty-first Century'. *American Journal of International Law* 96(2002)

Weiss, Thomas and Korn, David. *Internal Displacement: Conceptualisation and its Consequences.* Oxford: Rutledge, 2006

Weiss, Thomas. 'Internal Exiles: What Next for Internally Displaced Persons?' *Third World Quarterly* 24(2005): 429–447

Wet, Chris de. 'Improving Outcomes in Development-Induced Displacement and Resettlement Project'. *Forced Migration Review* 12(2002): 6–9

'World is Neglecting Major Internal Displacement Crises'. Office of the High Commissioner for Human Rights, 13 March 2009

Wyndham, Jessica. 'A Developing Trend: Laws and Policies on Internal Displacement'. *Human Rights Brief* (Winter 2006)

Zetter, Roger and Boano, Camillo. 'Planned Evacuation and the Right to Shelter During Displacement' in *Incorporating the Guiding Principles on Internal Displacement into Domestic Law: Issues and Challenges,* edited by Walter Kälin, Rhodri Williams, Koser Khalid and Andrew Solomon, 165–207. Washington, DC: The American Society of International Law and Brookings Institution, 2010

Zieck, Marjoleine. *UNHCR and Voluntary Repatriation of Refugees: A legal Analysis.* The Hague: Martinus Nighoff Pubisher, 1994

Zimmerman, Andreas and Boumler, Jalena. *The Current Challenges Facing the African Court on Human and Peoples' Rights.* KAS International Reports, 2010

Index